Heart Blessings

A scrapbook of Christian poetry & prose, for inspiration and daily devotion

Heart Blessings

A **scrapbook** of Christian poetry & prose, for inspiration and daily devotion

COMPILED BY EVANGELIST
DALE CROWLEY

PUBLISHED BY
THE KING IS COMING WORLDWIDE MINISTRIES, INC.
Washington, DC 20044-0001

PUBLISHED AND COPYRIGHTED © 2006 BY

THE KING IS COMING WORLDWIDE MINISTRIES, INC.

DALE CROWLEY JR., DIRECTOR AND RADIO SPEAKER

P. O. Box One

Washington, DC 20044-0001

20th Printing

First edition published in 1967

Library of Congress Catalog Card No. 73-87757

ISBN 0-940883-20-1

Printed in the United States of America.

Cover design and text by SCHUM & ASSOCIATES, McLean, Virginia

This dedication page is from the 1973 edition

Dedication

To the thousands of true friends who have encouraged me to use
a portion of my daily broadcast time on the RIGHT START FOR THE DAY
program for the reading of Christian poems, and who have
by their sacrificial gifts made possible the continuance of this faith
ministry since 1941, this book is affectionately dedicated.

Now in Heaven, this edition is offered in memory of my darling
wife, Marguerite, who helped tremendously in the preparation
of the First Edition of this book, and whose very life was
a psalm of blessing to all who knew her.

DALE S. CROWLEY   MARGUERITE M. CROWLEY

*On the air daily for a third of a century, the author
and compiler has diligently searched for a lifetime
for the best in Christian poetry and prose.*

Acknowledgments

The publishers acknowledge with deep appreciation the cooperation of so many authors and publishers in granting permission to use copyrighted material, and the kindness of many friends who have contributed many of these masterpieces. A diligent effort has been made to determine copyright ownership of all items used. If through lack of knowledge we have failed in any instance, and the same shall be brought to our attention, we promise to include this information in future editions of HEART BLESSINGS.

Many of these classical gems have come to us anonymously, and we are not able to give the proper credit to these contributors. Others we have gleaned from many old volumes, long since out of print. Some of these immortal gems are several hundred years old, with an even larger number from the nineteenth century. Much of this material is in public domain. Many poems, essays, and proverbs by the author and compiler are published for the first time.

We are especially indebted to the following publishers and authors for their permission to use much of the material in this book:

Harper and Row: Several poems by Grace Noll Crowell: "He That Keepeth Thee," "It Takes So Little," "He Thanks Thee Best," "Because of Thy Great Bounty" and "Wait."

Louizeau Brothers: Several poems from "Highways to the Hills" by Inez Kemper (copyright 1947).

Moody Press: From WMBI Scrapbook: "The Contrast," and "The Rest of the Way"; and from Martha Snell Nicholson's "Wings and Sky"; "Christmas Meditation," "Eternity," and "My Advocate."

American Tract Society: "The Incomparable Christ."

Good News Publishers: "The All Sufficient Saviour for All Earth's People" and "The Homeland."

Herald Press: Quotes from "Golden Hours With the Bible."

Pilgrim Tract Society: "When I Stand on the Streets of Gold."

Faith, Prayer & Tract League: "He Maketh No Mistake" by A. M. Chambers, "Songs in the Night" by S. G. Brondsema, "Disappointment," "The Refiner's Fire" by Arthur F. Ingler, "The Promises" by Geo. H. Talbert, "What Then?" (anon.), "Not Growing Old" by John E. Roberts, "If We Could See Beyond Today" by Norman J. Clayton, "I Needed the Quiet" by Alice H. Mortenson, "I Shall Not Want" by Mrs. J. R. Mott, "He Giveth More Grace" by Annie Johnson Flint, "Have You Taken It to Jesus" by Mrs. E. L. Hennessay, "God Ever Cares" by J. Danson Smith, "Chastening" by Grace E. Troy, "A Cry from Heathendom" by G. P. Turnbull, "Crown or Crucify" by Florence E. Johnson; and from unknown authors—"The Valley," "Consolation," "The Weaver," "Lean Hard" and "My Old Bible." All items in this paragraph available in tract form by Faith, Prayer & Tract League, 2627 Elmridge Dr., N.W., Grand Rapids, Michigan.

Back to the Bible Broadcast: Several inspiring items from "Poems for Sunshine and Shadow," Vols. I and II. (Permission granted by Ernest E. Lott, Administrative Director of Publishing).

Baptist Bible Tribune: Quotes of lasting value. (Permission granted by Editor Noel Smith).

The Evangelical Magazine: Several items (permission granted by Dr. Louis A. Jacobsen, editor).

The Christian Victory Publishing Co.: "The Miracle Man" and other items by the late Fred J. Meldau. (Permission granted by Dan Williams.)

Osterhus Publishing House: Several items from this firm's leaflets. (Permission granted by Ruth Osterhus.)

Our appreciation to the Wheeler City Rescue Mission for the privilege of including "Prescription for Your Need" and "Encouragement From a Rooster."

For permission from the publishers of Dale Crowley's books for several selected items, we are grateful. We are indebted to the following individuals for permission to include their valued poems: Mrs. Robert Ely's "Some Day I'll Be With You"; Frank Stollenwerck's "The Fear of God"; Florence Stellwagen's "Not So Easily Fixed"; Ramona Ray Woodson's "The Christ of Calvary and the Empty Tomb"; Jessie Whiteside Fink's "Our Flag"; Lillian Musick's "If the Bible Has No Answer"; T. Myron Webb's "Saved to Serve"; and for the contribution of A. C. Maxwell, "I'd Rather Say, 'I'm Fine.' "

Also, we are grateful to the following wonderful people for their permission to include certain choice compositions: Dorothy Wiles, for "The Christ of God"; W. L. Griffin, for "Grace, Love, Mercy"; Pastor M. H. Knoblock, for "My Bible and I"; Dora Johnson, "You Tell Me I Am Growing Old"; L. M. Zimmerman, "Herald of the Dawn"; Helen Haze, "For These I Am Thankful"; Jennie Wright, "A Psalm of Life"; Mabel E. Brown, "My Father Cares"; Dr. John E. Zoller, "Faithful Is He That Promised"; Josephine Long, "Take a Little Step Toward Me"; Connie Sandoz, "My Secret Stairway"; Lulu Minerva Schultz, "Miracle at Munda"; Mary Even, "My Prayer"; Myrtle Jones, "What's Your Story?"; Kathryn Bowsher, "Dare to Stand for Jesus"; Connie Calenburg, "Heaven"; and Dale Crowley, Jr., "Wait a Minute."

We have a sense of deep appreciation for the privilege of including the following classic gems: "Prayer for a Favor" by John J. Metcalfe; "No" by Dr. Frank Crane; "His Name Wonderful" by Mary Louise Leonard; "God's Loving Hand" by John Gilbert; "Things Just Don't Happen" and "Breaking Heart" by Esther Fields; "First Christmas in Heaven" and "Circumstances" by Albert S. Reitz; "My Hand in God's" by Florence Scripps Kellogg; "Counting on HIm" by Elsie Duncan Yale; "I Am Never Alone" by Carlos G. Fuller; "My Lord and I" by L. Shroey; "The Fellowship of Prayer" by Mary Stoner Wine; "Child of God" and "Tell Me What You Are" by Grenville Kleiser; "What Wilt Thou Have Me to Do" by T. O. Chisholm; "If I Had Prayed" by Joyce Rader; "Mizpah" by Julia Baker; and Myra Brooks Welsh's "The Touch of the Master's Hand."

We are indebted to Helen Steiner Rice for the use of several of her inspiring gems, so widely used on sympathy cards, and published by Gibson Company.

Other gems which serve to enrich this volume, for which we are thankful, are: "Living Sermons" by Florence Belle Anderson; "What Would He Say?" by Grace E. Troy; "Prayer" by James Montgomery; "Life's Mirror" by Madeline S. Bridges; "In Gratitude for Friends," "Our Own" and "At Sunset" by Margaret E. Sangster; "Give Up?" by Grace B. Renfro; "If" by Grace Clarkson; "Sometimes" by Mary Riley Smith; "No One Understands Like Jesus" by John Peterson; "Take My Life" by Frances Ridley Havergal; "The God Who Knows" by William Luff; "This, Too, Shall Pass" by Ella Wheeler Wilcox; "The Unknown Soldier's Prayer" by Frances Angermayer; "Mother Dear" by Oswald J. Smith; "Excuses" from Harold Leake's album; "God's Job for You" by Paul Lawrence Dunbar; "Trouble in the Amen Corner" by Archie Campbell; "Wait for Me" by Hovie Lister; "Should You Go First" by Rosy Roswell; "My Creed" by Dean Alfange; and "Pledge of Faith" by Rita S. Brehm (which received the 1962 George Washington Honor Medal from Freedom Foundation), and the classic gem, "The Secret" by Ralph Cushman.

We are particularly grateful to the Evangelical Publishers, Toronto, Ont., for permission to use several of the inspiring poems of Annie Johnson Flint, including "A Very Present Help," "He Giveth More Grace," "What God Hath Promised," "His Lamp Am I," "Where to Look," and "The World's Bible." And, for permission by The Abingdon Press to include poems of lasting worth from the book *Poems With Power* by James Mudge (original copyright 1909 by Eaton & Mains).

Also, we are most deeply grateful to the Rodeheaver Company for several of Homer Rodeheaver's gems from *Worthwhile Poems,* including "A Letter to Mother" by Mrs. D. A. Terradell, and "To My Mother" by Kate Douglas Wiggin; and for "Then Jesus Came," "No One Ever Cared for Me Like Jesus," "All the Way to Calvary," "Somebody Cares," "No One Understands Like Jesus," "He Lives," and "Mother's Prayers Have Followed Me."

SPECIAL CREDIT

As indicated in the first edition of HEART BLESSINGS, invaluable assistance was given me in the preparation of this book by my precious wife, Marguerite; and by my dear sister, Irene Harms. Both of these are now in Heaven "and their works do follow them."

In the unspeakably large task of enlarging this golden book of inspiration, no person deserves more credit than my loving granddaughter, Sharon Crowley, who spent weeks in assisting me in the assemblage of hundreds of choice gems clipped from the files of my Christian newspaper, *The Capitol Voice,* reaching over a period of many years. In addition, my faithful secretary, Pearl Cardinal, has rendered a tremendous service in much copy work, in letters to publishers and authors, and in preparing an exhaustive index. For these we are deeply grateful.

Dale Crowley, Author and Compiler

Washington, D.C., USA.
September 27, 1976

Table of Contents

The Greatness of God . . .

The Father, the Son, the Holy Spirit

Bless the Lord, O my soul. O Lord my God, thou art very great; thou art clothed with honour and majesty:

2. Who coverest thyself with light as with a garment: who stretchest out the heavens like a curtain:

3. Who layeth the beams of his chambers in the waters: who maketh the clouds his chariot: who walketh upon the wings of the wind:

4. Who maketh his angels spirits; his ministers a flaming fire:

5. Who laid the foundations of the earth, that it should not be removed for ever (Psalm 104).

How Great Thou Art

Oh, Lord, my God! When I in awesome
   wonder
Consider all the worlds Thy hands have
   made,
I see the stars, I hear the rolling thunder,
Thy power throughout the universe dis-
   played.

When though the woods and forest glades I
   wander
And hear the birds sing sweetly in the trees;
When I look down from lofty mountain
   grandeur,
And hear the brook and feel the gentle
   breeze.

And when I think that God, His Son not
   sparing,
Sent Him to die, I scarce can take it in;
That on the cross, my burden gladly bearing,
He bled and died to take away my sin.

When Christ shall come with shout of accla-
   mation
And take me home, what joy shall fill my
   heart!
Then I shall bow in humble adoration
And there proclaim, my God, how great
   Thou art!

(Chorus)
Then sings my soul, my Saviour, God to
   Thee;
How great Thou art, how great Thou art!
Then sings my soul, my Saviour, God to
   Thee;
How great Thou art, how great Thou art!

—S. K. Hine

God of the Earth, the Sky, the Sea

God of the earth, the sky, the sea,
Maker of all above, below,
Creation lives and moves in Thee;
Thy present life through all doth flow.

Thy love is in the sunshine's glow,
Thy life is in the quickening air;
When lightnings flash and storm winds
   blow,
There is Thy power, Thy law is there.

We feel Thy calm at evening's hour,
Thy grandeur in the march of night,
And when the morning breaks in power,
We hear Thy word, "Let there be light."

But higher far, and far more clear,
Thee in man's spirit we behold,
Thine image and Thyself are there,
Th' indwelling God, proclaimed of old.

—Samuel Longfellow

This Is My Father's World

This is my Father's world,
And to my listening ears
All nature sings, and round me rings
The music of the spheres.

—Maltbie Babcock

ALL THINGS BRIGHT AND BEAUTIFUL

All things bright and beautiful,
All creatures great and small,
All things wise and wonderful,
The Lord God made them all.

Each little flower that opens,
Each little bird that sings,
He made their glowing colors,
He made their tiny wings.

The purple-headed mountain,
The river running by,
The sunset, and the morning
That brightens up the sky.

The cold wind in the winter,
The pleasant summer sun,
The ripe fruits in the garden,
He made them every one.

The tall trees in the green wood,
The meadows where we play,
The rushes by the water,
We gather every day.

He gave us eyes to see them,
And lips that we might tell
How great is God Almighty,
Who has made all things well.
—*Cecil Frances Alexander*

In the beginning God created the heaven and the earth. . . . And God said, Let there be light: and there was light. . . . And God created man in His own image, in the image of God created He him; male and female created He them. And God blessed them, and God said, Be fruitful, and multiply, and replenish the earth, and subdue it: and have dominion over the fish of the sea, and over the fowl of the air, and over every living thing that moveth upon the earth (Gen. 1:1, 3, 27, 28).

God Moves in a Mysterious Way

God moves in a mysterious way
His wonders to perform;
He plants His footsteps in the sea
And rides upon the storm.
Deep in unfathomable mines
Of never-failing skills,
He treasures up His bright designs
And works His sovereign will.
Judge not the Lord by feeble sense,
But trust Him for His grace;
Behind a frowning providence
He hides a smiling face.
Blind unbelief is sure to err
And scan His work in vain;
God is His own Interpreter
And He will make it plain.

—*William Cowper*

"Behold your God!
"Who hath measured the waters in the hollow of His hand, and meted out heaven with a span, and comprehended the dust of the earth in a measure, and weighed the mountains in scales, and the hills in a balance? . . . Behold, the nations are as a drop in the bucket, and are counted as the small dust of a balance; behold, He taketh up the isles as a very little thing . . . All nations before Him are as nothing; and they are counted to Him less than nothing and vanity . . .

"Have ye not known? have ye not heard? hath it not been told you from the beginning? have ye not understood from the foundations of the earth? It is He that sitteth upon the circle of the earth, and the inhabitants thereof are as grasshoppers; that stretcheth out the heavens as a curtain, and spreadeth them out as a tent to dwell in . . .

"Lift up your eyes on high, and behold who hath created these things, that bringeth out their host by number: He calleth them all by names by the greatness of His might, for that He is strong in power: not one falleth" (Isaiah 40)

And So God Speaks

Have you stood entranced
    By the dazzling sight
Of a perfect rose
    Bathed in morning light,
And felt that only
    An artist rare
Could paint the loveliness
    Growing there?
And, then, dear friend,
    Did you whisper low
That this fragrant rose
    With its lovely glow
Was part of God's handiwork,
    Part of His plan
To speak through the beauty
    Of nature to man?

—*Cleo King*

The Spacious Firmament

The spacious firmament on high,
    With all the blue, ethereal sky,
And spangled heavens, a shining
    frame,
    Their great Original proclaim:
The unwearied sun, from day to day,
    Does his Creator's power display;
And publishes to every land
    The work of an almighty hand.

Soon as the evening shades prevail,
    The moon takes up the wondrous
    tale;
And nightly to the listening earth,
    Repeats the story of her birth;
While all the stars that round her
    burn,
And all the planets in their turn,
Confirm the tidings as they roll,
    And spread the truth from pole to
    pole.

—*Joseph Addison*

God of Our Fathers

God of our fathers, whose almighty hand
Leads forth in beauty all the starry band
Of singing worlds in splendor thru the
    skies.
Our grateful songs before Thy throne arise.

Thy love divine hath led us in the past;
In this free land by Thee our lot is cast.
Be Thou our ruler, guardian, guide and
    stay—
Thy word our law, Thy paths our chosen
    way.

—*Daniel C. Roberts*

Greatest Story

The maker of the universe
As man for man was made a curse;
The claims of laws which He had made
Unto the uttermost He paid.
His holy fingers made the bough
Where grew the thorns that crowned His
    brow;
The nails that pierced His hands were
    mined
In secret places He designed.

He made the forest whence there sprung
The tree on which His body hung;
He died upon a cross of wood,
Yet made the hill on which it stood.
The sky which darkened o'er His head
By Him above the earth was spread;
The sun which hid from Him its face
By His decree was poised in space.

The spear which spilt His precious blood
Was tempered in the fires of God;
The grave in which His form was laid
Was hewed in rocks His hands had made.
The throne on which He now appears
Was His from everlasting years,
But a new glory crowns His brow
And every knee to Him shall bow.

13

THE ALL-SUFFICIENT SAVIOUR
For All Earth's People

To the artist the Lord Jesus Christ is the One Altogether Lovely.

To the architect He is the Chief Cornerstone.

To the baker He is the Living Bread.

To the banker He is the Hidden Treasure.

To the biologist He is the Life.

To the builder He is the Sure Foundation.

To the carpenter, He is the Door.

To the doctor He is the Great Physician.

To the educator He is the Great Teacher.

To the engineer He is the New and Living Way.

To the farmer He is the Sower and the Lord of the Harvest.

To the florist He is the Rose of Sharon and the Lily of the Valley.

To the geologist He is the Rock of Ages.

To the horticulturist He is the True Vine.

To the judge He is the Righteous Judge, the Judge of all men.

To the juror He is the Faithful and True Witness.

To the jeweler He is the Pearl of Great Price.

To the lawyer He is the Counselor, the Law-giver, the Advocate.

To the newspaper man He is the Good News of Great Joy.

To the philanthropist He is the Unspeakable Gift.

To the philosopher He is the Wisdom of God.

To the preacher He is the Word of God.

To the sculptor He is the Living Stone.

To the servant He is the Good Master.

To the statesman He is the Desire of all nations.

To the student He is the Incarnate Truth.

To the theologian He is the Author and Finisher of our Faith.

To the laborer He is the Giver of Rest.

To the sinner He is the Lamb of God that takes away the sin of the world.

To the Christian He is the Son of the Living God, the Saviour, the Redeemer and Lord.

"He that hath the Son hath life; and he that hath not the Son of God hath not life" (I John 5:12).

To God Be the Glory

To God be the glory,
  Great things He hath done,
So loved He the world
  That He gave us His Son,
Who yielded His life
  An atonement for sin,
And opened the Life-gate
  That all may go in.

—Fanny J. Crosby

———————

"The Miracle Man! He came to us by a miracle and left by a miracle. His life was one continuous miracle. He was so full of power that all known laws of nature were counteracted at His wish; so full of life that the grave could not keep Him; so full of goodness that even the demons were forced to admit it; so great that years later one Augustine said of Him, 'His life is lightning, His words a thunder!' The Miracle Man is eternal in time, omnipotent in power, omniscient in intellect, sovereign in His actions. He is the Lord of Glory and the Lord of humanity, Master of nature and Master of providence, the coming Judge and the coming King. He is the only hope of mankind, and the only way to God; the Fountain of life; the Source of light, and the Author of liberty. He is full of grace, and full of truth. He sealed His tremendous claims and demonstrated His position by constant manifestations of miraculous power, by a sinless life, by a sacrificial death, and by His own resurrection from the dead."

—Fred J. Meldau

WHAT THINK YE OF CHRIST?

"Pharisees, with what have you to reproach Jesus?"

"He eateth with publicans and sinners."

"Is this all?"

"Yes."

"And you, Caiaphas, what say you of Him?"

"He is guilty: He is a blasphemer because He said, "Hereafter shall ye see the Son of Man sitting on the right hand of power and coming in the clouds of heaven.' "

"Pilate, what is your opinion?'

"I find no fault in this Man."

"And you, Judas, who have sold your Master for silver, have you some fearful charge to hurl against Him?"

"I have sinned in that I have betrayed the innocent blood."

"And you, centurion, who have led Him to the cross, what have you to say?"

"Truly, this was the Son of God."

"And you, demons?"

"He is the Son of God."

"John Baptist, what think you of Christ?"

"Behold the Lamb of God."

"And you, John the Apostle?"

"He is the Bright and Morning Star."

"Peter, what say you of your Master?"

"Thou art the Christ the Son of the Living God."

"And you, Thomas?"

"My Lord and my God."

"Paul, you have persecuted Him: What testify you of Him?"

"I count all things but loss for the excellency of the knowledge of Christ Jesus my Lord."

"Angels of heaven, what think you of Jesus?"

"Unto you is born a Saviour, which is Christ the Lord."

"And thou, Father in heaven, who knowest all things?"

"This is My beloved Son, in whom I am well pleased."

Dear reader, what think you of Christ?

Our Refuge

Are you drifting on life's ocean
Ere you sink beneath the wave?
Anchor to the Rock of Ages;
He will rescue, He will save.
There's no other friend like Jesus,
For He died to set us free.
If we'll only believe the record
Of His death and victory.

Then love the Lord with all your heart.
Love and lift your fellow men.
Turn from sin, and follow Jesus;
For you must be born again.
All have sinned. Not one is righteous.
All, like sheep, have gone astray.
Only Christ can save the lost one.
He's the Truth, the Life, the Way.

Christ's Will

HIS PURSE to Judas (John 12:4-6).

HIS BODY to Joseph of Arimathea (Mark 15:43; Luke 23:51-53).

HIS MOTHER to John, son of Zebedee (John 19:26, 27).

HIS SPIRIT back to His Father (Luke 23:46).

HIS CLOTHES to the soldiers (Matt. 27:35; Mark 15:24; Luke 23:34; John 19:23, 24).

HIS PEACE to His disciples (John 14:27).

HIS SUPPER to His followers (Luke 22:19).

HIMSELF an example as a Servant (John 13:15).

HIS GOSPEL for the world (Matt. 28:19).

HIS PRESENCE ALWAY, to the end of the world (Matt. 28:20).

My Prayer

Oh, Saviour on the cross,
  Help me to see, I pray,
That Thou didst bear my guilt
  And wash my sins away.

Oh, Risen Christ, Who conquered
  Death, I'm justified in Thee;
I cannot dread the judgment,
  For Thy vict'ry made me free.

Oh, Lord, Who didst ascend
  On high with priestly pow'r,
Thou art my Mediator,
  Interceding every hour.

O Lord, my coming King,
  In glory Thou wilt come;
And I shall wait for that blest word,
  "My child, well done"!

—Dale Crowley

Our Matchless Christ

To many, Jesus Christ is only a grand subject for a painting, a heroic theme for a pen, a beautiful form for a statue and a thought for a song; but to those who have heard His voice, who have felt His pardon, who have received His benediction, He is music, warmth, light, joy, hope and salvation, a Friend who never forsakes, who lifts us when others try to push us down. We cannot wear Him out; we pile on Him all our griefs and troubles. He is always ready to lift us; He is always ready to help us; He addresses with the same love; He beams upon us with the same smile; He pities us with the same compassion. There is no name like His. It is more inspiring than Caesar's, more musical than Beethoven's, more conquering than Napoleon's, more eloquent than Demosthenes', more patient than Lincoln's. The Name of Jesus throbs with all life, weeps with all pathos, groans with all pains, stoops with all love. Its breath is laden with perfume, Who like Jesus can pity a homeless orphan? Who like Jesus can welcome a prodigal back home? Who like Jesus can make a drunkard sober? Who like Jesus can illuminate a cemetery plowed with graves?

—Billy Sunday

GOD THE ARCHITECT

Thou hast made the flowers to bloom
  And the stars to shine;
Hid rare gems of richest ore
  In the tunneled mine;
But chief of all thy wondrous works
  Supreme of all thy plan,
Thou hast put an upward reach
  Into the heart of man.

—Harry Kemp

Jesus Christ Gave All

He gave His head to the crown of thorns.
He gave His back to the cruel lash.
He gave His cheeks to those who plucked out the hairs.
He gave His face to the rude human spittle.
He gave His shoulders to be draped with the robe of mock royalty.
He gave His clothes to His murderers.
He gave His mother to the Apostle John.
He gave His hands and feet to be transfixed with nails to the accursed Cross.
He gave His blood to this earth for the remission of sins.
He gave His body for the life of the world.
He gave His spirit to God.

Abandoned and desolate, without God, friend and acquaintance far from Him, He gave Himself unto death. The sun withdrew; behind the black pall of mourning a cold, cruel world shivered; nature itself refused to contribute anything—Jesus Christ "gave everything."

You know the grace of our Lord Jesus Christ, who was rich, yet for our sakes became poor—He "gave everything."

He loves me and gave Himself—"gave everything"—for me.

—William McCormick

Christ the Lord

Born to die was He;
Born to die, that we,
Though His precious blood,
Might be brought to God.

Lamb of God was He,
Dying on the tree,
Dying for our sin.
Life for us to win.

Raised from death was He,
His the victory;
Now He lives on high,
That we may not die.

Waiting now is He,
Coming soon is He,
Coming to the air,
We shall meet Him there.

King of Kings is He,
By divine decree;
One day He will reign,
When He comes again.

—W.L.P.

"Christ of God"

"The Christ of God," O wonderful claim,
    That Christ and God are one;
This Christ of God my Saviour became;
    God placed my sins on His Son.

"The Christ of God," O wonderful name,
    By men and angels adored;
In spirit and truth I worship Him;
    This Christ of God is my Lord.

"The Christ of God," Eternal One,
    The I AM of Thy word;
O send Thy message through Thine own,
    Until the world has heard.

"The Christ of God," our promised King,
    Will come to earth again;
This time to reign, o'er everything;
    Come quickly, Lord—Amen.

—Dorothy Wiles

"Bless the Lord, O my Soul,
    And all that is within me;
Bless His holy name.
    Bless the Lord, O my soul,
And forget not all His benefits."

(Psalm 103:1, 2)

The Incomparable Christ

More than nineteen hundred years ago there was born a man contrary to the laws of life. This man lived in poverty and was reared in obscurity.

He did not travel extensively. Only once did He cross the boundary of the country in which He lived; that was during His exile in childhood. He possessed neither wealth nor influence.

His relatives were inconspicuous, uninfluential, and had neither training nor education.

In infancy He startled a king. In childhood He puzzled the doctors. In manhood He ruled the course of nature, walking upon the billows as if pavements, and hushed the sea to sleep. He healed multitudes without medicine and made no charge for His service. He never wrote a book and yet all the libraries of the country could not hold the books that have been written about Him.

He never wrote a song and yet He furnished the theme for more songs than all the song writers combined. He never founded a college, but all the schools together cannot boast as having as many students. He never practiced medicine, yet He has healed more broken hearts than all the doctors, far and near.

He never marshalled an army, nor drafted a soldier, nor fired a gun, and yet no leader had more volunteers who have, under His orders made more rebels stack guns and surrender without a shot being fired. Every seventh day the wheels of commerce cease their turning and multitudes wend their way to worshipping assemblies to pay homage and respect to Him.

The names of the past proud statesmen of Greece and Rome have come and gone, but the name of this Man abounds more and more. Though time has spread nineteen hundred years between the people of this generation and the scene of His crucifixion, yet He still lives. Herod could not kill Him, Satan could not seduce Him, death could not destroy Him, and the grave could not hold Him.

He stands forth upon the highest pinnacle of heavenly glory, proclaimed of God, acknowledged by angels, adored by saints, and feared by devils, as the living personal Christ, our Lord and Saviour.

—Author Unknown

God Never Changes

God never changes! Things and people alter;
    And blessings, one time prized, with time grow dim;
He changes not—nor varies—nor doth falter;
    And we are ever rich in having Him.

God's love abides—though other loves may perish,
    Though streams, whereat we drank, may sadly dry;
Yea—though some love may fail, we much did cherish,
    We still may find in Him a sure supply.

And—to God's care there surely is no ending!
    He who gave Christ cannot withhold His care;
And we may know the joy of His attending—
    And in the hour of need shall find Him there!

—J. Danson Smith

Paradoxes and Contrasts

He was the Light, yet He hung in darkness on the Cross.

He was the Life, yet He "poured out His soul unto death."

He was the Rock of Ages, yet His "feet sank into deep waters."

He was the Son of God, yet He died a felon's death.

He was holy, undefiled, separate from sinners and knew no sin, yet He was "made sin" when He took the guilty culprit's place and suffered in his stead.

He bade the weary to come to Him for rest, yet not on earth could He find rest until He said, "It is finished," and gave up His life to God.

He was the Lion of the Tribe of Judah, yet He was led as a lamb to the slaughter.

He was the Ancient of Days, yet He was "cut off in the midst" of His days.

He was the Father of Eternity, yet He became the babe in the manger at Bethlehem.

He was the Mighty God, yet He became a man, and "was crucified through weakness."

He was the Image of the Invisible God, yet His visage was "marred more than any man."

All the fullness of the Godhead dwells bodily in Him, yet He took on Him the form of a servant, and was made in the likeness of men.

"He spake, and it was done; He commanded, and it stood fast," yet He humbled Himself and became obedient—even unto death.

He was the Desire of all nations, yet He was despised and rejected of men.

He is the Fountain of Life, yet upon the Cross He cried, "I thirst."

—*Dr. A. T. Pierson*

I Know a Name

I know a soul that is steeped in sin,
   That no man's art can cure;
But I know a Name, a Name, a Name
   That can make that soul all pure.

I know a life that is lost to God,
   Bound down by things of earth;
But I know a Name, a Name, a Name
   That can bring that soul new birth.

I know of lands that are sunk in shame,
   Of hearts that faint and tire;
But I know a Name, a Name, a Name
   That can set those lands on fire.

Its sound is a brand, its letters flame,
   Like glowing tongues of fire.
But I know a Name, a Name, a Name
   Of which the world ne'er tires.

—*Author Unknown*

CHRIST

Christ my Saviour, Christ my Friend;
Christ my Treasure without end;
Christ when waves of sorrow roll;
Christ the Comfort of my soul;
Christ when all around should fail;
Christ when enemies prevail;
Christ when false accusers rise;
Christ my Solace in the skies;
Christ when days are dark and drear;
Christ when all around is clear;
Christ when all the earth is gone;
Christ my King upon the throne;
Christ my home and Christ abroad;
Christ my Company on the road;
Christ in sickness, Christ in health;
Christ in poverty and in wealth;
Christ who once on earth has trod;
Christ the blessed "Son of God";
Christ for time and Christ for aye;
Christ for all eternity.

The Holy Spirit's Presence

Dear Holy Spirit, who can know
  The Comforter thou art,
Till they have felt deep need of Thee
  From out a broken heart.

Ten thousand griefs, dear Lord, have
    swept
  Across this heart of mine,
But every one has pushed me out
  Still deeper into Thine.

I know thou workest for my good,
  The soul's unfathomed pains,
The deep, dark dungeon's doleful cries
  Thou turn'st to mellow strains.

Thou art far sweeter than Thy gifts,
  Though they surpass all thought;
And yet thy presence in my breast
  With precious blood was bought.

O Comforter! It is Thyself
  Who shows the blood to me,
And in my mind revealest Christ
  Like an effulgent sea.

No creature in this world can know
  The way Thou leadest me,
Through storms and pangs and lonely
    griefs,
  From self out into Thee.

Dear, peaceful Spirit, Thou hast borne
  My sad heart far away
Into a gulf of tender love,
  Which melts it day by day.

Blest Holy Ghost, to me Thou art
  A boundless crystal sea,
And I can lose all loneliness
  When all alone with Thee.

I have no wish in all the world
  But to be filled with Thee,
And drink my being full of love
  From thine immensity.

—from *Beauty for Ashes*
by G. D. Watson

If Christ Had Not Come

by Edward L. Crane

Had Jesus not come to Bethlehem,
  On earth lived a perfect life,
There would not have been a
    "Calvary"—
  Nor Saviour from sin and strife.
A resurrection could never be
  For any one on the earth;
So I thank the Lord with all my heart,
  He came by a lowly birth.

My soul now joins in the angels' song
  Of praise to the Lord on high
Because of His birth in Bethlehem
  That I would not have to die.
The Saviour who went to Calvary
  Must be "related" to me:
And so it is, by His matchless grace,
  I am saved for eternity.

The atoning Cross could never have been
  Had Jesus not come to earth,
To Bethlehem, in a manger bed,
  From Glory to lowly birth.
His life was holy: without a flaw—
  The Lamb prepared to be slain—
My Saviour must live and die for me
  The love of God to proclaim.

His birth, life, death and resurrection
  Were each a part of God's Plan
To make salvation safe and secure
  To the Christ-believing man.
Soon He will come again for His own:
  The sound of trump will be heard;
The dead in Christ, and the living saints
  Will ascend to meet the Lord!

God's Answer

Light looked down and beheld darkness. "Thither will I go," said light.

Peace looked down and beheld war. "Thither will I go," said peace.

Love looked down and beheld hatred. "Thither will I go," said love.

So came light, and shone. So came peace, and gave rest. So came love, and brought life. And the word was made flesh, and dwelt among us.

—*Lawrence Houseman*

"The Word was made flesh, and dwelt among us, (and we beheld His glory, the glory as of the only begotten of the Father,) full of grace and truth" (John 1:14).

"And God so loved the world that He gave His only begotten Son, that whosoever believeth on Him should not perish, but have everlasting life" (John 3:16)

"But these are written that ye might believe that Jesus is the Christ, the Son of God; and that believing ye might have life through His name" (John 20:31).

"For the wages of sin is death, but the gift of God is eternal life through Jesus Christ our Lord" (Rom. 6:23).

"Neither is there salvation in any other: for there is none other name under heaven given among men, whereby ye must be saved: (Acts 4:12).

Come, Thou Almighty King

Come, Thou, Almighty King.
　Help us Thy name to sing.
Help us to praise,
　Father all glorious
　O'er all victorious,
　Come and reign over us
Ancient of Days.

Come, Thou Incarnate Word,
　Gird on Thy mighty sword.
Our prayer attend:
　Come and Thy people bless,
　And give Thy word success,
　Spirit of holiness
On us descend.

Come, Holy Comforter,
　Thy sacred witness bear
In this glad hour:
　Thou who almighty art
　Now rule in every heart,
　And n'er from us depart,
Spirit of power.

To the great One in Three
　Eternal praises be
Hence evermore.
　His sovereign majesty,
　May we in glory see,
　And to eternity
Love and adore.

—Author Unknown

"And His Name Shall Be Called Wonderful"

He's the One who paints the glory in the sunset,
He's the One who gilds the eastern sky with dawn,
He's the One who puts the silver in the moonlight,
He's the One who giveth grace unto the fawn.

He's the One who puts perfume in the lily,
He's the One who gives the rose its petals.
He's the One who giveth life to all the living,
He's the One who scattereth beauty everywhere.

He's the One who gives the stars their wondrous
　splendor,
He's the One who gives the bird its joyous song,
He's the One who spreads the dew upon the gar-
　den,
He's the One who rolls the mighty sea along.

He's the One who giveth to the field its flower,
He's the One in all the universe most fair,
He's the One who sends the sunshine and the
　shower,
He's the One with whom none other can compare.

He's the One who made the valleys and the moun-
　tains,
He's the One who gives the fields of golden grain,
He's the One who made the crystal flowing foun-
　tains,
He's the Lamb of God who for my sins was slain.

He's the One who blends the colors in the rainbow,
He's the One who draws the snowflakes' fair
　design,
He's the One who cares for me through sun and
　shadow,
And the wonder of it all is—He is mine!

—Mary Louise Leonard

21

Redemption . . .

The Cross, Salvation, Eternal Life

My Advocate

I sinned. And straightway, post-haste,
    Satan flew
Before the presence of the Most High
    God,
And made a railing accusation there.
He said, "This soul, this thing of clay
    and sod,
Has sinned. 'Tis true that he has named
    Thy name,
But I demand his death, for Thou has said,
'The soul that sinneth, it shall die.' Shall
    not
Thy sentence be fulfilled? Is justice dead?
Send now this wretched sinner to his
    doom.
What other thing can righteous ruler do?"
And thus he did accuse me day and night
And every word he spoke, O God was
    true!

Then quickly One rose up from God's
    right hand,
Before whose glory angels veiled their
    eyes.
He spoke, "each jot and tittle of the law
Must be fulfilled: the guilty sinner dies!
But wait. . . . Suppose his guilt were all
    transferred
To ME and that I paid his penalty!
Behold My hands, My side, My feet! One
    day
I was made sin for him, and died that he
Might be presented faultless, at Thy
    throne!"
And Satan fled away. Full well he knew
That he could not prevail against such
    love,
For every word my dear Lord spoke was
    true!

—*Martha Snell Nicholson*

Sin Revealed

By the Law is the knowledge of sin
        —*Rom. 3:20.*

Lord, how secure my conscience was,
    And felt no inward dread!
I was alive without the Law,
    And thought my sins were dead.

My hopes of heaven were firm and
        bright;
    But since the Precept came,
With a convincing power and might,
    I find how vile I am.

My guilt appeared but small before,
    'Till terribly I saw,
How perfect, holy, just and pure,
    Was Thy eternal Law.

Then felt my soul the heavy load—
    My sins revived again;
I had provoked a dreadful God,
    And all my hopes were slain.

'Till at the Cross of Calvary,
    I fell in deep despair,
Where Jesus bore the guilt for me,
    And I left my burden there.

—*Isaac Watts*

THE SOLID ROCK

My hope is built on nothing less
    Than Jesus' blood and righteousness.
    I dare not trust the sweetest frame
    But wholly lean on Jesus' name.
When darkness veils His lovely face,
    I rest in His unchanging grace;
In every high and stormy gale
    My anchor holds within the veil.
    On Christ the Solid Rock I stand;
    All other ground is sinking sand.

—*Edward Mote*

The Lost Sheep

The ninety and nine were counted,
  By the Shepherd at the close of the
    day.
But one of the number was missing;
  From the fold it had wandered away.

So the shepherd searched o'er the moun-
    tains
  And far in the valley below,
Crying out in great sorrow and anguish,
  Oh! where did my poor sheep go?

The night was dark and dreary,
  As he searched 'round many a rock.
For He loved the sheep of his bosom
  And wanted it back in his flock.

So he hunted on in the darkness,
  Till at last the poor sheep was found,
Bleeding, and torn, and helpless,
  He lifted it up from the ground.

He pressed it close to his bosom
  As he turned away in the cold,
And he wept with joy and gladness
  As he carried it back to the fold.

So Jesus the Shepherd is searching
  Over hills that are dark and cold,
Longing for the sheep of his bosom,
  To carry them back to the fold.

—*G. C. Golay*

Crowned or Crucified?

"What will ye then that I shall do
unto him?" (Mark 13:12). "You must
either crown Jesus or crucify Him."
—*Dr. G. Campbell Morgan*

I stood alone at the bar of God,
  In the hush of the twilight dim,
And faced the question that pierced
    my heart:
  "What will you do with Him?"
"Crowned or crucified? Which shall it
    be?"
No other choice was offered me.

He held out His loving hands to me,
  While He pleadingly said, "Obey!
Make Me thy choice, for I love thee
    so"—
  And I could not say Him nay.
Crowned, not crucified—this it must
    be;
  No other way was open to me.

I knelt in tears at the feet of Christ,
  In the hush of the twilight dim,
And all that I was, or hoped, or sought,
  Surrendered unto Him.
Crowned, not crucified—my heart shall
    know
  No king but Christ, who loveth me
    so.

The A B C of Salvation

"**ALL have sinned** and come short of the glory of God" (Romans 3:23). This is the first fact in God's redemption plan. The first chapters of the Bible tell us of the fall of man. As a result of Adam's transgressions, all men are lost. This is why all men need a Savior.

"**BEHOLD the Lamb of God** that taketh away the sin of the world" (John 1:29). Jesus Christ, God's only begotten Son, in His death on the cross offered His own blood as a Lamb slain before God for the remission of the sins of the world. Christ alone can take away our sin.

"**COME UNTO ME ALL YE**—and I will give you rest" (Matt. 11:28). It is there-fore coming unto Him, exercising faith in Him who is our sin bearer that will bring to us eternal salvation. "Him that cometh unto me I will in no wise cast out" (John 6:37).

The Message of the Cross

In the Cross of Christ I see,
   All the Love of God to me;
He it was who loved and gave,
   Guilty, sinful man to save.

In the Cross of Christ I know
   Something of my Saviour's woe.
I may surely read therein,
   All the sinfulness of sin.

In the Cross of Christ I learn
   Righteous judgment to discern;
See the Substitute for me
   Cursed and smitten on the Tree.

There I see my Surety die
   For a sinner such as I,
There my broken heart can trace
   All the riches of His grace.

At the Cross my soul finds peace
   From its burden full release;
There I may be reconciled,
   And confessed by God His child.

—George Goodman

Look Unto Jesus

Sweet the moments, rich in blessing
   Which before the cross we spend,
Life and health and peace possessing
   From the sinners' dying Friend.

Here we rest in wonder, viewing
   All our sins on Jesus laid;
Here we see redemption flowing
   From the sacrifice He made.

Here we find the dawn of heaven
   While upon the cross we gaze,
See our trespasses forgiven,
   And our songs of triumph raise.

Oh, that, near the cross abiding,
   We may to the Savior cleave,
Naught with Him our hearts dividing,
   All for Him content to leave!

Lord, in loving contemplation
   Fix our hearts and eyes on Thee
Till we taste Thy full salvation
   And Thine unveiled glory see!

He Did It All for You and Me

JESUS WAS LONELY (Matthew 14:23)
   That I might never be alone. (Matthew 28:20)
JESUS WAS TEMPTED (Matthew 4:1)
   That He might deliver me in temptation's hour. (Hebrews 4:15)
JESUS WAS FORSAKEN (Matthew 26:56)
   That I would never be forsaken. (Hebrews 13:5)
JESUS WAS CRUCIFIED (Matthew 27:50)
   That I might live forever (John 3:16)
JESUS BECAME A SERVANT TO MAN (Philippians 2:7)
   To make me a son of God. (I John 3:1)
JESUS TOOK UPON HIMSELF THE FORM OF MAN (Philippians 2:7)
   That I might have the image of God. (II Corinthians 3:18)
JESUS WAS SEPARATED FROM GOD (Matthew 27:46)
   That I might have eternal fellowship with God. (I John 1:8)
JESUS SUFFERED THE WRATH OF GOD (Mark 15:34)
   That I might know the love of God. (Ephesians 3:19)
JESUS ENDURED THE CROSS (Luke 23:33)
   That I might wear the crown. (II Timothy 3:8)

Wait a Minute . . .

*Before you do anything else
ask yourself
this important question . . .*

AM I READY TO MEET GOD?

"It is appointed unto men once to die, but after this the judgment" (Heb. 9:27).

"So then every one of us shall give account of himself to God" (Rom. 14:12).

Did you know that without trusting the Lord Jesus Christ as your Savior from sin you are not ready to meet God?

"He that believeth on the Son hath everlasting life: and he that believed not the Son shall not see life; but the wrath of God abideth on him" (John 3:36).

In God's sight you are a sinner,

"For all have sinned, and come short of the glory of God" (Rom. 3:23).

and God, being just, must punish sin.

"The wicked shall be turned into hell" (Psalm 9:17).

You cannot save yourself by anything that you can do.

"But we are all as an unclean thing, and all our righteousnesses are as filthy rags" (Isaiah 64:6).

TO STOP HERE WOULD LEAVE YOU WITHOUT HOPE!

But God loves you, and He Himself has provided for your salvation.

"For God so loved the world that he gave his only begotten Son, that whosoever believeth in him should not perish, but have everlasting life" (John 3:16).

To the sinner accepting Jesus Christ, God gives many promises.

Eternal life:

"And I give unto them eternal life; and they shall never perish, neither shall any man pluck them out of my hand" (John 10:28).

New standing before God:

"Therefore being justified by faith, we have peace with God through our Lord Jesus Christ" (Romans 5:1).

New nature:

"Therefore if any man be in Christ, he is a new creature: old things are passed away; behold, all things are become new" (II Cor. 5:17).

Forgiveness of sin:

"If we confess our sins, he is faithful and just to forgive us our sins, and to cleanse us from all unrighteousness" (I John 1:9).

Peace:

"Peace I leave with you, my peace I give unto you: not as the world giveth give I unto you. Let not your heart be troubled, neither let it be afraid" (John 14:27).

—*Dale Crowley, Jr.*

PARDON FOR ALL

Ruth M. Hawkes

*The One who reigns supreme on high,
   Whose mind conceived the plan
Of all this wondrous universe,
   Stoops down to pardon man.*

*A voice of penitence ascends,
   He bends with listening ear,
His gentle voice speaks to the soul—
   "Trust me, thou need'st not fear."*

*Though man is weak and scarred by
   sin,
   Has strayed far, far away—
"Come unto me, I'll give you rest,"
   He hears the Savior say.*

*How great our God! Omnipotent!
   His heart how good, how kind!
Oh, thou who know'st not His love,
   Seek Him, and thou shalt find!*

25

"The Blood"

John D. MacKinnon

There is a Cross all stained with blood,
　On Calvary's hill it stands,
That precious blood is flowing still
　Drawn from His feet and hands.
This precious blood that stained the
　Cross,
　It flows for you and me;
Come now and plunge beneath the flood
　And let your soul be free.

The blood that stained the rugged Cross
　On which my Savior died,
The blood that saves us from our sins
　Comes from His wounded side.
His blood it flowed down o'er the Cross
　Until it stained the ground,
Will cleanse your heart and make you
　free
　From sins that have you bound.

This flow of blood on Calvary's Hill
　Is from the Savior's heart;
When Satan had us at his will
　He died to take our part.
Then why not come to Him just now?
　He is waiting now for you.
Come to the Cross and call on Him
　And all things will be new.

Pastor Bob Crowley

Our Bible teaches the doctrine of *depravity.* While there is education and housing and higher wages and social security—all these things have not changed the nature of man; and the Bible teaches that it will not change: and if we are to blame evil, and crime, and broken homes, and all these things on the lack of economic progress, we are then taking an extreme unrealistic look at human nature.

We must have something *outside ourselves* to defeat the force of evil in this world: and this is exactly why Jesus Christ came into the world, and He alone can give to us the victory over evil. He declared, "I am come that ye might have life, and have it more abundantly."

A Seed, A Harvest

Except a corn of wheat fall
　To the ground and die,
It must remain just one small grain,
　It cannot multiply.
The germ of life within can never be
　Set free,
Until it go to death below,
　Until it cease to be.
These grains by hand of man are
　Cast into the earth:
Beneath the clod by touch of God,
　New life springs forth to birth:
Each green and tender blade is God's
　Own special care,
And harvest field will give the yield,
　Of full corn in the ear.
How slow we are to learn this mes-
　sage
　Of the Cross;
That we must die to bring forth fruit
　Receive our gain through loss.
As grain in Sower's hand, we yield
　Ourselves to Thee;
We own Thee, Lord, we claim Thy
　Word,
　A harvest we shall see.

When I Survey

When I survey the wondrous cross
　On which the Prince of Glory died,
My richest gain I count but loss,
　And pour contempt on all my pride.

Forbid it, Lord! that I should boast,
　Save in the death of Christ my God:
All the vain things that charm me most,
　I sacrifice them to His blood.

See, from His head, His hands, His feet,
　Sorrow and love flow mingled down;
Did e'er such love and sorrow meet,
　Or thorns compose so rich a crown."

Were the whole realm of nature mine,
　That were a present far too small;
Love so amazing, so divine,
　Demands my soul, my life, my all!

The Touch of the Master's Hand

'Twas battered and scarred, and the auc-
  tioneer
Thought it scarcely worth his while
To waste much time on the old violin,
  But he held it up with a smile.
"What am I bidden, good folk?" he
  cried.
  "Who'll start the bidding for me?
"A dollar—a dollar—then two, only
  two—
"Going for three"—but no—
  From the room far back, a gray-haired
  man
Came forward and picked up the bow,
  Then, wiping the dust from the old
  violin,
And tightening the loosened strings,
  He played a melody pure and sweet
  As a caroling angel sings.

The music ceased, and the auctioneer,
  With the voice that was quiet and low,
Said, "NOW what am I bid for the old
  violin?"
  And he held it up with the bow.
"A thousand dollars—and who'll make it
  two?
  "Two thousand—and who'll make it
  three?

"Three thousand once—three thousand
  twice—
  "And going and gone," cried he.
The people cheered, but some of them
  cried,
  "We do not understand.
"What changed the worth?"—Quick
  came the reply,
  "The touch of the Master's hand."

And many a man with life out of tune,
  And battered and scarred with sin,
Is auctioned cheap, to a thoughtless
  crowd,
  Much like the old violin.
A "mess of pottage"—a glass of wine,
  A game—and he travels on:
He is going once—and going twice—
  He's going—and almost gone!
But the Master comes, and the foolish
  crowd
Never can quite understand
The worth of a soul, and the change
  that's wrought
By THE TOUCH OF THE MAS-
  TER'S HAND.

—From "The Touch of the Master's Hand"
by Myra Brooks Welch, Brethren Publishing
House, Elgin, Ill., 1941.

ETERNITY

Once on a time I heard a preacher say:
"Suppose an angel were to start today
From some far star ten trillion miles away
And wing his way to earth through trackless
  space,
And pick one grain of sand, and then retrace
His weary journey to its starting place.
Each trip eons of time! So on and on,
'Til earth's last tiny grain of sand was gone,
And still eternity was just begun!"
The mind reels back from such immensity
Of time! . . . Undying soul, where will you be,
Where will you spend your long eternity!

—Marth Snell Nicholson

Call to Repentance

Say, where is thy refuge, you poor sinner,
And what is thy prospect today!
Why toil for the wealth that will perish,
The treasures that rust and decay?

O think of thy soul, that forever
Must live on eternity's shore,
When thou in the dust art forgotten,
When pleasures can charm thee no
    more.

The Master is calling thee, sinner,
In tones of compassion and love,
To feel that sweet rapture of pardon,
And lay up thy treasures above.

O kneel at the cross where He suffered,
To ransom thy soul from the grave:
The arm of His mercy will hold thee,
The arm that is mighty to save.

As summer is waning, poor sinner,
Repent, ere the season is past;
God's goodness to thee is extended,
As long as the day-beam shall last;

Then slight not the warning repeated
With all the bright moments that roll,
Nor say, when the harvest is ended,
That no one hath cared for thy soul.

'Twill profit thee nothing, but fearful
    the cost,
To gain the whole world, if thy soul
    should be lost.

"Then Jesus Came"

"When Jesus comes the tempter's power
    is broken,
    When Jesus comes, the tears are
      wiped away.
He takes the gloom and fills the life
    with glory,
    For all is changed when Jesus comes
      to stay."

At the Door

"Behold, I stand at the door, and knock; if any man hear my voice, and open the door, I will come in to him, and will sup with him and he with me" (Rev. 3:20).

I opened the door of my heart one day
And let the dear Christ in—
I asked Him henceforth to hold full sway
And leave no room for sin.
I am so glad I opened the door of my
    heart
To welcome this dearest Friend.
And I know He and I can never part
If I'm faithful and true to the end.
For never again will I bar the way
In His service my pleasure shall be
Till I knock for entrance, somewhere,
    someday
And He opens the door for me.

Joy of the New Birth

Written by a new Japanese Christian

(The following poem was written by Miss Kyoko Tsunoka afer her conversion to Christ in Noheji, Aomori Prefecture.)

Oh, the purity of being born again;
    I promise to follow the Lord.
Oh, the depth of the grace of being
    loved;
    Thankful to the Lord.
Oh, the pain of being chastened by
    Thee;
    Enduring in the Lord.
Oh, the joy of holding the glory of the
    Cross;
    I will lift up the name of the Lord.
Oh, the steadfastness of the founda-
    tion of the truth;
    It will never change throughout
    eternity.
Oh, the emptiness of my pride;
    Before the Lord it becomes dust.
Oh, the eternity of thankfulness;
    Praising the name of the Lord.

Jesus Alone Satisfies

Mary Helen Quinn

This world has nothing to offer
  To fill your longing soul—
Its pleasures are empty and hollow
  Sin and death are its goal.

This world has nothing to offer
  When sorrow has entered your gate—
No faith in a life immortal,
  No promise of a heavenly state.

This world has nothing to offer
  In times of distress and despair—
No courage to face life's battles,
  No strength to carry your care.

This world has nothing to offer
  When sin has ruined your life—
No hope for a full salvation,
  No victory o'er sin and strife.

This world has nothing to offer
  Even when all seems bright—
And your life is a gay round of pleasure,
  Remember—there cometh the night.

This world has nothing to offer
  When you come to the end of the road—
No light to brighten the valley,
  No hope of a happy abode.

Our Saviour has *all* to offer—
  He can fill your longing soul,
His balm can heal your heartache
  And make your broken life whole.

His strength can fill you with courage
  When facing life's battles afraid,
His blood can cleanse your sin-stains,
  On the cross He your ransom has paid.

Our Saviour has all to offer—
  His will is our joy and delight,
In His presence are pleasures forever,
  The pathway to heaven is bright.

So why will you not take our Saviour
  And leave this old world behind?
You see how vain are its offerings,
  But in Christ Jesus your all you will
    find.

Ring the Bells of Heaven

The theme of the Hour of Inspiration increases in popularity. Lyrics to the beautiful melody are:

> Ring the bells of heaven!
>   There is joy today
> For a soul returning from
>   From the wild.
> See, the Father meets him
>   Out upon the way,
> Welcoming His weary,
>   Wand'ring child.
>
> Ring the bells of heaven!
>   There is joy today,
> For the wand'rer now
>   Is reconciled';
> Yes, a soul is rescued
>   From his sinful way,
> And is born anew
>   A ransomed child.
>
> Ring the bells of heaven!
>   Spread the feast today!
> Angels swell the glad
>   Triumphant strain!
> Tell the joyful tidings,
>   Bear it far away!
> For a precious soul
>   Is born again.
>
> CHORUS:
> Glory! Glory! how the angels
>   sing,
> Gory! Glory! how the loud harps
>   ring!
> 'Tis the ransomed army,
> Like a mighty sea,
> Pealing forth the anthem of the
>   free.

"Therefore if any man be in Christ, he is a new creature: old things are passed away; behold all things are become new" (2 Cor. 5:17).

The Sea of God's Forgetfulness

Written by an Irish factory girl

I will cast in the depths of the fathomless sea,
 All they sins and transgressions, whatever they be;
Though they mount up to heaven; though they reach down to hell,
 They shall sink in the depths, and above them shall swell
All My waves of forgiveness, so mighty and free;
 I will cast all thy sins in the depths of the sea.

In the depths, in the depths, where the storm cannot come;
 Where its faint echo falls like a musical hum;
Where no mortal can enter, thy faults to deride;
 Far above them forever flows love's mighty tide.
Of their sepulcher vast—I, thy God, hold the key—
 I have buried them there in the depths of the sea.

In the deep, silent depths far away from the shore,
 Where they never may rise to trouble thee more;
Where no far-reaching tide with its pitiless sweep,
 Can stir the dark waters of forgetfulness deep—
I have buried them there, where no mortal can see—
 I have cast all thy sins in the depths of the sea.

BY THE CROSS

Oh, Lord, please let me see
How Thou didst suffer for me
In the garden of Gethsemane,
And die in such agony
On the cross of Calvary!

Oh, Lord, please let me feel
The pang of Thine ordeal
As Thou didst bleed to heal,
To purchase and to seal
My ruined soul to endless weal!

Oh, Lord, please let me taste
Of Thy reproach, of shame so base;
Of jeers and sneers cast in Thy face;
Of stinging scorn Thou didst embrace
To purchase life for a thankless race!

Oh, Lord, please let me hear
Thy groanings; and let me bear
To stand by Thy cross near,
Hear the drip of blood and tears
Fall forth proclaiming love so dear!

—Dale Crowley

No One Ever Cared for Me Like Jesus

I would like to tell you what I think of
 Jesus
  Since I found in Him a friend so
  strong and true;
I would tell you how He changed my
  life completely—
  He did something that no other one
  could do.

All my life was full of sin when Jesus
  found me;
  All my heart was full of misery and
  woe;
Jesus placed His loving arms around me,
  And He led me in the way I ought to
  go.

CHORUS:
No one ever cared for me like Jesus,
  There's no other friend so kind as He;
No one else could take the sin and dark-
  ness from me—
  Oh, how much He cared for me.

Every Hour and Every Day

Once in the stillness
    Of the late midnight hour
I felt the presence
    Of the Lord's saving power.

I fell on my knees
    And cried to Him there,
"O merciful Saviour,—
    Hear a lost sinner's prayer.

CHORUS:
Well, every hour, and every day;—
    Yes, every moment in every way,
I'm leaning on Jesus,
    The Rock of my soul.
I'm singing His praises
    Wherever I go.

I'll never forget
    That night on my knees—
The joy of that hour
    Has never left me.

It's my sweetest mem'ry
    That time can't erase:
I'm saved by His mercy,
    Redeemed by His grace.

You Cannot Hide From God

You cannot hide from God;
His eyes run to and fro;
He sees your every move—
He knows the way you go.

You cannot hide from God
No matter how you try;
Your every deed is seen
By His all-watchful eye.

You cannot hide from God;
He knows your every thought,
The intents of your heart,
The deeds that you have wrought.

You cannot hide from God
So why not seek His face?
He'll give you joy and peace,
And save you by His grace.

You cannot hide from God;
He loves you though you've strayed;
He's watching you today—
He wants you to be saved!

So lift your eyes to Jesus!
Behold the Lamb of God!
And cast you at His feet—
You cannot hide from God!

*"For God so loved the world that He gave His only begotten Son,
that whosoever believeth in Him should not perish,
but have everlasting life" (John 3:16).*

The Bible Declares of Jesus Christ

He is able to forgive our sins (Eph. 1:7).
He is able to deliver us from judgment (1 Thess. 1:10).
He is able to deliver us from the fear of death (Heb. 2:15).
He is able to reconcile us to God (II Cor. 5:20).
He is able to give us eternal life (John 10:28).
He is able to save ANYONE completely (Heb. 7:25).
He is able to give His peace and joy (John 14:27; 15:11).
He is able to take us to heaven (Jude 24).
He is able to help and save YOU (John 3:16).
"For whosoever shall call upon the name of the Lord shall
    be saved" (Rom. 10:13).

ACCEPTED

'Tis not for works which I have
   wrought,
'Tis not for gifts which I have brought,
Nor yet for blessings that I sought,
That I have been "Accepted."

'Tis not for tears that I have shed,
'Tis not for prayers that I have said,
Nor yet for slavish fear or dread,
That I have been "Accepted."

'Tis not for these, however right,
That God has formed intense delight,
Nor is it these that have made white
The robes of those "Accepted."

From these I turn my eyes to Him,
Who bore the judgment due to sin,
And by Christ's blood I enter in,
And share in his Acceptance.

His precious Blood was shed for me,
And in that precious Blood I see,
The righteous ground, the perfect plea,
For my complete Acceptance.

And when within that circle sweet,
Where God's eternal smile I meet,
I'll praise Him for the work complete,
Through which I am "Accepted."

Grace, Love and Mercy

How boundless is Thy sover-
   eign grace!
  No moral tongue can tell;
It seeks Thy children every
   place,
  And saves them all from hell.
O wondrous love, never ceas-
   ing,
  Rich in mercy, freely given;
Descending on the vilest sinner.
  And fitting him for heaven!

           —*W. L. Griffin*

"Forgiven"

1 John 2:12

Not far from New York, in a cemetery
   lone,
Close guarding its grave, stands a simple headstone
And all the inscription is one word
   alone—
      "Forgiven"

No sculptor's fine art hath embellished
   its form,
But constantly there, though the calm
   and the storm,
It beareth this word from a poor fallen
   worm—
      "Forgiven"

It shows not the date of the silent
   one's birth,
Reveals not his frailties, nor lies of his
   worth,
But speaks out the tale from his few
   feet of earth—
      "Forgiven"

The death is unmentioned, the name is
   untold,
Beneath lies the body, corrupted and
   cold,
Above rests his spirit, at home in the
   fold—
      "Forgiven"

And when, from the heavens, the Lord
   shall descend,
This stranger shall rise, and to glory
   ascend,
Well known and befriended, to sing
   without end—
      "Forgiven"

Why I Love Him

He walked the road to Calvary
  To take for me the blame.
Upon His head a crown of thorns
  He bore for me the shame.

He gave His all upon the cross
  That I might be set free.
He loved me more than His own life
  He shed His blood for me.

Such love as this binds all my wounds
  And soothes my troubled soul.
It gives me strength for all my needs,
  It makes me free and whole.

I mount up with wings as eagles
  To follow after Him.
I never grow tired or weary
  In loving and serving Him.

I'll walk the road with Him each day
  And hold His nail-pierced hand
Till I shall come at last to dwell
  In Heaven's happy land.
          —Mrs. Helen Hazel

All the Way to Calvary

I do not seek for diadem or scepter,
  I do not ask for worldly joy or fame;
I only want to follow my Redeemer,
  And tell abroad the wonders of His name!

CHORUS:
I will follow all the way to Calvary
  I will walk the road that Jesus walked for me;
I will serve Him to the end, for He is my dearest
    friend.
  I will travel ALL THE WAY TO CALVARY.

I know the path He trod was never easy
  It cost the Son of God His precious blood;
It leads on to the path of nameless anguish.
  But ever climbeth upward unto God.

So trusting in His love I'll toil and suffer,
  Supported by His everlasting grace;
Until at last I rise complete, perfected,
  Transformed to look upon His blessed face.

Profit or Loss

What will it profit, when life here is o'er
  Though great worldly wisdom I gain,
If, seeking knowledge—I utterly fail
  The wisdom of God to obtain?

What will it profit, when life here is o'er
  Though gathering riches and fame,
If, gaining the world I lose my own soul
  And in Heav'n unknown is my name?

What will it profit, when life here is o'er
  Though earth's farthest corners I see,
If, going my way, and doing my will
  I miss what His love planned for me?

What will it profit, when life here is o'er
  Though earth's fleeting love has been
  mine
If, seeking its gifts—I fail to secure
  The riches of God's love divine?

What will it profit? My soul, stop and
  think
  What balance that day will declare!
Life's record laid bare—will gain turn to
  loss,
  And leave me at last to despair?

SALVATION

God thought it—
Christ bought it—
The Bible taught it—
The mind caught it—
The soul sought it—
The Spirit wrought it—
The devil fought it—
But I've got it,
 —By the grace of God!
        —Dr. Andrew Jackson

The Bible

My Bible and I

I have a companion of infinite worth;
We travel together through this dreary
    earth.
    From pilgrimage here to a home in the
      sky.
    We're traveling together, my Bible and
      I.

I have a companion, a wonderful guide!
A solace and comfort, whatever betide;
    A friend never failing when others
      pass by—
    Oh, blessed communion—my Bible
      and I.

I have a companion, 'tis God's Holy
    Word,
Revealing from heaven the mind of my
    Lord;
    My rock and my refuge when danger
      is nigh—
    We've blessings eternal, my Bible
      and I.

I have a companion, a heavenly light,
A pillar by day and a fire by night;
    A lamp from the cradle until I shall
      die—
    What blessed communion—my
      Bible and I.

I have a companion, a faithful friend,
A union of blessing that never shall
    end,
    Till Jesus returns with His saints
      from on high,
    We'll travel together, my Bible and
      I.

O light of my pathway! Thou lamp to
    my feet!
O manna from heaven! So precious
    and sweet.
    For thee do I live, and for thee
      would I die,
    Forever and ever, my Bible and I.

               —M. H. Knobloch

"I Am the Bible"

I am God's wonderful library.
I am always—and above all—The Truth.
To the weary pilgrim, I am a good strong
    staff.
To the one who sits in gloom, I am a
    glorious light.
To those who stoop beneath heavy bur-
    dens, I am sweet rest.
To him who has lost his way, I am a safe
    guide.
To those who have been hurt by sin, I
    am a healing balm.
To the discouraged, I whisper glad mes-
    sages of hope.
To those who are distressed by the
    storms of life, I am an anchor.
To those who suffer in lonely solitude, I
    am a cool, soft hand resting on a
    fevered brow.
O, child of man, to best defend me, just
    use me!

               —John Clifford

HOW FIRM A FOUNDATION

How firm a foundation ye saints of the
    Lord.
    Is laid for your faith in His excellent
      Word;
What more can He say than to you He
    hath said,
    You who unto Jesus for refuge hath
      fled.

In every condition, in sickness, in
    health,
    In poverty's vale, or abounding in
      wealth;
At home, and abroad, on the land, on
    the sea,
    As your days may demand shall
      your strength ever be.

Thank God for the Bible

Thank God for the Bible whose clear shining ray
　Has lighted our path, and turned night to day;
Its wonderful treasures have never been told,
　More precious than rubies set round with pure
　gold.
Thank God for the Bible! In sickness or health,
　It brings richer comforts than honor or wealth;
Its blessings are boundless, an infinite store;
　We may drink at its fountain and thirst never-
　more.
Thank God for the Bible! Rich treasures untold
　Are laid up in store in its city of gold,
That beautiful home of the saved and the blessed,
　Where no sorrow can come, and where the
　weary find rest.
There are millions who wander in darkness
　today;
　No Saviour, no Bible, no knowledge to pray;
God, help us to feel and to act in His sight,
　To render our thanks, now, by giving them
　light!

The Anvil

Last eve I paused beside a blacksmith's door
　And heard the anvil ring the vesper chime;
Then, looking in, I saw upon the floor
　Old hammers worn with beating years of
　time.

"How many anvils have you had?" said I,
　To wear and batter all these hammers, so?"
"Just one," said he; then said, with twinkling
　eye,
　"The anvil wears the hammers out, you
　know."

And so, I thought, the anvil of God's Word
　For ages skeptic blows have beat upon:
Yet, though the noise of falling blows was heard
　The anvil is unharmed—the hammers, gone!
　　　　　　　　　　　　　　—*Anonymous*

The Bible

It is the traveller's map,
　The pilgrim's staff,
　The pilot's compass,
　The soldier's sword
　And the Christian's character.

Here Heaven is opened,
　The gates of hell disclosed.

Christ is its subject,
　Our good its design,
　The glory of God its end.

It should fill the memory,
　Rule the heart
　And guide the feet.

Read it slowly,
　Frequently, prayerfully.

It is a mine of wealth,
　And a river of pleasure.

It is given to you here in this
　life,
　Will be opened at the judg-
　ment
　And is established forever.

It involves the highest responsi-
　bility,
　Will reward the greatest labor,
　And condemns all who trifle
　with it sacred contents.

**"So shall my word be that
goeth forth out of my mouth: it
shall not return unto me void,
but it shall accomplish that
which I please, and it shall
prosper in the things whereto I
sent it" (Isaiah 55:11).**

The Bible Is

The charter of all true liberty.
The forerunner of all civilization.
The molder of institutions and governments.
The fashion of law.
The secret of national progress.
The guide of history.
The ornament and mainspring of literature.
The inspiration of philosophies.
The textbook of ethics.
The soul of all strong heart life.
The illuminator of superstition.
The enemy of oppression.
The uprooter of sin.
The comfort in sorrow.
The strength in weakness.
The pathway out of perplexity.
The escape from temptation.
The steadier in the way of power.
The embodiment of all lofty ideals.
The begetter of life.
The promise of the future.
The star of death's night.
The revealer of God.
The guide, hope, and inspiration of man.
The compass that points to Heaven.

My Bible

There is a book more precious
    Than anything on earth.
No wealth of gold or jewels
    Can equal its worth.
I go to it in trouble,
    And though my heart is sore,
It always gives me comfort,
    I love it more and more.

When doubtful what is best for me,
    I seek its guidance true;
And if I search with open mind,
    It tells me what to do.
I lay it on my pillow,
    Or I clasp it to my breast,
When I am sad or lonely,
    It always gives me rest.

My BIBLE is the WRITTEN WORD:
    The living Word, is He—
So my Bible, and my Saviour
    Are all the same to me.
His Holy Spirit leads me
    His Word to understand.
So as I hold my Bible
    The Saviour holds my hand.

          —*Emma Tubbs McChesney*

"The Book"

"I've found a big, old dusty thing high on a
    shelf, mother, look!"
"Be careful, Johnny dear, that's the Bible,
    God's Holy Book."
"God's Book?" the child replied.
"Then, Mother, before we lose it,
We'd better send it back to God,
For you know, we never use it."

Prescription for Your Need

By Dr. Sunshine
to be taken according to directions

Though you may view your work in tears,
    And count it all in vain,
Psalm one two-six will calm your fears,
    And make you sing again.

Though darkness shuts you in like night,
    You need not go astray;
John 8:12 tells about a Light
    That turns your night to day.

Are you restless, ever restless,
    Like the billows of the sea?
There is perfect peace and quiet
    In Isaiah two-six, three.

When assailed by foes unnumbered,
    And you know not what to do,
Flee, O flee to David's fortress
    Named in Psalm eighteen, verse 2.

When you're sick, be not discouraged,
    Though no earthly help is nigh;
In James five you'll find a Healer
    Who can hear your faintest cry.

If there's but little in your purse,
    (Or maybe nothing, which is worse!)
Your God will help you in your need,
    Psalm 37 find and read.

If those around you seem unkind,
    In John 15 your help you'll find,
So read of Christ, the Friend for aye;
    For He is with you every day.

Are you needing food and raiment?
    Are you poor as poor can be?
Take, ACCORDING TO DIRECTIONS,
    Matthew 6, verse 33.

Have you lost your faith in people,
    In yourself, and everything?
Take Mark 'leven, two and twenty,
    It will make you shout and sing.

Are there strange, conflicting sign-
    boards?
    All along your upward way?

Take John 10, verse 27,
    And you cannot go astray.

When death has claimed your loved
    ones,
    And you are torn with grief,
1 Thessalonians 4, helps,
    And gives one great relief.

Do you often feel unhappy?
    There's a safe and certain cure,
Found in Proverbs 16:20,
    That will happiness insure.

Are you starting on a journey?
    Does your heart sink with dismay?
Proverbs 3, verse 6, can strengthen,
    And direct you on your way.

When you are growing faint in heart,
    And would a tonic find,
Psalm 27 can impart
    New strength to heart and mind.

Are you oft inclined to worry?
    Have you more than you can bear?
In 1 Peter 5, verse 7,
    There's a balm for every care.

—Mrs. Clara S. Fisher

Unchained

There was a day when C. H. Spurgeon was criticized for not coming promptly enough to the defense of the Bible when it was being attacked. "Defend the Bible?" flamed the great preacher at his critics, "I would as soon think of defending a lion! Unchain it, and it will defend itself!"

This has been the true apostolic spirit from the first century to the twentieth. Unchain the Word of God, and it would go raging through the world and take the hearts of men by storm.

The Bible in the Schools

I'd like to see the Bible placed
    Where the Bible used to be:
Upon the top of the teacher's desk
    For every child to see.
I'd like to hear the teacher say,
    As my teacher used to do:
"Before we work or play, dear ones,
    I want to read to you."

I'd like to see the teacher stand
    Before the class again
And lift with reverent care the Book
    That makes God's purpose plain,
And ere the youngsters went to work,
    I'd like to hear her voice
Repeat those words of truth and faith
    That makes one's soul rejoice.

I'd like to see her face light up
    At each resplendent word,
And watch the children's souls shine out
    At the message they had heard;
I'd like to see the sweet content
    Fill the dear room, each nook,
And know that joy had come to each
    When teacher read the Book.

Yes, I'd like to see the Bible placed
    Where the Bible used to be,
I'd like to hear it read aloud
    In the schoolroom of the free.
I want my children taught to know
    God's matchless gift of love,
The Book of books is wisdom's gate
    To that bright home above.

MY OLD BIBLE

Though the cover be worn,
    And the pages are torn,
And though places bear traces of tears,
    Yet more precious than gold
Is the Book, worn and old,
    That can shatter and scatter my fears.

When I prayerfully look
    In the precious old Book,
Many pleasures and treasures I see;
    Many tokens of love,
From the Father above,
    Who is the nearest and dearest to me.

This old Book is my guide,
    'Tis a friend by my side,
It will lighten and brighten my way,
    Soothes and gladdens the mind,
As I read it and heed it today.

To this Book I will cling,
    Of its worth I will sing,
Though great losses and crosses be
    mind;
For I cannot despair,
    Though surrounded by care,
While possessing this blessing divine.

God's Wonderful Word

Thy Word is like a garden, Lord,
    With flowers bright and fair;
And everyone who seeks may pluck
    A lovely cluster there.
Thy Word is like a deep, deep mine;
    And jewels rich and rare
Are hidden in its mighty depths
    For every searcher there.
Thy Word is like a starry host:
    A thousand rays of light
Are seen to guide the traveler,
    And make his pathway bright.
Thy Word is like an armory
    Where soldiers may repair,
And find, for life's long battle day,
    All needful weapons there.
O may I love Thy precious Word,
    May I explore the mine,
May I its fragrant flowers glean,
    May light upon me shine.
O may I find my armor there,
    Thy Word my trusty sword;
I'll learn to fight with every foe
    The battle of the Lord.
        —Edwin Hodder

The Bible Stands

"The Bible stands like a rock
   undaunted
  'Mid the raging storms of time;
Its pages burn with truth eternal
   And they glow with a light sublime.

The Bible stands like a towering
   mountain
  Above the works of men;
Its truth by none can be refuted,
   And destroy it, they never can!

The Bible stands and it will forever
   When the world has passed away;
By inspiration it has been given,
   All its precepts I'll obey.

The Bible stands every test we give it,
   For its author is Divine,
By grace alone I hope to live it
   And prove it, and make it mine."
      —From *212 Victory Poems*

The Bible Has the Answer!

The Bible has the answer,
  It's the Word of life and light;
There's no groping in the darkness
  When your way is always bright.

The Bible has the answer,
  It's the compass and the chart;
You'll have the right directions
  When God's Word is in your heart.

The Bible has the answer,
  You'll have joy and vict'ry, too,
As you walk the pilgrim's pathway
  With the guide that's always true.

The Bible has the answer,
  It's the Book that shows the way.
It reveals the Christ of glory
  Who can change your night to day.

The Bible has the answer,
  Send the Word o'er land and sea:
It's the message of salvation,
  It's the power to make men free.
      —*Dale Crowley*

✣ ✣ ✣ ✣ ✣ ✣

The Bible—Yet It Lives

Generations follow generations—yet it
  lives.
Nations rise and fall—yet it lives.
Kings, dictators, presidents come and
  go—yet it lives.
Torn, condemned, burned—yet it lives.
Hated, despised, cursed—yet it lives.
Doubted, suspected, criticized—yet it
  lives.
Damned by atheists—yet it lives.
Scoffed at by scorners—yet it lives.
Exaggerated by fanatics—yet it lives.
Misconstrued and misstated—yet it
  lives.
Ranted and raved about—yet it lives.
Its inspiration denied—yet it lives.
Yet it lives—as a lamp to our feet.
Yet it lives—as a light to our paths.
Yet it lives—as the gate to heaven.
Yet it lives—as a standard for child-
  hood.
Yet it lives—as a guide for youth.
Yet it lives—as an inspiration for the
  matured.
Yet it lives—as a comfort for the aged.
Yet it lives—as food for the hungry.
Yet it lives—as water for the thirsty.
Yet it lives—as rest for the weary.
Yet it lives—as light for the heathen.
Yet it lives—as salvation for the sinner.
Yet it lives—as grace for the Christian.
  To know it is to love it.
  To love it is to accept it.
  To accept it means life eternal.
      —*Willard L. Johnson*

✣ ✣ ✣ ✣ ✣ ✣

The Bible Has *Your* Answer

If you are lonely, read Psalm 23.
If you need more faith, read Hebrews 11.
If you want new courage, read Joshua 1:9.
If you are harassed by doubts, read John 7:17.
If you are in danger, read Psalm 91.
If your sins are unconfessed, read 1 John 1:9.
If you want to conquer the adversary, read Ephesians 6:11-18.
If you want more confidence and assurance, read Romans 8.
If you are inclined to forget God's blessings, read Psalm 103.
If you want to be filled with joy and peace, read Philippians 4.
If you want to be a fruit-bearing Christian, read John 15.
If you have thoughts about death and the hereafter, read 1 Corinthians 15.
If you are sorrowful, read John 14:1-6; 1 Thessalonians 4:13-18.
If you are disposed to worry, read Matthew 6:19-34.
If you are fearful and afraid, read Psalms 27 and 46.
If you harbor bitterness or malice, read 1 Corinthians 13.
If you need some good rules for daily living, read Romans 12.
If you want a spiritual feast, read Psalm 19.
If you want more zeal and enthusiasm, read the book of Acts.

—From "The Bible Has the Answer,"
by Evang. Dale Crowley, page 121.

If the Bible Has No Answer

If the Bible has no answer
    We are doomed to dark despair.
Our lives are weak and worthless,
    If we can find no help there.

Have we come this toilsome way
    With sore and bleeding feet,
To discover the Old Book wanting,
    And there is no mercy seat?

Have we heard a mother's prayer
    In the still and silent night,
To learn for the burden on her heart
    There is no ray of light?

Have we looked on the faces of dear ones
    Who will greet us here no more,
Only to know we shall never meet them
    Over there on the Golden Shore?

If God's hand has ever led you
    Through surges wild and deep,
You KNOW the Bible has the answer,
    And every promise He will keep.

—Lillian Musick

Famous People on the Witness Stand

"The entrance of Thy words giveth light; they give understanding unto the simple" (Psalm 119:13).

A Great Astronomer:
"All human discoveries seem to be made only for the purpose of confirming more and more strongly the truths contained in the sacred Scriptures." —Sir William Herschel

A Noted Author:
"The most learned, astute and diligent student cannot, in the longest life, obtain an entire knowledge of this one volume—the Bible." —Sir Walter Scott

A Celebrated Jurist:
"The Bible has always been regarded as part of the Common Law of England." —Judge Blackstone, England

A Renowned Warrior:
"The Bible is no mere book, but a living Power that conquers all that oppose it." —Napoleon Bonaparte

A Famous Philosopher:
"There never was found, in any age of the world, either religion or law that did so highly exalt the public good as the Bible." —Sir Francis Bacon

A Distinguished Author:
"All that I have ever taught of art, everything that I have written, whatever greatness of mine, whatever I have done in my life, has simply been due to the fact that, when I was a child, my mother daily read with me a part of the Bible, and daily made me learn a part of it by heart." —John Ruskin

A Renowned Philosopher:
"The existence of the Bible, as a Book for the people, is the greatest benefit which the human race has ever experienced." —Immanuel Kant

A Famous British General
"I read my Bible every day, and recommend you, Gentlemen, to do the same." (Said to his military staff.) — Sir Bernard L. Montgomery

A Great Queen:
"The greatness of my empire, I owe to the Bible." Queen Mary of Britain

A Famous Statesman:
"I have known ninety-five great men of the world in my time, and of these, eighty-seven were followers of the Bible." Sir William E. Gladstone, Prime Minister of Great Britain.

Another Great Philosopher:
"It is a belief in the Bible, the fruits of deep meditation, which has served me as the guide of my moral and literary life. The further the ages advance in cultivation, the more can the Bible be used." —The German Writer, Geothe

A Celebrated Scientist:
"We account the Scriptures of God to be the most sublime philosophy. I find more sure marks of authority in the Bible than in any profane history whatever." —Sir Isaac Newton

A Supreme Court Justice:
"The American nation from its first settlement at Jamestown to this hour is based upon and permeated by the principles of the Bible." —Justice David Joseph Brewer

A Celebrated Scientist:
"I consider an intimate knowledge of the Bible an indispensable qualificfation of a well-educated man." —Dr. Robert A. Milliken

A Famous Educator:
"I thoroughly believe in a university education . . . but I believe a knowl-

edge of the Bible without a college course is more valuable than a college course without the Bible. Everyone who has a thorough knowledge of the Bible may truly be called educated." —Dr. Wm. Lyon Phelps, Yale University

A Great Statesman:
"The whole hope of human progress is suspended on the ever-growing influence of the Bible." —William Henry Seward

A Noted Surgeon:
"I have never in my whole life met a man who really knew the Bible and rejected it. The difficulty has always been an unwillingness to give it an honest trial." —Dr. Howard A. Kelly, Johns-Hopkins

A Famous Archaeologist:
"Of the hundreds of thousands of artifacts found by the archaeologists, not one has ever been discovered that contradicts, or denies one word, phrase, clause, or sentence of the Bible . . . but always confirms, and verifies the facts of the Biblical record." —Dr. J. O. Kinnaman

A Distinguished Leader:
"I believe the Bible because it is the Word of God." —William Jennings Bryan

A Famous Statesman:
"Whatever achievement of my life there is to be commended, the credit is due to my kind parents in instilling into my mind an early love of the Scriptures. —Daniel Webster

A Great General:
"In all my perplexities and distresses, the Bible has never failed to give me light and strength." —Robert E. Lee

A Noted Philosopher:
"In that final hour that comes to all men . . . this Book alone brings the word, like a bell in the fog, of Him who says, 'I am the resurrection and the Life.' " —Dr. Frank Crane

A Famous Poet
"We search the world for truth, we cull
The good, the true, the beautiful,
From graven stone and written scroll,
And all old flower-fields of the soul;
And weary seekers of the best,
We come back laden from our quest,
To find that all the sages said
Is in the Book our mothers read."

—John Greenleaf Whittier

God's Care . . .

His Goodness, Grace, Providence, Promises

"He That Keepeth Thee"

So often in the dark hours of the night
It comforts me to know of One who stays
Close by my side, Whose presence is a light
And a strength and solace through my nights
    and days.

And I am blest to know that as I sleep
He watches tenderly above me there,
And if I lie awake, He stays to keep
Me comraded and safe within His care.

O Love that will not slumber when my need
Is great through wearing pain or bitter loss.
O Love compassionate enough to heed
My cry, and with the strength to lift the cross
That otherwise might crush me. Love divine,
I thank Thee for this constant care of thine.
          —*Grace Noll Crowell*

God's Loving Hand

God's loving hand is everywhere,
  On every busy thoroughfare—
On mountain heights, in valleys low,
  On desert sands, in swirling snow;
In velvet green that clothes the hills,
  In tender buds, and song birds' trills;
And Summer, Winter, Spring and Fall,
  God's loving hand directs them all!
The things we see, touch, know and feel
  Prove God is present and He's real,
And, lo! how blest to understand
  We're kept by God's own loving hand!
          —*Jon Gilbert*

God's Kind Care

God hath not promised
  Skies always blue,
Flower-strewn pathways,
  All our life through;
God hath not promised
  Sun without rain,
Joy without sorrow,
  Peace without pain.

God hath not promised
  We shall not know
Toil and temptation,
  Trouble and woe;
He hath not told us
  We shall not bear
Many a burden,
  Many a care.

God hath not promised
  Smooth roads and wide,
Swift, easy travel,
  Needing no guide;
Never a mountain
  Rocky and steep,
Never a river
  Turbid and deep.

But God hath promised
  Strength for the day,
Rest for the labor,
  Light for the way.
Grace for the trials,
  Help from above,
Unfailing sympathy,
  Undying love.
          —*Annie Johnson Flint*

*"And we know that all things work together for good
to them that love God, to them who are the
called according to his purpose."*
Romans 8:28

As With Bounty

"The pastures are clothed with flocks; the valleys also are covered over with corn" (Psalm 65:13).

As with bounty
  Doth Thy hand
Give us, Father,
  Peace of land.

Fruitful season,
  Fields of grain,
Verdant pastures,
  Plenteous rain.

Wooded highlands,
  Flying birds,
Quiet meadows,
  Flocks and herds.

As in mercy
  Thou dost give,
Life abundant
  We would live.

As thy justice
  To forbear,
For our neighbor
  We could care.

Hands toil hardened,
  Lips that smile,
Steps that go
  The second mile.

Eyes that often
  Look above,
Souls awakened,
  Heart of love.

Of life's purpose
  Well aware,
This our earnest
  Humble prayer.
  —*J. Paul Sutton*

God's Serving Angels

'Tis written that the serving angels stand
Beside God's throne, ten myriads on each hand.
Waiting, with wings outstretched and watchful eyes,
To do their Master's heavenly embassies.
Quicker than thought His high commands they read,
Swifter than light to execute them speed,
Bearing the word of power from star to star—
Some hither and some thither, near and far.
And unto these naught is too high or low,
Too mean or mighty, if He wills it so;
Neither is any creature, great or small,
Beyond His pity which embraceth all.
Because His eye beholdeth all which are,
Sees without search, and cometh without care;
Nor any ocean rolls so vast that He
Forgets one wave of all that restless sea.
  —*Edwin Arnold*

Why Worry?

Why worry? Are tomorrow's skies more blue
  If on our beds we restless roll and toss
With burning sleepless eyes until the morning,
  Building bridges that we may never cross?

Does not the One who numbered every hair,
  And marks the little sparrow when it falls,
Give ear to us in His own image made,
  As well as to the raven when it calls?

And does He love the lilies of the field
  That do not toil and neither do they spin
More dearly than His helpless, storm-tossed child
  For whom He gave His life to save from sin?

Is He who weighs the mountains with His scales
  And measures in His hand the mighty deep,
Who meted out the heavens with a span,
  Not able every trusting soul to keep?

Then why these weary hours of nameless dread
  That bring but shattered nerves and hoary hair,
When He who rules the earth and restless seas,
  Bids us to cast on Him our every care?

44

God Cares for You

Trust God to care for you each day
    He knoweth all your needs
To Him you are far greater than
    The sparrow that He feeds.
Consider lilies of the field:
    They neither toil nor spin,
Yet are arrayed in robes so fair
    Not made by mortal men.
Take no thought about the morrow,
    What you shall eat or wear.
Seek first His Holy Kingdom, and
    Your burdens He will bear.
O, ye of little faith, look up
    And give your spirit wings.
Soar up above the clouds of doubt;
    Behold the King of kings.
You are His child, He cares for you.
    Receive His grace today
And know abiding peace and joy;
    There is no other way.
                —*Helen Hazel*

My Hand in God's

Each morning when I wake, I say,
"I place my hand in God's today";
I know He'll walk close by my side,
My every wandering step to guide.

He leads me with the tenderest care
When paths are dark and I despair—
No need for me to understand
If I but hold fast to His hand.

My hand in His! No surer way
To walk in safety through each day.
By His great bounty I am fed:
Warmed by His love, and comforted.

When at day's end I seek my rest
And realize how much I'm blessed,
My thanks pour out to Him; and then
I place my hand in God's again.

             —*Florence Scripps Kellogg*

Jesus Satisfies

There's not a craving of the mind
    Which Jesus cannot fill;
There's not a pleasure I would seek
    Aside from His dear will.
From hour to hour He fills my soul
    With peace and perfect love;
While rich supplies for ev'ry need
    He sendeth from above.

The joys which this vain world bestows,
    Have lost their charms for me;
Once I enjoyed its trifles too,
    But Jesus set me free.
Its joys will perish in a day,
    Its pleasures quickly fly;
Its mirth like mists will pass away,
    And all its honors die.

He stilled the angry tempests' power,
    Which raged within my heart;
And bade each sinful passion there,
    To speedily depart.
Yes, Jesus is my all in all,
    He satisfies my soul,
For me He died on Calvary,
    And now He makes me whole.

Yes, Jesus is my Saviour dear,
    My Rock, my Strength, my Song;
My Wisdom and my Refuge safe,
    To Jesus I belong.
He is my Advocate with God,
    My Way, my Life, my Light,
My Great Physician and my Friend,
    My Guide by day and night.

What of Tomorrow?

I do not know what still awaits,
    Or what the morrow brings;
But with the glad salute of faith,
    I hail its opening wings!
For this I know—that in my Lord
    Shall all my needs be met;
And I can trust the heart of Him
    Who has not failed me yet.
             —*Reinhard Jacob*

Things Don't Just Happen

Things don't just happen to us who love
   God,
   They're planned by His own dear
    hand.
Then molded and shaped, and timed by
   His clock,
   Things don't just happen, they're
    planned.
We don't just guess on the issues of life,
   We Christians just rest in our Lord.
We are directed by His sovereign will,
   In the light of His Holy Word.
We who love Jesus are walking by faith,
   Not seeing one step that's ahead.
Not doubting one moment what our lot
   might be,
   But looking to Jesus instead.
We praise our dear Saviour for loving us
   so,
   For planning each care of our life.
Then giving us faith to trust Him for all,
   The blessings, as well as the strife.
Things don't just happen to us who love
   God,
   To us that have taken our stand.
No matter what the lot, the course, or the
   price,
   Things don't just happen, they're
    planned.

           —*Esther L. Fields*
           copyrighted, 1944

Overheard

Said a Robin to a Sparrow,
   I should really like to know
Why these anxious human beings
   Rush around and worry so?

Said the Sparrow to the Robin,
   Friend, I think that it must be
That they have no heavenly Father
   Such as cares for you and me.

           —*Elizabeth Cheney*

Your Father Knoweth

Precious thought my *Father* knoweth,
   In His love I rest,
For whate'er my *Father* doeth,
   Must be always *best,*
Well I know the heart that planneth
   Nought but good for me;
Joy and sorrow interwoven—
   Love in all I see.

Precious thought, my Father *knoweth,*
   Careth for his child;
Bids me nestle closer to Him,
   When the storm beats wild.
Though my earthly hopes are shattered
   And the teardrops fall,
Yet He is Himself my solace,
   Yea, my "all in all"!

Sweet to tell Him all He knoweth,
   Roll on Him the care,
Cast upon Himself the burden
   That I cannot bear;
Then, without a care oppressing,
   Simply to lie still,
Giving thanks to Him for all things,
   Since it is His will.

Oh, to trust Him, then, more fully!
   Just to simply move
In the conscious, calm enjoyment
   Of the Father's love;
Knowing that life's checkered pathway
   Leadeth to His rest;
Satisfied the way He taketh
   Must be always best.

           L. W.

———————————

"Though the cause of evil prosper,
Yet this truth alone is strong,
Truth forever on the scaffold,
Wrong forever on the throne.
Yet that scaffold sways the future,
And behind the dim unknown,
Standeth God within the shadows,
Keeping watch above his own."

"Wits' End Corner"

Are you standing at "Wits' End Corner,"
  Christian with troubled brow?
Are you thinking of what is before you,
  And all you're bearing now?
Does all the world seem against you.
  And you in the battle alone?
Remember—to "Wits' End Corner"
  Is just where God's power is shown.

Are you standing at "Wits' End Corner,"
  Blinded with wearying pain,
Feeling you cannot endure it,
  You cannot bear the strain,
Bruised through the constant suffering
  Dizzy, and dazed, and numb?
Remember—to "Wits' End Corner"
  Is where Jesus loves to come!

Are you standing at "Wits' End Corner,"
  Your work before you spread,
All lying, begun, unfinished,
  And pressing on heart and head,
Longing for strength to do it,
  Stretching out trembling hands?
Remember—at "Wits' End Corner"
  The Burden Bearer stands.

Are you standing at "Wits' End Corner,"
  Yearning for those you love,
Longing and praying and watching,
  Pleading their causes above,
Trying to lead them to Jesus
  Wond'ring if you've been true?
He whispers at "Wits' End Corner"
  "I'll win them, as I won you."

Are you standing at "Wits' End Corner"?
  Then you're just in the very spot
To learn the wondrous resources,
  Of Him who faileth not!
No doubt to a brighter pathway
  Your footsteps will soon be removed,
But only at "Wits' End Corner"
  Is "the God who is able" proved!

My Heart Overflows

My heart overflows
With the goodness
I receive from the Lord
Day by day;
For the blessings
I count without number,
My spirit bursts forth
In His praise.

He giveth me life
With the morning,
And strength for the day
As I go;
And beauty unmeasured
About me,
All comes from His hand—
This I know.

The lark's brilliant song
At dawning,
The glistening dew
On the flower,
The fragrance
Of bursting new blossoms,
All speak
Of His wonder and power.

Then when evening sun fades
O'er the hilltops,
Purple shadows and mist
Hang below;
Then I think once again
Of His goodness and love,
And my heart
With its thanks overflows.
                    —*Oda M. Boyer*

————————

"And when he putteth forth his own sheep, he goeth before them, and the sheep follow him: for they know his voice" (John 10:4).

47

God Cares for Me

The way I may not
    Always see,
But this I know:
    God cares for me.

It matters not
    What seems to be,
Since this is true:
    God cares for me.

Though tempests rage
    On land and sea,
I'm safe because
    God cares for me.

From doubt and fear
    He keeps me free;
My surety this:
    God cares for me.
    —Glenville Kleiser

Nobody Walks Alone

Whenever the pathway of life seems rough
    And under your burdens you groan,
Just remember, wherever that path may go,
    Nobody walks alone.

When all of your friends have let you down,
    And all of your dreams have flown,
Just keep reminding your heart:
    Nobody walks alone.

Then suddenly you'll feel God's hand in yours
    And His eyes, uplifting your own . . .
And you'll hear His gentle, forgiving voice say,
    "Nobody walks alone."
    —Nick Kenny

He Maketh No Mistake

My Father's way may twist and turn,
    My heart may throb and ache,
But in my soul I'm glad I know,
    He maketh no mistake.

My cherished plans may go astray,
    My hopes may fade away.
But still I'll trust my Lord to lead
    For He doth know the way.

Tho' night be dark and it may seem
    That day will never break;
I'll pin my faith, my all in Him,
    He maketh no mistake.

There's so much now I cannot see,
    My eyesight's far too dim;
But come what may, I'll simply trust
    And leave it all to Him.

For by and by the mist will lift
    And plain it all He'll make.
Through all the way, tho' dark to me,
    He made not one mistake.

    —A. M. Overton

HE GOES BEFORE

"He goes before," what blessed words,
    Said Christ of Galilee;
And day by day its message stirs
    The hearts of you and me.

He goes before where'er you go
    About your daily task.
Why do you fret and worry so?
    Dear troubled soul, I ask.

He goes before when storms of life
    Sweep o'er you like a flood;
And when our days seem full of strife,
    He shelters with His blood.

He goes before each passing day,
    And leads to pastures green;
He gives protection in the way
    From dangers, though unseen.

He goes before when I shall tread
    The lonesome vale of death;
By Him I shall be safely led
    'Til ends my earthly breath.

He goes before when I shall stand
    Before my maker's face;
Then I shall dwell in that blest land
    With all those saved by grace.

God Knows Best

He knows best when days are sunny
  And the clouds have rolled away,
When laughter rules in all our dwelling
  And we are happy, glad and gay.
    HE KNOWS BEST.

He knows best when days are stormy
  And the clouds are thick and grey,
When hearts are bowed with grief and
    sorrows,
  Because loved ones went away.
    HE KNOWS BEST.

He knows best. O tell it often,
  When in peace, or battle's fray.
Whether joy or sadness touch thee,
  Tell it every night and day.
    HE KNOWS BEST.

"Father, Are You There?"

A little child lay in the dark;
  The room was strange, he saw
    nowhere.
He was afraid; but then he called,
  "Father, are you there?"

He felt a hand, so strong and warm,
  Close clasping his; then calm and
    clear
He heard his father's tender voice,
  "Yes, laddie, I am here."

Like that small child, we sometimes feel
  That we are in the dark of care;
In terror of some harm, we call,
  "O Father, are You there?"

We reach our hand to Him, and find
  A blessed answer to our fear;
His hand holds ours; we hear His voice,
  "Fear not, for I am here."

So though we tremble in the dark,
  In need of strength and help and
    cheer,
We have a tender Father's word,
  "Fear not, for I am here."
          —*Dinnie McDole Hayes*

I KNOW

I know not what the days may bring,
  Tomorrow waits unknown,
But this I know—the changeless Christ,
  My Lord, is on the throne.

I know not where my path may lead,
  How dark or rough the way,
But this I know—with Him I'm safe,
  He holds—I cannot stray.

I know not what my joys may be,
  What tears may silent fall.
But this I know—not fate unkind,
  But wisdom, measures all.

I know not as I voyage forth,
  What storms will menace, dark.
But this I know—He calmed the sea,
  So, trustful, I embark.

I know not when life's day will close
  As twilight darker falls.
But this I know—I fear no night,
  I'll answer when He calls.

THE PROMISES

My Savior's grace is promised me,
  His tender love and care,
His deep concern in every grief
  Each burden He will share.

My Father's care is promised me,
  His faithful, guiding hand,
To lead me on and bear me up,
  To heaven's golden strand.

My Father's wealth is promised me,
  Supplying all my need,
He is a King, and I, His own
  Am rich, yes, rich indeed.

The Holy Ghost is promised me,
  To in my heart abide;
To hold me steady, pray for me,
  And keep me sanctified.
          —*Geo. H. Talbert*

The Song of the Sparrow

"Are not five sparrows sold for two farthings, and not one of them is forgotten before God? But even the very hairs of your head are all numbered. Fear ye not therefore, ye are of more value than many sparrows" (Luke 12:6, 7).

I'm only a little sparrow,
   A bird of low degree;
My life is of little value,
   But the dear Lord cares for me.

He gives me a coat of feathers—
   It is very plain I know,
Without a speck of crimson,
   For it was not made for show.

But it keeps me warm in winter,
   And shields me from the rain;
Were it bordered with gold and purple,
   Perhaps it would make me vain.

And when the springtime cometh,
   I will build me a little nest,
With many a chirp of pleasure,
   In the spot I love the best.

I have no barn or storehouse,
   I neither sow nor reap;
God gives me a sparrow's portion,
   With never a seed to keep.

If my meat is sometimes scanty,
   Close pecking makes it sweet;

I have always enough to feed me,
   And life is more than meat.

I know there are many sparrows—
   All over the world they are found—
But our heavenly Father knoweth
   When ONE of us falls to the ground.

Tho' small, we are never forgotten;
   Tho' weak, we are never afraid;
For we know the dear Lord keepeth
   The life of the creatures He made.

I fly through city and country,
   I alight on many a spray;
I have no chart or compass
   But I never lose my way.

I just fold my wings at nightfall
   Wherever I happen to be;
For the Father is always watching
   And no harm can come to me.

I am only a little sparrow,
   A bird of low degree;
But I know that the Father loves me,
   Dost THOU know His love for THEE?

A PSALM OF LIFE

My Saviour, Lord Jesus, is with me alway.
His companionship is above all others.
He brightens my days with His spiritual beauty, and
Earth's loveliness about me.
My sleep is restful in His care.
Though dangers encompass me I know in whom I trust.
He is my Fortress, and no evil shall remove me from
His faithful protection.
He brings joy into my life and soothes my sorrows.
He gives me of the comforts of life, and raises up
Friends for companions.
To His lovingkindness there is no limit, and I am
His in this world and throughout Eternity.

          —*Jennie Esmond Wright*

Circumstances

(Philippians 1:12, 19)

Circumstances? How we pet them,
    How we give them right of way!
But the Master never planned that
    We should be beneath their sway.

We who know Him walk the highway
    Where the victors all have trod.
Circumstances cannot conquer
    In the presence of God.

Paul made circumstances serve him,
    Made them glorify His Lord;
Turned each trial into blessing
    As He boldly preached the Word.

"These things turned to my advantage,"
    This old warrior used to say.
"For our good they work together"
    Though the darkness shroud the day.

Why should Christians live beneath
    them,
    And not walk the heights with Him?
Circumstances? We're above them,
    Though they often seem so grim.

"More than victors"—this the promise,
    And Christ bids us cast out fear;
For we triumph o'er the testing
    With the Master ever near.
                    —*Albert Simpson Reitz*

Even Keel

I like to see a sailing-ship
    Go sailing out to sea;
The puffy sails are very white—
    It rides the breeze so free!

It hasn't any fear at all.
    It knows the skipper's hand,
So firm upon it all the time,
    Will bring it back to land.

Thus does our Father keep us safe;
    His hand's upon the wheel.
No matter how the winds may blow
    We'll keep an even keel.
                    —*Elizabeth Lyon*

GOD

There is an Eye that never sleeps
    Beneath the wing of night;
There is an Ear that never shuts
    When sinks the beams of light.

There is an Arm that never tires
    When human strength gives way;
There is a Love that never fails
    When earthly loves decay.

That Eye unseen o'erwatcheth all;
    That Arm upholds the sky;
That Ear doth hear the sparrows call;
    That Love is ever nigh.
                    —*James Cowden Wallace*

God Holds Your Hand

God understands the way you take,
He knows the trials of each day,
And sympathizing, lends an ear
To hear you e'en before you pray.
He walks with those who trust His love,
He holds them by the hand to guide;
What need to fear or be dismayed,
With His dear Presence by your side!

*"For the Lord thy God will hold thy right hand, Saying
unto thee, Fear not; I will help thee" (Isaiah 41:13).*

All Things Work Together for Good to Them That Love God

Romans 8:28

Just how this statement can be true,
  Perhaps has often puzzled you;
You've wondered how that "all things"
  could,
  Work out for your eternal good:
How trouble, sorrow and unrest,
  Could work together for the best;
How this could be, you did not know,
  And yet, you felt it must be so.

Now "all things" mean, both good and
  bad.
  Yea, things that really make you sad;
It means your sickness and your health,
  Your poverty as well as wealth;
Of trouble you will have your share,
  While in this world of toil and care;
But rest assured, you have a friend,
  Who knows your life from start to
  end.

Should God permit dark clouds some
  day,
  To cast a gloom across your way,
Just take it as your Father's will;
  You're in His care, He loves you still;
Be not alarmed, nor be cast down,
  'Tis through these trials you win a
  crown;
All earthly sorrow soon shall cease,
  While joys eternal shall increase.

There's much we do not understand,
  But "all things" are within His hand;
Remember God's mysterious plan,
  Cannot be solved by mortal man.
But when we reach the land of rest,
  We then shall see that He knew best.
The things we had not understood,
  We'll realize were for our good.

—By Uncle Charlie Cox

My Father Cares

My Father CARES. He cares for me;
Should I then ever careful be?
What if the way to me looks dark,
Has it not all by Him been marked?
And will He not give grace to me
To walk in it, whate'er it be?
He knows my weakness, knows my
  need,
Knows every thought and word and
  deed.
Knows all my longings and desires.
Oh, yes, He knows, but more He cares.
He cares. God cares. How grand the
  thought
In all my life that there is not
One detail not observed by Him!
Surely my cup o'erflows the grim.
Goodness and mercy, all my days
Shall follow me. To Him be praise!
He makes all things work for my good.
Oh, may I trust Him as I should!
My Father KNOWS, He LOVES, He
  CARES.
My Father hears and answers prayers.
Though iron gates my way doth block,
At His command, it will unlock.
No matter what my sight may dim,
I always have recourse to Him.
And, with Him, all my care will cease,
And He will fill me with His peace
And conscious knowledge of His love,
Which day to day, to me He'll prove.
My wants I will make known in prayer,
Then trust a loving Father's care.
His power, so great, His love, so strong,
Will fill my soul with endless song.
—*Mabel E. Brown*

Casting all your care
upon Him, for He
careth for you."

1 Peter 5:7

Counting on Him

His riches all abundantly surround me,
  His bounty to my every need is nigh.
The goodness of my God is ever
  round me;
    I know that I can count on His sup-
    ply.

And He will give the strength that I am
  needing.
    By circumstance I cannot be dis-
    mayed!
If I but follow where His love is leading,
  I know that I can count on Him for
  aid!

Whate'er the need, His promises are
  ready;
  And never yet has failed His faithful
  word.
Then may my trust be always strong
  and steady;
    I know that I can count upon my
    Lord.

—Elsie Duncan Yale

I Am Never Alone

I am never alone, by night or day,
For my Lord walks with me the entire
  way.
Though the storm clouds gather and
  night draws near,
I walk through the darkness untouched
  by fear.
I'm safe in His care, whatever betide,
I trust Him completely to be my guide.

I am never alone when burdens great
Seem to weigh me down with unkindly
  fate.
For always a Voice whispers in my ear:
"Faint not 'neath your burdens for I am
  near.
I will share the load that you have to
  bear,
I will lift from your heart depressing
  care."

I know my Saviour walks by my side,
In sorrow or trouble He is my guide.
I have light on my path in all distress,
For, by faith, His fellowship I possess.

—Carlos Greenleaf Fuller

What God Hath Promised

"Take no thought for your life, what ye shall eat or what ye shall drink; nor yet for your body, what ye shall put on. Is not the life more than meat, and the body than raiment? Behold, the fowls of the air: for they sow not, neither do they reap, nor gather into barns; yet your heavenly Father feedeth them. Are ye not much better than they? And why take ye thought for raiment? Consider the lilies of the field, how they grow; they toil not, neither do they spin, and yet I say unto you, that Solomon in all his glory was not arrayed like one of these. Wherefore, if God so clothe the grass of the field, which today is, and tomorrow is cast into the oven, shall he not much more clothe you, O ye of little faith? Therefore take no thought, saying, What shall we eat, or What shall we drink? or, Wherewithal shall we be clothed? . . . For your heavenly Father knoweth that ye have need of all these things. But seek ye first the kingdom of God, and His righteousness, and all these things shall be added unto you" (Matthew 6:25-33).

In This Hour

God is with me in this hour,
  I need not go alone
To meet the challenge of the day,
  For He has clearly shown
In other times, when to my soul
  The way was hard and steep,
That when I trusted Him I found
  All needed power to keep.

He shelters, guides, sustains and cheers,
  Whatever may betide,
I know—and in that knowing find
  That He is by my side.
Mine but to clear away the doubt,
  The fear, the dread, and then
He floods my soul with peace and I
  Serenely walk again.

Yes, God is with me in this hour,
My comfort, wisdom, faith and power.

—Author unknown

Somebody Cares

Somebody knows when your heart
    aches
And everything seems to go wrong;
Somebody knows when the shadows
Need chasing away with song;
Somebody knows when you're lonely,
Tired, discouraged and blue;
Somebody wants you to know Him,
And know that He dearly loves you.
Somebody knows when you're
    tempted,
And your mind grows dizzy and dim;
Somebody cares when you're weakest,
And farthest away from Him;
Somebody grieves when you've fallen,
You are not lost from His sight;
Somebody waits for your coming,
And He'll drive the gloom from the
    night.

—Fannie Stafford

Let's Not Complain

There never was a day so long
But what the Lord was there;
There to fill our hearts with song,
And take away our care;
There for us to lean upon—
His mighty arm so dear,
Let's not complain if days are long,
It brings the Lord so near.

There never was a night so dark
But what the Lord can see;
He's there to guide our little bark
Across the raging sea.
Tho' cloudy here and trials may come,
And skies be all but fair—
Let's not forget—God understands,
And He is always near.

Let's not forget—He knows the way,
Because the path He made
And if we're faithful, we shall find
We need not be afraid;
For God is there, yes God is there,
He hears and knows our call,
Let's trust Him, then, He'll answer
    prayer
And lead us, lest we fall.

Let days be long, and nights be dark;
We know they cannot last;
For every one we know of yet,
Has long ago been passed.
And now another day is here,
Let it be short or long;
Let's not complain, for God is there
To fill our hearts with song.

Give Me Trust

Give me the trust of a little child,
  Give me its simple faith;
Give the consciousness that God
  Will ever keep me safe.

Give me the trust of the birds that sing,
  Sing for their Master's praise;
Help me to recognize that God
  Keeps me through all may days.

Faithful Is He Who Has Promised

Are you passing through a testing?
  Is your pillow wet with tears?
Do you wonder what the reason,
  Why it seems God never hears?
Why it is you have no answer
  To your oft-repeated plea,
Why the heaven still is leaden
  As you wait on bended knee?

Do you wonder as you suffer,
  Whether God does understand,
And if so, why He ignores you,
  Fails to hold you in His hand?
Do black doubts creep in, assail you,
  Fears without, and fears within,
Till your brave heart almost falters
  And gives way to deadly sin?

All God's testings have a purpose—
  Someday you will see the light.
All He asks is that you trust Him,
  Walk by faith and not by sight.
Do not fear when doubts beset you,
  Just remember—He is near;
He will never, never leave you,
  He will always, always hear.

Faithful is He Who has promised,
  He will never let you fall.

God Will Be With You

God has not said life's pattern
  Is one we'll understand,
But He's promised He will keep us
  In the hollow of His hand!
He has not promised days serene
  And free from all alarms,
But he's said that underneath us
  Are "the everlasting arms"!
God has not promised mountain
  heights
  As on through life we go,
But He's promised to be with us
  In the valleys dark and low!

Daily will the strength be given,
  Strength for each and strength for all.
He will gladly give you peace,
Till your tired and weary body
  Finds its blessed, glad release.

When the darkened veil is lifted,
  Then, dear heart, you'll understand
Why it is you had to suffer,
  Why you could not feel His hand
Giving strength when it was needed,
  Giving power and peace within,
Giving joy through tears and trial,
  Giving victory over sin.

So till then just keep on trusting,
  Through the sunshine and the rain,
Through the tears and through the
    heartaches,
  Through the smiles and through the
    pain—
Knowing that our Father watches,
  Knowing daily strength He'll give,
Victory for each passing hour,
  This is life, so let us live!
                    —*John E. Zoller*

Someone to Care

When the world seems cold,
  And your friends are few,
There is Someone who cares for you.

When you've tears in your eyes,
  And your heart bleeds inside,
There is Someone who cares for you.

When your disappointments come,
  And you feel so blue,
There is Someone who cares for you.

When you need a Friend,
  A friend to the end,
There is Someone who cares for you.

Someone to care, Someone to share
  All your troubles like no other can do:
He'll come down from the skies,
  Brush the tears from your eyes—
You're His Child, and He cares for you.

A Solitary Way

There is a mystery in human hearts,
And though we be encircled by a host
Of those who love us well, and are
    beloved,
To everyone of us, from time to time,
There comes a sense of utter loneliness.
Our dearest friend is "stranger" to our
    joy
And cannot realize our bitterness;
"There is not one who really under-
    stands,
Not one to enter into all I feel":
Such is the cry of each of us in turn.

We wander in a "solitary way."
No matter what or where our lot may be;
Each heart, mysterious even to itself,
Must live its inner life in solitude.
And would you know the reason why
    this is?
It is because the Lord desires our love;
In every heart He wishes to be first.
He therefore keeps the secret key
    Himself,
To open all its chambers and to bless
With perfect sympathy and holy peace
Each solitary soul which comes to Him.

So when we feel this loneliness, it is
The voice of Jesus saying, "Come to Me,"
And every time we are "not understood,"
It is a call to us to come again;
For Christ alone can satisfy the soul,
And those who walk with Him from day
    to day
Can never have a solitary way.

And when beneath some heavy cross
    you faint,
And say, "I cannot bear this load alone,"
You say the truth. Christ made it pur-
    posely
So heavy that you must return to Him.
The bitter grief, which "no one under-
    stands,"
Conveys a secret message from the
    King,
Entreating you to come to Him again.

The Man of Sorrows understands it well,
In all points tempted He can feel with
    you.
You cannot come too often, or too near.
The Son of God is infinite in grace.
His presence satisfies the longing soul,
And those who walk with Him from day
    to day,
Can never have a solitary way.

—Author unknown

GOD EVER CARES

God ever cares! Not only in life's summer
When skies are bright and days are long and glad.
He cares as much when life is draped in winter,
And hearth doth feel bereft, and alone, and sad.
    God ever cares! His heart is ever tender!
    His love doth never fail nor show decay.
    The loves of earth, though strong and deep, may perish;
    But His shall never, never pass away.
God ever cares! And thus when life is lonely,
When blessings one time prized are growing dim,
The heart may find a sweet and sunny shelter—
A refuge and a resting place in Him.
    God ever cares! And time can never change Him.
    His nature is to care, and love, and bless.
    And drearest, darkest, emptiest days afford Him
    But means to make more sweet His own caress.

—J. Danson Smith

The Father's Hand

While through this changing world
    below
I would not choose my path to go;
'Tis Father's hand that leadeth me,
Then O how safe His child must be.

Sometimes we walk in sunshine bright,
Sometimes in a darkness of the night;
Sometimes the way I cannot see
But Father's hand still leadeth me.

Sometimes there seems no way to take,
But Father's hand a way doth make.
Sometimes I hear Him gently say,
"Come, follow Me, this is the way."

Why should I mind the way I go?
His way is best for me, I know.
He is my strength, my truth, my way,
He is my comfort, rod, and stay.

So on we travel hand in hand,
Bound for the heavenly promised land.
Always through all Eternity,
I'll praise His name for leading me.

—Ida L. Cornett

I know not where His islands lift
   Their fronded palms in air;
I only know I cannot drift
   Beyond His love and care.

—John Greenleaf Whittier

Fellowship With God . . .

Prayer, Devotion, Consecration

My Lord and I

I have a friend so precious,
  So very dear to me,
He loves me with such tender love,
  He loves so faithfully.
I could not live apart from Him,
  I love to feel Him nigh;
And so we dwell together,
  My Lord and I.

Sometimes I'm faint and weary;
  He knows that I am weak,
And as He bids me lean on Him
  His help I gladly seek.
He leads me in the paths of light
  Beneath a sunny sky,
And so we walk together,
  My Lord and I.

He knows how much I love Him,
  He knows I love Him well,
But with what love He loveth me
  My tongue can never tell.
It is an everlasting love
  In ever rich supply,
And so we love each other,
  My Lord and I.

I tell Him all my sorrows,
  I tell Him all my joys,
I tell Him all that pleases me,
  I tell Him what annoys.
He tells me what I ought to do,
  He tells me how to try,
And so we walk together,
  My Lord and I.

He knows how I am longing
  Some weary soul to win,
And so He bids me go and speak
  The loving word for Him.
He bids me tell His wondrous love,
  And why He came to die,
And so we work together,
  My Lord and I.

I have His yoke upon me,
  And easy 'tis to bear;
In the burden which He carries
  I gladly take a share.
For then it is my happiness
  To have Him always nigh;
We bear the yoke together,
  My Lord and I.

—*L. Shorey*

My Daily Prayer

Heavenly Father, we do not ask to always know the road,
  But we ask for strength to travel it.
We do not ask to see beyond the future's veil,
  But we ask for courage to face that future.
We do not ask that life shall bring us pleasure and ease,
  But we pray for patience and understanding so that,
  Come what may, our trust and confidence will be in Thee.

The Magic of Prayer

When the trials of this life make you weary,
And your troubles seem too much to bear,
There's a wonderful solace and comfort
In the silent communion of prayer.

When you've searched for the sun without
    ceasing,
And the showers continue to fall,
There's a heavenly lift in this wonderful gift
That God has extended to all.

From the magic of prayer there comes power
That will minimize all of your care.
And you'll gather new hope when you're able
    to cope
With the troubles that once brought despair.

So lift up your heart to the heavens.
There's a loving and kind Father there
Who offers release and comfort and peace
In the silent communion of prayer.

A Breath of Prayer

A breath of prayer in the morning
    Means a day of blessing sure.
A breath of prayer in the evening
    Means a night of rest secure.
A breath of prayer in our weakness
    Means a clasp of a Mighty Hand.
A breath of prayer when we're lonely
    Means Someone to understand.
A breath of prayer in our doubtings
    Assures us the Lord knows best.
A breath of prayer in our sorrows
    Means comfort and peace and rest.
A breath of prayer in rejoicing
    Gives joy an added delight.

For they that remember God's goodness
    Go singing far into the night.
There's never a year nor a season
    That prayer may not bless every hour,
And never a soul need be helpless
    When linked with God's infinite power.

—*Frances McKinnon Morton*

Daily

Walk daily with your Savior,
    And doubt will disappear;
You cannot be in darkness
    While He, the light, is near.

Walk daily with your Savior,
    And never leave His side;
For unto those who trust Him,
    No evil can betide.

Walk daily with your Savior,
    And love Him more and more;
And you will find the pathway
    Grow brighter on before.

Walk daily with your Savior,
    And trust His sov'reign grace;
Until at last He leads you
    To heav'n, His dwelling place.

Walk daily with your Savior,
    In fellowship of love;
And you shall share His friendship
    In yon fair land above.

—*Elisha A. Hoffman*

PRAYER

Prayer is the soul's sincere desire,
    Unuttered or expressed;
The motion of a hidden fire,
    That trembles in the breast.

Prayer is the burden of a sigh,
    The falling of a tear;
The upward glancing of an eye,
    When none but God is near.

Prayer is the simplest form of speech
    That infant lips can try;
Prayer, the sublimest strains that reach
    The Majesty on high.

O thou! by whom we come to God,
    The life, the Truth, the Way;
The path of prayer thyself hast trod:
    Lord, teach us how to pray.

—*James Montgomery*

"Take a Little Step Toward Me"

I stood one day in my lonely room
　With my heart full of grief and tears.
My memory turned like the hands on the
　　clock
　Back to the sinful years.

And I cried in my misery, "God, oh,
　　God,
　I need you so much—can't you see?
How far away you seem today,
　Can't you come closer to me?"

As I knelt a bit to pray, the words
　　wouldn't come,
　And my burden grew more and more,
The tears were streaming down my face
　And my heart was heavy and sore.

Then it seemed like a voice came
　　through to me,
　Like the rustle of leaves in a tree.
"Take a little step toward me, child,
　And I'll take a step toward thee."

I stood erect on my trembling feet
　And went forward to meet Him there.
I found the everlasting arms,
　And unburdened my load of care.

　　　　　　　　—Josephine Long

Worry vs. Prayer

Worry? Why worry? What can worry
　do?
It never keeps a trouble from overtaking
　you.
It gives you indigestion, and wakeful
　hours at night,
And fills the day with gloom, however
　fair and bright.
It puts a frown upon the face, and sharp-
　ness in the tone.
We're not fit to live with others, and
　unfit to live alone.
Pray? Why pray? What can praying do?
Praying really changes things, arranges
　life anew.
It's good for your digestion, gives peace-
　ful sleep at night,
And fills the grayest, gloomiest day with
　rays of glowing light.
It puts a smile upon your face, the love
　note in your tone,
Makes you fit to live with others, and fit
　to live alone.
Pray? Why pray? What can praying do?
It brings God down from Heaven to live
　and work with you.

　　　　　　　　—Author unknown

The Blessed Place

There is a place where thou canst touch the
　eyes
Of blinded men to instant perfect sight.
There is a place where thou canst say, "Arise,"
To dying captives bound in chains of night.
There is a place where thou canst reach the
　store
Of hoarded gold and free it for the Lord.
There is a place upon some distant shore
Where thou canst send the worker and the
　Word.
Where is that blessed place?—dost thou ask
　where?
O soul, it is the secret place of prayer.

　　　　　　　　—Adelaide Addison Pollard

Reward of Silence

In silence comes all loveliness,
　The dawn is ever still;
No noise accompanies the dew
　That glistens on the hill.

The sunrise slips up quietly,
　The moon is never heard,
And love that animates the eyes
　Surpasses any word.

And prayer is best in solitude—
　It seems so very odd
That long before I did not know
　In silence I'd find God.

　　　　　　　　—Jane Sayre

Power Conscious

Oh, dark is the land where the Evil One reigns,
   And strong is his citadel there!
Oh, deep are his dungeons and heavy the chains.
   That his long-enthralled prisoners wear!
What can brace up the arm and confirm the weak knee,
   The strong one to meet and o'ercome?
Like the message of cheer wafted over the sea—
   "There's somebody praying at home."
There are times when the enemy seems to prevail,
   And faintness creeps over the heart;
When courage and confidence quiver and quail
   At the glance of his fiery dart.
There are times when, exhausted, we can but stand still,
   When the sword-arm hangs nerveless and numb;
Oh then to the soul comes a whisper so chill—
   "Are they weary of praying at home?"
Oh, brothers, we toil in the twilight, perchance;
   Remember we wrestle in night!
Cry unto the Lord, would ye have us advance,
   And claim for us heavenly might?
Then back to the arm will its vigor be given,
   And the lips that in anguish were dumb
Shall shout as the foe from his stronghold is driven—
   " 'Tis because they are praying at home."

Lord, Teach Us to Pray

"The Lord looketh on the heart."
1 Samuel 16:7

We often say our prayers
But do we ever PRAY,
Or do the wishes of our HEART
Go with the words we say.
We may as well kneel down
And worship gods of stone
As offer to the LIVING GOD
A prayer of words alone.
For words, without the HEART
The Lord will never hear.
Nor will HE, to the one impart
Whose prayers are not SINCERE.
Lord, show us what we want,
And teach us HOW TO PRAY;
And help us, as we seek THY face
To FEEL the words we say.
"God, be merciful to me, a sinner."
Luke 18:13

Morning Prayer

I thank Thee, God,
For this new day,
Another chance
To do Thy way.
I pray Thee, God,
To so teach me,
That, childlike, I
May humble be.
When comes night,
May I then say:
"I know I walked
With God today."

How

Leave the How with
    Jesus—
   'Tis enough to know
Faithful to His promise,
   Help He will bestow.

Leave the How with
    Jesus—
   He will all explain;
Only trust Him fully
   'Til He comes again.
     —*The Bible Friend*

New Day Prayer

Ere thou risest from thy bed
Speak to God, whose wings were
   spread
O'er thee in the helpless night.
Lo, He wakes thee now with light!
Lift thy burden and thy care
In the mighty arms of prayer.
"Lord, the newness of this day
Calls me to an untried way.
Let me gladly take the road,
Give me strength to bear my load.
Thou my guide and helper be,
I will travel thru with Thee."
     —*Henry Van Dyke*

MY CAMEL

I loaded my camel rich and high,
And marched him up to the needle's
  eye.
He was laden with riches many fold,
With bales of silk, and sacks of gold.

I urged my camel with angry din,
I pressed my camel to enter in.
But far too large was his loading high,
He could not pass through the nee-
  dle's eye.

I rode the camel a night and day,
And sought to enter some other way;
But though I traveled a wearisome
  round,
Only the needle's eye I found.

I groaned because I did not have
  enough,
So I took from the camel the bulkier
  stuff,
And with gold and gems I would fain
  get by;
Still the camel stuck at the needle's
  eye.

So I left the camel alone outside,
And all by myself the entrance I tried.
But with my pockets stuffed—alas!
The needle still would not let me pass.

So at length I threw all my wealth
  away,
And sank upon lowly knees to pray.
I begged the Lord to forgive my sin,
And let a poor traveler enter in.

Lo, the marvelous needle's eye
Grew to an entrance wide and high.
And proud and glad, in a beggar's
  dress,
I passed through the portals of happi-
  ness.

But where the camel decided to go,
I did not care and do not know.

The Love of God

Unfathomed as the deep blue sea,
As boundless as the sky,
The greatness of a Father's love
Surrounds us from on high.

Protecting us from things that harm,
Inspiring us to praise,
Like sunshine are His rays of love,
That brighten all our days.

Though years may change the thoughts
    of men,
Experience confuse,
The love of God remains the same,
For those, His way would choose.

He satisfies with deepest joy,
His matchless love is giv'n.
That we experience on earth
The joy we'll find in Heav'n.

—*Ethel M. Miller*

The Secret

I met God in the morning,
    When my day was at its best;
And His Presence came like sunrise
    With a glory in my breast.

All day long the Presence lingered,
    All day long He stayed with me;
And we sailed in perfect calmness
    O'er a very troubled sea.

Other ships were blown and battered,
    Other ships were sore distressed,
But the winds that seemed to drive them
    Brought to us both peace and rest.

Then I thought of other mornings
    With a keen remorse of mind,
When I, too, had loosed the moorings,
    With the Presence left behind.

So I think I know the secret
    Learned from many a troubled way:
You must seek Him in the morning,
    If you want Him through the day.

—*Ralph Cushman*

The Fellowship of Prayer

We shall meet Him every morning,
  At the fellowship of prayer,
When we seek the heavenly Father,
  Bringing Him our joy and care.

To the secret inner closet,
  When the day is young and fair,
We shall bring our songs of worship,
  At the fellowship of prayer.

We shall bring our intercession,
  All our mutual askings share,
Knowing God the Father hears us,
  At the fellowship of prayer.

So each morning we touch heaven,
  And our loved ones some way bear
In their lives God's grace and glory,
  Through the fellowship of prayer.

—Mary Stoner Wine

The Difference

I got up early one morning
And rushed right into the day;
I had so much to accomplish
That I didn't take time to pray.

Problems just tumbled about me,
And heavier came each task;
"Why doesn't God help me," I won-
  dered.
He answered: "You didn't ask."

I wanted to see joy and beauty
But the day toiled on, gray and bleak;
I wondered why God didn't show me.
He said: "But you didn't seek."

I tried to come into God's presence.
I used all my keys at the lock.
God gently and lovingly chided,
"My child, you didn't knock."

I woke up early this morning,
And paused before entering the day;
I had so much to accomplish
That I had to take time to pray.

—Author unknown
from Log of the Good Ship Grace

This Morning

Did you meet your Lord this morning
  Ere you saw a human face?
Did you look upon His beauty
  Through His all-abounding grace?

Did you bow in prayer before Him
  Ere you went upon your way?
Did you ask for strength to carry
  All the burdens of the day?

Did you see His will in reading
  From His Holy Word, and take
Of His promises a portion,
  Blessed with love, for His Name's
    sake?

Oh, how weak and worthless are we,
  And our spirits quake within,
If we fail to meet our Master
  Ere the pathway we begin.

How He waits to give His blessing
  On our lives another day.
Christian, never start without Him.
  Let Him speak, and then, obey.

—La Von Doherty

A MORNING PRAYER

Lord, in the stillness of the dawn,
  Before the world breaks in
To flood the mind with its concerns,
  Its hurry and its din,
Let me breathe deep of heavenly air,
  And may mine inner ear
The music of that heavenly land
  In all its sweetness hear.

Oh, let my very soul inhale
  The fragrance of that place,
That every thought of mine today
  May be of peace and grace;
And may there echo in my voice
  That music from above,
So that the words that I shall speak
  May be in truth and love.

—A. M. Chambers

Hidden Manna

O child of God, awake! And
 See the radiant dawn of day.
The rising sun bids thee arise
 To meditate and pray.

All nature is responsive
 To God's summons to arise.
Ten thousand happy voices
 Raise a chorus to the skies.

The busy bee is searching
 For his honey from the flowers.
Let us search for "hidden manna"
 In the early morning hours.

There's a sweetness in the Lily,
 In the Rose of Sharon, too.
The Bible's leaves are petals, you must
 Search them through and through.

If you hunger for the nectar
 You will search in every flower;
And you'll find the manna sweeter
 In the early morning hour.

—Author unknown

My Secret Stairway

*I have a secret stairway
 That means so much to me,
For always at the head of it
 Jesus waits for me.*

*No matter what the day brings,
 I know that He will share
My burdens or my blessings,
 For He is always there.*

*'Tis wonderful, this stairway,
 Refreshing as the dew,
For when I'd be discouraged,
 My spirit He renews.*

*This stairway can belong to you,
 Just as it does to me,
Make room for it within your heart
 And then His face you'll see.*

—Connie M. Sandoz

Take Time to Be Holy

Take time to be holy;
 Speak oft with thy Lord;
Abide in Him always,
 And feed on His Word;
Make friends of God's children,
 Help those who are weak,
Forgetting in nothing
 His blessing to seek.

Take time to be holy;
 The world rushes on;
Spend much time in secret
 With Jesus alone;
By looking to Jesus
 Like Him thou shalt be;
Thy friends in thy conduct
 His likeness shall see.

Take time to be holy;
 Let Him be thy Guide,
And run not before Him
 Whatever betide;
In joy or in sorrow
 Still follow thy Lord.
And, looking to Jesus,
 Still trust in His Word.

Take time to be holy;
 Be calm in thy soul.
Each thought and each motive
 Beneath His control;
Thus led by His Spirit
 To fountains of love,
Thou soon shalt be fitted
 For service above.

—W. D. Longstaff

My Prayer

O God, this day be near us to defend us, within us to refresh us, around us to preserve us, before us to guide us, behind us to justify us, and above us to bless us. In Jesus' Name, Amen.

A Prayer for Quiet Time

Read slowly and thoughtfully

O Holy Spirit of God—
Come into my heart and fill me:
I open the windows of my soul to let
    Thee in.
I surrender my whole life to Thee.
Come and possess me, fill me with light
    and truth.

I offer to Thee the one thing I really
    possess:
My capacity for being filled by Thee.

I Prayed a Prayer Today

I prayed a prayer today.
I did not pray for wealth or even health
I did not pray for might or even sight
I did not pray for thee or even me
I prayed for God to work in me
I prayed for God to live in me
I prayed for God to be in me.

—Frank G. Kelly

The Heart That Prays

In cloistered stillness,
    or in crowded ways,
God breaths His nearness
    to the heart that prays;
His listening love flows in
    with calm, sweet power
To heal life's hurts, and
    light the troubled hour.

The heart that prays soars high
    on strong, glad wings,
And finds repose beyond earth's
    rending things.

"If you will be prayerful
You'll be careful."

PRAYER

I will not always pray, "Dear God, please give, and give to me." But sometimes ask, "Beloved Lord, what can I do for Thee?"

—Jennie Esmond Wright

In the Morning

Sweetly the holy hymn
    Breaks on the morning air;
Before the world with smoke is dim
    We must meet to offer prayer.

While flowers are wet with dews,
    Dew of our souls, descend;
Ere yet the sun the day renews,
    O Lord, Thy Spirit send.

Upon the battlefield,
    Before the fight begins,
We seek, O Lord, Thy sheltering shield
    To guide us from our sins.

—Charles H. Spurgeon

Prayer of St. Francis

"Lord, make me an instrument of Thy
    Peace;
Where there is hatred, let me sow love;
Where there is injury, pardon;
Where there is doubt, faith;
Where there is despair, hope;
Where there is darkness, light;
And where there is sadness, joy.
O Divine Master, grant that I may not so
    much
Seek to be consoled, as to console;
To be understood, as to understand;
To be loved, as to love;
For it is in giving that we receive;
It is in pardoning, that we are pardoned;
And it is in dying that we are born to
    eternal life."

"Prayer Before Singing"

A song is a beautiful thing!
Voices join in full-throated melody, and lift to blend
    in glorious harmony;
Men's hearts are moved—e'en lifted to ecstasy with
    a song
For a song is a beautiful thing.
But when I sing: Lord, let it not be for this alone,
Lest fruitless I be when day is done;
Touch Thou my lips,
Thy beauty let me see,
And fill my heart with love eternally,
That men may come to know and adore Thee.
Lord, this prayer I bring.
Lord, for Thee I sing.

—Don Hustad

The House Inside

I have a house inside of me;
A house that people never see;
It has a door through which none pass,
And windows, but they're not of glass.

"Where do you live?" asks folks I meet,
And then I say, "On such a street";
But still I know what's really me,
Lives in a house folks never see.

Sometimes I like to go inside,
And hide and hide and hide and hide
And "doctor up" my wounded pride
When I've been "treated rough" outside.

And sometimes, when I've been to blame
I go indoors and blush for shame;
And get my mind in better frame,
And get my tongue and temper tame.

I meet my heavenly Father there;
For He stoops down to hear my prayer;
To smooth my brow and cure my care
And make me brave to do and dare.

Then, after I have been made strong,
And have things right that were all wrong,
I come outside, where I belong,
To sing a new and happy song.

CHILD OF GOD

Dear child of God,
Be still and know
He walks with you
Where'er you go.

Dear child of God
You need not fear;
His power to help
Is always near.

Dear child of God
Know all is well,
Since in His love
You safely dwell.

Dear child of God
Trust Him today;
If dark the path
He lights the way.

Dear child of God
From worry cease;
He is right here,
Rest now in peace.

—Grenville Kleiser

*When the morning light you
   see,
  Don't forget to kneel and
   pray;
Ask the Lord to walk with thee,
  Every moment of the day.*

If I Had Prayed

Perhaps the day would not have seemed so
    long,
  The skies would not have seemed so gray,
If on my knees in humble prayer
  I had begun the day.
Perhaps the fight would not have seemed so
    hard—
  Prepared, I might have faced the fray
If I had been alone with Him,
  Upon my knees, to pray.

Perhaps I might have cheered a broken heart,
  Or helped a wand'rer on the way
If I had asked to be a light
  To some dark soul today.
I would remember just the pleasant things;
  The harsh words that I meant to say
I would forget, if I had prayed
  When I began the day.

I think I could have met life's harder trials
  With hopeful heart and cheerful smile
If I had spoken with my Lord
  Just for a little while.
And, if I pray, I find that all goes well.
  All care at His dear feet is laid;
My heart is glad—the load is light
  Because I first have prayed.

—M. Joyce Rader

The Ideal Prayer

Not more light I ask, O Lord,
  But eyes to see what is;
Not sweeter songs, but ears to
  hear
  The present melodies.

Not more strength, but how to use
  The power that I possess;
Not more of love, but skill to turn
  A frown to a caress.

Not more of joy, but how to feel
  The loving presence here,
To give to others all I have
  Of courage and of cheer.

Not other gifts, dear Lord, I ask,
  But only sight to see
How best those precious gifts to
  use
  Thou has bestowed on me.

Give me all fears to dominate,
  All purest joys to know.
To be the friend I wish to be,
  To speak the truth I know.

To love the pure, to seek the good,
  To help with all my might
All souls to dwell in harmony,
  In freedom's perfect light.

—Florence Holbrook

On Wings of Prayer

As, on a day when skies are overcast,
The sun is shrouded from our earth-bound sight,
Yet far above us, where a plane goes past,
We know the pilot skims a sea of light—
So, when our troubled thoughts, like clouds, press low
And we see only sadness and distress,
Beyond our range of vision we can know
That skies are bright with hope and happiness.
We need but rise on wings of faith and prayer
Through clouds that thin to mist and disappear.
Upborne and safe within the Father's care
We find the light of love has banished fear.

—Helen Reid Chase

Prayer

Obtaining God's Blessings for Ourselves and Others

"Is Prayer Essential?"

Prayer is just as essential for the child of God in the spiritual realm as breathing is for us in the natural. Without it God cannot move in our behalf for prayer is our avenue of approach to Him through Christ.

Scripture has much to say about this important subject. "The effectual fervent prayer of a righteous man availeth much" (James 5:16). Does it work? It surely does.

Jacob prays: The angel blesses him and Esau's revenge is changed to love.

Joseph prays: He is delivered from the prison in Egypt.

Moses prays: Amalek is discomfited and Israel triumphs.

Joshua prays: The day is lengthened and victory is gained.

David prays: God forgives him and he goes out to win others to the Lord.

Jehoshaphat prays: God turns away His anger and smiles.

Elijah prays: A little cloud appears, it begins to rain and the famine is broken.

Elisha prays: A widow's son is restored to life and food is provided.

Isaiah prays: The Assyrian army is put to flight.

Hezekiah prays: The sun dial is turned back and his life is prolonged.

Mordecai prays: Haman is hanged and Israel is set free.

Nehemiah prays: The king's heart is softened in a moment.

Daniel prays: The lions lose their appetite.

The Disciples pray: The Holy Spirit is poured out.

The Church prays: Peter is delivered by an angel.

Paul and Silas pray: The prison shakes, the doors are open, and the Philippian jailer is saved.

Jesus said: "If ye abide in Me, and My words abide in you, ye shall ask what ye will, and it shall be done unto you. **Ask,** and it shall be given unto you; **seek,** and ye shall kind; **knock,** and it shall be opened unto you. For everyone that asketh receiveth; and he that seeketh findeth; and to him that knocketh it shall be opened."

I Know God Answers Prayer

I know not how it will be done,
    Just how my God will answer prayer;
but I have faith that He will hear,
    That He will know and care.
As my prayer ascends to heaven,
    Back will come the answer sure;
If I pray for strength and wholeness,
    He will send His strength and cure.

If my need be food and shelter,
    He will send His prompt supply;
If I ask for His assistance,
    I can best on Him rely.
Ready, too, to take my burden
    When it seems to be a load,
And lead me gladly
    Along the heavenly road.

I know not how He works or answers,
    Know not how or when or why;
He has given His assurance
    That He's with me, ever nigh.
Giving help and love and substance
    When my heart lifts up its cry.
He will answer when I call Him;
    To my side in need will fly.

Prayer for a Favor

Dear God, I know that I have asked
 So many things of You;
To give me comfort in this life
 And make my dreams come true.
And I have not deserved the grace
 You have bestowed on me,
Or properly prepared myself
 For Your eternity.
But this one time I need your help
 More surely than before;
To be courageous and to keep
 Disaster from my door.
Dear God, You know my problem and
 The answer I must find.
And there are certain promises
 I cannot leave behind.
So I beseech You once again
 To hear the prayer I say,
And grant the favor I request,
 To help me out today.

—James J. Metcalfe

The Proof

Some tell us that prayer
 Is all in the mind,
That the only result
 Is the solace we find;
That God does not answer,
 Nor hear when we call:
We commune with our own hearts
 In prayer; that is all!
But we who have knelt
 With our burden and care,
And have made all our problems
 A matter of prayer,
Have seen God reach down
 From His heaven above,
Move mountains, touch hearts,
 In His infinite love;
We know that God works
 In a wonderful way
On behalf of His children
 Who trust Him and pray.

Prayer Answered

I asked for strength that I might achieve;
He made me weak that I might obey.
I asked for health that I might do greater
 things;
I was given grace that I might do better
 things.
I asked for riches that I might be happy;
I was given poverty that I might be wise.
I asked for power that I might have the
 praise of men;
I was given weakness that I might feel
 the need of God.
I asked for all things that I might enjoy
 life;
I was given life that I might enjoy all
 things.
I received nothing that I asked for, all
 that I hoped for.
My prayer was answered.

Prayer Time

There are many times when men have
 failed
 To take the time to pray.
And as they toil, they wonder why
 There's no success their way.
They strive so hard to reach the top
 By means of their own wit,
And forget to ask the Lord above
 To help out just a bit.
They wonder why their strength is not
 Sufficient to the task,
And just can't see the help He'd give
 If they would only ask.
His help is all we'll ever need
 To gain our every goal;
His strength can conquer all the fear
 Confronting any soul.
So when your troubles seem so great
 They can't be done your way,
Remember God above will help—
 If you'll take the time to pray.

—Ramon A. Prichard

Miracle at Munda

They were dying of thirst at Munda that day,
But God answers prayer, and they knew how to pray.
They were lost from their regiment, and blistering feet
March wearily on in the thick tropic heat.
No hunger had they, but each canteen was dry,
And a fiery sun glared from the deep tinted sky.
Some prayed as they marched, and night coming round
Brought rest, but no sparkling water they found;
Till the dew on the leaves in a brush thicket there
Served to moisten their lips and deepen despair;
But God had listened to each sincere word,
His miracle proving their prayers were heard.
A shell, from their own artillery sent
To blast the enemy, oddly went
A bit of a length, then fell to the ground,
Tore open the earth with a thunderous sound . . .
And water gushed over the trail in a stream,
This life-giving water-hole was real, no dream.
They waded in water, they drank until filled,
There was joy in their hearts that could not be stilled!
It happened at Munda . . . the Miracle, when
God answered the prayers of famishing men!

—Lulu Minerva Schultz

What Is Prayer?

Prayer
Is asking
A God
Who replies.
Prayer
Is seeking
For fire
From the skies.
Prayer
Is knocking
'Til Christ
Ope's the door.
Prayer
Is believing
In faith—
Nothing more.

—Gale Harris

My Prayer

God, take my hand,
    Please light the way;
My path make clear
    Through darkest day.
I ask Your light
    On act and deed,
To follow on
    Where'er You lead;
Your still small voice
    I will obey,
Stay close to You
    From day to day.
I pray that You will be
    My Guide for all eternity.

—Mary Even
(87 years young)

The Answer Is on the Way

Slowly I have learned God answers prayer.
Slowly I have learned this vital thing;
That my petition loosed upon the air,
Will reach its destination, and will bring
The answer that will be the best for me
Inevitably.

Slowly, oh, so slowly I have learned
To wait the answer coming soon or late;
So often in the past I prayed, then turned,
Refusing in my eagerness to wait,
And even so, the good God who had heard,
Answered every word.

Surely, I can wait patiently today,
Knowing the answered prayer is on its way.

—Grace Noll Crowell

God Answers Prayer

I know not by what methods rare,
But this I know: God answers prayer.

I know not when He sends the word
That tells us fervent prayer is heard.

I know it cometh soon or late;
Therefore we need to pray and wait.

I know not if the blessing sought
Will come in just the guise I thought.

I leave my prayers with Him alone
Whose will is wiser than my own.

—*Eliza M. H. Abbott*

SHUT IN WITH GOD!

So many things I cannot do
  That once were my delight.
From picnics on a sandy beach
  To walks through fog at night.

I cannot stroll along the street,
  Nor through a shady grove
To seek the wild bird's nesting place
  And nature's treasure-trove.

I cannot sail the restless sea,
  Nor ramble through the hills;
Nor can I coast down snowy slopes
  With heart-disturbing thrills.

So many things I cannot do
  Since I'm shut in at home.
"Shut in with God," and, praise His
    name,
  I do not need to roam—

For I can reach the throne of grace
  While seated in my chair,
Because He has bestowed on us
  The privilege of prayer.

And He has etched upon my heart
  His promises to me,
Of peace and comfort better far
  Than joys that used to be.

Have You Taken It to Jesus?

Have you taken it to Jesus?
  Have you left your burden there?
Does He tenderly support you?
  Have you rolled on Him your care?
O, the sweet unfailing refuge
  Of the everlasting arms;
In their loving clasp enfolded
  Nothing worries or alarms.

Have you taken it to Jesus,
  Just the thing that's pressing now?
Are you trusting Him completely
  With the when, and where and how?
Oh, the joy of full surrender
  Of our life, our plans, our all;
Proving, far above our asking,
  That God answers when we call.

Have you taken it to Jesus?
  'Tis the only place to go
If you want the burden lifted
  And a solace for your woe.
Oh, the blessedness to nestle
  Like a child upon His breast;
Finding ever, as He promised,
  Perfect comfort, peace and rest.

—*Mrs. E. L. Hennessay*

_____

This I Know

I know not by what methods rare,
But this I know—God answers prayer.
I know that He has given His Word,
Which tells me prayer is always heard,
And will be answered, soon or late,
And so I pray and calmly wait.
I know not if the blessing sought
Will come in just the way I thought,
But leave my prayers with Him alone,
Whose will is wiser than my own—
Assured that He will grant my quest,
Or send some answer far more blest.

The Call and the Answer

THE CALL

The way is dark, my Father!
  Cloud on cloud
Is gathering thickly o'er my head,
  And loud
The thunders roar above me. See,
  I stand
Like one bewildered! Father,
  Take my hand,
And through the gloom
  Lead safely home Thy child.

The path is rough, my Father!
  Many a thorn
Has pierced me and my feet all torn
  And bleeding mark the way;
Yet Thy command
  Bids me press forward. Father,
Take my hand and safe and blest
  Lead up to rest, Thy child!

The cross is heavy, Father!
  I have borne
It long, and still do bear it.
  Let my worn
And fainting spirit cross to
  That blessed land
Where crowns are given, Father!
  Take my hand
And, reaching down,
  Lead to the crown, Thy child.

THE ANSWER

The way is dark, My child, but
  Leads to light;
I would not always have thee
  Walk by sight.
My dealings now thou canst not
  Understand.
I meant it so; but I will take
  Thy hand
And through the gloom
  Lead safely home My child!

The path is rough, My child,
  But, oh, how sweet
Will be the rest for weary
  Pilgrim's feet.
When thou shalt reach the borders
  Of that land
To which I lead thee, as I take
  Thy hand
And safe and blest
  With Me shall rest My child!

The cross is heavy, child! Yet
  There is One
Who bore a heavier for thee;
  My Son,
My well-beloved. For Him bear
  Thine, and stand
With Him, at last, and from thy
  Father's hand,
Thy cross laid down,
  Receive a crown, My child!

—Author unknown

"Helping Together by Prayer"

I love to feel that though on earth we may never meet,
Yet we may hold heart-fellowship at God's dear feet.
I like to feel that in the work thou hast to do,
That I, by lifting hands of prayer, may help Thee, too.

I like to think that in the path His love prepares,
The steps may sometimes stronger prove through secret prayers.
I like to think that, when on high results we see,
Perchance thou wilt rejoice that I thus prayed for thee.

—Author unknown

72

A Little Talk With Jesus

A little talk with Jesus
How it smooths the rugged road;
How it seems to help me onward,
When I faint beneath my load.
When my heart is crushed with sorrow,
And mine eyes with tears are dim,
There's nought can yield me comfort
Like a little talk with Him.

I cannot live without Him,
Nor would I if I could;
He is my daily portion,
My medicine and food.
He's altogether lovely,
None can with Him compare—
The chief among ten thousand,
The fairest of the fair.

So I'll wait a little longer,
'Till His appointed time,
And glory in the knowledge
That such a hope is mine.
Then in my Father's dwelling,
Where "many mansions" be,
I'll sweetly talk with Jesus,
And He shall talk with me.

Secret Service

If the shut-ins all united
  In one voice of common prayer,
What a ceaseless shower of blessings
  Should be falling everywhere!

Though so weak and often helpless,
  They can wield a mighty power,
Lifting up their soul's petition
  To the Saviour, hour by hour.

They can importune the Father
  From the "secret place," and then
In the quiet of the stillness
  They can hear His voice again.

Never soldier in fierce conflict
  Could a higher honor bring
Than the shut-in who's performing
  "Secret service" for the King.

—*Author unknown*

Thankful for Unanswered Prayers

I thank Thee, Lord, for mine unanswered prayers, unanswered save Thy quiet, kindly, "Nay." Yet it seemed hard among my bitter cares that day.

I wanted joy, but Thou didst know that sorrow was the gift I needed most, and in its mystic depth I learned to see the Holy Ghost.

I wanted health, but Thou didst bid me sound the secret treasures of pain, and in the moans and groans my heart oft found Thy Christ again.

I wanted wealth; 'twas not the better part; there is a wealth with poverty oft given, and Thou didst teach me of the gold of heart, best gift of heaven.

I thank Thee, Lord, for these unanswered prayers, and for Thy word, the quiet, kindly "Nay." 'Twas Thy withholding lightened all my cares that blessed day.

—*Anonymous*

My Prayer for You

In thy journeys to and fro
  God direct thee;
In thy happiness and pleasure
  God bless thee;
In care, anxiety, or trouble
  God sustain thee;
In peril and in danger
  God protect thee.

Realization

Prayer does not bring God nearer us,
  For God is always near.
Prayer is the reverence of the heart
  Realizing He is here.

—*Jane Merchant*

Why Pray?

Why pray? Because we need spiritual and moral power in our lives, because we face world tasks in which we need the strength and cooperation of God, because we need communion with God in the exaltation of great hours and in the bitter depression of our sad and broken days.

"Lord, what a change within us one short hour
Spent in Thy presence will avail to make!
What heavy burdens from our shoulders take;
What parched lands refresh, as with a shower!
We kneel and all around us seems to lower;
We rise, and all the distant and the near
Stands forth in sunny outline, brave and clear!
We kneel, how weak! We rise, how full of
    power!
Why, therefore, should we do ourselves this
    wrong,
Or others, that we are not always strong;
That we are ever overborne with care;
That we should ever weak or heartless be,
Anxious or troubled, when with us is prayer,
And joy and strength and courage are with
    Thee?

DAILY PRAYER

If I can do some good today,
If I can serve along life's way,
If I can something helpful say,
    Lord, show me how.

If I can right a human wrong,
If I can help to make one
    strong,
If I can cheer by smile or song,
    Lord, show me how.

If I can aid one in distress,
If I can make a burden less,
If I can spread more happiness,
    Lord, show me how.

If I can do a kindly deed,
If I can help someone in need,
If I can show a fruitful seed,
    Lord, show me how.

If I can feed a hungry heart,
If I can give a better start,
If I can fill a nobler part,
    Lord, show me how.

—Grenville Kliser

Prayer and Radio

If radio's slim fingers
    Can pluck a melody
From night, and toss it over
    A continent or sea;
If songs, like crimson roses
    Are called from thin, blue air,
Why should mortals wonder
    If God hears prayer!

—Ethel Romig Fuller

"A Little Prayer"

Today I pray a little prayer,
    That God will keep you in His love
And bring you peace and smooth your
    way
And guide you safely day by day.

God's Way Is Best!

Praise

Natural Attitude of Grateful Hearts

We Will Praise Thee

Great Jehovah! we will praise Thee,
  Earth and heaven Thy will obey!
Suns and systems move obedient
  To Thy universal sway.

Deep and awful are Thy counsels;
  High and glorious is Thy throne;
Reigning o'er Thy vast dominion,
  Thou art God and Thou alone.

In Thy wondrous condescension
  Thou has stooped to raise our race;
Thou hast given to us a Saviour,
  Full of goodness and of grace.

By His blood we are forgiven,
  By His intercessions free,
By His love we raise to glory
  There to reign eternally.

God of Power—we bow before Thee;
  God of Wisdom—Thee we praise;
God of Love—so kind and tender
  We would praise Thee all our days.

Praise to Thee—our loving Father;
  Praise to Thee—redeeming Son;
Praise to Thee—Almighty Spirit;
  Praise to Thee—Thou Holy One.

—John White

WITH GOD FOREVER

The stars shine over the earth,
The stars shine over the sea;
The stars look up to the mighty God,
The stars look down on me,
The stars have lived for a million
  years,
A million years and a day,
But God and I shall love and live
When the stars have passed away.

The Thankful Heart

For all that God in mercy sends—
For health and children, home and
  friends,
For comforts in the time of need,
For every kindly word or deed,
For happy thoughts and holy talk,
For guidance in our daily walk—
  In everything give thanks!

For beauty in this world of ours,
For verdant grass and lovely flowers,
For song of birds, for hum of bees,
For the refreshing summer breeze,
For hill and plain, for stream and wood,
For the great ocean's mighty flood—
  In everything give thanks!

For the sweet sleep which comes with
  night,
For the returning morning light,
For the bright sun that shines on high,
For the stars glittering in the sky—
For these and everything we see—
O Lord, our hearts we lift to Thee.
  In everything give thanks!

—E. I. Tupper

I Thank Thee, Lord, for Everything

I am not satisfied to say,
"Thank Thee, Lord," three times a day;
For all around me everywhere,
There is so much to show His care;
So many good gifts I can see
That whisper of His love to me.
I want to run and laugh and shout
And let the gladness all come out.
So I have made this song to sing:
"I thank Thee, Lord, for everything."

We Thank Thee

For light on the way;
For peace in our day,
  We thank Thee!

For harvest and store;
For love at our door,
  We thank Thee!

For sunshine and cheer;
For friends we hold dear,
  We thank Thee!

For wisdom to know;
For courage to go,
  We thank Thee!

For freedom to live;
For substance to give,
  We thank Thee!
For vision to see;
For knowledge of Thee,
  We thank Thee!

—*Grenville Kleiser*

He Thanks Thee Best

He thanks Thee best who serves Thee
    best:
Who meets each glowing day
With grateful hearts and lifted face,
To toil and rest and play.

He thanks Thee best who loves Thee
    best:
And loving, loves each one
Who passes down the old high road
From sun to setting sun.

He thanks Thee best who trusts Thee
    best:
Whose faith shines through the dark.
A helpful, happy, hopeful thing
For way-tired hearts to mark.

He thanks Thee best who worships best:
Who prays where none may see,
Who humbly waits to hear Thy voice—
Who has no God but Thee.

—*Grace Noll Crowell*

God's Blessings Are Free

Meditate thankfully upon all things of God that are free—the air, the sunshine, the rain, the deep blue sky, the drifting billowing clouds, the fantastic massing of the snowflakes that make a world so new, the refreshing mountain streams, the sunsets, the green fields, the multicolored flowers that bedeck the borders, the marvelous music of the bird songs—the proud mocker, the faint call of the hermit thrush—that vie with all the vocals and fade the harpchords, the majestic trees with their dancing shadows, the silver moon while the day is resting, the winking stars that court in the nighttime, the sparkling crystal dewdrops that kiss the glass blades at the sunrise—His handiwork! His expressions of His love for me!

Because of Thy Great Bounty

Because I have been given much,
    I, too, shall give;
Because of Thy great bounty, Lord,
    Each day I live
I shall divide my gifts from Thee
    With every brother that I see
Who has the need of help from me.

Because I have been sheltered, fed,
    By Thy good care,
I cannot see another's lack
    And I not share
My glowing fire, my loaf of bread,
    My roof's shelter overhead,
That he, too, may be comforted.

Because love has lavished so
    Upon me, Lord,
A wealth I know that was not meant
    For me to hoard,
I shall give love to those in need,
    The cold and hungry clothe and feed,
Thus shall I show my thanks indeed.

—*Grace Noll Crowell*

Think and Thank

By Gilbert C. Temant

There are times when we feel
  We have reached the end;
The world has folded upon us
  Without a single friend.

And everyone around us pays
  No mind to how we feel;
Tho we have troubles to bear
  That seem so big and real.

But should we trade our troubles with
  Some others on this earth,
I'm sure we'd find just what
  Our blessings would be worth.

So if you have the ears to hear
  The robins' joyous call,
Remember there are those who live
  And never hear at all.

If you can see the sunshine
  And flowers in the park,
Just think of those who cannot see;
  To them it's always dark.

If you can take a daily stroll
  In the sunshine or in rain,
Just don't forget the millions
  Who shall never walk again.

And those who count their troubles,
  Oh so very far ahead,
Should learn to count their blessings
  Before they go to bed.

And thank God for those blessings
  And promise now that you
Will try to do a better job
  The next time He comes through.

—Submitted by Myrtle Jones

With Lesser Things?

There's never been a chance for me
To board a ship, to span a sea,
That I might tread a foreign shore
And drink my fill of ancient lore.
I've not been near the pyramids,
Nor walked the streets of old Madrid.

My eyes will likely never gaze
On priceless art of other days . . .
For these some folks have millions
    spent,
While I shall have to be content
With lesser things . . . in any case,
The things considered commonplace.

How could I say, "With lesser things"?
When God, through nature, beauty
    brings
To earthbound souls; yes, even I
Can view a cloud-swept summer sky—
Can revel in sheer ecstasy
At mountain heights and boundless sea.

Oh, many times, close by my side
I've found Him, when at eventide
With easel, brushes, colors fine,
He paints a canvas so divine
That even He seems loath to go—
So stays and does an afterglow.

Such matchless scenes to us unfurled.
Reveal the glories of His world.
Why, then, should I seek other sphere
When I've this Artist always near?
His works aren't found on museum
    wall—
Though He's the greatest of them all!

—Earl W. Oates

77

Forgive Me, Lord

Today upon a bus,
I saw a lovely maid with golden hair.
I envied her—she seemed so gay—
And wished I were as fair.
When suddenly she arose to leave,
I saw the cruel braces
As she hobbled down the aisle;
A victim of polio was she.
But as she passed—a smile!

Oh, God, forgive me when I whine.
I have two straight feet.
The world is mine.

And then I stopped to buy some sweets.
The lad who sold them had such charm.
I talked with him.
He said to me: "It's nice to talk
With folks like you.
You see," said he, "I'm blind."

Oh, God, forgive me when I whine.
I have two eyes.
The world is mine.

Then walking down the street,
I saw a child with eyes of blue.
He stood and watched the others play.
It seemed he knew not what to do.
I stopped a moment, then said to him,
"Why don't you join the others, dear?"
He looked ahead without a word,
And then I knew he could not hear.

Oh, God, forgive me when I whine.
I have two ears.
The world is mine.

With feet to take me where I'd go,
With eyes to see the sunset's glow,
With ears to hear what I would know—
Oh, God, forgive me when I whine.
I'm blessed indeed.
The world is mine.

I Got More Than My Share

As I travel down life's lonely road,
Sometimes I bear a heavy load.
Seems sometimes to me that life's
    unfair,
But when I think of what my Saviour's
    done,
And I count my blessings one by one,
Then I know I got more than my share.

CHORUS:
I gave my life to Him and he broke the
    power of sin.
I know I met Him there in prayer
When He bathed my soul at Calvary.
He saved my soul and He set me free.
Then I know I got more than my share.

Someday my journey here will end
Then I'll meet my blessed Friend,
And He'll give me there a crown to
    wear;
I will hear the Saviour say, "Well done,"
As I count my blessings one by one.
Then I'll know I got more than my
    share.

LET ME FORGET

One prayer, of all the prayers,
My heart might say,
Is, "Teach me to begin
All fresh today.
Lord, teach me to forget
The worry and the fret
That lies behind.
Each morning, born anew,
With vigor let me do
What's right and kind,
Unhampered by the wrong
Of yesterday.
Oh, teach me quick the song
To sing today,
Nor let my heart be sore
For what has gone before,
But cheerful say:
"Today the sun is bright!
Today I will do right!"

—*Helen Lockwood Coffin*

My Thanksgiving Psalm

I thank thee, Father, o'er and o'er
For all that thou hast done.
But, most of all, I thank thee for
The gift of thy dear Son.

I thank thee for the Christ who came
By way of human birth.
Thy love and power to proclaim,
By word and deed on earth.

I thank thee for the Christ who died
In my stead on the tree;
Who there poured out the crimson tide
Which wholly cleanses me.

I thank thee for the Christ who gives
Me life from death-fear freed—
The risen Christ who ever lives,
For me to intercede.

I thank thee for the Christ who comes
To human lives today,
Whereby his heavenly beauty blooms
Around our earthly way.

—Nobie Beall Dykes

Have You Forgotten God?

In the glare of earthly pleasure,
In the fight for earthly treasure,
'Mid your blessings without measure,
  Have you forgotten God?

You are thoughtful of the stranger
From the palace or the manger,
And the weak you shield from danger—
  Have you forgotten God?

While His daily grace receiving,
Are you still His Spirit grieving
By a heart of unbelieving—
  Have you forgotten God?

While His bounty you're accepting,
Are you His commands neglecting,
And His call to you rejecting—
  Have you forgotten God?

See the shades of night appalling,
On your pathway now are falling;
Hear ye not those voices calling—
  Have you forgotten God?

Praise

"Oh, that men would praise the Lord for his goodness, and for his wonderful works to the children of men." (Psalm 107:8).

How we need to praise our Saviour,
Giving glory to HIs name;
Whether things look bright or dreary,
We can praise Him just the same.

Praise Him for His great salvation,
For His blood that makes us clean,
For His wondrous keeping power,
For His arms on which to lean.

Praise Him for His love so boundless;
Praise Him for His matchless grace.
For His everlasting mercy,
Let us give Him ceaseless praise.

Praise Him for our daily blessings,
For our daily trials too;
'Tis in them He giveth triumph,
Shows us He can keep us true.

Praise Him for His Holy Spirit,
Teaching us to know the Word
And the love of God our Father,
Praise Him for Himself, our Lord.

—Naomi Ruth Randel

Christian Character . . .

Stability, Faithfulness, Perseverance

ONE SHIP SAILS EAST . . .

One ship sails east and another sails west,
By the very same wind that blows;
It's the set of a sail and not the gale,
Which determines the way a ship goes.

Like the winds of the sea are the ways of fate,
As we sail along through life;
It's the set of a soul that determines its goal,
Not human stress and strife.

If the ship of your soul is out on life's sea,
Tossed by the storms and distressed;
Set your sail for the harbor, wherever you be,
And drop anchor in the Haven of Rest.

BEGIN TODAY

Dream not too much of what
    you'll do tomorrow,
How well you'll work another
    year;
Tomorrow's chance you do not
    need to borrow—
Today is here.
Swear not someday to break
    some habit's fetter,
When this old year is dead and
    passed away;
If you have need of living,
    wiser, better
Begin today!

Give Us Men

"Give us men to match our moun-
    tains,
Give us men to match our plains,
Men with empires in their purpose
Men with throbbing, conquering
    brains.

Give us men to lead our nation,
Give us men with holy zeal,
Men aflame with truth and vision
Men who bear the heavenly seal.

Give us men who love the Bible,
And its precepts do obey,
Give us men who have convictions
And are Christians all the way.

Give us men who follow Jesus.
Give us men who love their Lord.
Men with hearts pure and courageous,
Men led by God's eternal Word."

Cross Currents

There are streams from the heart of the
    ocean,
That flow toward the rocks on this shore;
From the north and the south they are
    coming,
And they meet with a rush and a roar.

Far above on the crags I am watching
The conflict that never shall cease;
I can see how the struggle is faring,
Why that ocean can never know peace.

In our hearts there are conflicting currents
That rush in from here and from there.
We are warned that some will break on
    us,
But others steal up unaware.

In His heaven above, God is sitting;
And He sees every battle we fight.
He knows why there's always a struggle
In our lives as we strive for the right.

—Francis A. Hartley

MYSELF

I have to live with myself, and so
I want to be fit for myself to know.
I want to be able, as days go by
Always to look myself straight in the eye;
I don't want to stand with the setting sun,
And hate myself for things I have done.

I don't want to keep on a closet shelf
A lot of secrets about myself,
And fool myself, as I come and go,
Into thinking that nobody else will know
The kind of a man I really am:
I don't want to dress up myself in sham.

I want to go out with my head erect;
I want to deserve all men's respect;
But here in the struggle for fame and pelf
I want to be able to like myself.
I don't want to look at myself and know
That I'm bluster and bluff and empty show.

I can never hide myself from me;
I see what others may never see;
I know what others may never know;
I never can fool myself, and so,
Whatever happens, I want to be
Self-respecting and conscience free.

—*Edgar A. Guest*

Tell Me What You Are

Don't tell me what you will do
    When you have time to spare;
Tell me what you did today
    To ease a load of care.

Don't tell me what you will give
    When your ship comes in from sea;
Tell me what you gave today
    A fettered soul to free.

Don't tell me the dream you have
    Of conquest still afar;
Don't say what you hope to be,
    But tell me what you are.

—*Greenville Kleiser*

Be True

Thou must thyself be true
    If thou the truth wouldst teach;
Thy soul must overflow, if thou
    Another soul wouldst reach.
It needs the overflow of heart
    To give the lips full speech.

Think truly, and thy thoughts
    Shall the world's famine feed;
Speak truly, and each word of thine
    Shall be a fruitful seed;
Live truly, and thy life shall be
    A great and noble creed.

Horatius Bonar

The Builders

A builder builded a temple,
    He wrought it with grace and skill—
Pillars and groins and arches
    All fashioned to work his will.

Men said as they saw its beauty:
    "It never shall know decay,
Great is thy skill, O builder!
    Thy fame shall endure for aye."

A teacher builded a temple
    With loving and infinite care;
Planning each arch with patience,
    Laying each stone with prayer.

None praised her unceasing efforts;
    None knew of her wondrous plan.
For the temple the teacher builded
    Was unseen by the eyes of man.

Gone is the builder's temple,
    Crumbled into the dust;
Low lies each stately pillar,
    Food for consuming rust.

But the temple the teacher builded
    Will last while the ages roll.
For that beautiful unseen temple
    Was the child's immortal soul.

—*Hattie Vose Hall*

Just One Day

If I could live to God for just one day,
  One blessed day, from rosy dawn of light,
  Till purple twilight deepened into night,
  A day of faith unfaltering, trust complete,
  Of love unfeigned and perfect charity,
Of hope undimmed, of courage past dismay,
  Of heavenly peace, patient humility—
  No hint of duty to constrain my feet,
  No dream of ease to lull to listlessness,
  Within my heart no root of bitterness.
No yielding to temptation's subtle sway,
  Methinks, in that one day would so expand
  My soul to meet such holy, high demand
  That never, never more could hold me bound
  This shriveling husk of self that wraps me
    round.
So might I henceforth live to God alway.

                    —Susan E. Gammons

Sticking

There was a little postage stamp
No bigger than your thumb,
But still it stuck right on the job
Until its work was done.
They licked it and they pounded it
'Til it would make you sick.
But the more it took a lickin'
Why the tighter it would stick.
So, friend, let's be like the postage
    stamp
In playing life's rough game,
And just keep on a-sticking
Though we hide our heads in
    shame.
For the stamp stuck to the letter
'Til it saw it safely through.
There's no one could do better,
Let's keep sticking and be true."

Tapestry of My Life

I wonder what the other side will be, when I have finished weaving all my thread. I do not know the pattern, nor the end of this great piece of work which is for me. I only know that I must weave with care the colors that are given me day by day, and make of them a fabric firm and true, which will be of service for my fellowman.

Sometimes the colors are so dull and gray, I doubt if there will be one race of beauty there, but all at once there comes a thread of gold or rose so deep that there will always be that one bright spot to cherish or to keep, and maybe against its ground of darker hue it will be beautiful.

The warp is held in place by the Master's hand. The Master's mind the design for me. If I but weave the shuttle to and fro and blend the colors just the best I know, perhaps when it is finished, He will say, " 'Tis good," and lay it on the footstool of His feet.

                    —Author unknown

You Tell On Yourself

You tell on yourself by the friends you seek,
By the very manner in which you speak;
By the way you employ your leisure time;
By the use you make of dollar and dime.

You tell what you are by the things you
    wear,
By the spirit in which your burdens bear;
By the kind of things at which you laugh,
By the records you play on the phonograph.

You tell what you are by the way you walk,
By the things of which you delight to talk;
By the manner in which you bear defeat;
By so simple a thing as how you eat.

By the books you choose from the well-
    filled shelf;
In these ways and more, you tell on your-
    self;
So, there's really no particle of sense
In an effort to keep up a false pretense.

NO

No is next to the shortest word in the English language.

It is the concentrate Declaration of Independence of the human soul.

It is the central citadel of character and can remain impregnable forever.

It is the only path to reformation.

It is the steam gauge of strength, the barometer of temperament, the electric indicator of moral force.

It is the automatic safety-first device.

It has served more women than all the knights of chivalry.

It has kept millions of young men from going over the Niagara Falls of drunkenness, profligacy and passion.

It is the dragon that guards beauty's tower.

It is the high fence that preserves the innocence of the innocent.

It is the thick wall of the home, keeping the father from folly, the mother from indiscretion, the boys from ruin and the girls from shame.

It is the one word you can always say when you can think of nothing else.

It is the one answer that needs no explanation.

The mule is the surest footed and most dependable of all domestic animals. No is the mulepower of the soul.

Say it and mean it. Say it and look your man in the eye. Say it and don't hesitate.

A good round No is the most effective of known shells from the human howitzer.

In the great parliament of life the Noes have it.

The value of any Yes you utter is measured by the number of Noes banked behind it.

Live your own life. Make your own resolutions. Mark out your own program. Aim at your own mark. Determine your own conduct. And plant all around those an impregnable hedge of Noes with the jaggedest, sharpest thorns that grow.

The No-man progresses under his own steam. He is not led about and pushed around by officious tugboats.

The woman who can say No, carries the very best insurance against the fires, tornadoes, earthquakes and accidents that threaten womankind.

Be soft and gentle as you please outwardly, but let the center of your soul be a No, as hard as steel.

—Dr. Frank Crane

Life Is Too Short to Be Little

Often we allow ourselves to be upset by small things we should despise and forget. Perhaps some man we helped has proved ungrateful—some woman we believe to be a friend has spoken ill of us—some regard we thought we deserved has been denied us. We feel such disappointments so strongly that we can no longer work or sleep. But isn't that absurd? Here we are on this earth, with only a few more decades to live, and we lose many irreplaceable hours brooding over grievances that in a year's time will be forgotten by us and by everybody. No, let us devote our life to worthwhile actions and feelings, to great thoughts, real affections and enduring undertakings. For life is too short to be little.

MEN WANTED

The great want of this age is men:
Men who are not for sale;
Men who will condemn wrong in friend or foe—
    in themselves as well as others;
Men whose consciences are as steady
    as the needle to the pole;
Men who will stand for the right though the heavens totter,
    and the earth reels;
Men who can tell the truth and look the world right in the
    eye;
Men who neither brag nor run;
Men who neither flag nor flinch;
Men who can have courage without shouting it;
Men in whom the hope of everlasting life
    still runs deep and strong;
Men who know their message and tell it;
Men who know their business and attend to it;
Men who are not too lazy to work,
    nor too proud to be poor;
Men who are willing to eat what they have earned
    and to wear what they have paid for;
Men who are not ashamed to say No with emphasis.

Think Deeply
Speak Gently
Love Much
Laugh Often
Work Hard
Give Freely
Pay Promptly
Pray Earnestly
and Be Kind

—Raymond P. Murray

The Measure of a Man

Not—"How did he die?"
But—"How did he live?"
Not—"What did he gain?"
But—"What did he give?"
    These are the units
    To measure the worth
    Of a man, as a man,
    Regardless of birth.
Not—"What was his station?"
But—"Had he a heart?"
And—"How did he play his God-given
    part? Was He ever ready with a
    Word of good cheer,
    To bring back a smile,
    To banish a tear?"
Not—"What did the sketch in the
    newspaper say?"
But—"Did he accept Christ ere he
    passed away?"

The End of the Rope

When you've lost every vestige of hope,
    And you think you are beaten and
    done,
When you've come to the end of your
    rope,
    Tie and knot in the end and hang on.

Have courage, for here is the dope,
    When you stand with your back to the
    wall,
And you've come to the end of your rope,
    Tie a knot in the end and hang on.

You're not licked; do not sorrow and
    mope
    When your friends seem to all disap-
    pear;
Though you've come to the end of your
    rope,
    Tie a knot in the end—and hang on.

—Margaret Nickerson Martin

God Is Seeking for Men

God is seeking for men in this world's last hour,
For men who can love—and anointed with
    power—
Will stand in the gap, and make up the hedge
That many in darkness of sin may be led
To Christ the Redeemer who only can save
From the power of evil, despair and the grave.

God is seeking for men who can sorrow and feel
For the souls He created, whom no one can heal:
The poor, broken bodies, the sin-darkened souls
With none to deliver and none to make whole
The dear little children who cry in the night,
Who long for a Saviour to bring them the Light.

God called for a weapon to punish the lands
To put to the sword the work of His hands,
And bring revelation of sin through His Word,
That the nations far off may yet know the Lord.
But though they were punished by war's cruel hate,
So soon they forget their most terrible fate.

And ev'ry man wanders his own selfish way,
Enjoying his pleasure and failing to pray
For the pow'r of the Spirit that makes feeble man
An instrument, mighty to save, in the land.
O, where are the mighty, the holy and just
To whom God can proffer such high, noble trust?

Where, O where are the few to stand in the hedge,
To fill up the gap by a resolute pledge,
To carry the message of power to the weak,
The hungry, the sick, the forlorn and the meek?
My brother, my sister, won't you be the one
To tell the glad tidings of God's only Son?

Think not of tomorrow and what you may lose—
A throne and a crown is for those who will choose
To follow the Lamb anywhere He may go;
Rescuing souls out of darkness and woe;
Leading the lost in God's infinite plan—
Won't you tell Him today, "Lord, I'll be that man."
                  —Marion Haines

A Little Walk Around Yourself

When you're criticizing others,
  And are finding here and
    there
A fault or two to speak of,
  Or a weakness you can tear;
When you're blaming some-
    one's weakness,
  Or accusing some of pelf—
It's time that you went out
  To take a walk around your-
    self.

There are lots of human failures
  In the average of us all;
And lots of grave shortcomings
  In the short ones and in the
    tall;
But when we think of evils
  Men should lay upon the
    shelves—
It's time we all went out
  To take a walk around our-
    selves.

We need so often in this life,
  This balancing of scales;
This seeing how much in us
    wins
  And how much in us fails;
But before you judge another
  Just to lay him on the shelf—
It would be a splendid plan
  To take a walk around your-
    self.

Abraham Lincoln Said:

"I am not bound to win, but I am bound to be true. I am not bound to succeed, but I am bound to live up to the light I have . . . I must stand with anybody who stands right, stand with him while he is right, and part with him when he goes wrong."

One Here and There

*"Fear not, little flock; for it is your
Father's good pleasure to give you the
kingdom" (Luke 12:32).*

Of all we meet on life's great stream,
   There's but one here and there
Who treasures most the better things.
Each man to self most tightly clings.
For self he toils, of self he sings,
   Except one here and there.

The earth would be a darker place
   But for one here and there,
Whose heart with self has not been filled,
Whose love for God has not been killed,
Whose thankful praise has not been
      stilled;
   There's one here and there.

And this has been the Lord's wise will
   To find one here and there,
Who counting earthly gain but dross,
Would daily take the Christian cross
E'en at the risk of any loss;
   God finds one here and there.

'Tis not the many that He seeks,
   But just one here and there.
He seeks not all, but jewels fair;
For those who will His sufferings share,
And for His sake reproaches bear;
   They're few—one here and there.

But oh! the grandeur of the work
   For this one here and there!
To cheer those weary in the race,
To sinners speak of pardoning grace,
To shed heav'n's light in every place,
   Let's be one here and there.

Longfellow Said:

"The intellect of a man shows in
his eyes and forehead; the character of
a man is revealed in his face; but only
the voice of a man reveals his soul."

Just Keeping On

I've dreamed many dreams that never
   came true,
   And saw them vanish at dawn.
But I've realized enough of my dreams
   To make me keep dreaming on.

I've prayed many prayers when no
   answer came,
   Though patiently I waited long.
But answers have come to enough of my
   prayer
   To help me keep praying on.

I have trusted many a friend that failed,
   And left me to weep alone;
But I've found enough of my friends
   true blue
   To make me keep trusting on.

I've sown many seeds that fell by the
   way,
   For the birds to feed upon.
But I've held enough golden sheaves in
   my hand
   To help me keep sowing on.

Many blotches I've made in the great
   book of life,
   As the pages turn on.
But I find enough beauty in each turning
   page
   To make me keep turning on.

Beautiful Thoughts

"Think beautiful thoughts and set them
   adrift
On eternity's boundless sea!
Let their burden be pure; let their white
   sails lift,
And bear from you the comforting gift
Of Your heartfelt sympathy.
"For a beautiful thought is a beautiful
   thing,
And out on the infinite tide
May meet and touch and tenderly bring
To the sick and the weary and sorrowing
A solace long denied."

What You Are— Shows on Your Face

You don't have to tell
  How you live each day;
You don't have to tell
  If you work or play.
For a tried and true barometer
  Right in its place,
However you live, friend,
  It will show in your face.
The false, the deceit that you
  Carry in your heart
Won't stay down inside
  Where it first got its start:
For sinew and blood
  Are a thin veil of lace.
What you carry in your heart
  Will show in your face.
Now, if you dissipate nights
  Till the day is most nigh,
There is only one teller
  And one that won't lie.
Since your facial barometer
  Is right in its place,
However you live, my friend,
  It will show in your face.
Then, if your life is unselfish
  And for others you live,
Not for just what you can get,
  But for what you can give,
And if you live close to God
  In His Infinite Grace. . . .
You won't have to tell it,
  It will show in your face.

All the water in the world
  However hard it tried,
Could never sink a ship
  Unless it got inside.
All the evil in the world,
  The wickedness and sin,
Can never sink the soul's
    craft
  Unless it got inside.

Be the Best of Whatever You Are

If you can't be a pine on the top of the hill,
Be a shrub in the valley, but be
The best little shrub on the side of the rill.
Be a bush if you can't be a tree.
If you can't be a bush, be a bit of the grass—
Some highway the happier make—
If you can't be a muskie, then just be a bass,
But the liveliest bass in the lake.
We can't all be the captain,
Some must be the crew—
There is something for all of us here—
There's the big work to do, and there's the
    lesser to do,
And the task that is ours is the near.
If you can't be a highway, then just be a trail.
If you can't be the sun, be a star.
For it isn't by the size that you win or you fail.
Be the best of whatever you are.

God, Give Us Men

God, give us Men! A time like this demands
Strong mind, great hearts, true faith and ready
    hands;
Men whom the lust of office does not kill;
Men whom the spoils of office cannot buy;
Men who possess opinions and a will;
Men who have honor; men who will not lie;
Men who can stand before a demagogue
And scorn his treacherous flatteries without
    winking!
Tall men, sun-crowned, who live above the
    fog
In public duty and in private thinking;
For while the rabble, with their thumb-worn
    creeds,
Their large professions and their little deeds,
Mingle in selfish strife, lo! Freedom weeps,
Wrong rules the land and waiting justice
    sleeps.

—*Josiah Gilbert Holland (1819-1881)*

87

Children Learn What They Live

If a child lives with criticism,
  He learns to condemn.
If a child lives with hostility,
  He learns to fight.
If a child lives with ridicule,
  He learns to be shy.
If a child lives with shame,
  He learns to feel guilty.
If a child lives with tolerance,
  He learns to be patient.
If a child lives with encouragement,
  He learns confidence.
If a child lives with praise
  He learns to appreciate.
If a child lives with fairness,
  He learns justice.
If a child lives with security,
  He learns to have faith.
If a child lives with approval,
  He learns to like himself.
If a child lives with acceptance and
  friendship,
  He learns to find love in the world.
                    —*Dorothy Law Noltz*

What Matters Most

It matters not what others do,
  It is my task to see
My life is patterned in the mold
  The Lord has planned for me.

It matters not what others think,
  Or what the creed they claim;
It matters only that I live
  To glorify God's name.

It matters not what others say
  In ridicule or fun;
I want to live that I may hear
  His word, "My child, well done."

It matters not my lot in life,
  In sunshine, clouds or rain;
If only Jesus has control,
  Earth's greatest loss is gain.

10 Most Wanted Men

1. The man who tries to be the right example to every child, rather than merely talking about it.
2. The man who has a passion to help, rather than to be helped.
3. The man who is willing to say, "I was wrong, I'm sorry."
4. The man who will look at temptation squarely and say, "No."
5. The man who puts God's business above any other.
6. The man who throws himself totally into a project, then gives credit for its success to his helpers.
7. The man who has a ready smile and a pat on the back for others.
8. The man who goes with his children to church, rather than sending them.
9. The man who can see his own faults before he sees the faults of others.
10. The man who gives his money, time and talent without thought of return.

Things We Cannot Do

1. We cannot sow bad habits and reap a good character.
2. We cannot sow jealousy and hatred and reap love and friendship.
3. We cannot sow wicked thoughts and reap a good life.
4. We cannot sow wrong deeds and live righteously.
5. We cannot sow crime and get away with it.
6. We cannot sow dissipation and reap a healthy body.
7. We cannot sow crooked dealings and succeed indefinitely.
8. We cannot sow self-indulgence and not show it in our face.
9. We cannot sow disloyalty and reap loyalty from others.
10. We cannot sow dishonesty and reap integrity.

—*From Maywood Wesleyan "Call to Worship"*

Witnessing . . .

Personal Evangelism, Missions

Speak Out for Jesus

You talk about your business,
　Your bonds and stocks and gold;
And in all worldly matters
　You are so brave and bold.
But why are you so silent
　About salvation's plan?
Why don't you speak out for Jesus,
　And speak out like a man?

You talk about the weather,
　And the crops of corn and wheat;
You speak of friends and neighbors
　That pass along the street;
You call yourself a Christian,
　And like the Gospel plan—
Then why not speak for Jesus,
　And speak out like a man?

Are you ashamed of Jesus
　And the story of the cross,
That you lower His pure banner
　And let it suffer loss?
Have you forgot His suffering?
　Did He die for you in vain?
If not, then live and speak for Jesus,
　And speak out like a man.

I'd like to tell the story sweet
　Of Jesus. Wouldn't you?
To help some other folks to meet
　Their Saviour. Wouldn't you?
I'd like to travel all the way
　To where I'd hear my Jesus say:
"You've helped my work along today."
　I'd like that. Wouldn't you?

Hold High the Torch

You did not light its glow—
'Twas given you by other hands you
　know.
'Tis yours to keep it burning bright!
Yours to pass on when you no more
　need light.
For there are other feet that we must
　guide
And other forms go marching by our
　side.
Their eyes are watching every smile
　and tear,
And efforts which we think are not
　worthwhile
Are sometimes just the very help they
　need.
Actions to which their souls would
　give most heed,
So that in turn they'll hold it high,
And say, "I watched someone else
　carry it this way."
I think it started down its pathway
　bright
The day the Maker said, "Let there be
　light."
And He once said, who hung on
　Calvary's tree,
"Ye are the light of the world—Go
　Shine for ME."

**Be ready always to give an answer
to every man that asketh you a
reason of the hope that is in you,
with meekness and fear.**
1 Peter 3:15

I Had No Time

The day slipped by and time was spent
And all the good things that I meant
To do were left undone because
I had no time to stop and pause,
But rushed about, went here and there,
Did this and that, was everywhere.
I had not time to kneel and pray
For that lost soul across the way;
I had no time to meditate
On worthwhile things. No time to wait
Upon the Lord, and hear Him say:
"Well done, my child," at close of day.
And so, I wonder, after all
When life is o'er and I hear the call
To meet my Savior in the sky,
Where saints live on and never die,
If I can find one soul I've won
To Christ by some small deed I've done.
Or will I hang my head and whine,
"Forgive me, Lord, I had no time."

—Mrs. Herbert Bell

When I Enter the City

When I enter the beautiful city—
    Far removed from earth's sorrow
        and care,
I want to hear somebody saying,
    "It was you that invited me here."
When at home in those mansions in
        heaven,
    And the saved all around me
        appear,
I want to hear somebody saying,
    "It was you that invited me here."
To our Savior alone be the glory,
    Whose Spirit the witness did bear,
Yet I might not have heard the glad
        tidings,
    Had you not invited me here.

Evangelize!

Give us a watchword for the hour,
A thrilling word, a word of prayer;
A battle cry, a flaming breath,
That calls to conquest or to death.

A word to rouse the church from rest,
To heed her Master's high behest.
The call is given: Ye hosts arise,
Our watchword is Evangelize!

The glad evangel now proclaim
Through all the earth in Jesus' name;
This word is ringing through the skies,
Evangelize! Evangelize!

To dying men, a fallen race,
Make known the gift of Gospel grace;
The world that now in darkness lies,
Evangelize! Evangelize!

—Henry Grocker

Perpetual Life

The soul will never die. When this earth has crumbled to dust and passed away into the forgotten past, the soul will still be in the freshness of its youth.

When, in the fathomless future, eternity by human time concepts has become hoary with age, the soul will still be young.

When a million, million eternities have all lived out their endless ages and have rolled by into the forgotten past, and time is no more, the soul will still be living—a conscious, personal reality, endowed with perpetual life.

If Christians could see the value and immortality of a soul in contrast with the shortness of this earthly life, they would bend their greatest energies unceasingly to win even one for Christ.

"He that winneth souls is wise."

Diamond in the Rough

A diamond in the rough
Is a diamond sure enough.
For, before it ever sparkled,
It was made of diamond stuff.
Of course, someone must find it
Or it never will be found;
And then, someone must grind it,
Or it never will be ground!

But when it's found,
And when it's ground,
And when it's burnished bright,
That diamond's everlastingly
Flashing out its radiant light.

O Christian, please, whoe'er you be,
Don't say you've done enough;
That worst man on the street may be
A Diamond in the Rough.

—Unknown.

Gathering Jewels

Jewel gatherers for a crown,
    Know ye not the many a gem,
Now in darkness trampled down,
    Might bedeck a diadem?

Souls for which the Savior died,
    Souls enwrapped in sinful night,
Go and seek them far and wide,
    They will glitter in his sight.

With His blood washed white and pure,
    Graven with His name divine,
These our jewels shall endure,
    When the stars shall cease to shine.

The Man Next Door

Jesus died to bring salvation
    For the rich and for the poor:
Men of every tribe and nation—
    That includes the man next door.

Millions are in heathen darkness
    And with pleading hearts implore
For the Gospel of salvation—but
    What about the man next door?

"Go into all the world," said Jesus,
    "Tell them of My mighty power;
Bring our sheaves of every nation—
    And bring the man next door."

When we stand before our Savior
    On that glad eternal shore,
Heaven's glory will be brighter
    If we've brought the man next door.

—Selected

Nothing But Leaves

The Master is seeking a harvest
In souls He's redeemed by His blood.
He seeks for the fruit of the Spirit,
And works that will glorify God.
He looks for His likeness reflected
In lives that are yielded and true.
He's looking for zeal in the winning
Of souls He's entrusted to you.
He is yearning for someone to carry
His life-giving Word far and near.
He's waiting for hearts that are willing,
For ears that are open to hear.

Yes, What Else?

What are churches for but to make missionaries?
What is education for but to train them?
What is commerce for but to carry them?
What is money for but to send them?
What is life itself for but to fulfill the purpose of foreign
    missions enthroning Jesus Christ in the hearts of men?

—Josiah Strong

91

The Breaking of the Bread

Along the shores of Galilee,
   When Christ five thousand fed,
No one was omitted
   In the breaking of the bread.
Today they die in heathen lands,
   They die in want and dread,
For they have been omitted
   In the breaking of the bread.

Long years have passed and few have
     heard
   That Jesus Christ has bled,
That they might feed on Him who died
   To be the living Bread.
To gods of wood and stone they cry,
   Yet they are never fed,
For they have been omitted
   In the breaking of the bread.

Great God, Who gave Thy only Son,
   Help us now, Spirit-led,
To tell the story of Thy love
   To those who ask for bread.
Then gladly would we go or stay
   'Til this blest news has spread,
And they have been included
   In the breaking of the bread.

Your Daily Life

Is your daily life testifying to your interest
   in Missions?
Are you testifying to your Risen Lord with
   your interest in Missions?
Are you teaching your children to be
   interested in Missions?
Are you resisting the call for yourself or
   for your loved ones in Missions?
Are you praying for Missions?
Are you giving for Missions?

                      —A. L. L.

Call to Prayer

Care ye not that men are dying
   By the millions at our side,
And on far-flung fields are many
   Who the Gospel are denied!

Days are short in which to labor!
   Oh, the golden ripened grain,
And the need for willing workers,
   Who will count not cost or pain!

To your knees! Oh, Christian! Pleading
   That the Lord will quickly send
Laborers into the harvest
   E'er the span of time shall end!
                 —Edith Wilson

The Cry of the Heathen

A cry is ever sounding
   Upon the burdened ear.
A cry of pain and anguish,
   A cry of woe and fear;
It is the voice of millions
   Who grope in heathen night;
It is the cry of Jesus
   To rise and send them light.

With every pulse's beating,
   Another soul is gone,
With all its guilt and sorrow,
   To stand before the Throne.
And learn with awe and wonder
   The story of that grace
Which God to us had trusted
   For all our fallen race.

Oh, how the Master's bosom
   Must swell with love and pain
As evermore they meet Him—
   That sad and ceaseless train;
And if He holds us guilty
   For all our brothers' blood,
What answer can we offer
   Before the throne of God!
             —Author unknown

The True Missionary Motive

Why do we speak of missions?
　Why do missionaries go
To far off lands and countries,
　And people they don't know?
Why all the time and money,
　And sacrifice of lives?
Why care we so for others
　Beneath these starlit skies?

Well, here is just the reason:
　'Tis love—God's love within
The heart of any mortal,
　That has been cleansed from sin
When His great love is planted
　In the heart, a passion comes
To go and help our neighbors,
　Though in places or slums.

Jesus Christ is our example:
　'Twas love that led Him down
To lift us fallen creatures.
　He laid aside His Crown,
He gave up all to help us:
　Will we give all for Him
To share His love with others
　Whose lives are dark with sin?

How can we look at Jesus
　In dark Gethsemane,
Or see Him on Mount Calvary
　In greatest agony!
How can we read His message
　To go to all the world,
And preach His glorious gospel,
　And not His flag unfurl?

Oh, God, create within us
　A greater love for Thee,
And greater love for others
　Will come spontaneously.
A love that moves to action;
　A passion e'en unto death
To carry on Thy missions,
　And the lost and needy bless.

Yes, Master, breathe upon us
　Until we're more like Thee.
Until we cannot linger,
　But will work continually.
Pray for, give to, or hasten,
　To help those who need our hand,
That we all may live together
　In heaven's happy land.

—Mrs. Lura May Bustin

Stir My Heart

Stir my heart to prayer, Lord.
　Stir my feet to go.
Put the woe upon me
　That others Thee might know.

Make me discontented, Lord,
　To go the daily round.
Give me wings to go, Lord,
　Where hungry souls are found.

Into Thy dear hands, Lord,
　My life has found a place.
Oh, make it count for souls
　In this dark, needy place.

Fill me with Thy Spirit,
　Set my soul on fire;
Souls, for souls I'm pleading,
　Oh, grant me my desire!

—Hilda J. Davis

A Missionary's Equipment— Eleven Essentials

1. A life yielded to God and controlled by His Spirit.
2. A restful trust in God for the supply of all needs.
3. A sympathetic spirit.
4. A willingness to take a lowly place.
5. Tact in dealing with men.
6. Adaptability toward circumstances.
7. Zeal in service.
8. Steadfastness in discouragement.
9. Love for communion with God and for the study of His Word.
10. Some experience and blessing in the Lord's work at home.
11. A healthy body and a vigorous mind.

The Price of a Soul

A shilling? A pound?
   Pray what do you say?
Can that be the price of a soul
   today?
If that were the price
You'd be willing to pay,
   Come, follow these souls on
Their downward way.

Here's one with a skin
   That is dark and black
And he's burdened and fettered
   And hungry with lack.
He has stumbled and fallen
   And lives in a shack.
Now, what would you pay
   To bring this soul back?

Here's one who is red—
   On a jungle trail.
And his heart despises
   The face that is pale;
But eternal night
   Will be filled with his wail
And you hold the price
   Of his soul if you fail.

Here's one who is brown
   And his life is too,
But his soul is a
   Color of deeper hue.
To save him, kind friend,
   O what will you do?
The price of his soul,
   Perhaps, is with you.

My friend, ask yourself
   What it's worth to be saved.
Turn the light of the Cross
   On what you have craved.
Then 'vision the souls
   No lying enslaved.
You surely will pray
   And give till they're saved.

—Dean G. Felker

A Heart-Searching Question

What if your own were straying,
Fainting with famine pain,
And you should know where golden grow
Rich fruit and ripened grain;
Would you hear the wail as a thrice-told tale
And turn to your feast again?

What if your own were thirsting
And never a drop could gain,
And you would tell where a sparkling well
Poured forth melodious rain;
Would you turn aside while they gasped and
   died,
And leave them to their pain?

What if your own were darkened,
Without one cheering ray,
And you alone could show where shone
The purest sweet light of day.
Would you leave them there in their dark
   despair,
And sing on your sunlit way?

What if your own were prisoned
Far in a hostile land,
And the only key to set them free
Was held in your command;
Would you breathe free air while they stifled
   there,
And wait and hold your hand?

Yet what else are you doing,
Dear ones by Christ made free,
If you will not tell what you know so well
To those across the sea
Who have never heard one tender word
Of the Lamb of Calvary?

Go ye therefore and teach all nations, baptizing them in the name of the Father, and of the Son, and of the Holy Ghost; teaching them to observe all things whatsoever I have commanded you: and, lo, I am with you alway, even unto the end of the world" (Matthew 28:19-20).

What Would He Say?

(Luke 12:35-37)

If He should come today,
  And find my hands so full
  Of future plans, however fair,
  In which my Saviour has no share,
What would He say?

If He should come today,
  And find my love so cold,
  My faith so very weak and dim
  I had not even looked for Him,
What would He say?

If He should come today,
  And find I had not told
  One soul about my heavenly Friend,
  Whose blessings all my way attend,
What would He say?

If He should come today,
  Would I be glad—quite glad?
  Remembering He had died for all,
  And none, thro' me, had heard His
    call,
What would He say?

—*Grace E. Troy*

"Lord, Send Me!"

(Words and music by Mr. and Mrs. Robert Savage, written prior to their leaving for Ecuador, South America)

Lord Jesus, take this life of mine;
  I give to Thee my all.
Thy Spirit has made plain to me
  Thy urgent call.

The world says, "Stay, the cost is dear,
  And there is much to fear."
But Jesus whispers, "Go my child,
  For I am near."

No sweeter joy could my heart know,
  Than this, that He's called me
To tell abroad His wondrous grace
  That makes blind hearts to see.

Lord, send me, O send me forth I pray;
  The need is great, Thy call I will obey.
Thy love compels me, I must go;
  I'm willing, ready, longing to go.

Be a Missionary

(Mark 16:15)

Go, go, go; the Bible says to go
To every land till every man
And boy and girl shall know
That Jesus died on Calvary's tree,
To bring to all salvation free.
Oh, who will go? Oh, WILL YOU GO?

Pray, pray, pay; the Bible says to pray
That reapers brave may harvest save,
Lest souls should die today,
That boys and girls who never heard,
Be plainly told the blessed Word.
Oh, who will pray? Oh, WILL YOU
    PRAY?

Give, give, give; the Bible says to give
Your service true and money, too,
That boys and girls may live.
How much to give? With open hand,
For Jesus' sake, give all you can.
Oh, who will give? Oh, WILL YOU GIVE?

SUPPOSE

Suppose that Christ had not been born
That far-away Judean morn.

Suppose that God, whose mighty hand
Created worlds, had never planned
A way for man to be redeemed.
Suppose the Wise Men only dreamed
That guiding star whose light still glows
Down through the centuries. Suppose
Christ never walked here in men's sight,
Our blessed Way, and Truth and Light.

Suppose He counted all the cost,
And never cared that we were lost,
And never died for you and me,
Nor shed His blood on Calvary
Upon a shameful cross. Suppose,
That having died, He never rose,
And there was none with power to save
Our souls from death beyond the grave.
As far as piteous heathen know
These things that I've supposed are so.

—*Martha Snell Nicholson*

95

What Wilt Thou Say?

A hundred thousand souls a day
Are passing one by one away
In Christless guilt and gloom;
Without one ray of hope or light,
They're passing to their doom.

The Master's coming draweth near,
The Son of Man may soon appear.
His kingdom is at hand,
But ere that glorious day can be,
This Gospel of the Kingdom we
Must preach in every land.

Oh, let us, then, His coming haste,
Oh, let us end this awful waste
Of souls that never die.
A thousand million still are lost.
A Saviour's blood has paid the cost.
Oh, hear their dying cry;

They're passing, passing fast away,
A hundred thousand souls a day
In Christless guilt and gloom.
Oh, church of Christ, what wilt thou say
When in that awful judgment day
They charge thee with their doom?

—*A. B. Simpson*

Meditation at Midnight

"I cannot sleep,
    Dear God, I cannot sleep!
I cannot sleep
    Because so many hands keep
Beckoning me. And faces stare,
    And voices, piteous voices call
Upon the midnight air.
    And God, O can it be
That once upon a time, like me
    Thou couldst not sleep?
Because of many hands
    Outstretched from all the lands;
Because so many voices call—
    Voices and hearts and bodies all.
O, how they call! O, how they call."

—*Ralph Cushman*

My Father's Business

In the cool of a glad spring morning,
    The Master came unto me;
"My seed of TRUTH must be planted;
    Will you help in the work," asked He.
I answered, "Wait just a little;
    The day is so nice—so fair—
When the mornings are less enchanting
    In Thy fields I will do my share!"

In the dawn of a summer morning,
    I heard the Master say,
"My truth must be watched and tended;
    Will you work in My fields today?"
But I said, "The days are so dreamy
    And the Summer just begun;
I'll do my part in Thy labor
    When the glory of June is done!"

In the dew of an autumn morning,
    The Master quickly came;
"The harvest is white," He whispered,
    "Must the sowing be done in vain?"
But the fair autumn days, I pleaded,
    "Are so full of joys and gain—
After a few more weeks of sunshine—
    I will help Thee garner the grain."

In the chill of a winter morning,
    The Master came to me;
The ice-bound river was silent,
    The snow lay white on the lea.
"O Master, at last I am ready
    To work in Thy fields," I said.
But He gave me a look of pity—
    As He solemnly shook His head.

"The harvest is over," He answered,
    "Winter comes apace;
Precious wheat lies still ungarnered
    Because of your vacant place!
You've spent the past year in pleasure;
    My pleadings have been in vain,
But what of your guilty conscience—
    What of the wasted grain?"

A Missionary's Question

If only you knew when the sky turned gray,
  When the tempest raged, and the house gave
    way!
If only you knew of our fears that day—
  Would you have thought to pray?

If only you knew of that soul in pain,
  Who trembled in torment, to fear insane!
If only you knew he ne'er heard that Name—
  Would you have stopped to pray?

If only you knew in a low, hard bed
  Writhed the feverish form, so near to dead!
If only you knew of the tears we shed
  Would you have knelt to pray?

If only you knew of the toilsome speech
  Of the countless hours a pagan to reach!
If only you knew of this awesome breach—
  Would you've spared time to pray?

If only you knew that in heathen lands,
  Millions still perish with outstretched hands!
If only you knew it's your fault they're
  damned!
  Would you not weep and pray?

              —John Sanford, Philippines

The Gospel According to You

You are writing a gospel, a chapter each day,
  By deeds that you do, by words that you say.
Men read what you write, whether faithless or
  true.
  Say, what is the gospel according to you?
Men read and admire the Gospel of Christ,
  With its love so unfailing and true,
But what do they say, and what do they think
  Of the gospel according to you?
'Tis a wonderful story, that gospel of love,
  As it shines in the Christ-life divine.
And oh, that its truth might be told again
  In the story of your life and mine!
You are writing each day a letter to men:
  Take care that the writing is true.
'Tis the only gospel some men will read
  That gospel according to you.

The World's Bible

**"Ye are the epistles of Christ—
written with the Spirit of God"
(II Corinthians 3:3).**

Christ has no hands but our
  hands
  To do His work today;
He has no feet but our feet
  To lead men in His way;
He has no tongue but our
  tongues
  To tell men how He died;
He has no help but our help
  To bring them to His side.
We are the only Bible
  The careless world will read.
We are the sinner's gospel,
  We are the scoffer's creed.
We are the Lord's last mes-
  sage,
  Given in deed and word;
What if the type is crooked?
  What if the print is blurred?
What if our hands are busy
  With other work than His?
What if our feet are walking
  Where sin's allurement is?
What if our tongues are speak-
  ing
  Of things His lips would
    spurn?
How can we hope to help Him
  And hasten His return?

              —Annie Johnson Flint

ONLY A TRACT

It's only a Tract! You may tear it,
  And crumple it up in your hand;
The wind, as it passes, may bear it,
  And scatter it over the land.

It's only a Tract! But it telleth
  Of holiness, happiness, heaven;
Where God in Eternity dwelleth
  With sinners His love has forgiven.

It speaks of a future in glory,
  Of present enjoyment and bliss;
And will you neglect such a story,
  So loving, so joyous as this.

It whispers, "No matter how hardened,
  No matter how vile you have been;
You may at this moment be pardoned,
  And saved from the bondage of sin.

It points to the Substitute dying,
  The Sinless for sinners like you;
O soul, on His merits relying,
  Come, prove that its message is true!

It is but a Tract! Yet its warning
  Is whispered in Jesus' own voice;
And now, at the acceptance or scorning,
  Either HEAVEN or HELL will rejoice.

Why Didn't You Tell Us Sooner?

"Why didn't you tell us sooner?"
  The words came sad and low;
"O ye who knew the Gospel truths,
  Why didn't you let us know?
The Savior died for those who sin,
  He died to save from woe;
But we never heard the story,
  Why didn't you let us know?"

"You say you are Christ's disciples;
That you try His work to do;
And yet His very last command
  Is disobeyed by you.
'Tis indeed a wonderful story!
  He loved the whole world so,
But you didn't let us know!"

"Hear this pathetic cry of ours,
  O dweller in Christian lands!
For heathendom stands before you,
  With pleading, outstretched hands.
You may not be able to come yourself
  But some in your stead can go.
Will you not send us teachers?
  Will you not let us know?"

—G. P. Turnbull

Famous Missionary Mottoes

The same One Who said, "Come unto me," said also, "Go ye."

The supreme task of the church is the evangelization of the world. —Oswald J. Smith

---

To evangelize the world is so to present Christ that every human being will have a fair opportunity to intelligently accept or reject Him. —A. J. Gordon

---

Our job is not to bring the world to Christ, but to take Christ to the world.

Why should anyone hear the Gospel twice until everyone has heard the Gospel once?

Missionary Mothers

Dedicated to Other Missionary Mothers by Mrs. Dale Crowley

Behind great numbers of young missionaries on foreign fields today are their godly, praying mothers. the young people have heard and obeyed the call to "go . . . into all the world, and preach the gospel to every creature"; but who can estimate the value of their mothers' loving care, patient training, and persevering prayer for God's will in their lives, which prepared the way for that final act of obedience? There is a certain exhilaration for parents in standing with a large congregation, singing, "Give of thy sons to hear the message glorious," while enthusiastic missionary volunteers form a line across the front of an auditorium. But it is quite another thing when the day of departure finally comes. Here is a mother, standing on a dock. She hears the final blast on the ship's whistle, sees the longshoremen cast off the last hawsers, and watches the strip of water between the dock and the ship steadily widening, while a beloved son or daughter stands on the deck waving a handkerchief, until, down-river, even the fluttering handkerchief fades from sight.

Here is another, at an airport. She hears the door of the big plane close with a thud, sees the attendants wheel away the ramp, and then watches while the sleek aircraft taxies into position, and roars down the runway and up into the blue, taking away what seems like a part of her heart.

Or perhaps the farewell is said at home—and it isn't any easier. Boxes and trunks, which stood about anywhere and everywhere, have been packed and shipped. Now family prayers are over, the suitcases and handbags and the portable typewriter are in the car, and it is time to say good-bye. And then this is said with the full depth of its fine, old meaning, "God be with you"—and keep you, and bless you, and make you a blessing!

Some mothers are left practically alone; but others have at their sides husbands, and other sons and daughters, who share the heartaches of separation, and who, with them, believe that nothing is so sweet and satisfying for anyone as the whole will of God.

But the fathers go off to work, and the children and young folks to school and college, and it is the mothers who feel most keenly the sudden quiet of the home. Then come weeks and months of eagerly looking for the mails, with the ups and downs of praise and thanksgiving for good news, and agonizing prayer over bad news; and weeks without news. Godly fathers love their children dearly, and miss them, but their feelings toward sons and daughters on the field can never be quite so strong, full and deep as the mothers'.

But God fully understands, for He gave His only begotten Son, who had no furlough in thirty-three years. The heavenly Father must have a special love and care for missionary mothers. Just as He said to Moses, "I know their sorrows," so He says today; and He knows that these mothers have gladly given up the companionship of their sons and daughters for His name's sake, that they might tell others of His great love. May they take comfort in the fact that He knows and loves and cares, and that swifter than air mail, or telephone, or telegraph is the prayer that reaches the Throne of Grace on behalf of a loved one on the field.

—Sunday School Times

His Lamp Am I

His lamp am I,
To shine where He shall say;
And lamps are not for sunny rooms,
Nor for the light of day;
But for the dark places of the earth,
Where shame and wrong and crime have
    birth.
Or for the murky twilight gray
Where wandering sheep have gone
    astray.
Or where the lamp of faith grows dim
And souls are groping after HIm.
And as sometimes a flame we find,
Clear-shining, through the night,
So dark we cannot see the lamp—
But only see the light—
So may I shine, His love the flame,
That men may glorify His name.

              —*Annie Johnson Flint*

Our Missionaries' Needs

Do you hear them pleading, pleading
    Not for money, comfort, power,
But that you, O Christian worker,
    Will but set aside an hour
Wherein they will be remembered
    Daily at the Throne of Grace,
That the work which they are doing
    In your life may have a place?

Do you know that they are longing
    For the sympathetic touch
That is theirs when friends are praying
    In the homeland very much,
That our God will bless the efforts
    They are making in His Name,
And that souls for whom they're work-
    ing,
    With His love may be aflame?

Do you see them seeking, seeking
    For the gift of priceless worth
That they count of more importance
    Than all other gifts of earth?
Not the gold from rich men's coffers,
    Nor the relief from any care—
'Tis a gift that you can give them—
    'Tis the Christian's daily prayer.

Personality . . .

Example, Influence, Cheerfulness

Let Me SEE Your Sermon

I'd rather see a sermon than hear one
    any day,
I'd rather one should walk with me than
    merely show the way.
The eye's a better pupil and more will-
    ing than the ear;
Fine counsel is confusing, but example's
    always clear;
And the best of all the preachers are the
    men who live their creeds,
For to see the good in action is what
    everybody needs.
I can soon learn how to do it if you'll let
    me see it done,
I can watch your hands in action, but
    your tongue too fast may run.
And the lectures you deliver may be
    very wise and true;
But I'd rather get my lesson by observ-
    ing what you do.
For I may misunderstand you and the
    high advice you give,
But there's no misunderstanding how
    you act and how you live.

My Neighbor's Bible

I am my neighbor's Bible
    He reads me when we meet;
Today he reads me in my home—
    Tomorrow on the street.
He may be relative or friend
    Or slight acquaintance be;
He may not even know my name,
    Yet he is reading me.
And pray, who is this neighbor
    Who reads me day by day,
To learn if I am living right
    And walking as I pray?
O, he is with me always
    To criticize or blame;
So worldly-wise in his own eyes,
    And "Sinner" is his name.
Dear Christian friends and brothers,
    If we could only know
How faithfully the world records
    Just what we say and do,
O, we would write our record plain
    And come in time to see
Our worldly neighbor won to Christ
    While reading you and me.

—Joseph Wilson Barron

A Smile . . .

   . . . costs nothing, but gives much. It enriches those who receive, without making poorer those who give. It takes but a moment but memory of it sometimes lasts forever. None is so mighty that he can get along without it. And, none is so rich that he cannot be made richer by it. A smile creates happiness in the home, fosters goodwill in business . . . and is the countersign of friendship. It brings rest to the weary, cheer to the discouraged, sunshine to the sad, and is nature's best antidote for trouble. Yet, it cannot be bought, begged, borrowed or stolen. For it is given away. Some people are too tired to give you a smile. Give them one of yours—as none needs a smile so much as he who has no more to give.

—Ernest R. Conrad

SOWING SEEDS

I spoke a word,
And no one heard;
And no one cared
Or seemed to heed;
But after
Half a score of years
It blossomed
In a fragrant deed.

Preachers and teachers
All are we,
Sowers of seed
Unconsciously;
Our hearers
Are beyond our ken,
Yet all we give
May come again
With usury
Of joy or pain.

We never know
To what one little word
May grow.
See to it, then,
That all your seeds
Be such as bring forth
Noble deeds.

—*John Oxembaum*

IF YOU WILL

If God can make of an ugly seed,
  With a bit of earth and air,
And dew and rain, sunshine and
    shade—
  A flower so wondrous fair;
What can He make of a soul like
    you,
  With the Bible and faith and
    prayer,
And the Holy Spirit—if you do His
    will
  And trust His love and care?

—*A. D. Burkitt*

Lambs Follow Sheep

We oft hear the plea for trying to keep
  The lambs of the flock in the fold.
And well we may; but what of the sheep?
  Shall they be left out in the cold?

'Twas a sheep, not a lamb, that strayed away,
  In the parable Jesus told—
A grown-up sheep that had gone astray,
  From the ninety and nine in the fold.

Out in the wilderness, out in the cold,
  'Twas a sheep the Good Shepherd sought,
And back to the flock, safe into the fold,
  'Twas a sheep the Good Shepherd brought.

And why for the sheep should we earnestly long,
  And as earnestly hope and pray?
Because there is danger, if they go wrong,
  They will lead the young lambs away.

The lambs will follow the sheep, you know,
  Wherever the sheep may stray;
If the sheep go wrong, it will not be long
  Till the lambs are as wrong as they.

And so with the sheep we earnestly plead,
  For the sake of the lambs today.
If the lambs are lost, what a terrible cost
  Some sheep may have to pay!

YOUR LIFE TELLS

You tell on yourself by the friends you seek,
By the very manner in which you speak,
By the way you employ your leisure time,
By the use you make of dollar and dime.
You tell what you are by the things you wear,
By the spirit in which your burdens bear,
By the kind of things at which you laugh,
By the record you play on the phonograph.
You tell what you are by the way you walk,
By the things of which you delight to talk,
By the manner in which you bear defeat,
By so simple a thing as how you eat,
By the books you choose from the well-filled
    shelf,
In these ways and more you tell on yourself.
So there's really no particle of sense
In an effort to keep up false pretense.

I Lighted a Candle

I lighted a candle and looked at the tiny flame reaching up into the light, as I said a little prayer.

Once you have taken a step forward toward God, there is no turning back. We are all a part of Him.

I prayed for myself and for everyone everywhere.

It isn't easy to do right sometimes—it may mean loneliness, doing without things or maybe someone that we love.

It takes patience, love and sacrifice to do all of these—but every time we do right we are lighting a candle to show someone the right way to go—and when we do wrong we are putting out a little candle that guides someone safely and happily on life's journey.

We have our own free will. Some would hate God for the things that have happened in their lives and tell themselves they can't believe—that it is all a bag of tricks.

But if we pause to think, we realize that even the worst of us hate the things that are wrong.

God's love is the greatest love of all. He punishes and He rewards.

With the turning to Him comes a peace in your heart that surpasses all understanding and which without Him you never know.

Right living will bring rewards in many different ways.

To each of my children and everyone everywhere I would give my faith—knowing that earth has nothing as valuable—nor can anything offer the peace and happiness they seek but this.

It is the one thing that will endure until the end and assure safety on the last journey we will ever take.

When we say goodbye to the world and take a solo flight, when you kneel in a chapel, you'll find God there, and the more you go the more intrigued you will become.

You'll feel His presence and in the quiet of the place you'll find your way.

—*Emme Robbins*

It Is Better

To set a good example than to preach the finest sermon.

To be noted for living a pure life than to be admired for singing well.

To be called a fanatic by the world than to be its friend and a willful hypocrite at heart.

To be evil spoken of than to hear everybody speak well of you.

To please God than to please your friends.

To obey God than to backslide.

To have a conscience void of offense toward God than to be on good terms with the world.

To have a crown in heaven than a place on earth.

To give God all the glory than to take any of it yourself.

To do one thing well than to partly do several things.

To have 30 minutes of private prayer before the meeting than to have 30 minutes of useless conversation afterward.

To work for the salvation of souls than to seek to please yourself.

To love God and own nothing in this world than to be rich and lift up your eyes in hell.

I Know Something Good About You

Wouldn't this old world be better
If the folks we meet would say:
"I know something good about you,"
And treat us just that way?

Wouldn't it be fine and dandy,
If a handclasp warm and true,
Carried with it this assurance,
"I know something good about you"?

Wouldn't things here be more pleasant,
If the good that's in us all
Were the only things about us
That folks bothered to recall?

Wouldn't life be lots more happy
If we praise the good we see?
For there's such a lot of goodness
In the worst of you and me.

Wouldn't it be nice to practice
This fine way of thinking, too:
"You know something good about me,
I know something good about YOU"?

KINDNESS

If I can send some thought
Out into God's pure air,
His wings of love will speed it on
To help someone, somewhere.

If I can say a kindly word,
If only by one it is heard,
It may take root in a loving heart
And kindness to others impart.

If I can do a kindly deed,
Although 'tis small as a mustard seed,
It may grow and grow, and grow,
Until its blessings only God will know.

So let me be kind from day to day,
Smiling on others along the way,
And when the light of day is gone,
I will feel I have tried to help someone.

A fly can ruin the bottle of ointment. A harsh word or an unkind deed may darken many a day and cause quite a bit of pain, but on the other hand a cheerful word and a helping hand given at the proper time can revolutionize all of life. And one who lives and sees both he seamy side, and the better side of this thing called life can but agree with that potential poet of the rank and file, James Whitcomb Riley, when he says:

In a Friendly Sort of Way

"When a man ain't got a cent,
And he's feelin' sort o' blue,
And the clouds hang dark and heavy
And won't let the sunshine thru.
It's a great thing, O my brother,
For a fellow just to lay
His hand upon your shoulder
In a friendly sort o' way.

It makes a man feel curious,
It makes the teardrops start,
And you feel a sort o' flutter
In the regions 'round your heart.
You can't look up and meet his eyes,
You don't know what to say,
When a hand's laid on your shoulder
In a friendly sort o' way.

O, this world's a curious compound,
With its honey and its gall,
With its cares and bitter crosses,
But a good world after all.
And a good God must have made it;
Leastways that's what I say,
When a hand's laid on my shoulder
In a friendly sort o' way.

Influence of Small Things

Drop a pebble in the water, just a splash
    and it is gone;
But there's half a hundred ripples circling
    on and on and on—
Spreading, spreading, from the center,
    flowing on out to the sea;
And there's no way of telling, where the
    end is going to be.
But the little waves are flowing, and the
    ripples circling yet,
All the ripples flowing, flow to a mighty
    wave have grown;
And you've disturbed a mighty river, just
    by dropping in a stone.

Drop a word, unkind or careless, in a
    minute it is gone,
But there's half a hundred ripples circling
    on, and on, and on.
They keep spreading, spreading, spread-
    ing, from the center as they go,
And there's no way to stop them, once
    you've started them to flow.
Drop a word, unkind and careless, in a
    minute you forget,
But the little waves are flowing, and the
    ripples flowing yet.
And perhaps in some sad heart, a mighty
    wave of tears you've stirred,
And disturbed a life that's happy, when
    you've dropped an unkind word.

Drop a word of cheer and kindness, just a
    flash and it is gone,
But there's half a hundred ripples circling
    on and on, and on,
Bearing hope and joy and comfort on each
    splashing, dashing wave,
'Til you wouldn't believe the volume of
    the one kind word you gave.
Drop a word of cheer and kindness, in a
    minute you forget,
But the gladness still is swelling, and the
    joy is circling yet.
And you've rolled a wave of comfort,
    whose sweet music can be heard
Over the miles and miles of water, just by
    dropping one kind word.

How Others Know
We Are Christians

By our kindness and compassion,
By our help to those in need,
By our sympathetic patience,
By our willingness to heed,
By our happiness and gladness,
By unfailing charity,
By our tender ministrations,
Lord, may we interpret Thee.

By our eagerness to follow
Humbly in the Master's way,
By our loyalty and meekness,
By our courage day by day,
By our kind consideration,
By forgiveness full and free,
By our just appreciation,
Lord, may we interpret Thee.

By our strength in overcoming,
By refusing selfish gain,
By response to those who struggle,
By relieving woe and pain,
Just by daily, helpful service,
May we true disciples be,
Showing forth the love of Jesus,
Lord, and thus interpret Thee.

A Christian

Could I be called a Christian
    If everybody knew
My secret thoughts and feelings
    And everything I do?
Could they see the likeness
    Of Christ in me each day?
Could they hear Him speaking
    In every word I say?

Could I be called a Christian
    If everyone could know
That I am found in places
    Where Jesus would not go?
Could I be called a Christian
    If judged by what I read,
By all my words and actions,
    By every thought and deed?

Unconscious Influence

Sometimes, in your despondent moments, you may cry out, "What does it matter? My influence is of no consequence. There is nothing for me to do that cannot be a great deal better done by others." Not so. Not so. The light of a match may be insignificant compared with the blazing lenses of a lighthouse, but I once learned a lesson which has caused me from that day to be thankful for the light of a match!

One who has had the opportunity of an intimate acquaintance with the same Christian people for a quarter of a century cannot fail to have noticed how their growth had been like the blade, then the ear, then the full corn in the ear. Many times they are themselves unconscious of it and insist otherwise, but a careful observer will find evidence that it has been so.

Remember rather those who have so grown into the character of the Divine— and there are many such—that their every word and deed, aye, even the radiance of their countenances is unmistakable evidence of the indwelling Spirit.

The value of a Christian life cannot be measured by comparison; man's plain duty is to neglect not the gift that is in him, leaving the result with God.

—John R. DeMotte

Habit of Singing

Make a habit of singing.
  The day won't seem so long
As you sing, or even whisper
  The words of a beautiful song.
For God has given us music
  And has taught us how to sing
To chase away our worries and
  Find good in everything.

Helen Marshall Van Pelt

Just Being Happy

Just being happy is a fine thing to do.
Look on the bright side rather than the
  blue.
  Sad or sunny musing
  Is largely in your choosing,
And just being happy is a brave work
  and true.
Just being happy helps other souls
  along.
Their burdens may be heavy and they
  not strong.
  Your own skies will lighten
  If others' skies you brighten
By just being happy with a heart full of
  song.

—Ora Alexander

The Other Fellow

Don't think when you have troubles
  That your neighbor goes scot-free
Because he shows a smiling front
  And battles cheerfully.
No, man! He, too, has troubles,
  But herein the difference lies:
While you go idly moping 'round
  The other fellow tries.

Don't envy other people;
  Maybe, if the truth you knew,
You'd find their burdens heavier far
  Than is the case with you.
Because a fellow, rain or shine,
  Can show a smiling face,
Don't think you'd have an easier time
  If you would take his place.

'Tis hope and cheery courage
  That incite one to retrieve
One's past mistakes, to start afresh,
  To dare and to achieve.
So smile, and if perchance you light
  The spark of hope anew
In some poor sad and burdened heart,
  All honor be to you!

Pass on the Praise

"You're a great little wife, and I don't know what I would do without you." And as he spoke he put his arms about her and kissed her, and she forgot all the care in that moment. And, forgetting it all, she sang as she washed the dishes, and sang as she made the beds, and the song was heard next door, and a woman there caught the refrain and sang also, and two homes were happier because he had told her that sweet old story—the story of the love of a husband for a wife. As she sang, the butcher boy who called for the order heard it and went out whistling on his journey, and the world heard the whistle, and the man hearing it thought, "Here is a lad who loves his work, a lad happy and contented."

And because she sang, her heart was mellowed and as she swept about the back door the cool air kissed her on each cheek, and she thought of a poor old woman she knew, and a little basket went over to that home with a quarter for a crate or two of wood.

So, because he kissed her and praised her, the song came and the influence went out and out.

Pass on the praise.

A word and you make a rift in the cloud, a smile and you may create a new resolve, a grasp of the hand and you may repossess a soul from hell.

Pass on the praise.

A Frown or a Smile! Which?

A Frown went scowling down the
    street one pleasant morn in May.
And, Friend, would you believe it,
    everyone it met that day:
Man, woman, lad and lassie, it is
    queer but also true,
As soon as they came near it, went off
    a frowning, too!

Next day a smile went beaming down
    that selfsame street,
And every single person that it win-
    somely did meet:
Man, woman, lad and lassie, and it
    went for many a mile,
Jogged home all a-happy, wearing
    such a pleasant smile.

Now from this little fable, it is very
    plain to see,
There's no one but has influence who-
    ever he may be.
And if you're cross and crabbed, you
    make others crabbed too—
But if you smile on others, they will
    likewise smile on you.

Beautiful Lives

Beautiful faces are those that wear,
It matters little if dark or fair—
Whole-souled honesty printed there.
Beautiful eyes are those that show,
Like crystal panes where heart fires
    glow,
Beautiful thoughts that burn below.
Beautiful lips are those whose words
Leap from the heart like songs of birds,
Yet whose utterance prudence girds.
Beautiful hands are those that do
Work both earnest, and brave and true
Every moment the long day through.
Beautiful feet are those that go
On kindly ministries to and fro—
Down lowliest ways if God wills it so.
Beautiful shoulders are those that bear
Ceaseless burdens of homely care
With patient grace and daily prayer.
Beautiful lives are those that bless—
Silent rivers of happiness,
Whose hidden fountains few may guess.
Beautiful twilight, at set of sun,
Beautiful goal, with race well won;
Beautiful rest with work well done.

—R. S.

107

Try Smiling

When all things look gloomy, and seem to
    go wrong,
And everything pleasant has fled;
When the sighs and the tears drive away all
    your song,
Have you ever tried smiling, instead?

When heartaches oppress you, and burdens
    abound,
When the day seems so long and so dreary,
When you're weary, and tempted to scowl
    and to frown,
Have you ever tried smiling, my dear?

Oh, there's something so sweet in a sun-
    shiny smile,
God made them—to scatter life's rain!
So when you are tempted to frown any
    while,
My dear, just try smiling—again.
So smile, and the world will smile with
    you,
And smile, whether it smiles or not;
For the girl that's worthwhile is the girl
    with the smile—
So, dearie, try smiling—a lot!

Less of Me

Let me be a little kinder,
Let me be a little blinder
To the faults of those about me,
    Let me pray a little more.
Let me be, when I am weary,
Just a little bit more cheery,
Let me serve a little better,
    Those that I am striving for.
Let me be a little braver
When temptations bid me waver.
Let me strive a little harder
    To be all that I should be.
Let me be a little meeker
With the brother that is weaker.
Let me think more of my neighbor,
    And a little less of me.

—*Author unknown*

Living Sermons

There isn't a word that a preacher can say,
    No matter how lovely or true,
Nor is there a prayer that his eager lips pray
    That can preach such a sermon as you.

You vowed to serve Christ, and men know that you did.
    They're watching the things that you do;
There isn't an action of yours that is hid.
    Men are watching and studying you.

You say you're "no preacher"; yes, but you preach
    A wonderful sermon each day;
The acts of your life are the things that you teach,
    It isn't the things that you say.

Oh, Christians, remember, you bear His dear Name,
    Your lives are for others to view,
You are living examples; men praise you or blame,
    And measure all Christians by you.

—*Florence Belle Anderson*

Cheering Someone On

Don't you mind about the triumphs,
   Don't you worry after fame,
Don't you grieve about succeeding;
   Let the future guard your name.
All the best in life's the simplest;
   Love will last when wealth is gone;
Just be glad that you are living,
   And keep cheering someone on.

Let your neighbors have the blossoms,
   Let your comrades wear the crown;
Never mind the little setbacks
   Nor the blows that knock you down.
You'll be there when they're forgotten,
   You'll be glad with youth and dawn,
If you just forget your troubles,
   And keep cheering someone on.

There's a lot of sorrow round you,
   Lots of lonesomeness and tears,
Lots of heartaches and of worry
   Through the shadows of the years.
And the world needs more than tri-
   umphs,
   More than all the swords we've
   drawn;
It is hungering for the fellow
   Who keeps cheering others on.
                 —Otto A. Wurm

A GOOD CREED

Just to be tender, just to be true,
Just to be glad the whole day through;
Just to be merciful, just to be mild,
Just to be trusting as a child;
Just to be gentle and kind and sweet,
Just to be helpful with willing feet,
Just to be cheery when things go
   wrong,
Just to drive sadness away with a song,
Whether the hour is dark or bright,
Just to be loyal to God and right;
Just to believe that God knows best,
Just in His promise ever to rest;
Just to let love be our daily key—
This is God's will for you and for me!

Jewels of Life

Give me the man that says, "Hello,"
With a cheerful nod of his head,
And I'll show you a fellow that's never a
   foe,
But a friend of man instead.
His very presence enlightens the gloom,
That may surround you at the time;
Like a ray of sunshine into your room,
He comes with a smile sublime.

Give me the boy with the sparkling eye,
That whistles and sings 'long the road,
To the heaviness of his load.
Ah! He is the boy that is loved by all,
His coming is watched from afar,
His whistle is sweeter than a nightin-
   gale's call,
His face like the light of a star.

Give me the woman that caresses a child
As she passes it on the way,
I'll show you a woman that's not defiled
By the thoughtlessness of the day.
Ah! She is the woman that instills
Contentment and happiness into the
   heart,
One whose laughter ripples and thrills,
One with whom you regret to part.

Give me the girl with the smile so rare,
That it will lift a veil of sadness.
One that has evaded vanity's snare,
And I'll show you a maid of gladness.
She is a girl, like a beam of light,
That enters a home of sorrow,
Changing sorrow into that of delight,
Making glad the thoughts of tomorrow.
                —R. H. Sotherland

I Shall Not Pass This Way Again

The bread that giveth strength I want to
    give,
The water pure that bids the thirsty live:
I want to help the fainting day by day,
I'm sure I shall not pass again this way.

I want to give the oil of joy for tears,
The faith to conquer crowding doubts
    and fears,
Beauty for ashes may I give alway.
I'm sure I will not pass again this way.

I want to give good measure running
    over,
And into angry hearts I want to pour
The soft answer that turneth wrath away.
I'm sure I will not pass again this way.

I want to give to others hope and faith,
I want to do all that the Master saith;
I want to live aright from day to day.
I'm sure I will not pass again this way.

SMILE

*"A merry heart doeth good like
    medicine"* (Proverbs 17:22)

You're twice as attractive with a smile on your face!

It helps men too! Recently a friend came by my study after a civic club meeting where a doctor had pointed out what tension and temper tantrums could do to the heart. "I expect to go around smiling the rest of my life," this man said to me.

"Why all the smiles?" I inquired.

"Why that doctor told us that a temper tantrum—even a slight 'blowing of the top'—had such effect on the heart that it shortened your life by one week."

"On top of that," my friend continued, "it's easier to smile. It takes 66 muscles to frown and only 12 to smile. That's a scientific fact."

Think it over. It's easier to smile, and it looks much better!

—*A. P. Bailey*

Let Us Smile

The thing that goes the farthest towards making life worth while,
That costs the least and does the most, is just a pleasant smile,
The smile that bubbles from a heart that loves its fellowmen
Will drive away the cloud of gloom and coax the sun again.
It's full of worth and goodness, too, with manly kindness blent—
It's worth a million dollars, and doesn't cost a cent.
There is no room for sadness when we see a cheery smile;
It always has the same good look—it's never out of style—
It nerves us on to try again when failure makes us blue;
The dimples of encouragement are good for me and you.
It pays a higher interest, for it is merely lent—
It's worth a million dollars, and doesn't cost a cent.
A smile comes very easy—you can wrinkle up with cheer
A hundred times before you can squeeze out a soggy tear.
It ripples out, moreover, to the heart-strings that will tug,
And always leaves an echo that is very like a hug.
So, smile away. Folks understand what by a smile is meant.
It's worth a million dollars, and doesn't cost a cent.

—*W. D. Nesbit*

Radiant Faces

How lovely are the faces of
   Those who talk with God—
Lit with an inner sureness of
   The path their feet have trod;
How gentle is the manner of
   A man who walks with Him!

No strength can overcome him and
   No cloud His courage dim.
Keen are the hands and feet—ah, yes—
   Of those who wait His will;
And clear as crystal mirrors are
   The hearts His love can fill.

Some lives are drear from doubt and
   fear,
   While others merely plod;
But lovely faces are the mark of those
   Who walk and talk with God.

    "They looked unto Him and
    were radiant" (Psalm 34:5).

Just Smile

If the weather looks like rain—smile.
When you feel you must complain—
   smile.
Do not care if things seem gray,
Soon there'll come a brighter day.
You will find that it will pay
To smile.

If the world looks sad and drear—smile.
Banish every thought of fear—smile.
Do the very best you can,
Play your part now like a man,
Make each day a better plan—and smile.

If you taste life's bitter cup—smile.
Should the doctors give you up—smile.
You are very far from dead,
Waste no time in useless dread,
Put your trust in God instead—
And smile.

       —*Grenville Kleiser*

It Don't Take Much

It don't take much to make men glad,
To cheer folks up when folks get sad.
When crops look poor, and things go
   wrong,
It don't take much, it don't take long,
Whoever any fellah is,
To slip your arm inside of his
And let him know a friend he's got
Who's still a friend, no matter what.
He'll chirp right up at just a touch
Of friendliness—it don't take much.

It don't take much to make men smile—
Why, folks just want to all the while!
And all they need to make 'em start
Is just to meet one merry heart.

It don't take much to set men right;
One candle's bigger than the night.
If someone sees it who's astray
And finds the right and proper way,
You don't need scold, you don't need
   preach,
Just all you need to do is reach
Your hand and find some fellah's hand
And help him back to solid land.
A friendly hand, a kindly touch,
That's all they need—it don't take much.

       —*Source unknown*

HAPPINESS

Take a heaping cup of PATIENCE,
And a big heartful of LOVE.
Add two handsful of GENEROSITY
To all of the above.
Then blend in a dash of LAUGHTER
And some UNDERSTANDING too;
Sprinkle generously with KINDNESS
And MEMORIES, old and new;
Add a lot of FAITH and mix well
To make it rich and sweet,
And enjoy a heaping portion
With everyone you meet!

       —*Jon Gilbert*

Touching Shoulders

There's a comforting thought at the close of
the day,
When I'm weary and lonely and sad,
That sort of grips hold of my crusty old heart
And bids it be merry and glad.
It gets in my soul and it drives out the blue
And finally thrills through and through.
It is just a sweet memory that chants the
refrain:
I'm glad I touched shoulders with you.

Did you know you were brave, did you know
you were strong?
Did you know there was one leaning hard?
Did you know that I waited and listened and
prayed
And was cheered by your simplest word?
Did you know that I longed for that smile on
your face,
For the sound of your voice ringing true?
Did you know I grew stronger and better
because
I had merely touched shoulders with you?

I am glad that I live, that I battle and strive
For the place that I know I must fill.
I am thankful for sorrows. I'll meet with a
grin
What fortune may send, good or ill.
I may not have wealth. I may not be great,
But I know I shall always be true.
For I have in my life that courage you gave
When once I rubbed shoulders with you.

—Author unknown

When the Heart Is Full of Love

There is beauty in the forest
When the trees are green and
fair.
There is beauty in the meadow
When wild flowers scent the
air.
There is beauty in the sunlight
And the soft blue beams
above.
Oh, the world is full of beauty
When the heart is full of love.

—Author unknown

TEMPER

When I have lost my temper,
I have lost my reason too.
I'm never proud of anything
Which angrily I do.

When I have talked in anger
And my cheeks are flaming red,
I have always uttered something
Which I wish I had not said.

In anger I have never
Done a kindly deed or wise,
But many things for which I felt
I should apologize.

In looking back across my life,
And all I've lost or made,
I can't recall a single time
When fury ever paid.

So I struggle to be patient,
For I've reached a wiser age;
I do not want to do a thing
Or speak a word in rage.

I have learned by sad experience
That when my temper flies
I never do a worthy deed,
A decent deed or wise.

Your Speech

Be Careful What You Say

In speaking of a person's faults
  Pray don't forget your own;
Remember those with homes of glass
  Should seldom throw a stone.

If we have nothing else to do
  But talk of those who sin,
'Tis better we commence at home
  And from that point begin.

We have no right to judge a man
  Until he's fairly tried.
Should we not like his company
  We know the world is wide.

Some may have faults, and who has
    not?
  The old as well as young.
Perhaps we may for ought we know
  Have fifty to their one.

I'll tell you of a better plan,
  You will find it works full well:
Try your own defects to cure
  Before of other's tell.

Then let us all when we commence
  To slander friend or foe,
Think of the harm one word would do
  To those we little know.

Remember that faults sometimes like
  Our chickens roost at home;
So let's don't speak of other's faults
    until
  We have none of our own.

Watch Your Words

Keep watch on your words, my darlings,
  For words are wonderful things.
They are sweet like bee's fresh honey,
  Like bees they have terrible stings.

They can bless, like the warm, glad sun-
    shine
  And brighten a lonely life;
They can cut in the bitter contest
  Like an open, two-edged knife.

Keep them back if they're cold and
    cruel,
  Under bar and lock and seal;
The wounds they make, my darlings,
  Are always slow to heal.

May peace guard your lives, and ever,
  From the time of your earthly youth;
May the words that you daily utter
  Be the words of grace and truth.

                —Minnie E. Ludwig

Should You Feel Inclined to Censure

Should you feel inclined to censure
  Faults you may in others view,
Ask your own heart, ere you venture,
  If that has not failings, too.

Let not friendly vows be broken;
  Rather strive a friend to gain;
Many a word in anger spoken
  Finds its passage home again.

Do not, then, in idle pleasure
  Trifle with a brother's fame;
Guard it as a valued treasure,
  Sacred as your own good name.

Do not form opinions blindly;
  Hastiness to trouble tends;
Those of whom we thought unkindly,
  Oft become our warmest friends.

Is It Worth While?

Is it worth while that we jostle a brother,
  Bearing his load on the rough road of life?
Is it worth while that we jeer at each other—
  In blackness of heart, that we war to the knife?
  God pity us all in our pitiful strife.

God pity us all as we jostle each other:
  God pardon us all for the triumph we feel
When a fellow goes down 'neath his load on the heather
  Pierced to the heart: Words are keener than steel,
  And mightier far for woe than for weal.

Were it not well, in this brief little journey
  On over the isthmus, down into the tide,
We give him a fish instead of a serpent,
  Ere folding the hands to be and abide
  Forever and aye in dust at his side?

Look at the roses saluting each other;
  Look at the herds all at peace on the plain;
Man, and man only, makes war on his brother,
  And laughs in his heart at his peril and pain—
  Shamed by the beasts that go down on the plain.

Is it worth while that we battle to humble
  Some poor fellow down into the dust?
God pity us all! Time too soon will tumble
  All of us together, like leaves in a gust,
  Humbled, indeed, down into the dust.

—Joaquin Miller

THREE GATES

A careless word may kindle strife;
A cruel word may wreck a life.
A bitter word may hate instill;
A brutal word may smite and kill.
A gracious word may smooth the way;
A joyous word may light the day.
A timely word may lessen stress;
A loving word may heal and bless.

If you are tempted to reveal
  A tale someone to you has told
About another, make it pass,
Before you speak, three gates of gold.

Three narrow gates: First, "Is it true?"
  Then, "Is it needful?" In your mind
Give truthful answer. And the next
Is last and narrowest: "Is it kind?"

And if to reach your lips at last
  It passes thru these gateways three,
Then you may tell the tale, nor fear
What the result of speech may be.

A Kind Word

How little it costs, if we give it a
*   thought,*
*   To make happy some heart each*
*   day.*
Just one kind word or a tender smile,
*   As we go on our daily way.*

Perchance a look will suffice to
*   clear*
*   The cloud from a neighbor's face,*
And the press of a hand in sympathy,
*   A sorrowful tear efface.*

It costs so little, I wonder why
*   We give so little thought.*
A smile, kind words, a glance, a
*   touch—*
*   What magic with them is wrought!*

The Tongue

"The boneless tongue, so small and weak,
    Can crush and kill," declares the Greek.
"The tongue destroys a greater horde,"
    The Turk asserts, "than does the sword."

A Persian proverb wisely saith,
    "A lengthy tongue—an early death."
Or sometimes takes this form instead:
    "Don't let your tongue cut off your
    head."

"The tongue can speak a word whose
    speed,"
    The Chinese say, "outstrips the steed."
While Arab sages this impart:
    "The tongue's great storehouse is the
    heart."

From Hebrew hath this maxim sprung:
    "Though feet should slip, ne'er let the
    tongue."
The sacred writer crowns the whole,
    "Who keeps his tongue doth keep his
    soul!"

—*Philip B. Strong*

Your Life Today

One unkind word in the early morn
Will poison the thoughts for the day;
One unkind look to one we love
Will take all the sunshine away.
And twice all the sunshine we take away
From the lives of others at early day,
We steal from ourselves the whole day long,
And we lose the beauty of earth's glad song.
One little smile when things go wrong
Will drive off many a frown;
One pleasant look, though the thoughts do range,
Will put the temper down.
And twice all the pleasure that we give out,
At the time when we are most tempted to pout,
Will sweeten our lives like a breath of May,
And the sun will shine through the whole glad day.

—*Carrie May Nichols*

This Tongue of Mine

Oh, Spirit of the living God
Control this tongue of mine.
No knife is quite so sharp as words,
Yet words can be divine.
A tongue not yielded to God's will
Can stir up awful strife.
Lord, use this tongue of mine today
To speak Thy words of life.

I want my tongue to sing God's praise;
To tell His love for me,
To speak God's holy name in prayer
And thanks for Calvary.
Lord, help me that this tongue of mine
Shall speak Thy Word in love,
That what I say will be Thy will
Directed from above.

Oh, Holy Spirit faithful guide,
This tongue of mine inspire,
That only words that please the Lord
Shall be my heart's desire.
So may I lead some soul to Christ
By spoken words or songs.
Then as God leads, do not forget
My tongue to Him belongs.

—Edward L. Crane

THE ECHO

I shouted aloud and louder,
    While out on the plain one day;
The sound grew faint and fainter
    Until it had died away.
My words had gone forever—
    They left no trace or track—
But the hills nearby caught up the cry
    And sent an echo back.

I spoke a word in anger
    To one who was my friend.
Like a knife it cut him deeply—
    A wound that was hard to mend.
That word, so thoughtlessly uttered,
    I would we could both forget,
But its echo lives and memory gives
    The recollection yet.

How many hearts are broken;
    How many friends are lost
By some unkind word spoken
    Before we count the cost.
But a word or deed of kindness
    Will repay a hundredfold,
For it echoes again in the hearts of men
    And carries a joy untold.

—C. A. Lufburrow

Don't Repeat It

Speak of a man as you find him,
Censure alone what you see;
If a man be blamed, be reminded
From faults there are none of us free.

If the veil from the mind could be torn,
Thoughts written upon a brow;
Many would be passed by in scorn,
That are loaded with honors now.

Many a good man is ruined,
And many a good woman too,
By someone starting a rumor,
And not one word of it true.

So when you hear someone knocking,
A man's or a woman's good name;
Bet it's a lie . . . forget it,
Never repeat it again.

First to Throw a Stone

If there's one who often falters
  By the wayside in despair,
Seems unusual his shortcomings,
  Do you hold him up in prayer?
If the weak should stumble, brethren,
  If he cannot stand alone,
Let the perfect one among you
  Be the first to throw a stone.

If so often he has wavered,
  You cannot believe him true,
Have you mentioned it to Jesus
  As the strong one ought to do?
Do you ever stop, consider,
  Have you no faults of your own?
Let the perfect one among you
  Be the first to throw a stone.

Is there one with crosses heavy,
  Seems he cannot carry all,
And he doesn't keep step as we do;
  If he ever chance to fall,
Do you plead with God for mercy
  Till He answers from the throne?
Let the perfect one among you
  Be the first to throw a stone.

BEFORE

Before you say a word that stings,
Or rankles in some heart,
Before you toy with quarrellings,
And from some old friend part,
Remember that a kindly word
Will all the trouble end,
And that it's foolish and absurd
To banish a good friend.
Before you cloud the sky of love
With some unworthy deed,
Before you slay trust's peaceful dove,
Or make a fond heart bleed,
Remember that you'll need some day
The love you lightly spurn,
And that, tho' now you may be gay,
You'll suffer in your turn.
Before you chide a simple child,
Or cause a single tear,
Before you're tempted or beguiled
At innocence to sneer,
Think how much sunshine would be
  gone
But for the childlike mind,
And thank your stars for everyone
To whom you can be kind.

Don't Say It!

If all that we say,
In a single day;
With never a word left out,
Were printed each night,
In clear black and white,
'Twould prove queer reading, no doubt.

And, then, just suppose,
Ere our eyes we could close;
We must read the whole record through.
Then wouldn't we sigh,
And wouldn't we try
A great deal less talking to do?

And, I more than half think,
That many a kink
Would be smoother in life's tangled thread,
If half that we say,
In a single day,
Were left forever unsaid.

117

You Never Can Tell

You never can tell when you send a
  word—
  Like an arrow shot from a bow
By an archer blind—be it cruel or kind,
  Just where it will chance to go.
It may pierce the breast of your dearest
  friend,
  Tipped with its poison or balm;
To a stranger's heart in life's great mart
  It may carry its pain or its calm.

You never can tell when you do an act
  Just what the result will be;
But with every deed you are sowing a
  seed,
  Though its harvest you may not see.
Each kindly act is an acorn dropped

In God's productive soil;
Though you may not know, yet the tree
  shall grow
  And shelter the brows that toil.

You never can tell what your thoughts
  will do
  In bringing you hate or love;
For thoughts are things, and their airy
  wings
  Are swifter than carrier doves.
They follow the law of the universe—
  Each thing must create its kind;
And they speed o'er the track to bring
  you back
  Whatever went out from your mind.

Why Did You Do It?

I heard you take the name of my Lord in vain!
He is my best Friend.
That's why I'm interested.
When my best Friend is offended, so am I.
You would not *intentionally* offend either me
  or my Friend, would you?
He is your best Friend too.
He gives you life and every blessing.
He died to save you.
> *"Greater love hath no man than this, that
> a man lay down his life for his friends"
> (John 15:13).*

Friend, you have sinned against your best
  Friend!
> *"Thou shalt not take the name of the Lord
> thy god in vain; for the Lord will not hold
> him guiltless that taketh his name in vain"
> (Exodus 20: 7).*

But God loves you and will forgive you.
> *"If we confess our sins, He is faithful and
> just to forgive us our sins and to cleanse
> us from all unrighteousness . . . for the
> blood of Jesus Christ, His Son, cleanseth
> us from all sin" (1 John 1:7-9).*
>
> —Dale Crowley

Don't Judge Too Hard

"Brethren, if a man be overtaken in a fault, ye which are spiritual, restore such an one in the spirit of meekness; considering thyself, lest thou also be tempted" (Galatians 6:1).

Pray don't find fault with the man who
    limps
Or stumbles along the road,
Unless you have worn the shoes he wears
Or struggled beneath his load.
There may be tacks in his shoes that hurt,
Though hidden away from view,
Or the burden he bears, placed on your
    back,
Might cause you to stumble too.

Don't sneer at the man who is down today
Unless you have felt the blow
That caused his fall, or felt the shame
That only the fallen know.
You may be strong, but still the blows
That were his, if dealt to you
In the self same way at the self same time,
Might cause you to stagger too.

Don't be too harsh with the man who sins,
Or pelt him with words or stones
Unless you are sure, yea, doubly sure,
That you have not sins of your own.
For you know, perhaps, if the tempter's
    voice
Should whisper as soft to you
As it did to him when he went astray
'Twould cause you to falter, too.

Just Thoughtlessness

A little bit of hatred,
    can spoil a score of years,
And blur the eyes that ought to smile,
    with many needless tears.
A little bit of thoughtlessness,
    and anger for a day,
Can rob a home of all its joy,
    and drive happiness away.
A little bit of shouting,
    in a sharp and vicious tone,
Can leave a sting that will be felt,
    when many years have flown.
Just one hasty minute of uncontrolled
    ill temper can offend,
And leave an inner injury,
    that years may never mend.
It takes no moral fiber,
    to say harsh and bitter things,
It doesn't call for courage,
    to employ a lash that stings.
For cruel words and bitter,
    any fool can think to say,
But the hurt they leave behind them,
    many years can't wipe away.
Just a little bit of hatred,
    robs a home of all delight,
And leaves a winding trail of wrong
    that time may never right.
For only those are happy,
    and keep their peace of mind,
Who guard themselves from hatreds,
    and words that are unkind.

Service . . .

Compassion, Helpfulness, Works

What Did You Do?

Did you give him a lift? He's a brother of man and bearing
  about all the burden he can.
  Did you give him a smile? He was downcast and blue.
  And the smile would have helped him to battle it through.
  Did you give him your hand? He was slipping downhill.
  And the world, so I fancied, was using him ill.
  Did you give him a word? Did you show him the road?
  Or did you just let him go on with his load?

Did you help him along? He's a sinner like you.
  But the grasp of your hand might have carried him through.
  Did you bid him good cheer? Just a word and a smile
  Were what he most needed that last weary mile.
  Did you try to find out what he needed from you?
  Or did you just leave him to battle it through?

Do you know what it means to be losing the fight?
  When a lift just in time might set everything right?
  Do you know what it means—just the clasp of a hand
  When a man's borne about all that a man ought to stand?
  Did you ask what it was—why the look of despair,
  And the sad face deep lined with shadows of care.
  Were you a brother of his when the time came to be?
  Did you offer to help him—or didn't you see?

Don't you know it's part of the brother of man
  To find what the grief is and help, what you can?
  Did you stop when he asked you to give him a lift?
  Or were you so busy you left him to shift?
  Oh, I know what you meant: What you say may be true—
  But the test of your manhood is, WHAT DID YOU DO?
  Or did you just let him go on with his load?

—From the memories of John Considine, Jr.,
cousin of Bob Considine

120

Reason for Life

I don't know how to say it
   but somehow it seems to me
That maybe we are stationed
   where God wanted us to be;
That the little place I'm filling
   is the reason for my birth,
And just to do the work I do
   He put me on this earth.

If God had wanted otherwise,
   I reckon He'd have made
Me just a little different,
   of a worse or better grade.
And since God knows and understands
   all things of land and sea,
I fancy that He placed me here
   just where He wanted me.

Sometimes I get to thinking
   as my labors I review
That I should like a higher place
   with greater tasks to do.
But I came to the conclusion,
   when the envying is stilled
That the post to which God sent me
   is the post He wanted filled.

So I plod along and struggle
   in the hope when day is through
That I'm really necessary
   to the things God wants to do.
And there isn't any service
   I can give which I should scorn,
For it may be just the reason
   God allowed me to be born.

Helping Others

Just supposing we started this very day
To live our lives in a different way;
Just supposing we vowed and constantly
   tried
To help those in trouble—on life's way-
   side;
If we showed by our doings a hint of His
   love,
Wouldn't earth be a bit more like heaven
   above?

Others

Lord, help me live from day to day
   In such a self-forgetful way,
That even when I kneel to pray
   My prayer will be for others.

Help me in all the work I do
   To ever be sincere and true,
And know that all I do for You
   Must needs be done for others.

Let self be crucified and slain
   And buried deep, and all in vain
May efforts be to rise again,
   Unless to live for others.

PASS IT ON

Have you had a kindness shown?
   Pass it on;
'Twas not given for thee alone,
   Pass it on;
Let it travel down the years,
Let it wipe another's tears,
Till in heaven the deed appears
   Pass it on.

Did you hear a loving word?
   Pass it on;
Like the singing of a bird?
   Pass it on;
Let its music live and grow,
Let it cheer another's woe,
You have reaped what others sow—
   Pass it on.

Be not selfish in thy greed,
   Pass it on;
Look upon thy brother's need,
   Pass it on;
Live for self, you live in vain,
Live for Christ, you live again,
Live for Him, with Him you reign—
   Pass it on.

—Henry K. Burton

The House By the Side of the Road

There are hermit souls that live withdrawn,
  In the peace of their self-content;
There are souls, like stars, that live apart
  In a fellowless firmament.
There are pioneer souls that blaze their path
  Where highway never ran—
But let me live by the side of the road,
  And be a friend to man.

Let me live in a house by the side of the
  road,
  Where the race of men go by—
The men who are good, and the men who
  are bad,
  As good and as bad as I.
I would not sit in the scorner's seat,
  Nor hurl the cynic's ban;
Let me live in a house by the side of the
  road,
  And be a friend to man.

I see from my house by the side of the road,
  By the side of the highway of life,
The men who press with the ardor of hope,
  The men who are faint with strife.
But I turn not away from their smiles or
  their tears—
  Both parts of an infinite plan;
Let me live in my house by the side of the
  road,
  And be a friend to man.

—*Sam Walter Foss*

Pray With Your Hands

Talking to men for God is a great thing,
but talking to God for men is even greater;
but do not make your prayers all talk; pray
also with your hands and feet; that is, back
up your prayers with your works.

Service

A way there is to serve the Lord
  While living here below.
He this revealed within His word
  Grace, too, He will bestow.

To serve the Lord, it is the same
  As serve our fellow men,
"A cup of water in His name,"
  By such, you've served him then.

You service render to the Lord
  When hungry ones you feed,
In loving kindness, loving word
  You've served the Lord, indeed.

You serve the Lord, by serving man.
  You'll serve no other way.
So love and serve, serve all you can,
  You'll hear well done, some day.

Use Me, Lord

Someone is groping, Lord,
  Lost and astray:
Help me to light my lamp
  And show the way.

Someone is lonely, Lord,
  No friends are near;
Help me to be a friend
  And bring him cheer.

Someone's discouraged, Lord,
  His hope is dim;
Help me to lift his faith
  By helping him.

Someone is hungry, Lord,
  Hear, now, his prayer;
Give me a heart to help
  And gladly share.

My lamp I'll light and be a friend,
  And bear my brother's care;
To him I'll give a helping hand
  And freely with him share.

And thus I'll prove my love to Thee,
  And show a grateful heart
For everything Thou givest me—
  So rich in grace Thou art!

—*Dale Crowley*

Helpful Man

He never saw the trouble; he only saw the deed.
He never thought of distance; his mind was on the need.
He never reckoned money as a prize worth clinging to;
He said its only value was the good that it could do.
He never stopped to reckon what he'd miss, of joy to stay
And help a fellow-being who was stranded on the way—
Never paused to think of pleasures that he's cherished long and planned.
All he saw was one in trouble who must have a helping hand.

There seemed nothing so important that he wouldn't turn aside
For the man who needed friendship and was really trouble-tried;
He wasn't one to answer, "I have something else to do."
He thought his foremost duty was to help a man he knew.
He never saw the trouble; he only saw the deed.
He never thought of sacrifice; his mind was on the need.
And he had this simple motto, which he followed to the end:
"When the other man's in trouble, that's the time to be his friend."

If We Knew

If we knew the cares and crosses
  Crowding round our neighbor's way;
If we knew the little losses,
  Sorely grievous day by day,
Would we then so often chide him
  For the lack of thrift and gain—
Casting o'er his life a shadow,
  Leaving on his heart a stain.

If we knew the silent story
  Quivering through the heart of pain,
Would our womanhood dare doom them
  Back to haunts of guilt again?
Life hath many a tangled crossing,
  Joy hath many a break of woe,
And the cheeks tear-washed seem
    whitest,
  This the blessed angels know.

Let us reach into our bosoms
  For the key to other lives,
And with love to erring nature,
  Cherish good that still survives.
So that when our disrobed spirits
  Soar to realms of light again,
We may say, dear Father, judge us
  As we judged our fellowmen.

Make Me a Blessing, Lord

Make me a blessing, Lord! Help me
To help those needing help, to be
A blessing to my fellow men.
Instruct me when to speak and when
To hold my speech, when to be bold
In giving and when to withhold;
And if I have not strength enough
Then give me strength, Lord, make me
    tough.
With my own self but tender toward
All others. Let there be outpoured
On me the gentleness to bless
All who have need of gentleness.
Give me a word, a touch to fill
The lonely life, faith for the ill,
And courage to keep hearts up though
My own is feeling just as low.
When men have bitter things to meet
And quail and would accept defeat,
Then let me lift their eyes to see
The vision of Thy victory.
Help me to help; help me to give
The wisdom and the will to live!

—*James Dillet Freeman*

123

Kindness During Life

I would rather have one little rose
From the garden of a friend,
Than to have the choicest flower
When my stay on earth must end.

I would rather have one pleasant word
In kindness said to me,
Than flattery when my heart is still
And life has ceased to be.

I would rather have a loving smile
From friends I know are true,
Than tears shed around my casket
When this world I've bid adieu.

Bring me all your flowers today,
Whether pink or white or red.
I'd rather have one blossom now
Than a truck load when I'm dead.

—*Author unknown*

If you can fill one heart with joy,
Remove one cause of sadness,
There'll come to you without alloy
Full share of holy gladness.

Serve not for fame, but just be glad,
Not from sense of duty;
Unconsciously the fields are clad
With radiance and beauty!

Whoever in His name shall give
Of hope, of cheer, or ration,
And for man's good his life shall live,
Has found his proper station.

————————

Who shares his life's pure pleasures
   And walks the honest road,
Who trades with heaping measures
   And lifts his brother's load,
Who turns the wrong down bluntly
   And lends the right a hand,
He dwells in GOD'S OWN COUNTRY
He tills the HOLY LAND.

—*Louis F. Benson*

WISHING

Do you wish the world were better?
   Let me tell you what to do.
Set a watch upon your actions,
   Keep them always straight and true.
Rid your mind of selfish motives,
   Let your thoughts be clean and high.
You can make a little Eden
   Of the sphere you occupy.
Do you wish the world were wiser?
   Well, suppose you make a start
By accumulating wisdom
   In the scrapbook of your heart.
Do not waste one page on folly,
   Live to learn, and learn to live.
If you want to give men knowledge
   You must get it, ere you give.
Do you wish the world were happy?
   Then remember day by day
Just to scatter seeds of kindness
   As you pass along the way.
For the pleasures of the many
   May be oft times traced to one.
As the hand that plants an acorn
   Shelters armies from the sun.

But Didn't

Do you ever think at the close of the day
Of kindly words you meant to say—
   But didn't?
Do you ever think when day is done
Of errands kind you could have run—
   But didn't?
Do you ever think at daytime's leave
Of flowers gay you meant to give—
   But didn't?
Do you ever think when skies are red
Of hungry mouths you could have fed—
   But didn't?
Do you ever think at dawn or night
Of letters kind you meant to write—
   But didn't?
Do you think at life's last set of sun
You'll think of deeds you could have
   done—
   But didn't?

Saved to Serve

Read 2 Corinthians 5:14-20

We are not here to learn—but to lift —Galatians 6:10

We are not here to absorb—but to give forth — Luke 6:38.

We are not here to be ministered unto but to minister — Mark 10:35-45.

We are not here to be served but to serve others — John 21:15-17.

We are not here to hinder but to help — Mark 14:3-9.

We are not here to be a burden to others—but to bear the burdens of others — Galatians 6:2.

We are not here to stand on the sidelines and criticize the players—but to get into the game and help win the victory —Mark 16:15.

—Dr. T. Myron Webb

My Work

If I should fail to do the work
　Which God designed for me,
In all the world, there's not a soul
　To do my job, you see.

Some may accomplish what I could not,
　And gather much fame and wealth,
But no other creature which God has
　　made
　Can do my work but myself.

So, however humble my task may be,
　And how much tempted to quit,
I'll remember each day as I press along,
　There's nobody else to do it.

—Dale Crowley

Praying Hands

There are hands that help and comfort,
Hands that plan and teach
Hands that rest and hands that strive
For a goal just out of reach . . .
Hands that grasp and hands that give,
Hands that work and play.
Friendly hands and loving hands
That soothe life's cares away.
　But praying hands are dearest
　In the sight of God above.
　For in their sweet and earnest clasp
　Is reverence and love . . .
No hands can do an unkind act,
Nor cause another care,
Nor sin against our Father's love
When they are clasped in prayer.

What Of Your Life?

What is your life? As you go on your way?
Are you doing something for others each day?
What of your heart, is it clean in God's sight?
Or, is there something you should make right?
What of your mind; are the thoughts always pure?
Are you "storing up something" that's certain to endure?
What of your lips? Are words gentle and kind?
Or do you oft times "just speak out your mind"?
Are your hands busy in doing good deeds?
Your purse—is it open for others' needs?
Methinks if we all were right in these ways,
This old world would soon see much better days!

GO WORK

Go work in My vineyard,
  There's plenty to do;
The harvest is great,
  And the laborers are few.
There's weeding, and fencing,
  And the clearing of roots,
And plowing, and sowing,
  And gathering of fruits.
There are foxes to take,
  There are wolves to destroy,
All ages and ranks
  I can fully employ.
I've sheep to be tended,
  And lambs to be fed;
The lost must be gathered,
  The weary ones led.

Chorus:
Go work, go work,
Go work in My vineyard;
There's plenty to do;
Go work, go work.
The harvest is great,
And the lab'rers are few.

"Go work in My vineyard";
  I claim thee as Mine;
With blood did I buy thee,
  And all that is thine—
Thy time and thy talents,
  Thy loftiest powers,
Thy warmest affections,
  Thy sunniest hours.

Work, for the night is coming,
Work through the sunny noon;
Fill brightest hours with labor—
Rest comes sure and soon.
Give every flying minute
Something to keep in store;
Work, for the night is coming
When man works no more!

Service to Man

You may grow to great riches and glory;
  You may toil for yourself through the day;
You may write in your record the story,
  The struggles you have met on the way.
But vain is the fame that you boast of,
  And wasted the years that you can scan.
Your strength you have not made the most of
  If you've rendered no service to man.

If something of you isn't living,
  Long after your spirit has fled;
If your hand ceases toiling and giving
  The minute your body is dead,
You have quitted this world as a debtor,
  And failed in the Infinite Plan.
If you leave not one roadway that's better,
  You have rendered no service to man!

Now, Is the Time

If you have hard work to do,
  Do it now.
Today the skies are clear and blue,
Tomorrow clouds may come in view;
Yesterday is not for you:
  Do it now.

If you have a song to sing,
  Sing it now.
Let the notes of gladness ring
Clear as song of bird in spring,
Let every day some music bring,
  Sing it now.

If you have kind words to say,
  Say them now.
Tomorrow may not come your way,
Do a kindness while you may;
Loved ones will not always stay:
  Say them now.

If you have a smile to show,
  Show it now.
Make hearts happy, roses grow,
Let the friends around you know
The love you have before they go;
  Show it now.

—Author unknown

Worker and Shirker

"Come on!" cried the brook, as it hurried along,
  "There's ever so much that waits to be done;
There are meadows to water, and mill wheels to turn,
  And more things to work as the farther I run!"

"You can go if you choose," said the pond; "as for me,
  I will stay where I am; I hate effort and strife;
I've no fancy for work—no, indeed, not a bit!
  I shall lie here in comfort the rest of my life."

"Well, good-bye!" said the brook, and was off and away,
  To play with the children and freshen the earth;
It dimpled and rippled and sang at its work,
  And brightened the land with its toil and its mirth.

But the pond lay there idle, and slept at its ease,
  And thought itself clever, until, one fine day,
The farmer espied it, all stagnant and green,
  And—alas for its comfort! he drained it away.

—*Priscilla Leonard*

Let Me Know It Now

If you knew someone was thirsting for
  a drop of water sweet,
Would you be so slow to bring it?
  Would you step with laggard feet?
There are tender hearts all around us
  who are thirsting for our love;
Why withhold from them what nature
  makes them crave all else above?
I won't need your kind caresses when
  the grass grows o'er my face;
I won't crave your love or kisses in my
  last low resting place.
So, then, if you love me any, if it's but
  a little bit,
Let me know it now while living; I can
  own and treasure it.

———————

Do all the good you can,
By all the means you can,
In all the ways you can,
In all the places you can,
At all the times you can,
To all the people you can,
As long as ever you can.

—*John Wesley's Rule*

Lest I Be Blind

Lord, touch my eyes lest I be blind,
  And fail to know my neighbor's heart,
Or busy in my hurried mind,
  I fail to sense his harder part.

I would not shun to lift his load,
  Nor pass his wounded fortunes by,
But hasting down my own life's road,
  I might not hear his lonely cry.

Give me a heart, O Lord, like Thine,
  That feels the sorrows others bear,
And makes another's burdens mind,
  Because I really, truly care.

I take too much for granted, Lord,
  And trust he knows my secret care,
Yet fail to comfort with a word,
  Or tell him my concern is there.
Oh, let me weep with those who weep
  And laugh with men whose mirth
    o'erflows,
So that in Christliness I keep
  The feel of my good neighbor's woes!

—*Milo L. Arnold*

Give Them the Flowers Now

Closed eyes can't see the white roses,
  Cold hands can't hold them, you
    know.
Breath that is stilled cannot gather
  The odors that sweet from them blow.
Death, with a peace beyond dreaming,
  Its children of earth doth endow;
Life is the time we can help them,
  So give them the flowers now!

Here are the struggles and striving,
  Here are the cares and the tears;
Now is the time to be smoothing
  The frowns and the furrows and fears.
What to closed eyes are kind sayings?
  What to hushed heart is deep vow?
Naught can avail after parting,
  So give them the flowers now!

Just a kind word or a greeting;
  Just a warm grasp or a smile—
These are the flowers that will lighten
  The burdens for many a mile.
After the journey is over
  What is the use of them; how
Can they carry them who must be car-
    ried?
Oh, give them the flowers now!

What Wilt Thou Have Me Do?

Lord, what wilt Thou that I should do?
  What is my task?
This question, leaping from my heart,
  I kneel to ask.

What place of duty can I fill?
  Where can I go
To lighten, in Thy holy Name,
  Another's woe?

So many hearts are torn today,
  So many weep;
So many souls are passing now
  Through waters deep.

So many bear their loads alone,
  Without Thy grace;
So many have not found in Thee
  A resting place.

In such a world, with needs so vast,
  What can I do?
Fill Thou my heart with love like Thine;
  With pity, too.

Here are my hands, my feet, my all:
  Lead Thou the way,
Where I may do Thy works again,
  "While it is day."

—*T. O. Chisholm*

My Task

Another day God gives me, pure and white,
  How can I make it holy in His sight?
Small means have I, and but a narrow sphere,
  Yet work is 'round me, for He placed me here.
How can I serve Thee, Lord? Open my eyes,
  Show me the duty that 'round me lies.
Someone is sad—then speak a word of cheer;
  Someone is lonely—make him welcome here;
Someone has failed—protect him from despair;
  Someone is poor—there's something you can
    spare.
Thine own heart's sorrow mention but in prayer,
And carry SUNSHINE with thee EVERY-
  WHERE.

—*Author unknown*

REMEMBER

That nothing will run itself
  unless it is running
  downhill.
That to get anywhere it is
  necessary to start from
  where you are.
That the water in a well cannot be purified by painting the pump.
That the church will go no
  further than the mind
  and purpose of its
  members.

A Shut-In's Service

They say I am a shut-in now;
The truth of this I must avow;
Shut out from work; shut in with God,
I tread the path my Master trod.
The path of pain, and trials sore
That test my faith yet more and more.
Shut in with God, I still can be
A help to other waiting souls like me.

A light to shine upon their road;
A hand to lift their heavy load;
A guide, as we journey toward the West
To the paths of patience, peace, and rest.
And by my attitude I'll prove
There is a God of hope and love.
With the world shut out, with Christ
  shut in,
I still can serve my fellow men.

—Emma McNinch

RICH REWARDS ARE PROM-ISED THOSE WHO ARE FAITH-FUL: "Behold, I come quickly; and my reward is with me, to give every man according as his work shall be" (Revelation 22:12). Remember, in the parable of the talents, God's faithful ones are promised great rewards: "Well done, good and faithful servant; thou hast been faithful over a few things, I will make thee ruler over many things: enter thou into the joy of thy Lord" (Matthew 25:23).

GOD WILL NOT FORGET: "For God is not unrighteous to forget your work and labor of love, which ye have showed toward His name, in that ye have ministered to the saints, and do minister" (Hebrews 6:10). "For we are laborers together with God" (1 Corinthians 3:9).

It Takes So Little

It takes so little to put back the heart
  In anyone: a loving word of praise,
Uttered sincerely, oftentimes may start
  A light like sunshine running through
  the days.
It takes so little when the heart is sad
  To lift it up—some bright encourage-
  ment
May reach the sorrowing one and make
  him glad,
  Even when seemingly all hope is
  spent.
It takes so little, why should we with-
  hold
  That precious thing within our power
  to give?
Love, like a warm garment in the cold,
  And sympathy for others while we
  live?
It takes so little, ah, dear God, I pray,
  Help us to give it wisely day by day.

—Grace Noll Crowell

These Be My Offerings

These be my offerings today:
A smile to greet folk on my way,
A hand to clasp a hand whose need
God has made plain, a golden seed
Of truth that may rich harvest bring
To one who may be sorrowing,
And strength to lift another's load
Should he falter on the road.

These be my offerings today:
Prayer to be my steadfast stay,
Love that may in Christ's good stead
Sweeten another's daily bread,
Hope, that may with kindly cheer
Lift some heart oppressed by fear,
And faith whose mighty staff and rod
Are strengthened by the hand of God.
These be my offerings. Though small,
May His own kindness bless them all.

—Eleanor Halbrook Zimmerman

The Road of Life

One day as I was climbing up
   The road of Life to Home,
I met a stranger coming down
   With countenance sad and lone.

I had no time to help him then,
   I feared 'twould mean delay;
With guilty heart I turned aside—
   I dared not look his way.

To still my heart I hurried on,
   And then I heard a sigh;
I turned and looked, and then I saw
   A teardrop in his eye.

Forgetting time, I spoke to him,
   To share with him my cup.
"Dear friend, I fear you're going down
   When you should be going up."

With piteous look he turned to me,
   "How can I turn around?
For with this load upon my back,
   I can hardly make it down."

The joyful news I gladly told
   Of Christ who died for him
To take away the load he had
   If he would let Him in.

A gleam of hope came to his face,
   The tears began to flow.
The load of sin dropped from his back,
   His face began to glow.

And now he travels the road of life—
   Not down, but going up;
To see the glow upon his face
   Has more than filled my cup.

O Lord, forgive the times I've passed
   A stranger on life's road.
Not taking time to dry the tears,
   Nor helping lift the load.

And give me wisdom, Lord, I pray,
   That comes down from Thy throne,
That I might by Thy help and grace
   Lead some poor wanderer Home.

Human Relations

1. Speak to people. There is nothing as nice as a cheerful word of greeting.
2. Smile at people. It takes 72 muscles to frown and only 14 to smile.
3. Call people by name. The sweetest music to anyone's ears is the sound of his own name.
4. Be friendly and helpful. If you would have friends, be friendly.
5. Be cordial. Speak and act as if everything you do is a genuine pleasure.
6. Be genuinely interested in people. You can like almost everybody if you try.
7. Be generous with praise—be cautious with criticism.
8. Be considerate with the feelings of others. There are usually three sides to a controversy: yours, the other fellow's, and the right one.
9. Be alert to give service. What counts most in life is what we do for others.
10. Add to this a good sense of humor, a big dose of patience, and a dash of humility, and you will be rewarded many-fold.

—*Maranatha*

> "If you want to be rich, give.
> If you want to be poor, grasp.
> If you want an abundance, scatter.
> If you want to be needy, hoard."

MY PART

If any little word of mine
   Can make one life the brighter,
If any little song of mine
   Can make one heart the lighter,
God help us speak that little word,
   And take our bit of singing,
And drop it in some lonely vale,
   To set the echoes ringing.

—*Author unknown*

Somebody

Somebody did a golden deed;
Somebody proved a friend in need;
Somebody sang a beautiful song;
Somebody smiled the whole day long;
Somebody thought, " 'Tis sweet to live."
Somebody said, "I'm glad to give";
Somebody fought a valiant fight;
Somebody lived to shield the right.
WAS THAT SOMEBODY YOU?

Encouragement

If nobody smiled and nobody cheered,
 And nobody helped us along,
If each, every minute, looked after him-
 self,
 And the good things all went to the
 strong;
If nobody cared just a little for you,
 And nobody thought about me,
And we all stood alone in the battle of life,
 What a dreary old place this would be!

WORK

Let me but do my work from day to day,
 In field or forest, at the desk or loom,
 In roaring marketplace or tranquil room;
Let me but find it in my heart to say,
When vagrant wishes beckon me astray,
 "This is my work; my blessing, not my
 doom;
 Of all who live, I am the one by whom
This work can best be done in the right way."

Then shall I see it not too great, nor small,
 To suit my spirit, and to prove my powers;
 Then shall I cheerful greet the laboring
 hours,
And cheerful turn, when the long shadows
 fall
At eventide, to play and love and rest,
Because I know for me my work is best.

—First sonnet in "Three Best Things," *The Poems*
 of Henry van Dyke, 1911, page 256.

Prayer for Those Unheard

Lord, bless me with a listening mind.
 Attune me to the smaller sounds,
The whispered plea of loneliness,
 The whimper of an unloved child.

The sad, the sick, the lost. All these
 Ignored, unheard by passersby.
And use me, Lord, to meet their needs
 That I may, in a Christlike way,
Reflect Thy love for them each day.

—Irene Sharp

A Little More

A little more kindness,
A little less creed,
A little more giving,
A little less greed,
A little more smile,
A little less frown,
A little less kicking
A man when he's down,
A little more "we,"
A little less "I,"
A little more laugh,
A little less cry,
A little more flowers
On the pathway of life,
And fewer on graves
At the end of the strife.

—Author unknown

I expect to pass through this
world but once; any good thing,
therefore, that I can do, or any
kindness that I can show to any
fellow-creature, let me do it now;
let me not defer or neglect it; for I
shall not pass this way again.

—Henry Drummond

The Great Judge Sees All

Years ago, the office of my friend, the late Clinton N. Howard, Superintendent of the International Reform Federation, and affectionately known as "the Little Giant," was located on Constitution Avenue, just opposite the Supreme Court Building. One day on a close margin of time for an appointment in the Senate Office Building, he ran from his office to cross the street, but fell just beyond the curb. When he fell, this highly esteemed little old man, now about 80, dropped his brief case and an armful of papers he was trying to carry, and they scattered in different directions.

At that very moment, I was approaching the exact place in my car. I pulled to the right, stopped, got out of the car, and ran to Mr. Howard's side, in time to help him up, and to gather up the papers from the street. One day, a couple of years later, when I had all but forgotten the incident, I was attending the Fellowship Breakfast in the Senate Dining Room, in the Capitol, and Mr. Justice Burton of the Supreme Court rose to make some remarks complimentary to Mr. Howard. To my surprise, he related the incident of Mr. Howard's fall which he had watched from the window of his ornate chambers in the Supreme Court. He told of the fall, and of the man who rushed to the side of "the Little Giant," and helped him up.

Well, I got to thinking about that, and sat down and wrote this little song (which I certainly do not regard as a classic, but which I hope carries an important lesson):

O let us know that when we see a fallen neighbor
    And help him up when he needs a helping hand
That somewhere above there sits a Judge
    Who, Supreme in all the earth, looks down
    And sees when we have helped our fellow man.

Jesus told us of one who fell among the thieves,
    Who was beaten, and was robbed, and stripped of clothes;
Some heard his cry but passed him by—Scribes and Pharisees.
    Then came the Good Samaritan with compassion's cup—
    And Jesus praised the man who helped his brother up.

Chorus:
Oh, when you see your neighbor fall,
Help him up, calm his fear
Brush away the dirt from suit and shirt,
And send him on his way with friendly cheer.
Be a thoughtful, helpful friend;
It pays a bigger dividend,
And in Christ your reward will never end.

—*Dale Crowley*

Giving, Sharing . . .

"Let Us Give"

Let us give!
And remember by our gifts that we
May go to lands across the sea
And thru our missionaries there,
In loving service have a share
As dying people learn to live
Because we give!

Let us give!
Tithes and offerings—never less—
And God who sees and knows will
    bless.
And thru His power our gifts shall go
Beyond the world we see and know,
And we'll richer, better live
Because we give!

—Myrtle R. Creasman

The Joy of Sharing

Have you known the joy of sharing,
Known the thrill of burden-bearing;
Have you lifted from someone
    His load of care?

Have you felt in truest fashion
The rich meaning of compassion,
And the glory of your
    Privilege to share?

Oh, to be a friend and neighbor,
And to help thru toil and labor
With a heart that's always
    Set to do and dare!

Thus our lives will be refreshing
With the sunshine of God's blessing,
As we make it our main
    Business to SHARE.

—Dale Crowley

The Dead Sea

I looked upon a sea,
    And lo, 'twas dead,
Although by Hermon's snows
    And Jordan fed.

How came a fate so dire?
    The tale's soon told:
All that it got it kept
    And fast did hold.

All tributary streams
    Found here their grave
Because the sea received
    But never gave.

O Lord, help me my best,
    Myself, to give,
That I may others bless,
    And like Thee live.

The Coin and Currency Conversation

Fresh and crisp in his new green attire the dollar lay folded in the churchman's billfold. Jingling about with the pennies and nickels, a little dime plays. "You'd better have a good time," the dollar spoke through the partition, hearing the noise. "You won't be here long."

"How do you know?" The little dime stopped its frolicking, frightened at the idea.

"Because you are going to Sunday school."

"Do you go to Sunday school?" asked the dime of the dollar.

"I?" exclaimed the haughty dollar in surprise. "Of course not! I go to shows, and gasoline stations, and parks. Sunday is my big day, but I don't spend it in Sunday school. That's place for small fry like you."

—Moody Monthly

133

PROFIT AND LOSS

I counted dollars while God counted crosses;
I counted gains while He counted losses!
I counted my worth by the things gained in
　　store,
But He sized me up by the scars that I bore.
I coveted honors and sought for degrees;
He wept as He counted the hours on my
　　knees.
I never knew till one day by a grave
How vain are the things that we spend life to
　　save.

IF I WERE A DOLLAR BILL

　　I'd pray that my boss would take me to
church some Sunday and leave me there on
that little plate with the velvet cushion which
the usher passes around—you know. I think
I'd feel so kind of important and "snooty"
among those nickels and pennies. I've seen
enough of filling stations on Sundays to last
me for a lifetime anyway; I'd like to look up
a preacher for a change.

—Baptist Observer

Think It Over

God made the sun—it gives.
　　God made the moon—it gives.
God made the stars—they give.
　　God made the air—it gives.
God made the clouds—they give.
　　God made the earth—it gives.
God made the sea—it gives.
　　God made the trees—they give.
God made the flowers—they give.
　　God made the fowls—they give.
God made the beasts—they give.
　　God made the plan—He gives.
God made man—he . . . ?

Give It Now

If you have a rose for me
　　Give it to me now!
Do not wait till I am dead
　　My ambitions fully fed,
And I need no daily bread;
　　Give it to me now!

If you have some love for me,
　　Give it to me now!
Now, when it will make me strong,
　　As I'm battling with the wrong
Midst a worldly, wicked throng;
　　Give it to me now!

If you have a smile for me
　　Give it to me now!
It will give me strength today
　　For the tasks along my way
In the things I do and say;
　　Give it to me now!

If you have a kindly word
　　Give it to be now!
It will make my burden light;
　　It will help me do what's right;
It will help me win life's fight;
　　Give it to me now!

No Pocket in a Shroud

Spend your money while you're living;
　　Do not hoard it to be proud,
You can never take it with you,
　　There's no pocket in a shroud.

Gold can take you on no farther
　　Than the graveyard where you lie;
Tho' you're rich while you are living,
　　You're a pauper when you die.

Use it, then, some lives to brighten,
　　As thru life they weary plod
Place your bank account in Heaven,
　　And grow richer toward your God.

Use it wisely, use it freely;
　　Do not hoard it to be proud;
You can never take it with you;
　　There's no pocket in a shroud.

A Safe and Profitable Investment

Matthew 16:19-21

We've read about the man who built his house upon the sand,
And when the wind and tide arose, of course, it could not stand.
Why did he not dig to the rock, a good foundation lay?
It took a storm to teach him that such carelessness doesn't pay.
There was a man who worked and saved, great luxuries to buy.
He'd always wanted to be rich, and now the time was nigh.
But, oh! the bank his cash was in had closed its door one day;
And all his money and his dreams, at once were swept away.
Now where do you invest your gold? I pray you, count the cost.
Unless you place it in God's Bank, it's certain to be lost.
Some Christians labor to be great and earthly glories share;
Use what they have to please themselves: for others, have no care.
They lay their treasures up on earth, for they had rather be
Wealthy for just a little while, than for eternity.
And when they leave this world behind, to stand before the Lord,
They cannot take with them one mite of all their earthly hoard.
It does not really matter if our income's large or small;
The widow, with her little mite "cast in more than they all."
Just a few cents will buy some tracts to tell the story sweet:
Who knows how many souls 'twill gain to lay at Jesus' feet.
Must millions of poor souls be lost in heathen lands each year,
When such a little bit would send the Gospel far and near?
We say we want to follow Christ and walk the way He led,
Yet He who made the worlds had not a place to lay His head.
So why should we accumulate, and live in ease today,
And be impoverished in heaven, where we'll FOREVER stay?
Nay, take our all, dear Lord, and make each penny count for Thee.
And we will praise Thy matchless name throughout eternity.

—S.E.C.

GIFTS

'Tis not the gift which I receive
  That means so much to me.
It is the love that comes with it
  That brings me joy, you see.
No matter if the gift be small,
  It may not costly be,
Yet, if it comes with greatest love,
  It means the world to me.

—Madeline G. Wilson

A Happy Tither

I've formed a partnership with God,
It's free of all expense.
He furnishes all the capital
And I get nine tenths.
He gives me wisdom, guidance, and
  strength
And power for all details;
I pay one tenth for all of that,
My partner never fails.

The After Shock

When this life is over, and I pass along
    To the realms where the souls of men go,
I shall ask them up there, if it isn't unfair,
    One favor on me to bestow.
I'd just like to see, when the purse-proud
        arrive,
    The shock they will get when they find,
Be it early or late when they come to the gate,
    That they've left all their money behind.

When I get over there—can do as I please—
    If chuckling's permitted, I'll say,
"If you'll just let me wait at the side of the
        gate,
    I'll try not to get in the way.
But I do want to see the sad look that will be
    On the face of a money-mad gent,
Who was rich ere he died and was puffed up
        with pride,
    When he finds that he hasn't a cent.

Recalling the way mortals treasure their coin,
    Refusing to spend it or give,
And the boasting and flash which accompany
        cash,
    As if always their owners will live,
I am sure 'twill be fun, when the hoarding is
        done,
    And the once-wealthy hoarders arrive,
To be standing about and just see them find
        out
    That they didn't bring change for a five!

    —Edgar A. Guest

God gives us joy that we may give;
    He gives us love that we may share.
Sometimes He gives us loads to lift
    That we may learn to bear.
For life is gladder when we give,
    And love is sweeter when we share,
And heavy loads rest lightly, too,
    When we have learned to bear.

    —Author unknown

I Wonder Why

I wonder why the Lord did ask,
For tithes, from you and me;
When all the treasures of the
        earth
Are His—eternally?

And why should He depend on
        us,
To fill His house with meat,
When we have so very little,
And His storehouse is replete?

But He said to bring our little,
And He would add His much;
Then all the heavenly windows
Would be opened at His touch.

And blessings running over—
Even more than has been told—
Will be ours; but there's no
        promise
If His portion we withhold.

Are we afraid to prove Him?
Is our faith and love so small,
That we tightly grasp our little,
When He freely gave His all?

    —Roselyn C. Steere

What Do You Owe?

What do you owe God, you ask?
    Suppose He sent His bill:
One hundred thousand dollars for
    The sun upon the hill;
Two thousand for the little brook
    That runs along the way;
Five hundred for the night time
    And a thousand for the day;
Six hundred for the little birds
    That trill and chirp and sing;
Six hundred for the tiny flowers
    Which tell us that it's spring;
There are the bills which everyone
    Of every clime forget.
If God should charge you what
        you owe,
    You'd always be in debt.

Charge Your Gift With Prayer

There is a need that is greater than money,
For there's a gift that is still more rare;
Remember when giving your dollars,
To send each one off with prayer.

The rich man's great gift is a pauper,
Though given with pomp and with care;
When placed by the mite of a widow,
When that mite is charged with prayer.

The power of money is mighty,
And great things 'twill do and 'twill dare;
But it's naught by the side of the dollar
That's mightily charged with prayer.

Then pray as you give and keep praying,
This privilege the poorest may share;
Your dollars though few will do wonders
When each one is charged with prayer.

—*Mrs. D. E. Elby*

Out of This Life

Out of this life I shall never take
    Things of silver and gold I make.
All that I cherish and hoard away
    After I leave, on earth must stay.
Though I have toiled for a painting rare
    To hang on my wall, I must leave it
        there.
Though I call it mine and I boast its worth,
    I must give it up when I quit the earth.
All that I gather and all that I keep
    I must leave behind when I fall asleep.

And I wonder often, just what I shall own
    In that other life, when I pass alone.
What shall He find and what shall He see
    In the soul that answers the call for me?
Shall the great Judge learn, when my task
        is through,
    That my soul had gathered some riches,
        too?
Or shall at the last, it be mine to find,
    That all I had worked for I had left
        behind.

—*Author unknown*

When Your Latest Sun Goes Down

Carve your name high o'er the drift-
    ing sand,
Where the steadfast rocks defy
    decay;
All you can hold in your cold, dead
    hand
Is what you have given away.

Count your wide conquests o'er sea
    and land,
Heap up your gold, and hoard as you
    may;
All you can hold in your cold, dead
    hand
Is what you have given away.

Build your pyramids, skyward, let
    them rise,
Stand gazed at my millions, cultured
    they say;
All you can hold in your cold, dead
    hand
Is what you have given away.

Silver and gold and jewels so grand,
King of the saloon, or mart for a day;
Yet all you can hold in your cold,
    dead hand
Is what you have given away.

—*Joaquin Miller*

GIVING

"What, giving again?"
    I asked in dismay.
"And must I keep giving
    And giving away?"

"Oh, no," said the angel,
    Piercing me through;
"Just give until God stops
    Giving to you!"

—*Author unknown*

137

Life's Mirror

There are loyal hearts, there are spirits
    brave,
  There are souls that are pure and true;
Then give to the world the best you have,
  And the best will come to you.

Give love, and love to your life will flow,
  And strength in your inmost needs;
Have faith, and a score of hearts will show
  Their faith in your work and deeds.

Give truth, and your gifts will be paid in
    kind,
  And song a song will meet;
And the smile which is sweet will surely
    find
  A smile that is just as sweet.

Give pity and sorrow to those who mourn;
  You will gather in flowers again
The scattered seeds from your thought
    outborne,
  Though the sowing seemed in vain.

For life is the mirror of king and slave,
  'Tis just what we are and do;
Then give to the world the best you have
  And the best will come back to you.

—Madeline S. Bridges

Let Me Give

I do not know how long I'll live
  But while I live, Lord, let me give
Some comfort to someone in need
  By smile or nod—kind word or
    deed.
And let me do whate'er I can
  To ease things for my fellow man.
I want naught but to do my part
  To lift a tired or weary heart,
To change folks' frowns to smiles
    again—
  Then I will not have lived in vain;
And I'll not care how long I'll live
  If I can give—and give—and give.

Your Love Will Live

These have been such trying days
But our hearts are filled with
    praise;
Praise for precious friends like you,
Praise for all you've helped us do.

You do not know how much they
    meant,
Those loving gifts which you have
    sent;
They helped us with our heavy
    load,
And brightened up a lonely road.

Oh what a joy in life to find
Such helpful friends, so good and
    kind.
Although we have no gold to give,
Deep in our hearts your love will
    live.

The love for souls that you have
    shown,
Cause grateful praise to reach
    God's throne,
Brings courage in the bitter fight,
And life to those in heathen night.

May our dear Father up above
Reward you for your gifts of love;
Oh may He keep your heart aglow,
His very best on you bestow.

Your love will live long in the
    heart,
It never, never will depart.
This is our prayer until life ends:
"God, make us worthy of such
    friends."

—Dr. Fred Jarvis

All that I spend is gone—it is mine no
    longer;
All that I save is mine until I spend it,
    lose it, or leave it behind;
All that I give to God is added to my
    credit in the bank of heaven, and
    will be mine forever and ever.

Best Rules in Making Gifts

1. The **cause** must be **worthy.** You want your gift dollars to go to objects thoroughly worthwhile.
2. You want to give as you **want** to give, voluntarily, cheerfully—without constraint or coercion.
3. You should be convinced in your own mind that there is a real, **actual need.**
4. Give where your money will **reach the furtherest.** Make those gift dollars get the greatest results possible. Invest for time and eternity.
5. The **administration** of your gifts should be **trustworthy.** Your hard earned money must not be wasted, dissipated, or wrongly used.
6. Avoid putting your gifts into any institution where the **overhead** is too large.
7. Give as you **PRAY.** If you cannot pray about it, don't give to it.

Heart Gifts

It's not the things that can be bought
That are life's richest treasure.
It's just the little "heart gifts"
That money cannot measure . . .
A cheerful smile, a friendly word,
A sympathetic nod
Are priceless little treasures
From the storehouse of our God . . .
They are the things that can't be
bought
With silver or with gold.
For thoughtfulness and kindness
And love are never sold . . .
They are the priceless things in life
For which no one can pay.
And the giver finds rich recompense
In GIVING THEM AWAY.

—*Helen Steiner Rice*

There Are Two Seas

There are two seas in Palestine. One is fresh, and fish are in it. Splashes of green adorn its banks. Trees spread their branches over it, and stretch out their thirsty roots to sip of its healing waters.

Along its shores the children play, as children played when He was there. He loved it. He could look across its silver surface when He spoke His parables. And on a rolling plain not far away He fed five thousand people.

The river Jordan makes this sea with sparkling water from the hills. So it laughs in the sunshine. And men build their houses near to it, and birds their nests; and every kind of life is happier because it is here.

The river Jordan flows on south into another sea. Here is no splash of fish no fluttering leaf, no song of birds, no children's laughter. Travellers choose another route, unless on urgent business. The air hangs heavy above its waters, and neither man nor beast nor fowl will drink.

What makes this mighty difference in these neighbor seas?

Not the river Jordan. It empties the same good water into both. Not the soil in which they lie; not the country round about.

This is the difference. The Sea of Galilee receives but does not keep the Jordan. For every drop that flows into it another drop flows out. The giving and receiving go on in equal measure.

The other sea is shrewder, hoarding its income jealously. It will not be tempted into any generous impulse. Every drop it gets, it keeps.

The Sea of Galilee gives and lives. This other sea gives nothing. It is named The Dead.

There are two kinds of people in the world. The are two seas in Palestine.

—*Bruce Barton*

HIS OFFERING

'Twas a common congregation,
　Not many rich or poor,
And they settled back in their places
　When the sermon at length was o'er.

'Twas a missionary sermon,
　And the pastor tried, indeed,
To touch the hearts of his people
　For India's great need.

He asked for a large collection
　To send the precious Word,
And he raised the mute petition,
　"Touch their pocketbooks, O Lord!"

But " 'Twas only a begging sermon,
　One hears so many now!"
And a look of saddened patience
　Stole o'er the preacher's brow.

As they gave their dimes and nickels
　With a have-to-do-it air,
Instead of the look of helpful joy
　God's people ought to wear.

'Way down in front, on the free seat,
　Sat a shabby little boy,
No mother's pet and plaything,
　No father's pride and joy.

Poor child! He had no mother,
　And he was a drunkard's son,
Known to the congregation
　As "drunken Lacy's John."

Of course he had no offering,
　So the deacon passed him by.
"Let us ask a blessing on it,"
　Said the pastor with a sigh.

"Oh, wait," said the barefoot laddie,
　As he started to his feet,
"And ask one on my offering too!
　The deacon passed my seat."

So back went the good deacon,
　And his face wore a friendly smile
As he passed the box to the little lad
　Who was standing all the while.

"I haven't much to give," he said,
　"But I'll give all I can.
And I'll go out to India
　And preach when I'm a man."

And from his ragged jacket
　He drew his treasured pence,
And carefully he counted them—
　Just twenty-seven cents!

"There, that is every bit I have,"
　Said the shabby little lad,
"But I know that God'll bless it,
　'Cause I gave Him all I had!"

"Here, deacon, pass that box again!"
　Called honest Farmer Dorr.
"We haven't done the best we could;
　We want to give some more!"

And so the contribution box
　Went around the church once more,
And dollars now went dropping in
　Where nickels dropped before.

Men all unused to giving
　Gave now and softly smiled,
For now they gave to Jesus,
　Led by a little child.

And the pastor asked a blessing
　On a sum that made him glad,
And all because one little boy
　Gave Jesus all he had!

—*Elizabeth F. Guptill*

Friendship . . .

If You Have a Friend Worth Loving

The following poem was discovered by Mr. George Morgan, of the banking firm of Morgan, Drexel & Co., in a country newspaper. He carried it in his pocket for five years, occasionally reading it to his friends. Inquiries for copies of it were so frequent that he finally had it printed for distribution.

If you have a friend worth loving,
* Love him. Yes, and let him know*
That you love him, ere life's evening
* Tinge his brow with sunset glow.*
Why should good words ne'er be said
Of a friend—till he is dead?

If you hear a song that thrills you,
* Sung by any child of song,*
Praise it. Do not let the singer
* Wait deserved praises long.*
Why should one who thrills your heart
Lack the joy you may impart?

If you hear a prayer that moves you
* By its humble, pleading tone,*
Join it. Don't let the seeker
* Bow before his God alone.*
Why should not your brother share
The strength of "two or three" in
* prayer?*

If you see the hot tears falling
* From a brother's weeping eyes,*
Share them. And by kindly steering

Own your kinship in the skies.
Why should anyone be glad
When a brother's heart is sad?

If a silvery laugh goes rippling
* Through the sunshine on his face,*
Share it. 'Tis the wise man's saying—
* For both grief and joy a place.*
There's health and goodness in the mirth
In which an honest laugh has birth.

If your work is made more easy
* By a friendly, helping hand,*
Say so. Speak out brave and truly
* Ere the darkness veil the land.*
Should a brother workman dear
Falter for a word of cheer?

Scatter thus your seeds of kindness
* All enriching as you go—*
Leave them. Trust the Harvest-Giver;
* He will make each seed to grow.*
So, until the happy end,
Your life shall never lack a friend.

Prayer for a Friend

In the Book of God's remembrance
Our names are written there.
And it seems to bring you nearer
As I breathe your name in prayer;
And I thank the Heavenly Father
For your friendship sweet and true
And pray His richest blessings
Will ever rest on You!

A Friend's Greeting

I'd like to be the sort of friend that you
  have been to me;
I'd like to be the help that you've been
  always glad to be;
I'd like to mean as much to you each
  minute of the day
As you have meant, old friend of mine,
  to me along the way.

—*Edgar A. Guest*

Thank God for You

Thank God for you, good friend of mine,
Seldom is friendship such as thine;
How very much I wish to be
As helpful as you've been to me—
   Thank God for you.

When I recall from time to time
How you inspired this heart of mine,
I find myself inclined to pray,
"God bless my friend this very day"—
   Thank God for you.

Of many prayer quests, one thou art
On whom I ask God to impart
Rich blessings from His storehouse rare,
And grant to you His gracious care—
   Thank God for you.

So often at the throne of grace
There comes a picture of your face,
And then instinctively I pray
That God may guide you all the way—
   Thank God for you.

Some day I hope with you to stand
Before the throne at God's right hand,
And say to you at journey's end,
Praise God, you've been to me a
   friend—
   Thank God for you.

—Author unknown

   A friend whom you have been gaining during your whole life, you ought not to be displeased with in a moment. A stone is many years becoming a ruby; take care that you do not destroy it in an instant against another stone.

Tony Wons

If We Only Understood

Could we but draw back the curtains
   That surround each other's lives,
See the naked heart and spirit,
   Know what spur the action gives.

Often we should find it better,
   Purer than we judge we should;
We should love each other better,
   If we only understood.

Could we judge all deeds by motives,
   See the good and bad within,
Often we should love the sinner
   All the while we loathe the sin.

Could we know the powers working
   To overthrow integrity,
We should love each other's errors
   With more patient charity.

If we knew the cares and trials,
   Knew the efforts all in vain,
And the bitter disappointment,
   Understood the loss and gain—

Would the grim eternal roughness
   Seem—I wonder—just the same?
Should we help where now we hinder,
   Should we pity where now we
   blame.

Ah! we judge each other harshly,
   Knowing not life's hidden force;
Knowing not the fount of action
   Is less turbid at its source—

Seeing not amid the evil
   All the golden grain of good;
And we would love each other better
   If we only understood.

—Rudyard Kipling

A Good Friend

   To have a good friend is one of the highest delights of life; to be a good friend is one of the noblest and most difficult undertakings. Friendship depends not upon fancy, imagination or sentiment, but upon character. There is no man so poor that he is not rich if he have a friend; there is no man so rich that he is not poor without a friend. But friendship is a word made to cover many kindly, impermanent relationships. Real friendship is abiding. Like charity, it suffereth long and is kind.

When You Get to Know a Fellow

When you get to know a fellow, know his joys and his cares,
When you've come to understand him and the burdens that he bears,
When you've learned the fight he's making and the troubles in his way,
Then you find that he is different than you thought him yesterday.

You find his faults are trivial and there's not so much to blame
In the brother that you jeered at when you only knew his name.
You are quick to see the blemish in the distant neighbor's style;
You can point to all his errors and may sneer at him the while.

And your prejudices fatten and your hates more violent grow
As you talk about the failures of the man you do not know.
But when drawn a little closer, and your hands and shoulders touch,
You find the traits you hated really don't amount to much.

When you get to know a fellow, know his every mood and whim,
You begin to find the texture of the splendid side of him;
You begin to understand him, and you cease to scoff and sneer,
For with understanding always prejudices disappear.

You begin to find his virtues and his faults you cease to tell,
For you seldom hate a fellow when you know him very well.
When next you start in sneering and your phrases turn to blame,
Know more, before you censure, of his business and his name.

For it's likely that acquaintance would your prejudice dispel,
And you'd really come to like him if you knew him very well.
When you get to know a fellow and you understand his way,
Then his faults won't really matter, for you'll find a lot to praise.

The Reward of Friendship

There is no treasure like the treasure
  Of a faithful friend;
There is no pleasure like the pleasure
  Friendship can lend;
Fame and riches, other pleasures,
  These may quickly pass away—
Friendship and its golden treasures
  Last forever and a day.

Make It Friendly

Life is like a journey on a train,
With two fellow travelers at each window
  pane.
I may sit beside you all the journey through,
Or I may sit elsewhere, never knowing you.
But should fate mark me to sit by your side,
Let's be pleasant travelers—'tis so short a
  ride!

The Gift of Friends

God knew we needed something more than budding earth and sunlit sky,
And so He sent us friends to love, to lift our hearts and spirits high;
God chose to teach love's wond'rous art of comfort, cheer that never ends
By giving to the thankful heart the dear, good gift of faithful friends.
"I will mention the lovingkindness of the Lord" (Isaiah 63:7).

Friends That Count

The friends that love us always,
  In the good time and the bad;
The friends that love us always
  Are the friends that keep us glad.
The friends that cling in tempest
  As they do in calms, are those
That have made the paths of hardship
  Seem the paths of song and rose.
The friends that love us always,
  When we go their way or not,
Are the friends our hearts remember
  When the others are forgot.
The friends that stick the closest
  When the trouble grows the worst;
The friends that love us always,
  Just the way they did at first—
They are the crowning jewels
  Of the coronets we weave
In the dream of tender moments
  When the troubles start to leave.
We revere their names forever
  And we see their faces clear—
The friends that love us always,
  Whether sun or shadow's near.

DESTROYING OUR ENEMIES

Abraham Lincoln was once talking with a woman about how the North must treat the South. She disagreed with him, and said that she felt we must destroy our enemies. Lincoln replied: "What, madam? Do I not destroy them when I make them my friends?"

—*The Community News*

To Get the Most From Life

If you would get the most from life,
  You must put something in it,
And strive to help your fellow man
  Each day, each hour, each minute.
An act of kindness done by you,
  Will cheer the heart that's sad,
And when you cause someone to smile,
  It makes your own heart glad.
Be friendly with your brothers
  And extend a helping hand,
And each of them will grasp it
  In a way you'll understand.
Then when you travel down life's road
  And round the distant bend,
There'll be a host of people who
  Will say, "There goes my friend."

The Glory of Friendship

There is no greater earthly blessing than to claim
The faith and trust of those who know you well;
To be a kindly neighbor where you dwell,
To make a high example of your name,
And keep our humble doorway free from shame;
And let our worth each day's performance tell.

To freely give what honor would not sell,
For base advantage or the pomp of fame,
Some things there are which have no purchase price,
Yet rich or poor of these have daily need;
The comfort of some true friend's sacrifice,
His trust, his love, and every kindly deed.
God, grant I may be worthy while I live
Of all the joys my friends are glad to give.

—*Edgar A. Guest*

You're the Kind of Friend I'd Like to Be

You'll never know how thoughtful
A friend can really be
Until you meet one like the friend
That you have been to me!
I'd like to be that kind of friend,
But what I'll have to do
Is just be less and less like me
And more and more like you!

IN CONCLUDING

I am thankful, truly thankful,
    For kind and loving friends,
Who wait with willing heart and
    hands
    To help me gain my ends.
The faith which they repose in me
    Is strength, through thick and thin;
I must not disappoint them,
    So I feel I'm bound to win.

A FRIEND

You say you are my friend,
    A friend means, oh, so much!
I love to hear your footsteps
    I love to feel your touch.
I love the quiet, kindly way
    You tell me what to do.
The world would be a lonely place
    If it were not for you.
                    —*Caroline Ells Keeler*

Since it has been my lot to find
    At every parting of the road
The helping hand of comrade kind
    To help me with the load.
And since I have no gold to give,
    And love alone must make
        amends,
My humble prayer is, while I live,
    "God make me worthy of my
        friends."
                    —*Author unknown*

The Friend Who Just Stands By

When trouble comes your soul to try,
You love the friend who just "stands by."
Perhaps there's nothing he can do—
The thing is strictly up to you:
For there are troubles all your own,
And paths the soul must tread alone.
Times when love cannot smooth the road
Nor friendship lift the heavy load.
But just to know you have a friend
Who will "stand by" until the end,
Whose sympathy through all endures,
Whose warm handclasp is always yours—
It helps, someway, to pull you through,
Although there's nothing he can do.
And so with fervent heart you cry,
"God bless the friend who just stands by."

What Is a Friend?

A friend is a person of great understanding
    Who shares all our hopes and our schemes,
A companion who listens with infinite
    patience
    To all of our plans and our dreams.
A true friend can make all our cares melt
    away
    With the touch of a hand or a smile,
And with calm reassurance make everything
    brighter,
    And life always seem more worthwhile—
A friend shares so many bright moments of
    laughter
    At even the tiniest thing—
What memorable hours of light-hearted glad-
    ness
    And pleasure this sharing can bring!
A friend is a cherished and precious posses-
    sion
    Who knows all our hopes and our fears,
And someone to treasure deep down in our
    hearts
    With the closeness that grows through the
    years!

A Prayer for a Friend

Dear Lord, if I could only be
  Worthy of one wish from Thee,
I would not ask for wealth or fame—
  For I have more in Jesus' Name;
I would not ask for homes and lands—
  My treasures lie in Jesus' hands;
I would not ask for health or food—
  For Thou dost give me all that's good;
But I would that I could see
  Just how the greatest friend to be
To one Thou'st given me to love,
  Both here and in our home above—
That, Lord, the love Thou hast given me
  Might fill his life and soul, that he
Will never question, never fear,
  My love for him is just veneer—
But may each time I clasp his hand,
  Feel friendship true, and understand
That of Thy many gifts I see,
  He is a precious one to me. Amen.

You Came Into My World

You came into my world when I needed you most;
  You gave me a lift when my soul was cast
    down,
You breathed into my life a fresh inspiration,
  Gave me new hope to strive for the crown.

You inspired me to press on in the battle of life
  When the going was rough and skies were gray;
I was faltering and reeling under assaults by the
  foe
  When you came into my world that day.

I will never know why you came to me then
  With the encouragement and strength you gave,
Except that I know God sent you to me
  To help me in my trials to be brave.

Though the years since then have slipped by
  When you cheered me along life's way,
The memory of you shall never grow dim
  Since you came into my world that day!

—Dale Crowley

The Measuring Line

Measure your life by the joys that it
  brings—
  Not by the years—
Measure it, too, by the smiles and the
  songs—
  Not by the tears.
Measure your wealth by your friends
  and their love,
  You'll find that your measure is true;
And you'll be rich in the things that
  count
  Through the years ahead of you!

—Author unknown

Friends

A slender acquaintance with the world must convince every man that actions, not words, are the true criteria of the attachment of friends; and that the most liberal professions of good will are very far from being the surest marks of it.

—George Washington

Do not keep the alabaster boxes of your love and tenderness sealed up until your friends are dead. Fill their lives with sweetness. Speak approving, cheerful words, while their ears can hear them and their hearts can be thrilled by them.

—Henry Ward Beecher

"From a Friend"

My dear and much beloved friend
My best regards to you I send,
And from a heart sincere and true
All happiness I'm wishing you.

May you be free from all distress
And meet with real and true success.
May no misfortune come to you,
May all your friends prove kind and true.

But should your earthly friends depart
Remember still there is one heart
That beats for you with tender love;
'Tis your eternal friend above.

May God, "from whom all blessings
    flow,"
His benefits on you bestow
And save and keep you, day by day,
In His own good and pleasant way.

Let us in God put all our trust,
And seek His blessed Kingdom first.
To Him be true, and we shall meet
Some day upon the golden street.

In Gratitude for Friends

I thank you, God in heaven, for
    friends.
When morning wakes, when daytime
    ends,
    I have the consciousness
Of loving hands that touch my own,
Of tender glance and gentle tone,
    Of thoughts that cheer and bless!
If sorrow comes to me, I know
That friends will walk the way I go,
    And, as the shadows fall,
I know that I will raise my eyes
And see—ah, hope that never dies!—
    That dearest Friend of all.

—*Margaret E. Sangster*

We cannot tell the precise moment when friendship is formed. As in filling a vessel drop by drop, there is at last a drop which makes it run over; so in a series of kindnesses there is at last one which makes the heart run over.

—*Samuel Johnson*

THE FRIEND OF FRIENDS

Of all the many blessings that our gracious Father sends,
I thank Him most of all today for loyal-hearted friends:
Friends who know about my faults and keep on loving still,
Friends whose friendship changes not with happy days or ill,
Friends to whom my inmost secrets safely I confide,
Friends who make me happy just to have them by my side.
Yes! of all the many blessings that our gracious Father sends,
I thank Him most of all today for loyal-hearted friends.

I like my friends to meet each other—those for whom I care;
I feel their friendship's worth so much I want the rest to share;
Friendship's like the miracle of loaves in Galilee,
Though shared by many others, there's nonetheless for me.
And since I've thought of you, dear friend, in friendship's closest tie,
I've longed to introduce you to a friend, for he and I
Spend many hours together in a happy, solemn tryst.
How I wish you might know Him! my best friend, Jesus Christ.

—*Horace G. Halse*

Resolution, Courage . . .
Steadfastness, Victory

The Life That Counts

The life that counts must toil and fight;
Must hate the wrong and love the right;
Must stand for truth by day, by night—
This is the life that counts.

The life that counts must hopeful be;
In darkest night make melody;
Must wait the dawn on bended knee—
This is the life that counts.

The life that counts must aim to rise
Above the earth to sunlit skies;
Must fix its gaze on Paradise—
This is the life that counts.

The life that counts must helpful be;
The cares and needs of others see;
Must seek the slaves of sin to free—
This is the life that counts.

The life that counts is linked with God;
The turns not from the cross—the rod;
But walks with joy where Jesus trod—
This is the life that counts.

RESOLUTION

Just to be tender, just to be true,
Just to be glad the whole day through,
Just to be merciful, just to be mild,
Just to be trustful as a child;
Just to be gentle and kind and sweet,
Just to be helpful with willing feet,
Just to be cheery when things go wrong,
Just to drive sadness away with song.
Whether the hour is dark or bright,
Just to be loyal to God and right,
Just to believe that God knows best,
Just in His promise ever to rest.
Just to let love be our daily key,
That is God's will for you and me.

I Am Resolved

Let everyone of us who names the name of Christ enter into the spirit of (at least) these several resolutions:

BE IT RESOLVED:

That in the spirit of humble obedience I will seek God's will in my life;

That I shall prayerfully cultivate all Christian virtues, such as humility, gentleness, purity, patience and love, and thus be a worthy example of Christ my Lord;

That I shall daily pray for vision, discernment, and the spirit of compassion toward the souls of all people on this earth; and,

That I shall be, by His grace, an active witness for Christ, seeking the lost with the good news of salvation, both by my personal testimony, and by supporting Christian enterprises which are reaching the lost both at home and abroad; and,

That I shall make it a daily practice to study God's Word, and to pray, and to serve, so that I may fulfill the command to "grow in grace, and in the knowledge of our Lord and Saviour Jesus Christ; and,

That I shall live in daily expectancy of my Lord's return, "Looking for that blessed hope, the glorious appearing of the great God and our Saviour Jesus Christ."

❀ ❀ ❀ ❀ ❀

148

The Never Wavering Few

The easy roads are crowded, and the
　　level roads are jammed.
The pleasant little rivers with the drift-
　　ing folk are crammed.
But off yonder where it's rocky; where
　　you get a better view,
You will find the ranks are thinning,
　　and the travelers are few.

Where the going's smooth and pleasant
　　you will always find the throng.
For the many—more's the pity—seem
　　to like to drift along.
But the steps that call for courage and
　　the task that's hard to do,
In the end results in glory of the never-
　　wavering few.

Keep A-Goin'

Whether you strike thorn or rose,
　　Keep a-goin'.
If it hails or if it snows,
　　Keep a-goin'.
'Taint no use to sit an' whine,
When the fish ain't on the line,
Bait your hook an' keep a-tryin'
　　Keep a-goin'.

When the weather kills your crop,
　　Keep a-goin'.
When you tumble from the top,
　　Keep a-goin'.
S'pose you're out o' every dime,
Gettin' broke—that ain't no
　　crime.
Tell the world you're pullin' fine.
　　Keep a-goin'.

When it looks like all is up,
　　Keep a-goin'.
Drain the sweetness from the cup.
　　Keep a-goin'.
See the wild bird on the wing,
Hear the bells that sweetly ring,
When you feel like sighin', sing!
　　Keep a-goin'.

It Takes Courage

TO refrain from gossip when others
about you delight in it.

TO stand up for an absent person
who is being abused.

TO live honestly within your means
and not dishonestly on the means of others.

TO be talked about and yet remain
silent when a word would justify you in
the eyes of others, but which you cannot
speak without injury to another.

TO be a real man, a true woman, by
holding fast to your ideals when it causes
you to be looked upon as strange and
peculiar.

TO refuse to do a thing which is
wrong, though others desire it.

TO dress yourself according to your
income, and to deny yourself what you
cannot afford to buy.

TO live always according to your
convictions.

*(This was found on the fly leaf of an
old Bible.)*

---

*Give unto us, O Lord the spirit
of brightness and of courage.
Let not any shadow oppress our
spirits lest our gloom should
darken the light by which
others have to live.
Help us to play the man,
and so to help others to face
courageously whatsoever
tomorrow may bring them
for the sake of
Jesus Christ our Lord.*

Life

When your heart is sad and weary,
And your eyes with tears are dim;
When you feel all hope has left you
And your chance in life seems slim,
Try to pull yourself together,
Scatter sand along our track;
Get a grip on life, then hold it . . .
Don't waste time in looking back.

When you feel life's not worth living
And you hope the end is near;
When you think you've lost your best
    friends
And all else that you hold dear,
Gather all your strength and courage,
Let no weakness bar your way;
Just forget the thorns and briars
That you found along the way.

Lift yourself from out the meshes
Of the tangled threads of woe
Ever pressing onward, upward,
Though the task seems hard and slow.
Keep your head up, climbing ever,
Till you reach the very top;
He who'd gain the highest apex
Must not idle time nor stop.

Life is short, but worth the living
And you need not live in vain;
If your efforts prove a failure,
Start anew and try again.
Life is just what we would make it,
Be it happiness or woe,
Or success or many failures;
We choose the path on which to go.

—Margaret Reigh Martz

MY AIM

I shall aim high.
The stars are there
And God is too,
Who answers prayer!

—Lulu M. Schultz

Opportunity

If yesterday you made mistakes,
    Don't sit and brood
And spend today regretting them
    'Twill do no good.

By errors be not overthrown,
But make each one a steppingstone.

For the the new day's dawning light,
    Another chance
Will come to you; oh, let it not
    Escape your glance.

Blind is the man who cannot see,
Each day, an opportunity.

—Kind Words

I Would Be True . . .

I would be true, for there are those
who trust me. I would be pure, for there
are those who care. I would be strong,
for there is much to suffer. I would be
grave, for there is much to dare. I would
be a friend to all—the foe, the friendless.
I would be giving, and forget the gift. I
would be humble, for I know my weakness. I would look up—and laugh, and
love, and lift.

My Daily Prayer

May God grant me the knowledge to
    know the true from the false,
May He grant me the wisdom to
    know His will, and
Give me the power, the courage, the
    strength and the desire to do it.
In Jesus name, I pray.

It Can Be Done

Somebody said that it couldn't be done;
  But he, with a chuckle, replied,
That maybe it couldn't but he would be one
  Who wouldn't say so till he'd tried.
So he buckled right in, with a trace of a grin
  On his face. If he worried he hid it.
He started to sing as he tackled the thing
  That couldn't be done—and he did it.

Somebody scoffed: "Oh, you'll never do that;
  At least, no one ever has done it."
But he took off his coat and he took off his hat,
  And the first thing we knew, he'd begun it.
With a lift of his chin, and a bit of a grin,
  Without any doubting or quiddit,
He started to sing as he tackled the thing
  That couldn't be done—and he did it.

There are thousands to tell you it can't be done;
  There are thousands to prophesy failure;
There are thousands to enumerate, one by one,
  The dangers that wait to assail you;
But just buckle in with a bit of a grin,
  Then take off your coat and go to it;
Just start in to sing as you tackle the thing
  That cannot be done—and you'll do it.

—Edgar A. Guest

Dare to Stand for Jesus

Dare to stand for Jesus;
  Dare to face the foe;
Dare to be like Jesus,
  Everywhere you go;
Christ will go before you;
  He will see you through;
Dare to stand for Jesus;
  No matter what others do!

Dare to serve the Saviour;
  Dare to let friends know;
Dare to follow Jesus;
  He would have it so;
Christ, the Lord, will guide you—
  He is ever true;
Dare to stand for Jesus;
  No matter what others do!

Dare to go to battle;
  Fight for Christ, your King;
Dare to have convictions;
  Victory He will bring;
Dare to be a Daniel;
  Christ will stand by you;
Dare to stand for Jesus;
  No matter what others do!

Kathryn Bowsher

Not Backward

I would not turn backward—my face as "a
    flint,"
I've set to go onward with Holy intent.
I'm trusting in Jesus, who never can fail;
Who pleads for me there in the heavenly vale.

I would not turn backward. "I press to the
    prize"
That waiteth the victor beyond the blue skies;
A crown never fading, a robe of pure white,
A home with my Savior—eternally bright.

Oh, soul, when tempted to turn from "the way,"
When night's deepest sorrow has followed the
    day;
Look up, and take courage, be strong in the
    Lord,
And trust in the promises found in His Word.

—Wilbur J. Powell

There are ruts in the Road of
    Life's stony street,
There are dangerous places for
    stumbling feet—
Where the strongest have fallen
    and cowards turned back
To look for a safer and easier
    track.
But remember that under
    Time's rutted clay
The steps of the Master have
    marked the way—
His footprints are there on the
    path ahead
For He, too, once traveled the
    road we tread.

COURAGE

Courage is enduring for just one minute longer,
Courage is just holding on though others may be
    stronger.
Courage is a grappling hand when dreams we've had
    are facing,
Courage is keeping on enheartening and persuading.
Courage is certain faith expressed in act heroic,
Something deeper, much more live than simply being
    stoic.
Courage is a sensing of our destiny, a tightening
Of the belt of circumstance though all its face be
    frightening.
Courage is a midnight song through the deep darkness
    singing.
Till the music born of faith sets all life's rafters ringing.
Courage is a sensing that in spite of pain and sorrow
God will see us through today and meet our need
    tomorrow.

—*Ruth Winant Wheeler*

God, give me Strength
So that I may
Complete the tasks
I should this day.

God, give me Faith
Always to see
Your loving hand
Directing me.

God, give me Hope
Through these dark ways
Shall come the light
Of better days.

Give me Courage,
Dear God, to smile
And, come what may—
Feel life worthwhile.

Encouragement to "Keep on Keeping On"

We've all dreamed dreams that have never come true. We've seen them vanish at dawn. But we've realized enough of our dreams, thank God, to make us want to dream on. We've prayed many prayers when no answers came, though we've waited, patient and long. But answers have come to enough of our prayers, to make us keep praying on.

We've trusted many a friend that failed, and left us to weep alone. But we've found enough of our friends true blue, to make us keep trusting on. We've sown many seeds that fell by the way, for the birds to feed upon. But we've held enough golden sheaves in our hands to make us keep sowing on. We've drained the cup of disappointment and pain, and gone many days without song. But I've sipped enough nectar from the roses of life, to make me want to go on.

—*Adapted by Tim Spencer*

Give Up?

Give up because the cross is heavy,
   Sink down in weakness 'neath its
    load?
Give up and say you can't endure it,
   Too rough, too toilsome is the road?
Ah, no; rejoice you have a cross,
   A cross which none but you may
    bear;
Why, you are rich, when by that cross
   You earn your right a crown to
    wear.
Give up while there is still in heaven
   A God who notes the sparrow's fall?
Give up when He so longs to help you,
   But only wants to hear you call?
He clothes the lilies, feeds the birds;
   Would He to you, then, pay less
    heed?
Look up to Him with prayerful heart,
   He will supply your every need.

—*Grace B. Renfrow*

"Lord, Let Us Stand"

Lord, let us stand in the thick of the fight,
    Let us bear what we must without whining;
Grant us the vision to do what is right,
    Though a thousand false beacons are
      shining.
Let us be true as the steel of a blade.
    Make us bigger than skilled and clever;
    Teach us to cling to our best, unafraid,
    And hearken to false gospels, never.
Let us be grave when the burden is great,
    Faithful when wounded by sorrow;
Teach us, when troubled, with patience to
    wait
The better and brighter tomorrow.
Spare us from hatred and envy and shame.
    Open our eyes to life's beauty;
Let not the glitter of fortune or fame
    Blind us to what is our duty.
Let us be true to the right to the end,
    Let us stand to our task without whining;
Let us be right, as a man, as a friend,
    Though a thousand false beacons are
      shining.

—Author unknown

Be Strong for Battle

BE STRONG!
We are not here to play, to dream, to drift.
We have hard work to do, and loads to lift.
Shun not the struggle; face it. 'Tis God's gift.

BE STRONG!
Say not the days are evil—Who's to blame!
And fold the hand and acquiesce—O
    shame!
Stand up, speak out, and gravely, in God's
    name.

BE STRONG!
It matters not how deep entrenched the
    wrong,
How hard the battle goes, the day, how long,
Faint not, fight on! Tomorrow comes the
    song.

—Maltbie D. Babcock

See It Through

When you're up against a trouble,
    Meet it squarely, face to face;
Lift your chin and set your shoulders,
    Plant your feet and take a brace.
When it's vain to try to dodge it,
    Do the best that you can do;
You may fail, but you may conquer,
    See it through!

Black may be the clouds about you
    And your future may seem grim,
But don't let your nerve desert you;
    Keep yourself in fighting trim.
If the worst is bound to happen,
    Spite of all that you can do,
Running from it will not save you,
    See it through!

Even hope may seem but futile,
    When with troubles you're beset,
But remember you are facing
    Just what other men have met.
You may fail, but fail still fighting;
    Don't give up, whate'er you do;
Eyes front, head high to the finish.
    See it through!

—Edgar A. Guest

Don't Give Up

Twixt failure and success
    The point's so fine,
Men sometimes know not when
    They touch the line.
Just when the pearl was waiting
    One more plunge,
How many a struggler has
    Thrown up the sponge.
Then take his honey
    From the bitterest cup:
There is no failure
    Save in giving up!

—Author unknown

IF

(with apologies to Kipling)

If you can trust when everyone about you
  Is doubting Him, proclaiming Him untrue;
If you can hope in Christ, tho' all forsake you
  And say 'tis not the thing to you to do;
If you can wait on God, nor wish to hurry,
  Or, being greatly used, keep humble still;
Or if you're tested, still refuse to worry,
  And so remain within His sovereign will;
If you can say 'tis well, when sorrow greets you,
  And death has taken those you hold most dear;
If you can smile when adverse trials meet you,
  And be content e'en tho' your lot be drear;
If you can be reviled and never murmur,
  Or being tempted, not give way to sin;
If you can fight for right and stand the firmer,
  Or lose the battle when you ought to win.
And go to tell the story of the Savior
  To souls in darkness o'er the desert dust;
If you can pray when Satan's darts are strongest,
  And take the road of faith instead of sight;
Or walk with God, e'en tho' His way be longest,
  And swerve not to the left nor to the right;
If you desire Himself alone to fill you,
  For Him alone you care to live and be;
Then 'tis not you, but CHRIST Who dwelleth in
  you,
  And that, O child of God, is victory!

—*Grace Reynolds*

Hanging On

It's hanging on that does it,
  When others faint and tire;
To keep a-going onward,
  To climb a little higher.
Some folks are always weary.
  They say it can't be done,
While others keep on trying,
  And find in Work their fun.

It's hanging on that does it;
  It takes a lot of grit;
But the more of that you're
  spending,
  The more you have of it.
And soon it gets as easy
  As singing an old, old song.
Forget that you are plugging,
  And days just slide along.

It's hanging on that does it;
  Folks see you standing pat,
They say you are a wonder,
  A genius, and all of that.
You laugh at their exclaiming
  Superior brain or brawn,
And know that all the difference
  Is just in hanging on.

—*R. Walter Wright*

If you *think* you are *beaten,* you *are;*
  If you *think* you dare not, you don't.
If you'd like to win, but think you can't,
  It's almost a cinch you won't.
If you think you think you'll lose, you're lost,
  For out in the world we find
Success *begins* with a fellow's *will;*
  It's all in the state of mind.
Life's battles don't always go
  To the stronger or faster man;
But soon or late the man who wins
  Is the one who *thinks* he can.

—*Walter Wintle*

De da'kest hour, dey allus say,
  Is jes' befo' de dawn.
But it's moughty ha'd a-waitin'
  When do night goes frownin' on;
An' it's moughty ha'd a-hopin'
  W'en de clouds is big and black,
An' all de t'ings you's waited fo'
  Has failed, or gone to wrack—
But jes' keep on a-joggin
  Wid a little bit o' song,
De mo'n is allus brightah
  W'en de night's bin long.

—*Paul Lawrence Dunbar*

Don't Quit

When things go wrong, as they some-
   times will,
When the road you're trudging seems all
   uphill,
When funds are low and debts are high,
And you want to smile, but you have to
   sigh,
When care is pressing you down a bit,
Rest if you must, but don't you quit.
Life is queer with its twists and turns,
As everyone of us sometimes learns;
And many a failure turns about,
When he might have won had he stuck it
   out.
Don't give up, though the pace seems
   slow—
You may succeed with another blow.
Often the goal is nearer than
It seems to a faint and faltering man.
Often the struggler has given up,
When he might have captured the victor's
   cup,
And learned too late, when the night
   slipped down
How close he was to the golden crown.
Success is failure turned inside out—
The silver tint of the clouds of doubt.
And you never can tell how close you are;
It may be near when it seems afar.
So stick to the light when you're hardest
   hit—
It's when things seem worst that you
   mustn't quit.

—*Author unknown*

Marching On

Before the world we're on parade
   And march along our way;
Remember too before our Lord
   Each day's Inspection Day.
It makes you stand up straighter too,
   And hold yourself just so
To keep in mind we're being watched
   And checked on by the foe.

The heroes of the ages past
   Who left their mark on high,
Now watch us go marching by.
And angels looking down above
   Upon the host arrayed
Rejoice with those that love the Lord
   And march in this parade.

Let heads be high and shoulders
      straight,
   It's surely more than pride,
For we are filling now the gaps
   Where once the martyrs died.
And we were chosen just as they;
   Our orders from on high.
Their battle and their cause is ours
   Our destiny the sky.

Let's tune our ears to hear the voice
   Our Captain speaks on high,
And mind the way our Captain went
   When He came here to die.
Forsaking all that holds us back
   And reaching on before,
We press toward that Promised Land
   And to that Golden Shore.

—*Roland H. DaVall*

"And let us not be weary
in well doing: for
in due season we shall
reap, if we faint not."
—Galatians 6:9

155

The Mystic Path

There's a path filled with mystery,
With strange wonders it is rife—
It's the trail all mortals travel,
It's the pilgrimage of Life.

We do not choose to tread this path,
But when once on it we've entered,
We find the journey so alluring
That our heart on it is centered.

Tho' this path is rough and rugged,
Clad with many thorns and briars,
Yet the flowers on the byways
Inspire our tread with fond desires.

There's winding and there's climbing
O'er the slopes of many a hill;
Bruised and sore we'd fain grow weary
But for scenes and sounds that thrill.

All the sorrows and the heartaches
We experience on the way
Cannot conceal or overshadow
All the joys we find each day.

There's a phantom, mystic something
Just before us as we tread
That is beckoning us onward
To the prize that's just ahead.

We must not pause or halt our steps;
To look backward would be vain;
To reflect upon our hardships
Would serve only to detain.

Let us therefore not grow weary
From the heartaches that we meet,
But with vig'rous tread, and steady,
March on our journey to complete.

For this mystic path of Life,
Shrouded by the mists of time,
Offers every weary pilgrim
Deepest griefs and joys sublime.

Hark! There'll be a glad tomorrow
When our pilgrimage shall end;
There'll be a crowning of the faithful
By our Savior, Lord, and Friend.

So, be strong, my fellow pilgrim,
Though your heartaches here be sore.
Soon the mystic path will lead you
Up to Heaven's blessed door!

—Dale Crowley

Stay Firm

Stay firm—
He has not failed thee,
    In all the past
And will He go and leave thee
    To sink at last?
Nay, He said He will hide thee
    Beneath His wing;
And sweetly there in safety
    Thou mayest sing.
"The Lord is Thy Keeper."
    Ps. 121:5

If there be one thing upon earth that mankind loves and admires better than another, it is a grave man—a man who dares look the devil in the face and tell him he is the devil.

—James A. Garfield

Because a fellow has failed once or twice, or a dozen times, you don't want to set him down as a failure till he's dead or loses his courage—that's the same thing.

—George Horace

That's the Pay-Off!

You may be able to load the bases every
    inning—
BUT—If you don't cross home plate,
    you don't score a run.
                THAT'S THE PAY-OFF.

You may have the best golf clubs,
    clothes, and stance—
BUT—If you can't sink your shots, you
    won't get the prize.
                THAT'S THE PAY-OFF.

You may have the best car and win all
    the trial heats—
BUT—If your motor fails in the big
    race, you don't get the purse.
                THAT'S THE PAY-OFF.

You may make twice as many first
    downs as your opponent
BUT—If you can't cross the goal line,
    you don't get a point.
You may have an excellent education—
You may have a host of friends—
You may have a top paying job—
You may have a good reputation—
You may give much to charity—
You may have perfect health—
BUT—
If you haven't settled your account with
    God—
If you haven't accept Jesus Christ as
    God's Son—
If you haven't asked Him to forgive
    your sins—
You won't win the prize!
You won't have real peace!
You won't get to heaven!
What is a man profited if he gain the
    whole world and lose his own soul?
                —Matthew 16:26

Believe on the Lord Jesus Christ, and
thou shalt be saved. —Acts 16:31
            —Faith, Prayer, Tract League

GROWTH

For every hill I've had to climb,
    For every stone that bruised my
        feet,
For all the blood and sweat and
        grime,
    For blinding storms and burning
        heat,
My heart sings but a grateful song—
    These were the things that made
        me strong!
For all the heartaches and the tears,
    For all the anguish and the pain,
For gloomy days and fruitless years,
    And for the hopes that lived in
        vain,
I do give thanks, for now I know
    These were the things that helped
        me grow!
'Tis not the softer things of life
    Which stimulate man's will to
        strive;
But bleak adversity and strife
    Do most to keep man's will alive.
O'er rose-strewn paths the weak-
    lings creep,
    But brave hearts dare to climb the
    steep.
                —Author unknown

    The highest type of heroism is
not the courage and nerve of the warrior, facing the foe, but the courage to
face the daily issues of life, opposing
wrong and upholding right.
                —Roswell C. Long

Value of Time . . .

My Times Are in Thy Hands

I take my pilgrim staff anew,
Life's path, untrodden, to pursue,
Thy guiding eye, Lord, I view;
    My times are in Thy hand.

Throughout the year, my heavenly
    Friend,
On Thy blest guidance I depend;
From its commencement to its end
    My times are in Thy hand.

Should comfort, health, and peace be
    mine,
Should hours of gladness on me shine,
Then let me trace Thy love divine;
    My times are in Thy hand.

But shouldst Thou visit me again
With languor, sorrow, sickness, pain,
Still let this thought my hope sustain,
    My times are in thy hand.

Should those this year be called away
Who lent to life its brightest ray,
Teach me in that dark hour to say,
    My times are in Thy hand.

A few more days, a few more years—
Oh, then a bright reverse appears,
Then I shall no more say with tears,
    My times are in Thy hand.

"I must work the works of him that sent me while it is day, for the night cometh when no man can work" (John 9:4).

MY TIME

Generations have come and gone,
    Drank the cup of life, then fled!
Made their Eternal Record,
    Then joined the army of the dead!

They're gone! Oh frightful words!
    Where, where have they quietly
        fled?
Gone from our sight and memory,
    The millions of forgotten dead!

Each chased his favorite phantom,
    In his own respective age;
Or, in the light of eternity,
    Carefully wrote life's sacred page.

TIME is the momentous hour,
    When Eternal character is formed;
When we divest ourselves of hope,
    Or, like victors, are adorned.

Ages have rolled their rusty centuries
    Along through the vista of Time,
'Till now has come the AWFUL HOUR,
    When it's your turn to live and mine!

MY TIME! O dreadful thought!
    My time to act! My moment to live!
Great God, in this stupendous hour,
    Infinite inspiration give!

Shall I, in this fearful hour,
    Break sin's fantastic spell?
Or, with the reckless millions,
    Will I BARTER Heaven for Hell?

On the volition of my will,
    I can reach the realms of light;
Or, I can forge infernal chains
    To bind me in Eternal Night!

Wasted Hours

O how many hours I've wasted
Of the day God gave to me—
And I wonder when I face Him
What my answer then shall be?

In the bright and golden morning
There was work I should have done:
"A cup of water" to be given—
A hand to help some fallen one.

I should through all the morning hours
Have toiled on with a song;
With Jesus close, the way's not hard.
He makes the weak ones strong.

In the bright and sunny noontime
Should I have slumbered on in ease?
Jesus said, "To Me you did it
As you did it unto these."

Now I'm facing toward the sunset
And my heart aches so with pain
As I think of hours I've wasted,
Hours that ne'er will come again.

O, my Savior dear, forgive me.
I've not meant to grieve thee so,
And I promise I will serve Thee
As I through the evening go.

All these twilight hours I'll labor,
Never murmur nor complain,
If I may win, and bring to Thee,
A few sheaves of golden grain.

*"Whereas ye know not what shall
be on the morrow? For what is
your life? It is even a vapor,
that appeareth for a little time,
and then vanisheth away"
(James 4:14).*

A Day So Passeth

(*Translated from the Swedish: Sion's
Basun No. 591*)

A day so passeth from our time
    And cometh nevermore.
And yet a night with peace divine
    The earth doth settle o'er.

But as Thou wast, Thou wilt remain,
    O Lord, so full of grace.
And Thou hast fixed within Thy plan
    Our nights as well as days.

Secure I then shall rest in Thee
    When night hath from us gone;
And praises give Thee joyfully
    When day again doth dawn.

But if still death doth summon me
    E'er night hath hastened by,
Assured, I am that Thine I'll be
    If I should live or die.

—*Translated by J. Paul Bennett*

Time for Everything

Take time to work—
    it is the price of success.
Take time to think—
    it is the source of power.
Take time to play—
    it is the secret of perpetual youth.
Take time to read—
    it is the fountain of wisdom.
Take time to be friendly—
    it is the road to happiness.
Take time to dream—
    it is hitching your wagon to a star.
Take time to love and be loved—
    it is the privilege of us all.
Take time to look around—
    it is too short a day to be selfish.
Take time to laugh—
    it is the music of the soul.

—*Old English Prayer*

No Time for God?

No time for God?

What fools we are to clutter up
Our lives with common things
And leave without Heart's gate
The Lord of life, and life itself—

No time for God?

As soon to say, no time
To eat or sleep or live or die.
Take time for God
Or you shall dwarf your soul
And then the angel death
Comes knocking at our door,
A poor misshapen thing you'll be
To step into eternity.

No time for God?

That day when sickness comes
Or troubles find you out
And you cry out for God,
Will He have time for you?

No time for God?

The Clock of Life

The clock of life is wound but once,
    And no man has the power
To tell just where the hands will stop,
    At late or early hour!
To lose one's wealth is sad indeed;
    To lose one's health is more;
To lose one's soul is such a loss
    As no man can restore!
So live, love, and pray,
    And toil with a will:
Place no faith in tomorrow—
    For "the clock" may then be still!
                    —*Author unknown*

It is better to live rich, than to die rich.
                    —*Samuel Johnson*

When I Have Time

When I have time so many things I'll do
To make life happier and more fair
For those whose lives are crowded now with
    care;
I'll help to lift them from their low despair
        When I have time.

When I have time, the friend I love so well
Shall know no more these weary, toiling
    days;
I'll lead her feet in pleasant paths always
And cheer her heart with words of sweetest
    praise,
        When I have time.

When you have time! The friend you hold so
    dear
May be beyond the reach of all your sweet
    intent;
May never know that you so kindly meant
To fill her life with sweet content
        When you had time.

Now is the time! Ah, friend, no longer wait
To scatter living smiles and words of cheer
To those around whose lives are now so
    drear;
They may not need you in the coming year—
        Now is the time!

Three Days

So much to do; so little done!
Ah! yesternight I saw the sun
Sink beamless down the vaulted gray—
The ghastly ghost of yesterday.

So little done; so much to do!
Each morning breaks on conflicts new;
But eager, brave, I'll join the fray,
And fight the battle of today.

So much to do; so little done!
But when it's o'er—the victory won—
O then, my soul, this strife and sorrow
Will end in that great, glad tomorrow
                    —*James Roberts Gilmore*

What Have We Done Today?

We shall do so much in the years to come,
  But what have we done today?
We shall give our gold in a princely sum,
  But what did we give today?
We shall lift the heart and dry the tear.
We shall plant a hope in the place of fear,
We shall speak the words of love and cheer,
  But what did we speak today?

We shall be so kind in the afterwhile,
  But what have we been today?
We shall bring each lonely life a smile,
  But what have we brought today?
We shall give to truth a grander birth,
And to steadfast faith a deeper worth.
We shall feed the hungering souls of earth,
  But whom have we fed today?

We shall reap such joys in the by and by,
  But what have we sown today?
We shall build us mansions in the sky,
  But what have we built today?
'Tis sweet in idle dreams to bask,
But here and now do we do our task?
Yes, this is the thing our souls must ask,
  "What have we done today?"

          —*Nixon Waterman*

Matter is based on units. Time has for its basic foundation the second. The spirit has for its foundation the dividing of a crust of bread, the administering of a cup of water, or the widow's mite. A kind word spoken in the time of need, a smile, the care of a little child, sometimes means more than great deeds. It is not for us to judge which actions are worthwhile and which do the most toward establishing the Kingdom in God's sight. "The first shall be last, and the last shall be first."

        —Dorothea S. Kopplin, in
          Something To Live By

A PSALM OF LIFE

Tell me not in mournful numbers,
  "Life is but an empty dream!"
For the soul is dead that slumbers,
  And things are not what they seem.

Life is real! Life is earnest!
  And the grave is not its goal;
"Dust thou art, to dust returnest,"
  Was not spoken of the soul.

Not enjoyment and not sorrow,
  Is our destined end or way;
But to act, that each tomorrow
  Find us farther than today.

Art is long, and time is fleeting,
  And our hearts, though stout and brave,
Still, like muffled drums are beating
  Funeral marches to the grave.

In the world's broad field of battle,
  In the bivouac of life,
Be not like dumb, driven cattle!
  Be a hero in the strife!

Trust no future, howe'er pleasant!
  Let the dead past bury its dead!
Act, act in the living present!
  Heart within and God o'erhead!

Lives of great men all remind us
  We can make our lives sublime.
And, departing, leave behind us
  Footprints in the sands of time.

Footprints, that perhaps another,
  Sailing o'er life's solemn main,
A forlorn and shipwrecked brother,
  Seeing, shall take heart again.

Let us, then, be up and doing,
  With a heart for any fate;
Still achieving, still pursuing,
  Learn to labor and to wait.

        —*Henry W. Longfellow*

Live As You Pray

I knelt to pray when day was done,
And prayed: "O Lord, bless everyone;
Lift from each saddened heart the pain,
And let the sick be well again."

And when I woke another day
And carelessly went on my way,
The whole day long I did not try
To wipe a tear from any eye;
I did not try to share the load
Of any brother on the road;
I did not even go to see
The sick man just next door to me.

Yet once again when day was done,
I prayed: "O Lord, bless everyone."

But as I prayed, into my ear
There came a voice that whispered clear:
"Pause, hypocrite, before you pray;
Whom have you tried to bless today?
God's sweetest blessings always go
By hands that serve Him here below."

And then I hid my face and cried,
"Forgive me, God, for I have lied;
Let me but live another day
And I will live the way I pray."

—*Author unknown*

How Did You Spend the Day?

Did you waste the day or lose it?
Was it well or poorly spent?
Did you leave a trail of kindness
Or a scar of discontent?
As you close your eyes in slumber,
Do you think God would say,
"You have earned one more tomorrow"
By the good you did today?

—*Author unknown*

Moment By Moment

Time slips away
  It's never held,
  It's never caught,
  It's never kept,
  It never ceases,
  It only vanishes
    Moment by moment.

Time slips away
  Memories are formed,
  Memories are written,
  Memories to recall,
  Memories to cherish
    Moment by moment.

Time slips away
  Wasted opportunities,
  Thoughtless living,
  Searching and longing
    Moment by moment.

Time slips away
  Inevitable path—
  Returning to dust
    Moment by moment.

Time slips away
  Hearing eternity
    Moment by moment.

An account is given, for
  Time that slipped away
    Moment by moment.

—*Beth Maryanne*

Success and Rewards . . .

God's Hall of Fame

Your name may not appear down here
  In this world's Hall of Fame;
In fact, you may be so unknown
  That no one knows your name.
The Oscars here may pass you by,
  And neon lights of blue;
But if you love and serve the Lord,
  Then, I have news for you!

This Hall of Fame is only good
  As long as time shall be;
But keep in mind, God's Hall of Fame
  Is for Eternity!
To have your name inscribed up there
  Is greater, yes, by far,
Than all the Halls of Fame down here,
  And every man-made star.

This crowd on earth, they soon forget
  The heroes of the past,
They cheer like mad until you fall,
  And that's how long you last!
But God, He never does forget,
  And in His Hall of Fame,
By just believing in His Son,
  Inscribed you'll find your name.

I tell you, friend, I wouldn't trade
  My name, however small,
That's written there beyond the stars
  In that celestial Hall
For every famous name on earth
  Or glory that they share:
I'd rather be an unknown here,
  And have my name up there!

—Walt Huntley

At the Top

Whenever you see someone up at the
  top,
  Don't imagine he got there by luck.
For back of his glory lies many a story
  Of battle and struggle and pluck.
He may seem to be taking things easy
  today
  And dodging the trials which irk,
But the years of his past, from the first
  to the last,
  Were a constant succession of work.

Whenever you see someone crowned by
  success,
  Don't fancy he won it by chance;
Though he's walking today on an easier
  way,
  And you cannot behold with a glance
The scars of his battle, just to keep this
  in mind—
  Life's laurels don't go to the shirk.
And if you but knew his life history
  through,
  You'd know that he once had to
  work.

Success doesn't come to the indolent
  hand,
  With busy men life is concerned;
Be the man who he may, he will find on
  the way
  That its prizes all have to be earned.
So whenever you gaze on a leader of
  men,
  Up on top where the glory is fair,
You can know with his luck there were
  courage and pluck—
  You can bet that he worked to get
  there.

—Edgar A. Guest

His Monument

He built a house, time laid it in the dust;
  He wrote a book, its title now forgot;
  He ruled a city, but his name is not
On any tablet graven, or where rust
Can gather from disuse, or marble bust.

He took a child from out a wretched cot;
Who on the State dishonor might have
    brought;
  And reared him in the Christian's hope
    and trust.
The boy, to manhood grown, became a light
  To many souls and preached to human
    need
The wondrous love of the Omnipotent.
The work has multiplied like stars at night
  When darkness deepens; every noble
    deed
Lasts longer than a granite monument.

             —*Sarah Knowles Bolton*

❧ ❧ ❧ ❧ ❧

GOD WANTS A MAN—

Courageous like Joshua.
Self-reliant like Nehemiah.
Full of faith like Abraham.
Persevering like Jacob.
Decisive like Moses.
Above reproach like Daniel.
Long suffering like Paul.
Prayerful like Elijah.
Master of passions like Joseph.
Bold like Peter and John.
Godlike like Enoch.

What It Takes

    On a card in a church in the city
of London is to be found the follow-
ing list of qualifications said to be
needed by a pastor:
  The strength of an ox.
  The tenacity of a bulldog.
  The daring of a lion.
  The patience of a donkey.
  The industry of a beaver.
  The versatility of a chameleon.
  The vision of an eagle.
  The meekness of a lamb.
  The hide of a rhinoceros.
  The disposition of an angel.
  The resignation of an incurable.
  The loyalty of an apostle.
  The heroism of a martyr.
  The faithfulness of a prophet.
  The tenderness of a shepherd.
  The fervency of an evangelist.
  The devotion of a mother.

Brace Up!

Get out of the rut and into the work—
  There's always hope for the man who will.
You'll be left behind if you sulk and shirk,
  This world of ours isn't standing still.

Don't say, "I can't!" when you haven't tried;
  At least be honest and say, "I won't!"
Don't admit defeat ere you've caught your
    stride;
  There's always room for another—in front.

When things look bluest, brace up and laugh;
  The sky is happiest when it's blue.
Things aren't as bad as they look, by half;
  Surely, half a trouble can't trouble YOU.
Brace up! Tomorrow's another day.

  With another chance for the heart that's
    stout.
The world will think things have gone YOUR
    way,
  Till YOU admit that you're down and out.

             —*Charles R. Barrett*

Rise Above the Circumstances

Old Jim had been a faithful horse,
  But he was growing old.
So Uncle Lem made up his mind:
  The horse should not be sold.

But turned out in the pasture land
  To roam and feed at will,
Or rest beneath the shady trees,
  Down by the waters still.

Lem loved his faithful servant Jim,
  And watched him day by day.
And when he whistled to the horse,
  Jim gave an answering neigh.

One day the horse had disappeared,
  So Lem went out to see
What had become of faithful Jim—
  Where could the creature be?

Lem thought of an abandoned well
  Which had uncovered been;
He hurried down the path to see.
  Yes, Jim had fallen in!

If he should try to pull him out
  A leg might broken be;
So he would go and get his gun
  And end Jim's misery.

Lem brought the gun but couldn't bear
  To shoot old faithful Jim.
So brought a shovel and a pick
  With which to bury him.

Lem took a shovel full of dirt
  And rolled it in the well.
It slid down on the horse's back
  And to the bottom fell.

As fast as every load was sent,
  The horse would stamp it down;
And as they both thus worked away,
  At last the well was gone!

Out jumped the horse, all whole and
    sound;
  Kicked up his heels and ran.
Let's get from out this simple tale
  A moral, if we can.

When people try to crush us down
  And cover us with dirt,
Let's stamp it underneath our feet
  And never let it hurt.

Let's be like Jim and rise above
  The troubles that beset.
If we are on the side of right,
  We'll gain the victory yet.

Money Will Buy

A bed but not sleep.
Books but not brains.
Food but not appetite.
Finery but not beauty.
A house but not a home.
Medicine but not health.
Luxuries but not culture.
Amusements but not happiness.
A crucifix but not a Savior.
A church but not a heaven.

But what you cannot buy you can
  receive as a gift.
*"For the wages of sin is death; but the
gift of God is eternal life through Jesus
Christ our Lord" (Romans 6:23).*

Achieving Success

He has achieved success who has lived well, laughed often, and loved much; who has gained the respect of intelligent men and the love of little children; who has filled his niche and accomplished his task; who has left the world better than he found it, whether by an improved poppy, a perfect poem, or a rescued soul; who has never lacked appreciation of earth's beauty, or failed to express it; who has always looked for the best in others and given the best he had; whose life was an inspiration, his memory a benediction.

—*Bessie A. Stanley*

SUCCESS

Success is being friendly when another
    needs a friend;
It's in the cheery words you speak, not
    in the coins you lend.
Success is not alone in skill and deeds of
    daring great;
It's in the roses that you plant beside
    your garden gate.
Success is in the way you walk the paths
    of life each day;
It's in the little things you do and in the
    things you say.
Success is in the glad hello you give
    your fellow man;
It's in the laughter of your home and all
    the joys you plan.
Success is not in getting rich or rising
    high to fame;
It's not alone in winning goals which all
    men hope to claim.
It's in the man you are each day, through
    happiness or care;
It's in the happy words you speak and in
    the smile you wear.
Success is being big of heart and clean
    and broad of mind;
It's being faithful to your friends, and to
    the stranger kind.
It's in the children whom you love, and
    all they learn from you—
Success depends on character and every-
    thing you do.

REWARDS

Who does God's work will get God's
    pay;
No human hand God's hand can stay.
He does not pay as others pay,
But God's high wisdom knows a way;
And this is sure, let come what may:
Who does God's work will get God's
    pay!

Garden of Life

Do you know that each life is a garden,
And we sow as the days go by
Seeds, for a future harvest
To be gathered with smiles or a sigh?

Then what of the soil of our garden?
Is it fertile, or stony and old?
Will it bring forth the thorn and the thistle,
Or "the grain of a thousand fold"?

Have we planted the rose of "forgive-
    ness,"
And the lily of purest white
That sends forth its sweetest fragrance
Through the long, dark hours of the
    night?

Have we planted that rare little blossom
That blooms when the days are hot;
Ever echoing the voice of its Master,
"Dear friends, forget Me not?"

Have we planted much in our gardens
From His wonderful Book of Life?
Have we sown the seeds of "obedience,"
His assurance of help through the strife?

Have we also sown the seeds of "truth"?
Have we done the best that we can
To'ard sowing that marvelous seed of
    "love,"
Love for both God and man?

You know that in this world's sowing
'Tis true, and will ever be,
There will come into every garden
Some grief . . . from Gethsemane.

But after the grief in the garden
The harvest we'd hoped to see
Will blossom in all its beauty,
Through the glory of Calvary.

Then know that your life is a garden,
And you sow as the days go by
Seeds . . . for a future harvest,
To be gathered with smiles, or a sigh.

—Harriette Flora Gray

The Better Way

It is better to lose with a conscience clean
  Than win with a trick unfair;
It is better to fail and to know you've been,
  Whatever the prize was, square,
Than to claim the joy of a far-off goal
  And the cheers of the standers by,
Than to know down deep in your inmost soul
  A cheat you must live and die.

Who wins by tricks may take the prize,
  And at first he may think it sweet.
But many a day in the future lies
  When he'll wish he had met defeat.
For the man who lost shall be glad at heart
  And walk with his head up high;
While his conqueror knows he must play the
  part
Of a cheat and a living lie.

The prize seems fair when the fight is on.
  But save it is truly won
You will hate the things when the crowds are
  gone.
  For it stands for a false deed done.
And it's better you never should reach your
  goal
  Than ever success to buy
At the price of knowing deep down in your
  soul
  That your glory is all a lie.

Sowing and Reaping

In the name of God advancing,
  Sow thy seed at morning light;
Cheerily the furrows turning,
  Labor on with all thy might.

Look not to the far-off future,
  Do the work which nearest lies;
Sow thou must before thou
  reapest,
  Rest at last is labor's prize.

Standing still is dangerous ever;
  Toil is meant for Christians
  now;
Let there be, when evening
  cometh,
  Honest sweat upon thy brow.

And the Master shall come smil-
  ing,
  At the setting of the sun,
Saying, as He pays thy wages,
  "Good and faithful one, well
  done!"

          —*Author unknown*

Wanted—A Worker

God never goes to the lazy or idle when He needs men
  for His service—
Moses was busy with his flocks at Horeb.
Gideon was busy threshing wheat.
Saul was busy searching for his father's lost sheep.
Elisha was busy plowing with twelve yoke of oxen.
Amos was busy following the flock.
Nehemiah was busy bearing the king's cup.
Peter and Andrew were busy casting a net into the sea.
James and John were busy mending their nets.
Matthew was busy collecting customs.
Saul was busy persecuting the friends of Jesus.

How to Succeed in the Christian Life

1. Rely upon the Holy Spirit. —Eph. 5:18, Acts 1:8
2. Confess Jesus as Lord. —Rom. 10:9, 10; Phil. 2:11
3. Pray without ceasing. —1 Thess. 5:17; Luke 18:8
4. Search the Scriptures daily. —John 5:39; Acts 17:11
5. Attend public worship regularly. -Heb. 10:25; Psa. 50:5
6. Give liberally without grudging. —2 Cor. 9:7; Luke 6:38
7. Give attention to missions. —John 4:35, 36; Matt. 28: 19, 20
8. Forget self—live for others. —Matt. 20:26-28; 1 John 3:16
9. Witness to someone daily. —Acts 2:42, 46, 47
10. Keep growing in grace. —2 Pet. 3:18; Eph. 4:12-16
11. Memorize one verse daily. —Psa. 119:11; Dan. 12:3
12. Carry your Bible or Testament with you always. —Titus 1:9; Phil. 2:16

If I Gained the World

If I gained the world but had not Jesus
Who endured the cross and died for me,
Could then all the world afford a
    refuge,
Whither, in my anguish, I might flee?

Had I wealth and love in fullest measure,
And a name revered both far and near,
Yet no hope beyond, no harbor waiting,
Where my storm-tossed vessel I could
    steer.

Oh, what emptiness—without the
    Savior,
'Mid the sins and sorrows here below!
And eternity, how dark without Him!
Only night and tears and endless woe.

What though I might live without the
    Savior,
When I come to die, how would it be?
Oh, the face the valley's gloom without
    Him,
And without Him, all eternity!

COMPENSATION

For everything you have missed, you have gained something else. —Emerson

Straight through my heart this fact today
By truth's own hand is driven:
God never takes one thing away
But something else is given.

I did not know in earlier years
This law of love and kindness:
But without hope, through bitter tears,
I mourned in sorrow's blindness.

And ever following each regret
For some departed treasure,
My sad, repining heart was met
With unexpected pleasure.

If all were easy, if all were bright,
Where would the cross be—where
    would the fight?
But, in the hard place, God gives to you
Chances for proving what HE can do.
                                    —*Anon.*

The fellow who is willing to
climb upward —ONE STEP
at a time — usually reaches
the TOP of the ladder.

"Little Things" Count . . .

Life's Smaller Tasks

There is never a lost moment in the
Life of a person who really tries.
And no labor is ever wasted if the
Person who does it is wise.

There are times when small tasks go
    unnoticed
By others too busy to praise.
But the little tasks linked to the big ones
Show in oh so many ways.

If we set our hearts toward the highway
And make just one guidepost today,
It will give others a sense of direction
Who are following in our way.

The Lord only expects us to keep busy
And never lament the small deed.
For it could prove a light of inspiration
That somebody else might need.

—Mrs. Daisy Lambright
from Union Signal

Little Things Matter

It's the little things that matter
  As you travel down the road.
And there's joy and great contentment
  In sharing someone's load.
To you it's such a little thing
  And hardly worth the time,
But, brother, it can mean a lot
  With a long hard hill to climb.
Our lives are filled with ups and downs;
  More downs than ups, it seems.
And often times a helping hand
  Brings closer still our dreams.
If there be that which we may do
  To lighten someone's way,
Let's do it, then, and thank the Lord
  This was our lucky day.

—L. Noyes

Your Mission

If you cannot on the ocean
  Sail among the swiftest fleet,
Rocking on the highest billows,
  Laughing at the storms you meet;
You can stand among the sailors,
  Anchored yet within the bay.
You can lend a hand to help them
  As they launch their boats away.

If you are too weak to journey
  Up the mountain, steep and high,
You can stand within the valley
  While the multitudes go by.
You can chant in happy measure
  As they slowly pass along—
Though they may forget the singer,
  They will not forget the song.

If you have not gold and silver
  Ever ready at command;
If you cannot toward the needy
  Reach an ever-helping hand,
You can succor the afflicted,
  O'er the erring you can weep;
With the Savior's true disciples
  You a tireless watch may keep.

Do not, then stand idly waiting
  For some greater work to do;
Fortune is a lazy goddess—
  She will never come to you.
Go toil in the Lord's great vineyard;
  Do not fear to do or dare—
If you want a field of labor
  You can find it anywhere.

—Ellen M. H. Gates

Little deeds of kindness
  Little words of love
Help to make earth happy
  Like the heaven above.

—Julia A. Carney

The BEST That I Can

"I cannot do much," said a little star,
  "To make the dark world bright;
My silver beams cannot struggle far
  Through the folding gloom of night.
But I am a part of God's great plan,
And I'll cheerfully do the best that I can."

"What is the use," said a fleecy cloud,
  "Of these dew-drops that I hold?
They will hardly bend the lily proud,
  Though caught in her cup of gold.
Yet I am a part of God's great plan,
My treasures I'll give as well as I can."

A child went merrily forth to play,
  But a thought, like a silver thread,
Kept winding in and out all day
  Through the happy, busy head:
"Mother said, 'Darling, do all you can,
For you are a part of God's great plan.'"

So she helped a younger child along,
  When the road was rough to the feet;
And she sang from her heart a little song,
  A song that was passing sweet.
And her father, a weary, toil-worn man,
  Said, "I too will do the best that I can."

"For Them, or for Me?"

"Where shall I work today, dear Lord?"
  And my love flowed warm and free.
So the Lord, He pointed to a tiny place
  And said, "You tend that for me."

I answered, "Oh, no, dear Lord.
  Why, no one could ever see,
No matter how well my work was done.
  Not that little place for me."

And the Lord answered—He was not
  harsh—
  He answered me tenderly,
"Tell me, precious child of mine,
  Are you working for them, or for me?
Nazareth was a little place,
  And so was Galilee."

Little Things

Little drops of water,
  Little grains of sand,
Make the mighty ocean
  And the pleasant land.
So the little moments,
  Humble though they be,
Make the mighty ages
  Of eternity.
So our little errors
  Lead the soul away
From the path of virtue
  Far in sin to stray.

The Little Lad

'Twas a little lad that stood in the crowd
With his lunch of fishes and bread.
But that lunch was multiplied many
  times o'er,
And more than five thousand were fed.

It's the little things that we do each day
That count in this life here below.
From the smallest of acorns, we all know,
The mightiest of oaks do grow.

It may be the little talent we have,
If we've only the patience to wait,
That God, with His power, may magnify
And make into something that's great.

So, the little deeds and little thoughts
We should watch with the utmost care,
For the things that we count as little
  "down here"
May be judged as the largest "up there."
          —Cyril W. Wommack

My Little Gift

I am but a tid-bit
Coming to your door.
As regular as any clock
I come each month to store

My tithe in heaven's kingdom
Knowing it will be
Help for someone laboring
In life's troubled sea.

The journey will be lighter
Knowing I have shared
Of my blessings, God will know
That someone truly cared.

—Minerva Schultz

God's Great Treasure

God took a pebble and made a mountain;
    From a drop He made the seas—
Took a petal and made the flowers;
    From a twig He made the trees;
Hung a flaming sun in the heavens,
    Made the valleys and the plains;
Made the grass green, endless prairies;
    Made the fields rich with grain.
He gathered His treasures around Him,
    And gazed at His wonders unfurled;
He showered them richly with blessings—
    Said, Lo, I've created a world.

—Edith Frazier

God's Minute

I have only just a minute,
Only sixty seconds in it,
Forced upon me, can't refuse it.
Didn't seek it, didn't choose it.
I must suffer if I lose it,
Give account if I abuse it.
Just a tiny little minute
But eternity is in it.

He that is faithful in that which is least, is faithful also in much; and he that is unjust in the least is unjust also in much (Luke 16:10).

Who hath despised the day of small things? (Zech. 4:10).

The Tiny Acorn

"Little by little," an acorn said,
    As it slowly sank in its mossy bed;
"I am slowly growing every day,
    Hidden deep in the earth away."
Little by little each day it grew;
    Little by little it sipped the dew;
Downward it sent out a thread-like root;
    Up in the air sprung a tiny shoot.
Day after day, and year after year,
    Little by little the leaves appear;
And the slender branches spread far and
    wide,
    Till the mighty oak is the forest's
    pride.

—Anonymous

The broomcorn broom in the American kitchen owes its origin to Benjamin Franklin.

A friend once sent him a small whisk broom from India. Franklin discovered a few seeds in some of the straws and planted them. From the tiny crop that resulted, he took seeds and distributed them among several friends in different parts of the country.

Thus broomcorn was grown, and a healthy industry resulted. Isn't that like life itself? We can never measure what a kind act, a thoughtful word, or a gesture of sympathy will do in this fertile world. God made us all to be planters.

171

Thank God for Little Things

Thank you, God, for little things that
    often come our way,
The things we take for granted but don't
    mention when we pray.
The unexpected courtesy, the thoughtful,
    kindly deed,
A hand reached out to help us in the time
    of sudden need—
Oh, make us more aware, dear God, of
    little daily graces
That come to us with "sweet surprise"
    from never-dreamed-of places.

        —Helen Steiner Rice

YOUR PLACE

Is your place a small place?
    Tend it with care—
He set you there.
Is your place a large place?
    Guard it with care—
He set you there.
Whate'er our place, it is
    Not yours alone, but His
Who set you there.

        —John Oxenham

There's never a rose in all the world
    But makes some green spray sweeter;
There's never a wind in all the sky
    But makes some bird wing fleeter;
There's never a star but brings to heaven
    Some silver radiance tender;
And never a rosy cloud but helps
    To crown the sunset splendor;
No robin but may thrill some heart,
    His dawn like gladness voicing;
God gives to all some small sweet way
    To set the world rejoicing.

        —Anonymous

God's Discipline . . .

Affliction, Chastisement, Suffering

When Thou Passest Through the Waters

Is there any heart discouraged
   As it journeys on its way!
Does there seem to be more darkness
   Than there is of sunny days?

Oh, it's hard to learn the lesson
   As we pass beneath the rod,
That the sunshine and the shadow
   Serve alike the will of God.

But there comes a world of promise
   Like the promise of the bow—
That however deep the waters,
   They shall never overflow.

When the flesh is worn and weary,
   And the spirit is depressed,
And temptations sweep upon it, like
   A storm on ocean's breast,

There's a haven ever open
   For the tempest-driven bird;
There's a shelter for the tempted
   In the promise of the Word.

For the standard of the Spirit
   Shall be raised against the foe,
And however deep the waters,
   They shall never overflow.

When a sorrow comes upon you,
   That no other soul can share,
And the burden seems too heavy
   For the human heart to bear,

There is one whose grace can comfort
   If you'll give Him an abode;
There's a burden-bearer ready
   If you'll trust Him with your load.

For the precious promise reaches
   To the depth of human woe,
That however deep the waters,
   They shall never overflow.

When the sands of life are ebbing
   And I know that death is near,
When I'm passing through the valley,
   And the way seems dark and drear;

I will reach my hand to Jesus,
   In His bosom I shall hide,
And 'twill only be a moment
   Till I reach the other side.

It is then the fullest meaning
   Of the promise I shall know:
"When thou passest through the waters,
   They shall never overflow."

A Christian man's life is lain in the loom of time, to a pattern which he does not see, *but God does;* and his heart is in the shuttle. On one side of the loom is sorrow, and on the other is joy; and the shuttle, struck alternately by each, flies back and forth carrying the thread, which is white or black as the pattern needs; and in the end, when God shall lift up the finished garment, and all its changing hues shall glance out, it will then appear that the dark and deep colors were as needful to beauty as the bright and high ones.

—Henry Ward Beecher

Gladness Out of Affliction

Can gladness come out of affliction?
Can joy out of sorrow be born?
  And after a night of bereavement,
  Can happiness come in the morning?
God's presence is found in affliction,
He's ready to answer the cry;
To banish the fears and the doubtings
With "Be of good cheer, it is I."

His love for His child is unchanging,
Although it seems veiled in a cloud.
'Tis only with purpose of blessing
Affliction is ever allowed.

Continue to trust through the trial,
To murmur not, nor be dismayed.
The Lord will not leave nor forsake
  thee,
He comforts with, "Be not afraid!"

God's instrument oft is affliction,
For moulding and training His own;
But all through the trial and testing
His love and His mercy are shown.

Affliction is "but for a moment,"
But after its purpose is wrought,
The blessing will go on forever,
The fruit that the trial has brought.

God holdeth the key of affliction.
The end from beginning is known.
'Tis not that He willingly sends it,
But in faithfulness unto His own.

Yes, gladness can come through
  affliction,
And joy out of sorrow is born.
The night may be heavy with
  weeping,
But happiness comes in the morn.

"Many are the afflictions of the righteous; but the Lord delivereth him out of them all" (Psalm 34:19).

Emptied and Filled

One by one He took them from me,
  All the things I valued most;
Until I was empty handed
  Every glittering toy was lost.

And I walked earth's lonely highways
  In my rags and poverty;
Till I heard His voice entreating,
  "Lift your empty hands to me."

Empty hands I lifted heavenward
  And He filled them with a store
Of His own transcendent riches
  Till my hands could hold no more.

And at last I comprehended,
  With my mind so slow and dull,
That God could not pour His riches
  Into hands already full.

A Crushed Rose

O, beautiful rose, please tell me,
  For I would like to know
Why I must crush your petals
  That the sweet perfume may flow.
O life that is clothed in beauty,
  Perhaps like that wonderful rose
You will need to be crushed by suffering
  If the radiance of your life must glow.
A life that is crushed by sorrow
  Can feel for another's grief,
And send out that fragrance of love
  That will bring some heart relief.
O, do not repine at your testing
  When called to pass under the rod;
For your life the sweeter will be
  If blest by the hand of God.
Then let us rejoice when He sendeth
  Some sorrow or hardship that tries;
And be glad to be crushed as the rose leaf
  That a sweeter perfume may arise.

—Flora Osgood

174

The Potter's Hand

To the Potter's house I went down one day
And watched Him while moulding the vessels of
*   clay.*
And many a wonderful lesson I drew,
As I noted the process the clay went through.

Trampled and broken, downtrodden and rolled,
To render more plastic and fit for the mold.
How like the clay that is human, I thought,
When in heavenly hands to perfection is brought.

For self must be cast as the dust at His feet,
Before it is ready for service made meet.
And pride must be broken, and self-will lost—
All laid on the altar, whatever the cost.

But lo! by and by, a delicate vase
Of wonderful beauty and exquisite grace.
Was it once the vile clay? Ah, yes; yet how
*   strange,*
The Potter has wrought so marvelous a change!

Not a trace of the earth, nor mark of the clay,
The fires of the furnace have burned them away.
*   —M. F. Clarkson*

Now I want you to think that in life troubles will come, which would seem as if they never would pass away. The night and storm look as if they would last forever; but the calm and the morning cannot be stayed; the storm in its very nature is transient. The effort of nature, as that of the human heart, ever is to return to its repose, for God is peace.
                    —George McDonald

And when God, who sees all and wishes to save us, upsets our designs, we stupidly complain against Him, we accuse His providence. We do not comprehend that in punishing us, in overturning our plans and causing us suffering, He is doing all this to deliver us, to open the infinite to us.
                    —Victor Hugo

It Matters to Him

My child, I know thy sorrows,
Thine every grief I share;
I know how thou art tested,
And, what is more—I care.

Think not I am indifferent
To what affecteth thee;
Thy weal and woe are matters
Of deep concern to Me.

But, child, I have a purpose
In all that I allow;
I ask thee then to trust Me,
Though all seems dark just
    now.

How often thou hast asked Me
To purge away thy dross!
But this refining process
Involves for thee—a cross.

There is no other pathway
If thou wouldst really be
Conformed unto the image
Of Him who died for thee.

Thou canst not be like Jesus
Till self is crucified.
And as a daily process
The cross must be applied.

Just as the skillful gard'ner
Applies the pruning knife,
E'en so, I, too, would sever
The worthless from thy life.

I have but one sole object—
That thou shouldst fruitful be—
And is it not thy longing
That I much fruit should see?

Then shrink not from the train-
    ing
I needs must give to thee;
I know just how to make thee
What I would have thee be.

Crushed

A red rose drooping to the ground
With a delicate beauty, touched
By a careless foot at eventide
Was trampled on a crushed.

Christlike, the injured flower returned
No thorn prick for the blow,
But gave instead a rich perfume
To him who laid it low.

Disappointment

"Disappointment—His appointment."
  Change one letter, then I see
That the thwarting of my purpose
  Is God's better choice for me.

His appointment must be blessing,
  Though it may come in disguise.
For the end, from the beginning,
  Open to His vision lies.

"Disappointment—His appointment,"
  Whose? The Lord's who loves me
    best,
Understands and knows me fully,
  Who my faith and love would test.

For, like loving, earthly parents,
  He rejoices when He knows
That His child accepts unquestioned
  All that from His wisdom flows.

"Disappointment—His appointment,"
  "No good things will He withhold."
From denials oft we gather
  Treasures of His love untold.

Well He knows each broken purpose
  Leads to fuller, deeper trust;
And the end of all His dealings
  Proves our God is wise and just.
                —*Edith L. Young*

SORROW

I learn as the years roll onward and leave
  the past behind,
That much I have counted as sorrow, but
  proves that the Lord is kind;
That many a flower I longed for had a
  hidden thorn of pain;
And many a rugged bypath led to fields
  of ripened grain.

The clouds but cover the sunshine, they
  cannot banish the sun,
And the earth shines out the brighter
  when the weary rain is done.
We stand in the deepest shadow to see the
  clearest light,
And often from wrong's own darkness
  comes the very strength of right.

So the heart from the hardest trial gains
  the purest joy of all,
And from lips that have tasted sadness,
  the sweetest songs will fall.
For as peace comes after suffering, and
  love is reward of pain,
So after earth comes heaven, and out of
  our loss the gain!
                —*Maurie G. Clay*

The Reason

If our lives were always easy,
If no troubles came our way,
If each day was filled with gladness,
We might then neglect to pray.
So, when sorrow crowds our pathway,
When our woes seem multiplied,
It may be God's way to draw us
Back again close to His side.

CHASTENING

Chastening breaks us and makes us in order that we may be fit vessels for the Lord's service.

When God wants to drill a man,
　and thrill a man, and skill a man;
When God wants to mold a man
　to play the noblest part;
Watch His methods,
　Watch His ways!
How He hammers him
　and hurts him,
And with mighty blows converts him
Into trial shapes of clay which God
　only understands.
How He uses whom He chooses,
　and
　with every purpose fuses,
By every act induces him to try His
　splendor out—
GOD KNOWS WHAT HE'S ABOUT!

Friendly Obstacles

For every hill I've had to climb
　Or every stone that's bruised my feet;
For all the blood and sweat and grime,
　For blinding storms and burning heat,
My heart sings but a grateful song:
These were the things that made me
　strong.

For all the heartaches and the tears,
　For all the anguish and the pain,
For gloomy days and fruitless years,
　And for the hopes that lived in vain,
I do give thanks; for now I know
These were the things that help me grow.

'Tis not the softer things of life
　Which stimulate man's will to strive,
But bleak adversity and strife
　Do most to keep man's will alive.
O'er rose-strewn paths the weaklings
　creep,
But brave hearts dare to climb the steep!

The Refiner's Fire

He sat by a furnace of seven-fold heat,
　As He watched by the precious ore;
And closer He bent with a searching gaze
　As He heated it more and more.

He knew He had ore that could stand the
　test
　And He wanted the finest gold,
To mold as a crown, for the King to wear,
　Set with gems of price untold.

So He laid our gold in the burning fire,
　Tho' we fain would say Him, "Nay";
And watched the dross that we had not
　seen
　As it melted and passed away.

And the gold grew brighter and yet more
　bright,
　But our eyes were dim with tears.
We saw but the fire—not the Master's
　hand,
　And questioned with anxious fears.

Yet our gold shone out with a richer glow
　As it mirrored a Form above,
That bent o'er the fire, tho' unseen by us,
　With a look of ineffable love.

Can we think it pleases His loving heart
　To cause us a moment's pain?
Ah, no! but He sees through the present
　cross
　The bliss of eternal gain.

So He waited there with a watchful eye,
　With the love that is strong and sure,
And His gold did not suffer a bit more
　heat
　Than was needed to make it pure.
　　　　　　　—*Rev. Arthur F. Ingler*

He Leadeth Me

He leadeth me.
In pastures green? No, not always.
Sometimes He Who knoweth best
In kindness leadeth me in weary ways
Where heavy shadows be;
Out of the sunshine warm and soft and bright,
Out of the sunshine into darkest night.
I oft would yield to sorrow and to fright
Only for this: I know He holds my hand.
So, whether led in green or desert land,
I trust, although I cannot understand.

He leadeth me.
Beside still waters? No, not always so.
Oft times the heavy tempest round me blow,
And o'er my soul the waves and billows go.
But when the storm beats wildest, and I cry
Aloud for help, the Master standeth by
And whispers to my soul: "Lo, it is I."
Above the tempest wild I hear Him say:
"Beyond the darkness lies the perfect day;
In every path of thine I lead the way."

So, whether on the hilltops, high and fair,
I dwell, or in the sunless valleys, where
The shadows lie—what matter? He is there.
And more than this; where'er the pathway lead
He gives to me no helpless, broken reed,
But His own hand, sufficient for my need.
So where He leads me I can safely go.
And in the blest hereafter I shall know
Why in His wisdom He hath led me so.

Broken Things

A broken body on the cross,
A wound whence blood and water flow;
That every fettered child of sin
Might full deliverance know.
How dear to God are broken things,
What power in His hand they gain;
Then trust Him with your shattered hopes,
And bodies racked with pain.

PROGRESS

Until I learned to trust,
I never learned to pray.
And I did not fully learn to trust
Till sorrows came my way.

Until I felt my weakness,
His strength I never knew;
Nor dreamed till I was stricken,
That He could see me through.

Who deepest drinks of sorrow
Drinks deepest too of grace;
He sends the storm so He, Himself
Can be our hiding place.

His heart, that seeks our highest
good,
Knows well when things annoy;
We would not long for heaven
If earth held only joy.

The Pattern of Life

If the pattern of life
looks dark to you,
And the threads seem
twisted and queer,
To the One who is planning
the whole design,
It's perfectly plain and clear—
For it's all a part of
God's loving plan,
When He works in
His threads of gray,
And they'll only make brighter
The rose and gold
Of another happier day.

The Valley

I have been through the valley of
   weeping,
The valley of sorrow and pain;
But the "God of all comfort" was with
   me,
   At hand to uphold and sustain.

As the earth needs the clouds and the
   sunshine,
   Our souls need both sorrow and joy;
So He places us oft in the furnace,
   The dross from the gold to destroy.

When He leads through some valley of
   trouble,
   His powerful hand we can trace;
For the trials and sorrows He sends us
Are part of His lessons of grace.

Oft we shrink from the purging and
   pruning,
   Forgetting the husbandman knows
The deeper the cutting and paring,
   The richer the cluster that grows.

Well He knows the affliction is needed;
   He has a wise purpose in view.
And in the dark valley He whispers,
   "Hereafter thou'lt know what I do."

As we travel through life's shadowed
   valley,
   Fresh springs of His love ever rise;
And we learn that our sorrows and
   losses
Are blessings just sent in disguise.

So we'll follow wherever He leadeth,
   Though pathways be dreary or
   bright;
For we've proof that our God can give
   comfort;
   Our God can give songs in the night.

—From Streams in the Desert

God-Given Thorns

Strange gift indeed—a thorn to prick—
   To pierce into the very quick,
To cause perpetual sense of pain.
   Strange gift! And yet, 'twas given for
   gain.

Unwelcome, but it came to stay;
   Nor could it e'en be prayed away.
It came to fill its God-planned place—
   A life-enriching means of grace.

O much-tried saint, with fainting heart,
   The thorn with its abiding smart,
With all its wearing, ceaseless pain
   Can be thy means of priceless gain.

And so whate'er thy thorn may be,
   From God accept it willingly.
But reckon Christ—His life—His power
   To keep, in thy most trying hour.

And sure—thy life will richer grow;
   His grace sufficient will bestow.
And in Heav'n's morn thy joy 'twill be
   That by His thorn, He strengthened
   thee.

---

*Tears are the showers
that fertilize this world;
And memory of things
precious keepeth warm
The heart that once
did hold them.*

—Jean Ingelow

SOMETIME

Sometime, when all life's lessons have been learned,
And sun and stars for evermore have set,
The things which our weak judgments here have spurned,
The things o'er which we grieved with lashes wet,
Will flash before us, out of life's dark night,
As stars shine most in deeper tints of blue;
And we shall see how all God's plans are right,
And how what seemed reproof was love most true.

And, we shall see how, while we frown and sigh,
God's plan goes on as best for you and me;
How, when we called, He heeded not our cry,
Because His wisdom to the end could see.
And even as wise parents disallow
Too much of sweet to craving babyhood,
So God, perhaps, is keeping from us now
Life's sweetest things, because it seemeth good.

And if, sometimes commingled with life's wine,
We find the wormwood, and rebel and shrink,
Be sure a wiser hand than yours or mine
Pours out this potion for our lips to drink.

And that sometimes the sable pall of death
Conceals the fairest boon His love can send.
If we could push ajar the gates of life,
And stand within and all God's workings see,
We could interpret all this doubt and strife,
And for each mystery find a ready key.

But not today. Then be content, sad heart!
God's plans, like lilies, pure and white unfold.
We must not tear the close-shut leaves apart;
Time will reveal the calyxes of gold,
And if, through patient toil, we reach the land
Where tired feet, with sandals loosed may rest,
When we shall clearly see and understand,
I think that we shall say, "God knew the best."

—*Mary Riley Smith*

A B C of Afflictions

As gold is tried — 1 Peter 1:7; Job 23:10
But joy cometh in the morning — Psalm 30:5
Cure for troubled hearts — John 14:1, 2
Devil's part in testings — Job 1:6, 2:6
Everything in Father's care — Matthew 6:25
Father in heaven knows — Matthew 10:29
God's peace and supply — Philippians 4:6, 19
Heart searching a must — Psalm 119:67
I will restore health — Jeremiah 30:17
Joy and security in Christ — Romans 8:18ff
Kindness in disguise — Psalm 40:1; 94:12
Lord's presence a comfort — Isaiah 43:2
Magnifying Christ — Philippians 1:19-23
No chastisement pleasant — Hebrews 12:11
Our victory in Christ — 1 Corinthians 15:57
Purpose of suffering — John 9:3; 15:2
Quietness via waiting — Isaiah 40:31
Rejoice as partakers — 1 Peter 4:12, 13
Suffering to comfort others — 2 Corinthians 1:4
Tribulation works patience — Romans 5:3
Under His wings — Psalm 36:7; 91:4
Victory lies in faith — 1 John 5:4
When weak I am strong — 2 Corinthians 12:7ff
X-Ray eyes of God — Psalm 139:16
Your Savior suffered more — Isaiah 53
Zealous to suffer — Philippians 3:10

God's Purposes

God would never send you the dark-
ness
  If He felt you could bear the
  light;
But you would not cling to His
guiding hand
  If the way were always bright;
And you would not care to walk by
faith
  Could you always walk by sight.

'Tis true He has many an anguish
  For your sorrowful heart to bear,
And many a cruel thorn crown
  For your tired head to wear.
He knows how few would reach
  heaven at all
  If pain did not guide them there.

So He sends you the blinding dark-
ness
  And the furnace of sevenfold heat;
'Tis the only way, believe me,
  To keep you close to His feet.
For 'tis always so easy to wander
  When our lives are glad and
  sweet.

Then nestle your hand in your
  Father's
  And sing if you can as you go.
Your song may cheer someone
  behind you
  Whose courage is sinking low.
And well, if your lips do quiver,
  God will love you better so.

Comfort in Sorrow . . .

Bereavement, Heartaches, Loneliness

God's Flower Garden

It's hard to lose the ones we love,
  To see them pass away,
The sweetest and the kindest gone
  While others are left to stray!

But if we had a garden
  With roses fair and bright,
We'd often pick the loveliest
  And think it to be right.

And so it is with Jesus
  In His earthly garden here;
He often picks the fairest flowers,
  The ones we love so dear.

The flowers that are picked by Him
  Will never fade away.
We know they'll live forever, and
  We'll see them some sweet day.

—*Marjorie Staata*
*(Written by a young girl after the death
of both parents)*

His Own Way

There is no way but His own way
  To give us comfort day by day;
He'll lift the veil of doubt and fear
  And brush away each lonely tear.

There is no hand but His own hand
  To lift us up and let us stand
In all our grief with head unbowed,
  To see above the anguished crowd.

There is no light but His own light
  To guide us through the darkest
  night.
When shadows fall, there is no fear;
  In His own way He is ever near.

—*Susan Hicks*

Sometime We'll Understand

Not now, but in the coming years,
  It may be in the Better Land,
We'll read the meaning of our tears,
  And there, sometime, we'll understand.

We'll catch the broken threads again,
  And finish what we here began;
Heav'n will the mysteries explain,
  And then, ah then, we'll understand.

We'll know why clouds instead of sun
  Were over many a cherished plan;
Why song has ceased, when scarce begun;
  'Tis there, sometimes, we'll understand.

God knows the way, He holds the key;
  He guides us with unerring hand.
Sometimes with tearless eyes we'll see;
  Yes, there, up there, we'll understand.

Then trust in God through all thy days;
  Fear not, for He doth hold thy hand;
Though dark the way, still sing and praise;
  Sometime, sometime, we'll understand.

—*Maxwell N. Cornelius*

Just Away

I cannot say, and I will not say
  That she is dead—she is just away!
With a cheery smile, and a wave of the hand,
  She has wandered into another land,
  And left us dreaming how very fair
It needs must be, since she lingers there.
And you—O you, who the wildest yearn
For the old time step and glad return,
  Think of her faring on, as dear
In the love of There as the love Here;
Think of her still as the same, I say:
  She is not dead—she is just away!

—*James Whitcomb Riley*

Life's Deeper Meaning

Father, to thee we look in all our sorrow;
　Thou art the fountain whence our healing flows;
Dark though the night, joy cometh with the morrow;
Safely they rest who on thy love repose.

When fond hopes fail and skies are dark before us,
　When the vain cares that we our lives increase,
Comes with its calm the thought that thou art o'er us,
　And we grow quiet, folded in thy peace.

Nought shall afright us, on thy goodness leaning;
　Low in the heart faith singeth still her song;
Chastened by pain we learn life's deeper meaning,
　And in our weakness thou dost make us strong.

—*F. L. Hosmer*

The Other Side

This isn't death, it's glory!
It isn't dark, it's light;
It isn't stumbling, groping,
Or even faith—it's sight!

This isn't grief, it's having
My last tear wiped away.
It's sunrise, it's the morning
Of my eternal day.

This isn't even praying,
It's speaking face to face;
It's listening, and it's
　glimpsing
The wonders of His grace.

This is the end of pleading
For strength to bear my pain;
Not even pain's dark memory
Will ever live again.

How did I bear the earth life
Before I came up higher,
Before my soul was granted
Its every deep desire.

Before I knew this rapture
Of meeting face to face
That One who sought me,
　saved me,
And kept me by His grace.

Heartaches

When your heart is aching,
　Turn to Jesus;
He's the dearest Friend
　That you can know.
You will find Him standing
　Close beside you,
Waiting peace and comfort
　To bestow.
Jesus understands
　Whate'er the trouble,
And He waits to heal
　Your wounded soul:
Will you trust His love
　So strong and tender?
He alone can make
　Your spirit whole.
Heartaches, take them all
　To Jesus—
Go to Him today,
　Do it now with delay.
Heartaches, take them all
　To Jesus.
He will take your heartaches
　All away.

The Breaking Heart

When your lonely heart is breaking
　'Neath a heavy load of care,
And your tears have been exhausted,
　But the pain still lingers there—
Then take it to the Mender,
　Commit it all to Him—
And let Him bind the broken chords,
　And give new joy within.
For underneath the burden sore,
　Your spirit cries aloud.
And Jesus' ear is tuned to hear
　Your cry above the crowd.
Why hold it then, within your heart,
　To eat your soul away,
When Jesus beckons you to come
　And hide in Him today?
He wants to heal your broken heart,
　He died from one you know—
And in His dying, met your need,
　And conquered every foe.

—*Esther L. Fields*

Wait for Me

Wait for me up in glory,
　Wait by the river of life;
Tell Jesus for me that I'm longing
　And ready to cease from my sighs.
Just tell Him I'll see you in glory
　After this life here is through.
Just wait for me up in glory,
　And soon I'll be coming to you.

When the Lord called you home,
　How it broke my heart
To see you go away,
　Although I knew right from the start
We'd meet again some day.

So I'll watch and pray,
　Each night and day,
Until my work is through—
　Then I shall hear my Master say,
"Come home, we're waiting for you!"

—Hovie Lister

"Comfort Ye My People"

Behold, happy is the man whom God correcteth: therefore despise not thou the chastening of the Almighty: for he maketh sore, and bindeth up: he woundeth, and his hands make whole (Job 5:17, 18).

Now no chastening for the present seemeth to be joyous, but grievous; nevertheless AFTERWARD it yieldeth the peaceable fruit of righteousness unto them which are EXERCISED thereby (Hebrews 12:11).

Before I was afflicted I went astray: but now have I kept thy word . . . I know, O Lord . . . that thou in thy faithfulness has afflicted me (Psalm 119:67, 75).

My soul, wait thou ONLY upon God; for my expectation is from him (Psalm 62:5).

The eternal God is thy refuge, and underneath are the everlasting arms (Deuteronomy 33:27).

On the Death of a Believer

In vain our fancy strives to paint
　The moment after death,
The glories that surround the saints,
　When yielding up their breath.

One gentle sigh their fetters breaks;
　We scarce can say, "They're gone!"
Before the willing spirit takes
　Her mansion near the throne.

Faith strives, but all its efforts fail
　To trace her in her flight!
No eye can pierce within the veil
　Which hides that world of light.

Thus much (and this is all) we know,
　They are completely blest;
Have done with sin, and care, and woe,
　And with their Saviour rest.

On harps of gold they praise His name,
　His face they always view;
Then let us foll'wers be of them,
　That we may praise Him too.

Their faith and patience, love and zeal
　Should make their mem'ry dear;
And, Lord, do Thou the pray'rs fulfill
　They offer'd for us here.

While they have gain'd, we losers are,
　We miss them day by day;
But thou canst ev'ry breach repair,
　And wipe our tears away.

We pray, as in Elisha's case,
　When great Elijah went,
May double portions of thy grace
　To us who stay, be sent.

—I. Newton, d. 1807

No One Understands Like Jesus

No one understands like Jesus—
　He's a friend beyond compare:
Meet Him at the throne of mercy,
　He is waiting for you there.

No one understands like Jesus
　When the days are dark and drear;
No one is no near, so dear as Jesus!
　Cast your every care on Him.

—John Peterson

ONLY TODAY

Help me to place in Thy hands today
  The things that my heart most fears:
Tomorrow's anguish and bitter pain,
  Tomorrow's sorrow and tears,
The long, long years, and the loneliness,
  The silence, the vacant chair.
The grief of today is enough, dear Lord,
  But tomorrow's I cannot bear!

Ease Thou my burden and lighten my load,
  Till only today is left.
Soft comes His voice in the hush of my soul,
  "Oh, broken heart, and bereft,
My grace is sufficient for thee TODAY;
  Pillow upon My breast
Thy weary hand, in My circling arms
  Today thou shalt find rest.

Today I can meet thine every need,
  Today My love can fill
The echoing chambers of thy heart.
  Then rest thee, and be still.
Be still and trust—tomorrow's tears
  May all be wiped away
By God Himself. O grieving heart,
  Thy Lord may come today!"
          —Martha Snell Nicholson

Love Can Never Lose Its Own

Yet love will dream, and faith will trust
  (Since He who knows our need is just),
That somehow, somewhere, meet me must.
  Alas, for him who never sees
The stars shine through his cypress-trees!
  Who, hopeless, lays his dead away,
  Across the mournful marbles play!
Who hath not learned in hours of faith
  The truth to flesh and sense unknown,
That life is ever lord of death,
  And love can never lose its own!
          —John G. Whittier

OUR COMFORT

Christ mourned at tomb of Lazarus,
  He realized the loss—
The darkness of "the valley,"
  The shadows of the cross.
The bitter grief at parting,
  The pain that mothers feel;
He wept, though He was ready
  The human grief to heal.

Oh, there are tears for dying,
  And heart-break by the grave;
There's a loneliness and sighing;
  But Christians should be brave.
For One who passed before us
  Came back that we might see
That soul-life is eternal;
  Let this your comfort be.
          —Dorothy Dix Porges

Love's Ministry Rewarded

Through life's highway I was plodding
  'Neath a weight of many woes;
Saw I aught of life and beauty,
  Knew I naught of soul repose.
For my thoughts were turned within me,
  Where secure upon his throne
Selfishness supreme sat brooding,
  Thinking of himself alone.
Soon my burdens so oppressed me
  That for help I cried aloud,
When before my wakened vision
  Rose a vast and friendless crowd:
Helpless men and widowed mothers,
  Starving children by the score—
All were burdened with some heartache,
  Each one Sorrow's vestments wore.
Notwithstanding all my troubles,
  Touched with pity, moved by love,
Sought I then—O blessed moment!—
  Other's sadness to remove.
Then my soul waxed light and radiant,
  And my eyes with gladness shone,
For in lifting others' burdens,
  Somehow I had lost my own!
          —Arthur S. Gray

Some Day I'll Be With You!

Someday I'll be with you, Sweetheart,
And you will hold my hand.
And then, I know, that God will show
Me how to understand
Just why He took you far away
When knowing all the while
The way we'd miss you every day
And long to see your smile.

You loved to live and work and plan
And help your fellowmen,
And speak a word of comfort
To strangers as well as friends.
And though your life in years was short,
In service it was long.
So God just thought He'd take you
Where chosen ones belong.

But, way beyond the sunset, dear,
I'll see again your loving face
Smiling so sweetly down at me;
How proud to take my place
Beside you, knowing all the while
We'll never have to part,
But just pal along together
Like we did right from the start.

I want to know the road you took,
So I can take it, too,
And you can meet me part the way,
Then I'll go back with you.
For that time won't be long, Sweetheart,
Gets closer every day,
When I'll take leave of earthly things
And quietly slip away.

—*Mrs. Robert Ely*

GETHSEMANE

All those who journey, soon or late,
Must pass within the Garden gate;
Must kneel alone in darkness there,
And battle with some fierce despair.

God pity those who cannot say,
"Not mine, but Thine"; who only
pray,
"Let this cup pass," and cannot see
The purpose of Gethsemane.

—*Ella Wheeler Wilcox*

She Left It for My Comfort

Before going to be with the Lord, my dear wife left within her Bible a poem for me. She left it for my consolation. Each day I have read it as I have stood before her portrait. It is called "Mizpah," the covenant between Jacob and Laban, meaning, "The Lord watch between thee and me while we are absent, one from another." I was asked to recite it before the great congregation of the World Bible Conference at the Caesarea Amphitheater.

Mizpah

Go thou thy way and I go mine,
Apart, yet not afar:
Only a thin veil hangs between
The pathways where we are.
And God keeps watch 'tween thee and me,
This is my prayer:
He looketh thy way, He looketh mine,
And keeps us near.
I know not where thy road may lie,
Or which way mine will be.
If mine will lead thru parching sands,
And thine beside the crystal sea;
Yet God keeps watch 'tween thee and me;
We cannot fear.
He holds thy hand, He claspeth mine,
And keeps us near.
I sigh oft'times to see thy face,
But since this may not be,
I'll leave thee to the care of Him
Who cares for thee and me.
"I'll keep you both beneath My wings."
This comforts, dear;
One wing o'er thee, and one o'er me—
So we are near.

—*Julia A. Baker*

Thank God for Mizpah! —D.C.

Among my list of blessings infinite
Stands this the foremost:
That MY HEART HAS BLED.

—*Edward Young*

Why Should We Weep?

Why should we weep for those who die;
   They fall—their dust returns to dust;
Their souls shall live eternally
   Within the mansions of the just.

They die to live—they sink to rise,
   They leave this wretched mortal shore;
But brighter suns and bluer skies
   Shall smile on them for evermore.

Why should we sorrow for the dead?
   Our life on earth is but a span;
They tread the path that all must tread,
   They die the common death of man.

The soul, the eternal soul, must reign
   In worlds devoid of pain and strife;
Then why should mortal man complain
   Of death, which leads to happier life.

—Alfred Lord Tennyson

A Message From Paradise

What mean you by this weeping
   To break my very heart?
We both are in Christ's keeping,
   And therefore cannot part.
You there—I here, tho' parted,
   We still at heart are one;
I only just in sunshine,
   The shadow scarcely gone.

What though the clouds surround you,
   You can the brightness see.
'Tis only a little way
   That leads from you to me.
I was so very weary,
   Surely, you could not mourn,
That I a little sooner
   Should lay my burden down.

Then weep not—weep not, Darling,
   God wipes away all tears.
'Tis but a little while
   Thou you may call it years.

—Author unknown

Songs in the Night

There is never a day so dreary
But God can make it bright.
And unto the soul who trusts Him
He giveth songs in the night.

There is never a path so hidden
But God will lead the way,
If we seek for His Spirit's guidance
And patiently wait and pray.

There is never a cross so heavy
But the nail-scarred hands are there,
Outstretched in tender compassion
The burden to help us bear.

There is never a heart so broken
But the loving Lord can heal.
For the heart that was pierced on
   Calvary
Doth still for His loved ones feel.

Looking This Way

Over the river faces I see,
   Fair as the morning, looking for me.
Free from their sorrow, grief and despair,
   Waiting and watching patiently there.

Father and mother, safe in this vale,
   Watch for the boatman, wait for the sail
Bearing their loved ones over the tide,
   Into the harbor, near to their side.

Brother and sister, gone to that clime,
   Wait for the others, coming some time.
Safe with the angels, whiter than snow,
   Watching for dear ones, waiting below.

Sweet little darling, light of the home,
   Looking for someone—beckoning come;
Bright as a sunbeam, pure as the dew,
   Anxiously looking, mother, for you.

Looking this way, yes, looking this way;
   Loved ones are waiting, looking this
     way;
Fair as the morning, bright as the day,
   Dear ones in glory, looking this way!

—J. W. Van De Venter

Should You Go First

Should you go first, and I remain
    To walk the road alone,
I'll live in memory's garden, dear,
    With happy days we've known.
In spring, I'll wait for the roses red,
    In summer, lilacs blue;
In autumn, when the brown leaves fall,
    I'll catch a breath of you.

Should you go first, and I remain
    For battles to be fought,
Each thing you've touched along the way
    Will be a hallowed spot.
I'll hear your voice, I'll see your smile
    Though blindly I may grope;
The memory of your loving hand
    Will buoy me on, with hope.

Should you go first, and I remain
    To finish with the scroll,
No dark shadows shall creep in
    To make this life seem droll.
We've known so much of happiness,
    We've had our cup of joy;
The memory is one gift of God
    That death cannot destroy.

Should you go first, and I remain,
    One thing for sure we know;
We'll meet again in that bright land
    Beyond the golden shore.
God's great salvation we've received
    Through Jesus' matchless Name,
And in heaven, reunited,
    We shall never part again!

—Rosy Rosewell

I opened the old, old Bible,
And looked at a page of Psalms,
Till the wintry sea of my troubles
Was soothed as by summer calms;
For the words that have helped so many,
And the ages have made more dear,
Seemed new in their power to comfort,
As they brought me their word of cheer.

Does Jesus Care?

Does Jesus care when my heart is
    pained
    Too deeply for mirth or song?
As the burdens press, and the cares
    distress
    And the way grows weary and long.

Does Jesus care when my way is dark
    With the nameless dread and fear?
As the daylight fades into deep night
    shades,
    Does He care enough to be near?

Does Jesus care when I've said
    "Good-bye"
    To the dearest on earth to me?
And my sad heart aches till it nearly
    breaks—
    Is it aught to Him? Does He care?

O, yes, He cares; I know He cares;
    His heart is touched with my grief;
When the days are weary, the long
    nights dreary,
    I know my Saviour cares!

—Frank E. Graeff

Life's Lessons

I learn, as the years roll onward,
    And leave the past behind,
That much I had counted sorrow
    But proved that God is kind;
That many a flower I'd longed for
    Had hidden a thorn of pain,
And many a rugged by-path,
    Led to fields of ripened grain.
The clouds that cover the sunshine
    They cannot banish the sun.
And the earth shines out the brighter
    When the weary rain is done.
We must stand in the deepest shadow
    To see the clearest light;
And often through wrong's own darkness
    Comes the welcome strength of right.

—Anonymous

Someday Soon I'll Be There With You!

(A poem written by David Crowley, with the inscription: *Dedicated to Grandfather Crowley in memory Grandmother."* David also composed the music for these lyrics, and sang the song to the family.)

It's been many years, my wife.
They were happy years, my love.
I can't say how much I'll miss you.
Guess I'll have to finish the course alone.
The fragrant flowers around your hair,
Your favorite flowers when love was
     young,
And as I kiss your lifeless lips,
I remember the first time we kissed.
O memories, memories, how sweet they are.
Our dear children, all grown, standing by.
Times we cried, the times we laughed.
You, my love, how I love you!
And as I stare at your hands
Folded over your breast,
I can't hold back the tears.
But then I stop and think,
Someday soon I'll be there with you.
Someday . . . someday . . . soon . . .
I'll be there . . . with you!

When Trouble Comes, Let Go and Let God

When you're troubled and worried and
     sick at heart;
And your plans are upset, and your world
     falls apart,
Remember, God's ready and waiting to
     share
The burden you find much too heavy to
     bear—
So with faith, "LET GO" and "LET GOD"
     lead the way
Into a brighter and less-troubled day.

—*Helen Steiner Rice*

Yielding to God

O Love that will not let me go,
  I rest my weary soul in thee;
I give thee back the life I owe,
That in thine ocean depths its flow
  May richer, fuller be.

O Joy that seekest me through pain,
  I cannot close my heart to thee;
I trace the rainbow through the rain,
And feel the promise is not vain
  That morn shall tearless be.

—*George Matheson*

The Traveler

She has put on invisibility.
Dear Lord, I cannot see—
But this I know, although the road
     ascends
And passes from my sight,
That there will be no night;
That You will take her gently by the hand
And lead her on
Along the road of life that never ends,
And she will find it is not death but dawn.
I do not doubt that You are there as here,
And You will hold her dear.
Our life did not begin with birth,
It is not of the earth;
And this that we call death, it is no more
Than the opening and closing of a door—
And in Your house how many rooms
     must be
Beyond this one where we rest momently.
Dear Lord, I thank You for the faith that
     frees,
The love that knows it cannot lose its
     own;
The love that, looking through the
     shadows, sees
That You and she and I are ever one!

—*James Dillet Freeman*

189

The Now of Life . . .

Faith, Dedication, Hope

NOW!

This little now is all the time that's given
  To anyone of high or low degree;
And how one spends it, for himself or heaven,
  Decides his own eternal destiny.

This little now, could I but grasp its meaning,
  Its mighty import, as the days go by,
I should be more awake, have less of
    dreaming—
  I should live now instead of by and by.

The only time in which to serve my Master,
  In which to help my helpless fellow men!
Oh, let me labor just a little faster;
  In serving others I may heaven win.

This little space holds in its narrow limits
  The grandest of achievements time can know.
The utmost failures human life exhibits,
  The highest joy, the deepest depths of woe.

He who completes his task assigned by heaven,
  Who wins unfading laurels for his brow,
Will heed the great Commander's orders given,
  To watch and pray and work for others now.

—Mrs. A. N. Loper

FAITH

Lord, give me faith!—
      to live from day to day,
With tranquil heart to do
      my simple part,
And, with my hand in Thine,
      just go Thy way.

Lord, give me faith!—to trust,
      if not to know;
With quiet mind in all things
      Thee to find.
And, childlike, go where Thou
      wouldst have me go.

Lord, give me faith!—
      to leave it all to Thee.
The future is Thy gift,
      I would not lift
The vail Thy love has hung
      'twixt it and me.

—John Oxenham

Salutation to the Dawn

Look to this day.
For it is the very life of life.
In its brief course lies all the varieties and realities of your existence:
The bliss of growth; the glory of action; the splendor of beauty;
For yesterday is already a dream, and tomorrow is only a vision;
But today, well lived, makes every yesterday
A dream of happiness, and every tomorrow a vision of hope.
Look well, therefore, to this day.

—The Sanskrit

Yesterday, Today and Tomorrow

There are two days in every week about which we should not worry—two days which should be kept from fear and apprehension.

One of these days is Yesterday with its mistakes and cares, its aches and pains, its faults and blunders. Yesterday has passed forever beyond our control.

All the money in the world cannot bring back Yesterday. We cannot undo a single act we performed; we cannot erase a single word we said. Yesterday is gone.

The other day we should not worry about is Tomorrow with its possible adversities, its burdens, its large promise and poor performance. Tomorrow is beyond our immediate control.

Tomorrow's sun will rise either in splendor or behind a mask of clouds—but it will rise. Until it does, we have no stake in Tomorrow, for it is as yet unborn.

That leaves only one day—Today. Any man, by the grace of God, can fight the battles of just one day. It is only when you and I add the burdens of those two awful eternities—Yesterday and Tomorrow—that we break down.

It is not the experience of Today that drives men mad—it is remorse or bitterness for something which happened Yesterday and the dread of what Tomorrow may bring. Let us, therefore, journey but one day at a time.

—*Illinois Medical Journal*

Alphabet of Life

Act promptly.
Be courteous.
Cut out worry.
Deal squarely.
Eat what is wholesome.
Forgive and forget.
Get religion.
Hope always.
Imitate the best.
Judge generously.
Knock nobody.
Love somebody.
Make friends.
Never despair.
Owe nobody.
Play occasionally.
Quote your mother.
Read good books.
Save something.
Touch no liquor.
Use discretion.
Vote regularly.
Watch your step.
X-ray yourself.
Yield to superiors.
Zealously live.

God's Lamp

When skies are dark,
  And the road ahead
Seems rough and all uphill;
  God sets a lamp on a
Heavenly window sill.
  So just look, look up,
And every time you do,
  You'll find the lamp
Of Faith and Hope
  Glowing with love for you!

I Shall Have Faith

I shall have faith through a mountain may stand,
  Seeming impossible; at His command
I shall go forward expecting that He
  Who promised a pathway, will clear one for me.

I shall have faith though an ocean may rise,
  Hiding the opposite shore from my eyes.
I shall not falter, for I have been shown
  That God never fails to take care of His own.

I shall have faith, placing all I hold dear
  Under His care; there is nothing to fear.
Night has no terrors; storms cannot appall;
  Shadows are veils that the sunbeams let fall.
Dawn scatters darkness; it brings a new day
  And I shall have faith because God walks my way.

—*Eugenia Finn*

The Eternal Now

We can never reach tomorrow,
Yesterday is dead and gone;
Yet the now of happy living
Marches on and on and on.

So I do not see tomorrow
And its worries when I pray;
But instead I pray that Jesus
Will stay close to me, today.

It will keep me very busy;
It will keep me happy, too—
If I work along with Jesus
At the task He helps me do.

So I do not see tomorrow—
For its needs I do not pray—
Each tomorrow always brings me
Just another glad today!

—Author unknown

A Perfect Faith

O for a faith that will not shrink
  Tho' pressed by every foe.
That will not tremble on the brink
  Of any earthly woe!

That will not murmur nor complain
  Beneath the chastening rod;
But in the hour of grief or pain
  Will lean upon its God.

A faith that shines more bright and
    clear
  When tempests rage without;
That when in danger knows no fear,
  In darkness feels no doubt.

Lord, give us such a faith as this,
  And then, whate'er may come,
We'll taste, e'en here, the hallowed
    bliss
  Of our eternal home.

—William H. Bathhurst

The Bridge Builder

An old man trav'ling a lone highway
Came at the evening cold and gray
To a chasm vast and deep and wide.
The old man crossed in the twilight dim;
The swollen stream had no fear for him.
But, he turned when safe on the other side,
And built a bridge to span the tide.

"Old man," said a fellow pilgrim near,
"You are wasting your strength in building
    here.
Your journey will end with the ending day.
You never again will pass this way.
You've crossed the chasm deep and wide,
Why build you this bridge at evening tide?"

The builder lifted his old grey head.
"Good friend, in the path I have come," he
    said,
"There followeth after me today,
A youth whose feet must pass this way.
This chasm that has been as naught to me,
To that fair-haired youth may a pitfall be.
He, too, must cross in the twilight dim.
Good friend, I am building the bridge for
    him."

Faith Is a Bridge

Faith is a bridge over which we may
walk from unknown to the known, from
sunlight to darkness and on to sunlight
again. And though we cannot see the far
end of the bridge, we step confidently,
knowing that others have gone before us
and the way is sure. Let us not stand at the
chasm's edge and despair of the mist and
the dark. For all though life this bridge
will hold. If we but step on it, we shall
find the way across.

—Esther Baldwin York

HOW MUCH I OWE

When this passing world is done,
When has sunk yon glowing sun,
When we stand with Christ in Glory,
Looking o'er life's finished story,
Then, Lord, shall I fully know—
Not till then—how much I owe.

When I stand before the throne,
Dressed in beauty not my own,
When I see Thee as Thou art,
Love Thee with unsinning heart,
Then, Lord, shall I fully know—
Not till then—how much I owe.

When the praise of heaven I hear,
Loud as thunder to the ear,
Loud as many waters' noise,
Sweet as harp's melodious voice,
Then, Lord, shall I fully know—
Not till then—how much I owe.

Even on earth, as through a glass
Darkly, let Thy glory pass;
Make forgiveness feel so sweet;
Make Thy Spirit's help so meet—
Even on earth, Lord, make me know
Something of how much I owe.

—Robert Murray McCheyne

I know not when I go or where
    From this familiar scene;
But He is here and He is there,
    And all the way between;
And when I leave this life, I know,
    For that dim vast unknown,
Though late I say, or soon I go,
    I shall not go alone.

—Anonymous

The Eye of Faith

I do not ask for earthly store
    Beyond a day's supply;
I only covet more and more
    The clear and single eye.
To see my duty face to face,
And trust the Lord for daily grace.

Whate'er the crosses mine shall be,
    I will not dare to shun;
I only ask to live for Thee,
    And that Thy will be done.
Thy will, oh Lord, be mine each day,
While passing on my homeward way.

And when at last my labor o'er,
    I cross the narrow sea,
Grant, Lord, that on the other shore
    My soul may dwell with Thee.
And learn what here I cannot know:
Why Thou has ever loved me so.

—J. J. Maxfield

First Place in Your Heart

The earth is the Lord's and the fullness
        thereof,
    All the land, and the silver, and gold;
The cattle and sheep upon thousands of hills,
    And all the wealth, and the riches untold.
God giveth us richly all things to enjoy
    From out of His bountiful store;
For "every good gift cometh down from
        above,"
    And daily He blesses us more.
He gave unto us the unspeakable gift,
    Of Jesus, the Son of His love.
To ransom our souls from the bondage of sin,
    And bring us to glory above.
Such wonderful love! 'tis the least we can do,
    And a very small thing on our part,
To render the worship and praise due to Him,
    And grant Him first place in the heart.

—Author unknown

Take my life, and let it be
  Consecrated, Lord, to Thee;
Take my hands and let them move
  At the impulse of Thy love.
Take my lips, and let them be
  Filled with messages for Thee;
Take my silver and my gold,
  Not a mite would I withhold.
Take my love, my God, I pour
  At Thy feet its treasure store;
Take myself and I will be
  Ever, only, ALL for Thee!

—Frances Ridley Havergal

My Faith

I need not worry, I need not fear;
The Lord my God is very near.
He holds my hand and makes me glad;
He wipes my tears when I am sad.
He fills my heart with love and peace,
And all my troubles begin to cease.
He points his finger to show the way;
And from this path I will not stray!

—Vincent Lorenzo

I Can Trust

I cannot see, with my small human sight
Why God should lead this way or that for me;
I only know He saith, "Child, follow Me."
  But I can trust.

I know not why my path should be at times
So straitly hedged, so strongly barred before:
I only know God could keep wide the door;
  But I can trust.

I find no answer, often, when beset
With questions fierce and subtle on my way.
And often have but strength to faintly pray;
  But I can trust.

I often wonder, as with trembling hand
I cast the seed along the furrowed ground,
If ripened fruit will in my life be found;
  But I can trust.

I cannot know why suddenly the storm
Should rage so fiercely round me in its wrath;
But this I know—God watches all my path;
  But I can trust.

I may not draw aside the mystic veil
That hides the unknown future from my sight;
Nor know if for me waits the dark or light;
  But I can trust.

I have no power to look across the tide,
To see, while here, the land beyond the river,
But this I know, I shall be God's forever;
  So I can trust.

—Author unknown

Just for Today

Lord, for tomorrow and its needs
  I do not pray;
Keep me, my God, from stain of sin
  Just for today.
Help me to labor earnestly,
  And duly pray;
Let me be kind in word and deed,
  Father, today.

Let me no wrong or idle word
  Unthinking say;
Set thou a seal upon my lips
  Through all today.
Let me in season, Lord, be grave,
  In season gay;
Let me be faithful to thy grace,
  Dear Lord, today.

And if, today, this life of mine
  Should ebb away,
Give me thy sacrament divine,
  Father, today.
So for tomorrow and its needs
  I do not pray;
Still keep me, guide me, love me,
  Lord
  Through each today.

—Ernest R. Wilberforce

Where to Look

I don't look back: God knows the fruitless efforts,
  The wasted hours, the sinning, the regrets;
I leave them all with Him who blots the record,
  And mercifully forgives and then forgets.

I don't look forward: God sees all the future,
  The road that short or long will lead me home.
And He will face with me its every trial,
  And bear for me the burdens that may come.

I don't look round me; then would fears assail me
  So dark the tumult of earth's restless seas.
So dark the world, so filled with woe and evil,
  So vain the hope of comfort or of ease.

I don't look in, for then am I most wretched;
  Myself has naught on which to stay my trust.
Nothing I see, save failures and shortcomings,
  And weak endeavors crumbling into dust.

But I look up—into the face of Jesus,
  For there my heart can rest, my fears are stilled;
And there is joy and love and light for darkness,
  And perfect peace, and every hope fulfilled.

—Annie Johnson Flint

The God Who Knows

I do not know the future,
  But I know the God who
    knows,
And in His perfect wisdom,
  Unknowing, I repose.
What good could come of
  knowing?
  How little I could do
To meet the joys or sorrows
  That I am coming to!
I do not know the future,
  But I know the God who
    knows.
I make His love my study,
  And follow where He goes.
The path, its joy and sorrows,
  I do not care to trace;
Content to know His goodness,
  His mercy, and His grace.

—William Luff

Herald of the Dawn

If we could see, as we are seen,
  By Him who watches from above,
If we could look into His plans
  And comprehend His wondrous love,
We would not murmur 'neath our load,
  Nor question whether He doth care,
But we would hope and trust and wait,
  Each weary day relieved by prayer.

If we could glimpse the far-off land
  Where He shall gather in His own,
If we could hear His angels sing
  Before the golden shining throne,
We would not find our journey hard,
  As now through life we travel on,
For we would know the night we're in,
  Is but the herald of the dawn.

—L. M. Zimmerman

A Highway to Heaven

Sung by Doris Akers, this is one of the most frequently requested songs. She sings it with real spirit, and the beating drums make you feel that you are marching right up to heaven.

It's a highway to heaven—
  None can walk up there
  But the pure in heart.
It's a highway to heaven—
  I'm walking up the King's highway.

My way gets brighter,
  My load gets lighter
Walking up the King's highway—
  There's joy in knowing,
  With Him I'm going,
Walking up the King's highway.

Oh, it's a highway to heaven—
  None can walk up there
  But the pure in heart.
I'm walking up the King's highway:
  I am walking, I am talking,
Shouting glory, hallelujah—
  Walking up the King's highway!

TODAY!

With every rising of the sun
Think of your life as just begun.

The Past has cancelled and buried
  deep
All yesterdays. There let them sleep.

Concern yourself with but Today.
Grasp it, and teach it to obey

Your will and plan. Since time began
Today has been the friend of man.

You and Today! A soul sublime
And the great heritage of time.

With God himself to bind the twain,
Go forth, brave heart! Attain! Attain!

What's Your Story?

No matter what else you are doing—
From cradle days through to the end—
You're writing your life's secret story.
Each day sees another page penned,
Each month ends a thirty-page chapter,
Each year means the end of a part,
And never an act is misstated,
Nor ever a wish from the heart.
Each day when you wake, the book opens
Revealing a page clean and white.
What thoughts and what words and what
  actions
Will cover its surface by night?
God leaves that to you—you're the writer,
And never one word shall grow dim
Till some day you write the word "Finis,"
And give back your life book to Him.

                —*Author unknown*

The Silver Cord

Some day the silver cord will break
  And I no more as now shall sing;
But, O, the joy when I shall wake
  Within the palace of the King.

Some day my earthly house will fall;
  I cannot tell how soon 'twill be.
But this I know, my All in All
  Has now a place in heav'n for me.

Some day when fades the golden sun
  Beneath the rosy-tinted west,
My blessed Lord will say, "Well done!"
  And I shall enter into rest.

Some day, till then I'll watch and wait,
  My lamp all trimmed and turning
  bright,
That when my Saviour opes the gate,
  My soul to Him may take its flight.

                —*Fanny J. Crosby*

Carry On

Hope is the song within my heart,
The shield 'twixt me and harm;
Hope is the blanket of my faith
That keeps my spirit warm.

Hope is the shining beacon light
Burning through darkest night,
Holding me ever to purpose high,
Guiding my feet aright.

Hope is the gleaming, twinkling star,
Shining and glowing bright;
Cheering me on my lonely way,
Piercing the gloom of night.

Hope is the banner of courage brave,
Help and strength to us giving;
Were it not for hope springing ever new,
Life were not worth the living.

It is hope that makes our lives
   worthwhile,
Though all else may be gone;
Hope holds her torch before our eyes,
A challenge to carry on.

       —*Myrtie Fisher Seaverns*

O Master, Let Me Walk with Thee

O Master, let me walk with Thee
In lowly paths of service free;
Tell me Thy secret, help me bear
The strain of toil, the fret of care.

Help me the slow of heart to move
By some clear winning word of love.
Teach me the wayward feet to stay,
And guide them in the homeward way.

Teach me Thy patience; still with Thee
In closer, dearer company.
In work that keeps faith sweet and
   strong,
In trust that triumphs over wrong.

In hope that sends a shining ray
Far down the future's broadening way.
In peace that only Thou cast give,
With Thee, O Master, let me live.

       —*Washington Gladden*

This Day Is Thine

This day is thine, a shining gift from heaven,
   Gleaned for thy use from treasuries of time,
Given in trust to hold until the even.
   This day is thine, a sacred charge sublime.

This day is thine, to be what thou shalt make it,
   Hidden in self or used in service fine;
When thou shalt bring it back to Him who gave it.
   What will it be, this golden day of thine?

This day is thine, thy yesterdays are finished.
   Soon will the present join the changeless past;
Will its bright hours be greater for thy keeping
   Or by the dreaded rust of waste o'er cast?

This day is thine, there may be no tomorrows.
   This day is thine from dawn till setting sun;
May thou at even, like a worthy steward,
   Hear in thy heart the Master's words, "Well done."

       —*Verna Whinery*

Something to Live For

You must have a hope to inspire you.
You must have path to pursue.
You must have an object to work for,
A plan and a purpose in view.

You must have a sense of direction
Or else you'll go drifting along.
You must have a faith that will guide you
When life holds no light and no song.

You must have a stake in the future,
Though swiftly the years may depart.
You'll always have something to live for
If you have a dream in your heart.

—*Patience Strong*

Don't Carry the Burdens of Tomorrow

God broke our years into hours and days,
That hour by hour, and day by day,
Just going on a little way,
    We might be able, all along,
    To keep quite strong.

Should all the weight of life be laid
Across our shoulders at just one place,
And the future, rife with woe and struggle,
Meet us face to face:
We could not go;
Our feet would stop, and so
God LAYS A LITTLE ON US EVERY
    DAY.

And never, I believe, in all life's way,
Will burdens bear so deep,
Or pathways lie so steep,
But we can go, if, by God's power,
We ONLY BEAR THE BURDEN OF
    THE HOUR.

—*Author unknown*

Lean Hard

Cast thy burden upon the Lord
and He shall sustain thee
(Psalm 55:22).

CHILD of My love, lean hard,
And let Me feel the pressure of thy
    care;
I know thy burden, child, I shaped it;
Poised it in Mine own hand, made no
    proportion
In its weight to thine unaided strength.
For even as I laid it on, I said,
I shall be near, and while he leans on
    Me,
This burden shall be Mine, not his;
So shall I keep My child within the
    circling arms
Of My own love. Here lay it down, nor
    fear
To impose it on a shoulder which
    upholds
The government of worlds. Yet closer
    come;
Thou art not near enough; I would
    embrace thy care
So I might feel My child reposing on
    My breast.
Thou lovest Me? I knew it. Doubt not
    then;
But, loving Me, lean hard.

Casting all your care upon Him;
for He careth for you.
(1 Peter 5:7)

—*Paul Pasnor*

One of His Own

I may not know what lies ahead for me;
    But this I know, I'm not alone.
I found a Friend who always stands by me,
    And claims me as one of His own.
One of His own is all I want to be—
    Where He may lead, I'll follow on;
What if I know, whatever comes to me,
    I'll always be one of His own.

This, Too, Shall Pass Away

A mighty monarch in days of old
Made offer of high honor, wealth and gold,
To one who should produce in form concise
A motto for his guidance, terse, yet wise;
A precept soothing in his hours forlorn,
Yet one that in his prosperous days should warn.
Many the maxims sent the king, men say;
The one he chose: "This, too, shall pass away."

Has some misfortune fallen your lot?
This, too, will pass away; absorb the thought,
And wait—your waiting will not be in vain,
Time gilds with gold the iron links of pain.
The dark today leads into light tomorrow;
There is no endless joy, no endless sorrow.

Are you upon earth's heights, no cloud in view;
Go read your motto once again: "This, too,
Shall pass away." Fame, glory, and power,
They are but little bubbles of the hour,
Flung by the ruthless years down in the dust.
Take warning and be worthy of God's trust.

—*Ella Wheeler Wilcox*

Age and Death . . .

As I Grow Older

Lord, Thou knowest, better than I know myself, that I am growing older.

Keep me from becoming talkative, and from the habit of thinking that I must say something on every occasion.

Release me from the craving to straighten out other people's affairs.

Keep my mind free from endless detail; give me wings to get to the point.

Give me grace to listen to the recital of others' tribulations. Help me to endure with patience.

Seal my lips against my own aches and pains. They are increasing, and Thou knowest my love of rehearsing them is becoming pleasanter as the years go by.

Teach me that occasionally it is possible that I may be mistaken.

Make me thoughtful, but not moody; helpful, but not bossy. Give me an awareness of the limits to my own store of wisdom. It seems a pity not to use it all, but Thou knowest, Lord, that I want a few friends at the end. Amen.

TIME SPEEDS ON

When as a child, I laughed and wept,
    Time crept.
When as a youth, I dreamed and talked,
    Time walked.
When I became a full grown man,
    Time ran.
When older still I daily grew,
    Time flew.
Soon I shall find in traveling on
    Time gone.

"So teach us to number our days, that we may apply our hearts unto wisdom."
Psalm 90:12

A Prayer

When my hair is thin and silvered, and
    my time of toil is through,
When I've many years behind me, and
    ahead of me a few,
I shall want to sit, I reckon, sort of
    dreaming in the sun,
And recall the roads I've traveled, and
    the many things I've done.
I hope there'll be no picture that I'll
    hate to look upon
When the time to paint it better or to
    wipe it out, is gone.
I hope there'll be no vision of a hasty
    word I've said
That has left a trail of sorrow, like a
    whip welt, sore and red.
And I hope my old age dreaming will
    bring back no bitter scene
Of a time when I was selfish, or a time
    when I was mean.
When I'm getting old and feeble, and
    I'm far along life's way,
I don't want to sit regretting any
    bygone yesterday.
I am painting now the picture that I'll
    want some day to see.
I am filling in a canvas that will soon
    come back to me.
Though nothing great is on it, and
    though nothing there is fine,
I shall want to look it over when I'm
    old, and call it mine.
So I do not dare to leave it, while the
    paint is warm and wit,
With a single thing upon it that I later
    will regret.

—Author unknown

Not Growing Old

They say that I am growing old,
I've heard them tell it times untold.
In language plain and bold—
But I'm not growing old.

This frail old shell
In which I dwell
Is growing old, I know full well—
But I am not the shell.

What if my hair is turning gray?
Gray hairs are honorable, they say.
What if my eyesight's growing dim?
I still can see to follow Him
Who sacrificed His life for me upon
  the Cross of Calvary.

What should I care if time's old plow
Has left its furrows on my brow?
Another house, not made by hand
Awaits me in the Glory Land.

What though I falter in my walk?
What though my tongue refuse to talk?
I still can tread the narrow way,
I still can watch and praise and pray.

My hearing may not be so keen,
As in the past it may have been.
Still, I can hear my Savior say
In whisper soft, "This is the way."

The outward man—do what I can
To lengthen out this life's short span—
Shall perish, and return to dust,
As everything in nature must.

The inward man, the scriptures say,
Is growing stronger every day.
Then how can I be growing old
When safe within my Savior's fold?

Ere long my soul shall fly away
And leave this tenement of clay.
"This robe of flesh I'll drop and rise
To seize the everlasting prize"—
I'll meet you on the streets of gold,
And prove that I'm not growing old.

      —*John E. Roberts*

How I Can Tell

How do I know my youth is all spent?
Well, my get up and go has got up and
  went.
But in spite of it all, I'm able to grin,
When I think where my get up and go has
  been.
Old age is golden, so I've heard it said.
But sometimes I wonder when I get into bed
With my ears in a drawer, my teeth in a cup,
I realize that I'm not still a pup.
Ere sleep dims my eyes, I say to myself,
Is there anything else to be put on the
  shelf?
And I'm happy to say as I close the door,
My friends are the same way, perhaps
  even more.
When I was young, my slippers were red.
I could kick my heels right over my head.
And when I grew older my slippers were
  blue,
But still I could dance the whole night
  through.
Now I am old, my slippers are black.
I walk to the store and puff my way back.
The reason I know my life is near spent:
My get up and go has got up and went.
But really, I don't mind, and I think with
  a grin
Of all the grand places my get up has been.
Since I have retired from life competition,
I busy myself with complete repetition—
I get up each morning, and I dust off my
  wits,
Pick up my paper and read the obits—
If my name is missing, I know I'm not
  dead,
So I eat a good breakfast, and go back to
  bed.

      —*Author unknown*

"This Old House"

Has your "get up and go" "got up and went"?

We dedicate this item to some of our senior citizens who are not yet ready to admit that years are creeping up.

Everything is farther than it used to be. It's twice as far to the bus stop, for instance, and they have added a hill, I've noticed. I've given up running for a bus—it leaves faster than it used to.

Seems to me they are making staircases steeper than they used to make them in the old days. And have you noticed the small print they are using? Newspapers are getting farther away when I hold them, and I have to squint to make out the news. No sense to have them read aloud; everyone speaks in such a low voice that I can hardly hear them.

The barber doesn't hold a mirror behind me any more so I can see the back of my head. The material in my suits is always too skimpy around the waist and in the seat. And shoe laces are so short they are almost impossible to reach.

Even people are changing. They are so much older than I am. I ran into an old classmate the other night and he had aged so that I didn't recognize him. I got to thinking about the poor fellow while I was shaving this morning. While doing so, I glanced in the mirror at my own reflection. Confound it! They don't use the same kind of glass in mirrors any more!

Something is haywire, topsy-turvy, or just plain crazy, and I just can't figure what it is!

At Sunset

It isn't the thing you do, dear,
It's the thing you've left undone
Which gives you a bit of heartache
At the setting of the sun.
The tender word forgotten,
The letter you did not write,
The flower you might have sent, dear,
Are your haunting ghosts tonight.

The stone you might have lifted
Out of a brother's way,
The bit of heartsome counsel
You were hurried too much to say,
The loving touch of the hand, dear,
The gentle and winsome tone
That you had no time or thought for,
With troubles enough to your own.

The little act of kindness,
So easily out of mind;
Those chances to be angels,
Which every mortal finds—
They come in night and silence—
Each chill, reproachful wraith—
When hope is faint and flagging,
And a blight has dropped on faith.

For life is all too short, dear,
And sorrow is all to great
To suffer our slow compassion
That tarries until too late.
And it's not the thing you do, dear,
It's the thing you leave undone,
Which gives you the bit of heartache
At the setting of the sun.

—Margaret E. Sangster

God, keep my heart attuned to laughter
　　When youth is done;
When all the days are gray days, coming after
　　The warmth of sun.
God, keep me then from bitterness, from grieving,
　　When life seems cold;
God, keep me loving and believing
　　As I grow old.

End of Life's Book

When we near the end of the writ of life,
And are near to the close of the book,
Our thoughts give the pages a backward
    turn,
With many a lingering look.
And memory paints from the written
    page
Those pictures that stay on her walls.
And while present things fade,
Those undimmed by age remain, 'till the
    temple falls.
Then we lift our gaze to the hills beyond,
That are rosy with sunset glow;
And we only dream as we linger here,
Of the things we then will know.

—Mrs. Thos. E. Boorde

Eventide

I want to know, when day is done,
That life has been worth living—
That I have brought somebody joy
Through kind, unselfish living.

I want to feel, when evening falls
And shadows quickly lengthen,
That I have made somebody glad,
Some weakness I have strengthened.

I want to know, that come what may,
I've left some cheer and gladness;
I want to feel, at close of day
I've banished someone's sadness.

I want to feel at close of day,
That someone's cares were lighter.
Because of kindness I have done,
May someone's life be brighter.

—Raymond Orner

PACKING UP

I need to pack for a coming journey,
And must not forget important things...
For it's not a round trip passage;
There will be no way to come back!...
I shall take faith and pack it tightly
Among the folds of daily life,
And hold before me courage
To give strength when shadows come.
Too long I have wrestled with small
    things
That would not stay packed to the end...
But crumble they would,
And could not be used
At the end of my destination!
O, I would pray daily to keep in store
The vital things I need for my soul
That when my journey starts
I shall be packed and ready.

—Clara S. Hoff

SUNSET

When I stand in the glow of life's sunset
    And think on the things of the day,
Will tears of regret roll down my cheek
    For the things I have missed on the way?

Will my life be just a hodgepodge
    Of carelessness, greed and doubt,
Or will it tell the story
    Of taking the easy way out?

Will it be like a business ledger
    With figures neat and trim,
And over against the things of self
    Will there be a few items for Him?

God, help me to live in the daytime
    A life that is dotted with good;
That the Master Accountant who audits
    the books,
    Will say, "She has done what she
    could."

—Mae Conat Hill

At Evening Time

So many things I cannot do
  That once were my delight.
From picnics on a sandy beach
  To walks through fog at night.

I cannot stroll along the street,
  Nor through a shady grove
To seek the wild bird's nesting place
  And nature's treasure-trove.

I cannot sail the restless sea,
  Nor ramble through the hills;
Nor can I coast down snowy slopes
  With heart-disturbing thrills.

So many things I cannot do
  Since I am shut at home.
"Shut in with God," and praise His name,
  I do not need to roam.

For I can reach the throne of grace
  While seated in my chair,
Because He has bestowed on us
  The privilege of prayer.

And He has etched upon my heart
  His promises to me
Of peace and comfort, better far
  Than joys that used to be.

—Ella B. Jones

NOT RETIRING

Growing old, but not retiring,
  For the battle still is on;
Going on without relenting
  Till the final victory's won.
Ever on, nor think of resting,
  For the battle rages still
And my Saviour walks beside me,
  As I seek to do His will.

Let me labor in Thy harvest
  More than ever in the past.
Reaping in what Thou hast planted,
  Till I dwell with Thee at last;
That before Thy throne eternal,
  I may have some fruit to bring;
Not my work—the fruit of Calvary,
  All Thine own, my Lord and King.

—From "Our Daily Bread"

You Tell Me I Am Getting Old

You tell me I am getting old.
  I tell you that's not so!
The "house" I live in is worn out,
  And that, of course, I know.

It's been in use a long, long while;
  It's weathered many a gale;
I'm really not surprised you think it's
  Getting somewhat frail.

The color changing on the roof,
  The window getting dim,
The walls a bit transparent and
  Looking rather thin.

The foundation not so steady as
  Once it used to be—
My "house" is getting shaky, but my
  "House" isn't ME!

My few short years can't make me old.
  I feel I'm in my youth.
Eternity lies just ahead, a life of
  Joy and truth.

I'm going to live forever, there;
  Life will go on—it's grand!
You tell me I am getting old!
  You just don't understand.

The dweller in my little "house"
  Is young and bright and gay;
Just starting on a life to last
  Throughout eternal day.

You only see the outside, which is
  All that most folks see.
You tell me I am getting old?
  You've mixed my house with ME!

—Dora Johnson
(88 years young)

204

The Way Home

Years and years ago, when I was just a little lad,
And after school hours used to help around the farm with Dad;
I used to get so very tired when eventide would come,
That I'd get kind of fearsome-like
   About the journey home.

But Dad would always lead the way, and once in awhile turn 'round and say,
So tender-like, so cheering—"Come on, my lad, we're nearing home";
That always kind of helped me some,
   Following Father home.

I'm getting old and feeble now, and trembly at the knee,
But life is just the same today as then it used to be;
And I am very weary now that eventide has come,
And sometimes still get fearful-like,
   About the journey home.

But still my Father leads the way, and once in awhile I hear Him say,
So tender like, so cheering—"Come on, my child, you're nearly home";
And still that kind of helps me some,
   And so I'm following Father's Son.

—Anonymous

Crossing the Bar

Sunset and evening star,
   And one clear call for me!
And may there be no moaning of the bar,
   When I put out to sea.

But such a tide as moving seems asleep,
   Too full for sound or foam.
When that which drew form out the
     boundless deep
Turns again home.

Twilight and evening bell,
   And after that the dark!
And may there be no sadness of farewell,
   When I embark.

For though from out our bourne of Time
     and Place
   The flood may bear me far,
I hope to see my Pilot face to face
   When I have crossed the bar.

—Alfred Lord Tennyson

My latest sun is sinking fast,
   My race is nearly run;
My strongest trials now are past,
   My triumph is begun.

I know I'm nearing the holy ranks
   Of friends and kindred dear;
For brush the dews on Jordan's
     banks,
   The crossing must be near.

I've almost gained my heavenly
     home,
   My spirit loudly sings;
Thy holy ones, behold, they come!
   I hear the noise of wings.

O, bear my longing heart to Him
   Who bled and died for me;
Whose blood now cleanses from all
     sin,
   And gives me victory.

—J. Hascall

The Heart's Cry for Sympathy

If I should die tonight
My friends would look upon my quiet face
Before they laid it in its resting place,
And deem that death had left it almost fair,
And laying snow-white flowers against my
hair
Would smooth it down with tearful tender-
ness,
And fold my hands with lingering caress;
  Poor hands, so empty and so cold tonight.

If I should die tonight
My friends would call to mind with loving
thought
Some kindly deed the icy hand had wrought,
Some gentle word the frozen lips had said,
Errands on which the willing feet had sped.
The memory of my selfishness and pride,
My hasty words, would all be set aside,
  And I should be loved and mourned
    tonight.

If I should die tonight,
E'en hearts estranged would once more turn
to me,
Recalling other days remorsefully;
The eyes that chill me with averted glance
Would look upon me as of yore, perchance,
And soften in the old, familiar way;
For who would war with dumb, unconscious
clay?
  So I might rest forgiven of all tonight.

O, friends, I pray tonight,
Keep not your kisses for my dead, cold brow;
The way is lonely; let me feel them now;
Think gently of me; I am travel worn,
My faltering feet are pierced with many a
thorn;
Forgive! ah, hearts estranged, I plead!
When dreamless rest is mine, I shall not need
  The tenderness for which I long tonight.
                    —*Henry Ward Beecher*

There Was a Man

*"What doth it profit a man, to gain
the whole world, and forfeit his life?"*

There was a man in our town,
  And he had wondrous health;
But recklessly he squandered it
  Accumulating wealth.
And when he saw his health was
    gone,
  With all his might and main,
He squandered all the wealth he'd
    won
  To get his health again.
And when with neither health nor
    wealth
  He in his coffin lay,
The preacher couldn't say a thing
  Excepting, "Let us pray!"

Around the Corner

Around the corner I had a friend,
In this great city, that has no end.
Yet days go by and weeks rush on
And before I know it, a year has gone,
And I never see my old friend's face,
For life is a swift and terrible race.
He knows I like him just as well
As in the days when I rang his bell,
And he rang mine; we were younger
    then.
And now we are busy, tired men,
Tired of playing the foolish game.
Tired of trying to make a name.
"Tomorrow," I say, "I'll call on Jim
Just to show him that I think of him."
But tomorrow comes, and tomorrow
    goes,
And the distance between us grows
    and grows.
Around the corner—yet miles away,
"Here's a telegram, sir." Jim died
    today.
And that's what we get and deserve
    in the end.
Around the corner, a vanished friend.
                    —*C. Henson Towne*

206

He Comes to Church

At last he came to church today;
Six neighbors carried him that way;
But when he passed the portals
    straight,
Another had to swing the gate,
Another open wide the door,
For he could open it no more.
But now at last he came in search
Of something that they have in
    church.

The preacher spoke a helpful word,
And yet I wonder if he heard.
Or, if he heard, he understood?
His hearing now was not so good.
He was made welcome, even then;
And yet he would have been, I
    know,
As welcome years and years ago.

We all must go to church some day,
But some of us too long delay.
The words of comfort by our bier
We could have come in life to hear.
For here to greet us waits a Friend
At the beginning, not the end.
Religion is for living—aye,
To live by, not alone to die.

—*Douglas Malloch*

SAILS

I watched a sail until it dropped from sight
Over the rounding sea. A gleam of white,
A last far-flashed farewell, and, like a thought
Slipt out of mind, it vanished and was not.

Yet the helmsman standing at the wheel
Broad seas still stretched beneath the gliding keel.
Disaster? Change? He felt no slightest sign,
Nor dreamed he of that far horizon line.

So may it be, perchance, when down the tide
Our dear ones vanish. Peacefully they glide
On level seas, nor mark the unknown bound.
We call it death—to them 'tis life beyond.

SAY IT NOW

What silences we keep year after year,
    With those who are most near to us and dear!
We live beside each other day by day,
    We speak of myriad things, but seldom say
The full sweet word that lies just in our reach,
    Beneath the commonplace of common
        speech:
Then out of sound, and out of reach they go—
    These dear, familiar ones who loved us so;
And sitting in the shadow they have left,
    Alone with loneliness, and sore bereft,
We think with vain regret of some kind word
    That once we might have said and they
        have heard.

—*Nora Perry*

How Old Are You?

Age is a quality of mind—
If you have left your dreams behind,
If hope is lost,
If you no longer look ahead,
If your ambitions' fires are dead—
    Then you are old!

But if from life you take the best,
And if in life you keep the jest,
If love you hold—
No matter how the years go by,
No matter how the birthdays fly,
    You are not old!

—*Author unknown*

My Twilight Years

*May I not forget the strength that comforted me in the desolation of other darkened
    hours of despair;*
Spare me from bitterness and sharp passion of unguarded moments;
May I not forget that poverty and riches are of the spirit;
May my thoughts and actions keep me friendly with myself;
Let me not follow the clamor of the world but walk calmly down my path;
Give me a few friends who love me for what I am;
Keep ever burning before my vagrant steps the kindly light of hope;
*Though age and infirmity overtake me and I come not within sight of the castle of my
    dreams, teach me still to be thankful for life and sweet memories.*
May the evening's twilight find me gentle, still.

—*J. R. Runkle*

To the Older Christian

You may be growing older,
And your step a mite bit slow;
You may not move as fast as once,
But oh, God loves you so.
You may think that you're not needed,
That your work down here is through;
But, my beloved oldster,
God has a plan for you.
Your white hair shows the wisdom
You've gathered through the years;
Your patience stands for victories,
Proves you've conquered many fears.
Your sweetness shows that Christ
    indwells,
His love in you abides;
As these virtues flow out from you,
You're blessing other lives.
Oh, don't ever be discouraged
If others must wait on you;
You've done your share of service,
Just let His light shine through.
So rejoice and live for Jesus
And to others His kindness show;
You're still wanted and still needed,
You're God's messenger, you know!

—*Claire Belle Steinmiller*

Abide With Me

Abide with me! Fast falls the eventide,
The darkness deepens; Lord, with me
    abide!
When other helpers fail, and comforts
    flee,
Help of the helpless, O, abide with me!

Swift to its close ebbs out life's little day;
Earth's joys grow dim, its glories pass
    away;
Change and decay in all around I see;
O Thou, who changest not, abide with me!

I need Thy presence every passing hour,
What but Thy grace can foil the tempter's
    power?
Who, like Thyself, my guide and stay can be?
Through cloud and sunshine, Lord, abide
    with me!

Hold Thou Thy cross before my closing
    eyes;
Shine through the gloom and point me to
    the skies;
Heaven's morning breaks, and earth's
    vain shadows flee.
In life, in death, O Lord, abide with me!

—*Henry Lyte*

DYING WORDS OF CHRISTIANS

"Our God is the God from whom cometh salvation. God is the Lord by whom we escape death." —Martin Luther.

"Live in Christ, die in Christ, and the flesh need not fear death." —John Knox.

"The best of all, God is with us." —John Wesley.

"I have pain—there is no argument against sense; but I have peace, I have peace." —Richard Baxter.

"More praise still. O help me to praise Him. I have nothing else to do. I have done with prayers and other ordinances." —John Janeway.

"The battle's fought—the battle's fought and the victory is won! The victory is won forever! I am going to bathe in an ocean of purity and benevolence and happiness to all Eternity. Faith and patience, hold out." —Payson.

"Glory of God! I see Heaven sweetly opened before me." —Abbott.

"Glory! Glory! Glory!" —Joseph Everett. (These exclamations of rapture continued for twenty-five minutes and then only ceased with life itself.

"Earth recedes and Heaven opens . . . This is my coronation day." —Dwight L. Moody.

"Look, I see the angels coming with Jesus . . . They're coming after me." —My mother, Mrs. R. R. Crowley.

———

If I think I may scatter some comfort and cheer,
I'll be willing to tarry one more little year.
But then if, like Moses, my work is all done,
I pray the dear Father to gather me home.

DYING WORDS OF SINNERS

"All my possessions for a moment of time!" —Queen Elizabeth.

"I am suffering the pangs of the damned." —Talleyrand.

"Hell is a refuge, if it hide me from Thy frown." —Altamonth, the infidel.

"I would gladly give 30,000 pounds to have it proved there is no hell!" —Chartres, the atheist.

"Give me more laudanum that I may not think of eternity." —Mirabeau, agnostic.

"I am taking a fearful leap into the dark." —Hobbs, the atheist.

"I am abandoned by God and man! I shall go to Hell! O Christ, O Jesus Christ!" —Voltaire, the infidel.

"The devil is ready to seduce us, and I have been seduced." —Cromwell.

"When I lived, I provided for everything but death; now I must die, and I am unprepared to die." —Caesar Borgia.

"What blood, what murders, what evil councils have I followed. I am lost! I see it well!" —Charles IX, King of France.

"Until this moment I thought there was neither God nor a hell; now I know and feel that there are both and I am doomed to perdition by the just judgment of the Almighty!" —Sir Thomas Scott.

"I would give worlds, if I had them, if the 'Age of Reason' had never been published. O Lord, help me! Christ, help me! Stay with me! It is hell to be left alone!" —Tom Paine.

"Oh, my poor soul! What will become of thee? Wither wilt thou go?" —Cardinal Mazarin.

I'd Rather Say, "I'm Fine"!

There is nothing whatever the matter with me,
  I am just as healthy as can be.
I have arthritis in both my knees,
  And when I talk, I talk with a wheeze;
My pulse is weak, my blood is thin,
  But I'm awfully well for the shape I'm in.
My teeth eventually have to come out,
  And my diet . . . I hate to think about.
I'm overweight and I can't get thin,
  But I'm awfully well for the shape I'm in.
I think my liver is out of whack,
  And a terrible pain is in my back,
My hearing is poor, my sight is dim,
  And everything seems to be out of trim.
My food and saliva don't seem to blend,
  But I'm awfully well for the shape I'm in.
I have arch supports for both my feet,
  Or I wouldn't be able to walk the street.
Sleeplessness I have night after night,
  And in the mornings I look a sight.
I'm practically living on aspirin,
  But I'm awfully well for the shape I'm in.
THE MORAL IS, as this tale we unfold,
  That for you and me who are growing old,
It's better to say, "I'm fine" with a grin,
  Than to let them know the shape we're in.
  —*Contributed by A. C. Maxwell, Houston, TX*

Heaven and Immortality . . .

HEAVEN

HEAVEN, the home of mansions fair,
Here are some of the things that will not
    be there:
No sin can enter the portals fair,
The vile and the unclean shall not be
    there;
No sickness, no death, suffering or pain,
No devil, no demons can entrance gain;
No darkness, no night, woe or despair,
No cares or heavy burdens to bear;
No disappointment in that Fair Land,
No tears or sighs on the Golden Strand;
No fear of evil our peace to annoy,
Nothing to hurt, mar or destroy;
No heartache or grief, no not a trace
Will ever be found in that Holy Place;
Yea, fairer than mortals here have known,
Are the things God hath prepared for
    His own!

Heaven, the place so wondrously fair,
Here are some things that will be there:
God's throne where the glorified pros-
    trate fall,
Jesus, the Saviour, fairest of all!
Saints of all ages, lovers of God,
All who have been washed in the Blood;
Loved ones and friends dear to the heart,
Will meet in that land nevermore to part;
Children of all kinds will be seen,
Joyful and happy on swards of green;
Amid the flowers that never fade,
Gorgeous colors of every shade;
The River of Life and streets of gold,
Oh, the beauties of Heaven can never be
    told;
Such music and singing on earth is not
    heard,
Nor can be described by pen or word;

The Tree of Life, with trees blooming fair,
All manner of fruit will be found there;
Perfect love and perfect rest,
Companionship with all the blest;
Perfect peace, freedom from strife,
Everlasting joy, eternal life!
Yea, more than mortals here have known,
Are the things God hath prepared for
    His own!

—Catherine Dongell

A Child of the King

My Father is rich in houses and lands,
He holdeth the wealth of the world in
    His hands!
Of rubies and diamonds, of silver and
    gold,
His coffers are full, He has riches untold.
My Father's own Son, the Savior of men,
Once wandered o'er earth as the poorest
    of men;
But now He is reigning forever on high,
And will give me a home in heav'n by
    and by.
I once was an outcast stranger on earth,
A sinner by choice, an alien by birth!
But I've been adopted, my name's writ-
    ten down,
An heir to a mansion, a robe, and a crown.
A tent or a cottage, why should I care?
They're building a place for me over
    there!
Tho' exiled from home, yet still I may
    sing;
    All glory to God, I'm the child of a
    King.

That Beautiful Land
Called Heaven

I read of a land more fair than this.
  It's free from sin and shame.
It is a land of perfect bliss,
  Where none are sick or lame.
It is a land forever free
  From disappointment sad;
Where all the saints in love agree
  In things that make them glad.
It is a land where strife will end,
  Where greed and pride will cease,
Where all will join in heart and hand
  In universal peace.
It is a land of true success,
  Where all are doing well,
Where all rejoice and praise the Lord,
  Who saved their souls from hell.
It is a land of no regrets
  That cast their shadows round.
It is a bright and happy land,
  In which no clouds are found.
The unkind word will never sting
  Within this land above,
For all will speak like Christ their
    King,
  The King of peace and love.
Here broken hearts will all be healed,
  And friends will part no more.
Eternal joys are here revealed
  On those celestial shores.
Though countless ages onward roll,
  Its pleasures never cease.
Then let the Christ into your soul,
  And share His eternal peace.

Heaven!

Heaven's promise; O what comfort!
Land which knows no pain nor strife—
Shores of beauty—dawn unending,
Goal, toward to press, thru life!
Oh what joy in Jesus' presence!
Christ, whose love is freely mine!
He—Who came to earth to save me,
Precious Savior—King Divine!
There before His throne I'll worship,
Gaze upon His lovely face;
Thank Him! For my soul's salvation,
Praise Him for His wondrous grace.
I shall kneel before my Maker—
List to heaven's choirs, sweet,
Hear the angels sing His praises—
Cast my crowns before His feet!
Sinless—perfect—Holy City!
Gates of pearl . . . oh streets of gold!
Death shall never draw her curtain,
Night shall not its mantle fold.
I shall walk and talk with Jesus,
He who waits on yonder shore;
Oh, my soul doth long for HEAVEN,
There to dwell forevermore!

—*Connie Calenberg*

When the Mists
Have Rolled Away

When the mists have rolled in splendor
  From the beauty of the hills,
And the sunlight falls in gladness
  On the river and the rills,
We recall our Father's promise
  In the rainbow of the spray:
We shall know each other better
  When the mists have rolled away.

We shall come with joy and gladness,
  We shall gather round the throne;
Face to face with those that love us,
  We shall know as we are known:
And the song of our redemption
  Shall resound through endless day
When the shadows have departed,
  And the mists have rolled away.

—*Annie Herbert*

Looking for a House?

This house is a mansion, made of stone, precious stones. The stones are all different in color, the walls are jasper. The foundation is solid rock, garnished with precious stones. The gates are made of one pearl. Driveway—transparent gold. Running water, clear as a crystal coming from the Throne of God. Many rooms are in this great mansion; all of this put together without the sound of a hammer. Beautifully landscaped. The trees are monthly, bearing twelve manner of fruit. There are no electric bills to pay—this house is never dark—has new lighting system. The Lamb is the light thereof. Rev. 21:23—This house is so clean, there's no sickness or death. This house is so pleasant, you cannot cry—for God wipes away all your tears. Rev. 21:4.

The best insurance ever, guaranteed against any destruction such as lightning, tornadoes, or earthquakes. There's no bloodshed or bombing in this house. Communists cannot come through the front or back gate. Highly restricted neighborhood—restrictions that cannot be broken. There aren't any neighbors that are robbers, thieves, drunkards, adulterers or liars; in fact, all commandment breakers are restricted from this area.

The payment of this purchased possession was made at Calvary. The Holy Ghost is the Administrator. By grace you become an inheritor through the shed blood of Jesus. By repentance of sin, the shed blood is applied to the heart. Then you give your heart.

—Audrey Dorer

Think of It!

Think of stepping on shore
　And finding it Heaven.
Of taking hold of a hand
　And finding it God's hand.
Of breathing a new air
　And finding it celestial air;
Of feeling invigorated
　And finding it immortality.
Of passing from storm and
　　tempest
　To perfect calm.
Of waking and knowing
That I am Home!

When His Glory Paints the Sky

I can see Him through the twilight
　At the closing of the day.
I could almost hear Him whisper
　As to Him I knelt to pray.

Only wait a little longer.
　Falter not in faith or sight.
I will meet you in the morning
　When His glory paints the sky.

With my eye of faith upon Him,
　Though the shadows thicken fast,
For the darkness cannot hide Him,
　Till the morning break at last.

In my times of deepest anguish,
　When with bitter tears I pray,
I can hear His gentle whisper,
　I am near you all the way.

Only wait a little longer.
　Falter not in faith or sight.
I will meet you in the morning
　When His glory paints the sky.

Where the Rainbow Never Fades

It cannot be that the earth is man's only abiding place. It cannot be that our life is a mere bubble cast up by eternity to float a moment on its waves and then sink into nothingness. Else why is it that the glorious aspirations which leap like angels from the temple of our heart are forever wandering unsatisfied? Why is it that all the stars that hold their festival around the midnight throne are set above the grasp of our limited faculties, forever mocking us with their unapproachable glory? And, finally, why is it that bright forms of human beauty presented to our view are taken from us, leaving the thousand streams of our affections to flow back in Alpine torrents upon our hearts? There is a realm where the rainbow never fades; where the stars will be spread out before us like islands that slumber in the ocean, and where the beautiful beings which now pass before us like shadows will stay in our presence forever.

—George D. Prentice in "Man's Higher Destiny"

No Disappointment in Heaven

There's no disappointment in Heaven,
  No weariness, sorrow or pain.
No hearts that are bleeding and broken,
  No song with a minor refrain.
The clouds of our earthly horizon
  Will never appear in the sky,
For all will be sunshine and gladness
  With never a sob or a sigh.

There'll never be crepe on the door knob,
  No funeral train in the sky;
No grave on the hillside of glory,
  For there men shall nevermore die.
The old will be young there forever
  Transformed in a moment of time;
Immortal we'll stand in His likeness
  The stars and the sun to outshine.

I'm bound for the beautiful city
  My Lord has prepared for His own,
Where all the redeemed of all ages
  Sing glory because they are home.
Sometimes I grow homesick for heaven
  And the glories I there shall behold.
What a joy that will be when my Savior
  I see
In that beautiful city of gold.

—F. M. Lehman

Love Keeps Its Own Eternally

I cannot think of them as dead
  Who walk with me no more.
Along the path of life I tread,
  They have but gone before.

The Father's house is mansioned fair
  Beyond my vision dim;
All souls are His, and here or there
  Are living unto Him.

And still their silent ministry
  Within my heart hath place,
As when on earth they walked with me
  And met me face to face.

Their lives are made forever mine;
  What they to me have been,
Hath left henceforth its seal and sign
  Engraven deep within.

Mine are they by an ownership
  Nor time nor death can free;
For God hath giv'n to Love to keep
  Its own eternally.

—Frederick Hosmer

We'll All Be Together Again

When dear ones have left us to journey afar
O'er mountain or prairies or sea,
Our thoughts travel oft where the loving ones are
And lonely we often must be.
But sweet is the thought of the homecoming time
To women, and children and men.
It rings, like the bells, with a musical chime;
We'll all be together again!

When sickness and trouble break into our lives,
When cares throng in manifold ways,
When many a wearisome burden contrives
To mar the sweet peace of our days,
When lives have been sundered by death's cruel
      hand,
When dear ones no more have our care,
All happy and safe in the beautiful land;
So safe, no more needing our prayer.
Oh, blessed thoughts of the meeting once more
Beyond all sorrow and pain;
Where nothing is wrong on the heavenly shore
And we'll all be together again!

—J. M. Wylie

IN MEMORIAM

So live, that when thy summons comes to join
The innumerable caravan, that moves
To that mysterious realm, where each shall take
His chamber in the silent halls of death,
Thou go not, like the quarry-slave at night,
Scourged to his dungeon; but, sustained and
      soothed
By an unfaltering faith, approach thy grave,
Like one who wraps the drapery of his couch
About him, and lies down in resurrection faith.

—Adapted from William Cullen Bryant

You May Go to Heaven

Without health,
Without wealth,
Without fame,
Without a great name,
Without an education,
Without big earnings,
Without culture,
Without beauty,
Without friends,
      BUT
**Remember, you
can't go to heaven
without Christ.**

Just Around the Corner

Just around the corner,
    a little out of sight
Your loved one walked ahead
    into Eternal Light.

Just around the corner,
    there is a brighter view,
Where many other loved ones
    at last can see God, too!

And tho' your work's
    not finished here,
Just know God hears
    your prayer.

Someday just around
    the corner
You will find your
    loved one there!

"Behold, I show you a mystery; we shall not all sleep, but we shall all be changed, in a moment, in the twinkling of an eye, at the last trump: for the trumpet shall sound, and the dead shall be raised incorruptible, and we shall be changed. For this corruption must put on incorruption, and this mortal must put on immortality. So when this corruptible shall have put on incorruption, and this mortal shall have put on immortality, then shall be brought to pass the saying, Death is swallowed up in victory" (1 Cor. 15:51-54).

Safely Home!

I am home in Heaven, dear ones;
   All's so happy, all's so bright!
There's a perfect joy and beauty
   In this everlasting light.

All the pain and grief are over,
   Every restless tossing passed;
I am now at peace forever,
   Safely home in Heaven at last.

Did you wonder I so calmly
   Trod the Valley of the Shade?
Oh! but Jesus' love illumined
   Every dark and fearful glade.

And He came Himself to meet me
   In that way so hard to tread;
And with Jesus' arm to lean on,
   Could I have one doubt or dread?

Then you must not grieve so sorely,
   For I love you dearly still;
Try to look beyond earth's shadows,
   Pray to trust our Father's will.

There is work still waiting for you,
   So you must not idle stand;
Do your work while life remaineth—
   You shall rest in Jesus' land.

When that work is all complete,
   He will gently call you home;
Oh, the rapture of the meeting!
   Oh, the joy to see you come!

Immortality of the Soul

Victor Hugo's great soul found utterance in his later years for these thoughts, which will find an echo in many hearts:

"I feel in myself the future life. I am like a forest once cut down; the new shoots are stronger and livelier than ever. I am rising, I know, toward the sky. The sunshine is on my head. The earth gives me its generous sap, but heaven lights me with the reflection of unknown worlds.

"You say the soul is nothing but the resultant of the bodily powers. Why, then, if my soul more luminous when my bodily powers begin to fail? Winter is on my head, but eternal spring is in my heart. I breathe at this hour the fragrance of the lilacs, the violets and the roses, as at twenty years. The nearer I approach the end the plainer I hear around me the immortal symphonies of the worlds which invite me. It is marvelous yet simple. It is a fairy tale, and it is history.

"For half a century I have been writing my thoughts in prose and in verse; history, philosophy, drama, romance, tradition, satire, ode and song; I have tried all. But I feel I have not said the thousandth part of what is in me. When I go down to the grave, I can say like many others—'I have finished my day's work.' But I cannot say, 'I have finished my life.' My day's work will begin again the next morning. The tomb is not a blind alley; it is a thoroughfare. It closes on the twilight, it opens on the dawn."

216

My Heavenly Home

The destination of my God
Is not within the grave's cold walls;
But where the bells of heaven toll,
I'll soar whene'er my Savior calls!

Yea, far beyond the starry sky
There is a land bereft of care;
When to its glories I draw nigh
I'll see my Savior standing there!

With smiling face he'll bid me come,
And lead me to a mansion fair;
O day of days! When I reach home—
What joy! What bliss beyond compare!

The destination of my Soul
Is not beneath the cold, gray sod;
But when the bells of heaven toll,
I'll soar to meet my Living God.

HEAVEN

And God shall wipe away all tears from their eyes (Rev. 21:4).

A City without tears—God wipes away all tears up yonder. This is a time of weeping, but by and by there will be a time when God shall call us where there will be no tears. A City without pain, a City without sorrow, without sickness, without death . . . Think of a place where temptation cannot come. Think of a place where we shall be free from sin . . . and where the righteous shall reign forever. Think of a City that is not built with hands, whose inhabitants are numbered by no census, except the Book of Life. . . Think of a city where no hearses with their nodding plumes creep slowly with their sad burdens to the cemetery; a city without griefs or graves, without sins or sorrows, without marriages or mournings, without births or burials; a city which glories in having Jesus for its King, angels for its guards, and whose citizens are saints.

—Dwight L. Moody

WITH GOD

More homelike seems the vast unknown
　Since loved ones entered there;
To follow them were not so hard,
　Wherever they may fare.
They cannot be where God is not,
　On any sea or shore;
What'er betides, Thy love abides,
　Our God, forevermore.

—John W. Chadwick

When I Stand on the Streets of Gold

"He shewed me that great city, the holy Jerusalem" (Rev. 21:10-27).

The burdens of life may be many,
　The frowns of the world may be cold.
To me it will matter but little,
　When I stand on the Streets of Gold.
With joy I shall enter the city,
　The face of my Saviour behold;
And I shall be changed and be like Him,
　When I stand on the Streets of Gold.
What wonderful visions of beauty,
　What glorious scenes shall unfold,
What dazzling splendors surround me,
　When I stand on the Streets of Gold.
Earth's sorrows will all be forgotten,
　And I shall be safe in His fold;
Shut in with my Lord and the angels,
　When I stand on the Streets of Gold.
I'll see the white throne of His glory,
　The names of the saints enrolled.
The mansions that Christ is preparing,
　When I stand on the Streets of Gold.
For ages on ages I'll praise Him,
　And never grow weary or old.
Love crowned, I'll abide in His presence,
　When I stand on the Streets of Gold.

Climbing White Rose

My garden beds were blooming.
  Yet now all I can see
Is my little fragrant white rose
  Growing eternally high for me.

So in life's wider garden
  There are buds of promise, too,
Beyond our reach to gather,
  But not beyond our view.

As sunbeam, and as shadows
  Fall from Christ's pierced hands,
We can surely trust His wisdom
  Since our heart He understands.

And maybe in the morning
  When His blessed face you see,
He will tell you why your white rose
  Has climbed up to eternity.

A Sunset Lesson

This evening I saw the sun set
  Behind the mountain dim;
It dropped from behind a beautiful
    cloud,
  All gold around its rim.
And as the sun sank down to rest,
  Beneath its bed of gold,
It filled my soul with rapture,
  Its beauty to behold.
O that my life, at close of day,
  May be as supremely bright,
As I pass on from this present world
  To the realms of endless light;
That a golden crown may await me
    there,
  As bright as this golden sky,
And that I may dwell forever there,
  In that beautiful home on high.

—*Etta M. Spicer*

SOMEDAY

Someday I'm gonna walk those streets of gold,
  Someday I'm gonna talk with saints of old;
Someday I'm gonna be forever
  In that Land so bright and fair;
Someday I'm gonna see the mansions
  He has promised to prepare.
Someday I'll see my Saviour
  Face to face, someday;
Someday I'll tell the story
  Saved by grace, someday.
Someday, till then, I don't know when,
  But until then He'll lead me all the way
To that eternal Homeland—someday!

—*Sharon and Donna Parschauer*

The Return of Christ . . .

Coming Soon

In the glow of early morning,
In the solemn hush of night;
Down from heaven's open portals,
   Steals a messenger of light.
Whispering sweetly to my spirit,
While the hosts of heaven sing!
This the wondrous thrilling story,
   Christ is coming, Christ my King.

Oft me thinks I hear His footsteps,
Stealing down the paths of time;
And the future dark with shadows,
   Brightens with the hope sublime.
Sound the soul-inspiring anthem
Angel hosts, your harps attune;
Earth's long night is almost over,
   Christ is coming—coming soon.

Long we've waited, blest Redeemer,
Waited for the first bright ray
Of the morn when sin and sorrow
   At thy Presence flee away;
But our vigil's nearly over;
Hope of heaven, oh, priceless boon!
In the east the glow appearing,
   Christ is coming—coming soon.

                  —*W. Macomber*

When we see Jesus
   Coming in glory;
When He comes from
   His home in the sky,
Then we shall meet Him
   In that bright mansion;
We'll understand it
   All by and by.

And They Shall See His Face

Rev. 22:4-10

"Shall see His Face," how wonderful!
That Face once "marred" on Calvary.
When standing in our room and stead,
He bore the curse and set us free.

"Shall see His Face" mid angel throngs,
What rapt'rous joy the thought affords.
There myriad hosts shall Him acclaim,
The King of kings and Lord of lords.

"Shall see His Face" where earthly sounds
No longer fall upon our ears,
Where sorrows end and conflicts cease,
And God shall wipe away our tears.

"Shall see His Face," His lovely Face,
Without a darkling veil between.
In the full blaze of Glory light,
His matchless beauty will be seen.

"Shall see His Face," O blessed hope,
It thrills our soul with ecstacy.
Not just a passing look or glance,
But GAZING through eternity.

Lord, haste that day when face to face,
We shall behold Thee as Thou art.
And in that new Eternal song,
Cleansed by Thy blood, we'll have a part.

There in that land of cloudless day,
Adoring at Thy feet we'll fall.
And with ten thousands of Thy saints,
Rejoicing, crown Thee Lord of all.

                  —*M. E. Rae*

Christ Returneth

It may be at morn when the day is awaking,
When sunlight thru darkness and shadow is
    breaking,
That Jesus will come in the fullness of glory
To receive from the world "His own."

It may be at mid-day, it may be at twilight,
It may be, perchance, that the blackness of
    midnight
Will burst into light in the blaze of His glory,
When Jesus receives "His own."

Oh joy, oh delight! should we go without
    dying.
No sickness, no sadness, no dread and no
    crying.
Caught up through the clouds with our Lord
    into glory
When Jesus receives "His own."

—*H. Turner*

NOW and THEN

NOW as through a glass, but darkly,
    Future hopes by faith we trace;
THEN in realms of radiant glory
    We shall see our Savior's face.

NOW by faith we see Him only,
    Our reflections may be dim;
THEN when He appears to call us,
    We shall really be like Him.

NOW, by scientific findings,
    Men attempt to conquer space;
THEN, our mighty Lord will take us
    Where He has prepared our place.

NOW, by His command, we spread
    His great Gospel Truth abroad;
THEN, we'll see in His blest presence
    Those we lead to Christ our Lord.

—*Mabel E. Palmer*

"Your Redemption Draweth Night"

Lift up your heads, rejoice,
    Redemption draweth nigh;
Now breathes a softer air,
    Now shines a milder sky;
The early trees put forth
    Their new and tender leaf;
Hushed is the moaning wind
    That told the winter's grief.

Lift up your heads, rejoice,
    Redemption draweth nigh;
Now mount the laden clouds
    Now flames the darkening sky;
The early scattered drops
    Descend with heavy fall,
And to the waiting earth
    The hidden thunders call.

Lift up your heads, rejoice,
    Redemption draweth nigh;
O note the varying signs
    Of earth, and air, and sky;
The God of glory comes
    In gentleness and might,
To comfort and alarm,
    To succor and to smite.

He comes, the wide world's King,
    He comes, the true heart's
        Friend,
New gladness to begin,
    And ancient wrong to end;
He comes to fill with light
    The weary waiting eye:
Lift up your heads, rejoice,
    Redemption draweth nigh.

If Christ Had Come Today

Our Lord has told us all to watch
  His coming to discern:
For in an hour when we think not,
  Our Savior shall return.

Suppose that He had come today,
  At morning or at noon,
Or in the evening? For we know
  It will be very soon.

Would I have been ashamed before
  Him, as He looked on me?
Have I been glorifying Him
  Who died to set me free?

What thoughts possessed me, as about
  My daily task I went?
What of those hasty words I spoke,
  When I was tired and spent?

That visit which I meant to make,
  That word of comfort say;
I'd ne'er have had another chance,
  If Christ had come today.

When pausing on the step to greet
  My neighbor with a word,
How strange I did not say one thing
  About my precious Lord.

Why is my time so occupied
  With every trifling thing?
Will I not gain a single soul
  As trophy for my King?

I know that all around me, souls
  Are dropping into hell,
And yet I go my tranquil way,
  As though all things were well.

Lord, as I contemplate these facts,
  I hide my face with shame.
Oh, wake me, rouse me, Lord, I pray
  And stir me into flame!

I once was lost and doomed myself,
  But someone prayed for me,
And someone told me of the Lord,
  Who died to set us free.

Can I withhold from others that
  Which I received so free?
And thus neglect the work which Christ
  Entrusted unto me?

Nay, help me, Lord, to live for Thee,
  My privileges prize;
That I may never be ashamed
  To meet Thy loving eyes.

REJOICE

Rejoice, rejoice, believers,
  And let your lights appear;
The evening is advancing,
  And darker night is near.
The Bridegroom is arising,
  And soon He draweth nigh;
Up, pray, and watch, and wrestle,
  At midnight comes the cry.

See that your lamps are burning;
  Replenish them with oil;
And wait for your salvation,
  The end of earthly toil.
The watchers on the mountain
  Proclaim the Bridegroom near.
Go meet Him as He cometh,
  With alleluias clear.

Our hope and expectation,
  O Jesus, now appear!
Arise, Thou Sun so longed for,
  O'er this benighted sphere!
With hearts and hands uplifted,
  We plead, O Lord, to see
The day of earth's redemption
  That brings us unto Thee.

—Laurentius Laurenti
Translated, Sarah B. Findbater

QUITE SUDDENLY

Quite suddenly—it may be at the turning of a lane,
Where I stand to watch a skylark from out the swelling grain,
That the trump of God shall thrill me, with its call so loud and clear,
And I'm called away to meet Him, whom of all I hold most dear.
Quite suddenly—it may be as I tread the busy street,
Strong to endure life's stress and strain, its every call to meet,
That through the roar of traffic, a trumpet, silvery clear,
Shall stir my startled senses and proclaim His coming near.

Quite suddenly—it may be in His house I bend my knee,
When the kingly voice, long hoped for, comes at last to summon me;
And the fellowship of earth-life that has seemed so passing sweet,
Proves nothing but the shadow of our meeting round His feet.
Quite suddenly—it may be as I lie in dreamless sleep,
God's gift to many a sorrowing heart, with no more tears to weep,
That a call shall break my slumber and a voice sound in my ear;
"Rise up, my love, and come away! Behold, the Bridegroom's here!"

The Two Comings of Christ

A CONTRAST

When Christ comes the second time, it shall not be as it was on His first advent.

He came the first time to die in the sinner's place. He is coming the second time to execute judgment on the sinner.

He came the first time to seek and to save that which was lost. He is coming the second time "in flaming fire to execute judgment on all them that know not God."

He came the first time to be man's representative before a God of love and grace. He is coming the second time as God's representative against a rebellious world.

He came the first time in great humility; He is coming the second time in great power and glory.

He came the first time as the lowly Nazarene; He is coming the second time as the King of kings and Lord of lords.

He came the first time to be "despised and rejected of men." He is coming the second time to be acknowledged by all, both high and low, rich and poor, bond and free.

He came the first time to ride the lowly ass into Jerusalem. He is coming the second time to ride the great white horse, leading the armies of heaven.

He came the first time to submit to the unjust judgment of earthly potentates. He is coming the second time to compel all earthly rulers to yield their scepters to Him.

He came the first time to shed His blood on the cross. He is coming again as the mighty Conqueror whose "vesture is dipped in blood."

He came the first time to save men from a devil's hell. He comes the second time to say to all the workers of iniquity, "Depart ye, into everlasting fire, prepared for the devil and his angels."

—From "The Soon Coming of Our Lord"

As Darkness Falls

Though the shades of night grow
    deeper
O'er this sinful, strife-filled world;
Lo, there's still a blessed banner
There on Calv'ry's mount unfurled!
'Tis the word that God has spoken;
All salvation's work is done—
Life eternal now He giveth
To believers in His Son.
Satan rages, shadows lengthen,
Millions wander in the night.
Many souls in many nations
Seek for comfort, help, and light.
Forward, then, ye God-blessed sol-
    dier,
Serving Christ where'er He say.
Time is short to do His bidding,
And He may return today!
Know no ill can ever harm you
If you live His Word to share
With the world He loves so dearly:
He will keep you everywhere.
E'en the martyr's death means bless-
    ing:
Sooner than His face you'll see!
E'en the martyr's death means riches,
Now and in eternity!
Forward, then, redemption's story
Has not lost its ancient pow'r!
Share it with earth's hosts of lost ones
In this world's eleventh hour.
Forward, then, the foe is ruthless,
Yet the battle is so sweet,
For we know that soon in triumph
Jesus in the air we'll meet!

—Cornelius Vanderbreggen, Jr.

When the World Is Ablaze

Day of judgment—day of wonders!
Hark the trumpet's awful sound,
Louder than a thousand thunders,
Shakes the vast creation round!
How the summons
Will the sinner's heart confound!

See the Judge our nature wearing,
Clothed in majesty divine!
You, who long for His appearing,
Then shall say, "This God is mine!"
Gracious Savior!
Own me in that day for Thine!

At His call the dead awaken,
Rise to life from earth and sea:
All the powers of nature, shaken
By His looks, prepare to flee;
Careless sinner!
What will then become of thee?

Horrors, past imagination,
Will surprise your trembling heart,
When you hear your condemnation,
"Hence, accursed wretch, depart!
Thou with Satan
And his angels hast thy part!"

But to those who have confessed,
Loved and served the Lord below,
He will say, "Come near, ye blessed.
You, forever,
Shall my love and glory know!"

Under sorrows and reproaches,
May this thought our courage raise!
Swiftly God's great day approaches,
Sighs shall then be changed to praise!
We shall triumph,
When the world is in a blaze!"

It Won't Be Long, It May Be Soon

Someday I'll cross the mystic stream,
  It won't be long, it may be soon;
Someday I'll lay my burden down,
  It won't be long, it may be soon.

Someday I'll reach the golden shore,
  And dwell with Jesus evermore—
I'll meet the ones who've gone before;
  It won't be long, it may be soon.

He's coming back with glory rare,
  It won't be long, it may be soon;
We'll rise to meet Him in the air,
  It won't be long, it may be soon.

If He should call me, this I know,
  I'm safe and ready, now, to go;
I'm waiting with my heart aglow—
  It won't be long, it may be soon.

Then as you travel on life's way,
  Thru waters deep and billows cold,
You may have Jesus as your stay,
  He'll walk with you and lead you home.

Oh, brother, will you let Him in?
  He'll save and keep you free from sin,
'Till heaven's door you enter in:
  It won't be long, it may be soon.

—Parschauer Sisters

A Little While

A little while—then Christ will come
  The glorious hour draws nigh
When He will come to take His bride
  To dwell with Him on high;
Our trials then will all be o'er,
  Our tears be wiped away,
The darkest night of earth will be
  Dispelled by endless day.

A little while—and Christ will come,
  He will not tarry long.
Though days be drear, my heart can
  sing
A glad triumphant song.
Bright rays of hope now fill my soul,
  They pierce the gloom of night,
And shadows dark forevermore
  Will vanish with the light.

A little while—O glorious thought—
  Soon we shall hear His voice,
And while we watch and serve Him
  here,
  Our longing hearts rejoice.
In heavenly realms we'll sing His
  praise
  For wonders of His love,
As with the saints, we worship Him
  Around the throne above.

Some Golden Daybreak

Some glorious morning sorrow will
  cease,
Some glorious morning all will be peace;
Heartaches all ended, school days all
  done,
Heaven will open—Jesus will come.

CHORUS:
Some golden daybreak, Jesus will
  come;
Some golden daybreak, battles all won,
He'll shout the vict'ry, break thro' the
  blue,
Some golden daybreak, for me, for you.

Sad hearts will gladden, all shall be
  bright,
Good-bye forever to earth's dark night;
Changed in a moment, like Him to be,
Oh glorious daybreak, Jesus I'll see.

Oh, what a meeting, there in the skies,
No tears nor crying shall dim our eyes;
Loved ones united eternally,
Oh what a daybreak that morn will be.

WHAT THEN?

When the choir has sung its last anthem,
    And the preacher has made his last prayer,
When the people have heard their last sermon
    And the sound has died out on the air;
When the Bible lies closed on the altar,
    And the pews are all empty of men,
And each one stands facing his record—
    And the Great Book is opened—what then?

When the actors have played their last drama,
    And the mimic has made his last pun;
When the film has flashed its last picture,
    And the scoreboard displayed its last run,
When the crowds seeking pleasure have vanished
    And gone out in the darkness again—
When the Trumpet of the Ages has sounded,
    And we stand up before Him—what then?

When the bugle's call sinks into silence,
    And the long-marching columns stand still;
When the captain has given his last orders,
    And they've captured the last fort on the hill,
And the flag has been hauled in from the masthead,
    And the wounded afield have checked in,
And a world that rejected its Saviour,
    Is asked for a reason—what then?

Golden Nuggets . . .

Pungent Paragraphs, Sentence Sermons

How to Live

Worry less, work more;
Ride less and walk more;
Frown less and laugh more;
Drink less and breathe more;
Eat less and chew more;
Preach less and practice more.

> —*The above was found in the handwriting of the late Effie B. Browne*

The Minds of Men

If we work upon marble, it will perish.
If we work upon brass, time will efface it.
If we rear temples, they will crumble to dust.
But if we work upon men's immortal minds,
If we imbue them with high principles,
With the just fear of God and love of their fellowman,
We engrave on those tablets something which no time can efface,
And which will brighten and brighten unto eternity.

Things to Think About . . .

To admit you are wrong is the first step toward getting right.

If your foot slips, you may recover your balance, but if your tongue slips, you cannot recall your words.

His heart cannot be pure whose tongue is not clean.

There is no greater mistake than to suppose that Christians can impress the world by agreeing with it.

My Shepherd

The Lord is my Shepherd,
I'm one of His sheep.
I'm safe in His pasture
Awake or asleep.
His watching is constant,
He knows me by name.
He knows every weakness
Yet He loves me, the same.

A GOOD COMBINATION

If you could get Religion like a Baptist
Experience it like a Methodist
Be loyal to it like a Catholic
Sacrifice for it like a Jew
Be proud of it like an Episcopalian
Pay for it like a Presbyterian
And enjoy it like a Negro
What a great religion you would have.

"I am the WAY, the TRUTH, and the LIFE" (John 14:6)

Without the WAY there is no Going;
Without the TRUTH there is no Knowing;
Without the LIFE there is no Living.

> —*Thomas á Kempis*

"No man cometh unto the Father but by Me" (John 14:6)

Full many a gem of purest ray serene,
The dark unfathomed caves of ocean bear.
Full many a flower is born to blush unseen,
And waste its sweetness on the desert air.

A Religion

That does nothing
That gives nothing
That costs nothing
That suffers nothing
Is worth nothing.

I am only one; but I AM ONE;
I cannot do everything;
but I can do something.
What I can do, I ought to do;
and what I ought to do,
By the Grace of GOD,
I WILL DO!!

"TAINT"

'Taint what we have,
But what we give.
'Taint where we are,
But how we live;
'Taint what we do,
But how we do it—
That makes this life
Worth goin' through it.

Five Little Words

There are five little words, I'd have you to
    know;
They are: "Pardon me," "Thank you," and
    "Please."
Oh, use them quite often wherever you go;
There are few words more useful than these.
These five little words are filled with a power
That money or fame cannot give.
So commit them to memory this very hour
And use them as long as you live!

A Christian is a mind through which Christ thinks, a heart through which Christ loves, a voice through which Christ speaks, a hand through which Christ helps.

It isn't hard to make a mountain out of a molehill. Just add dirt.

The Invincible Truth

Truth crushed to earth shall rise again,
    The eternal years of God are hers;
But Error, wounded, writhes with pain,
    And dies among his worshipers.
                    —*William Cullen Bryant*

Remember
that if the OUTLOOK
may not be bright, at times—
the UPLOOK IS
ALWAYS BRIGHT!

A retreat from the
WRONG DIRECTION
is the only wise move in the
RIGHT DIRECTION.

"God governs the affairs of men."
            —Benjamin Franklin.

"It takes a heart to share."

"Little is much if God is in it."

That Ten Dollar Bill

It's not what I'd do with a million,
   If riches e'er fell to my lot;
But it's what I will do at the present
   With the Ten Dollar Bill that I've got.

We are as young as our faith and hope and as old as our fear and despair.

Got a Problem?

Feel glum? Keep mum.
Don't grumble. Be humble.
Trials cling? Just sing.
Can't sing? Just cling.
Don't fear. God's near!
Money goes—He knows.
Honor left—not bereft.
Don't rust—work, trust!

—*Ernest B. Allen*

When a man has to make an admission,
That his temper got the best of him;
He's really making a sad confession,
That his worst, is the best of him!

—*C. W. Renwick*

The Old Evangelist Bud Robinson's Daily Prayer

"O Lord, give me a backbone as big as a saw log, and ribs like the sleepers under the church floor. Put iron shoes on me and galvanized breeches. And give me a rhinoceros hide for a skin, and hang a wagon load of determination up in the gable end of my soul, and help me to sign the contract to fight the devil as long as I've got a tooth, and then gum him till I die. Amen.

There is a lot of difference between thinking and worrying. Every businessman must spend much time thinking—but he has no time for worrying. Thinking develops ideas. It plans big things. It builds. Thinking is constructive. It makes men strong. But as soon as thinking becomes disorganized, worry begins.

Most evolutionists seem to know everything about the missing link except that it is still missing.

Life is nothing else but the working of the Spirit of God within us.

—*William Law*

QUOTABLE QUOTES

It is high time to awake out of sleep (Romans 13:11).

A man may die and leave upwards of a million without taking any of it upwards.

Yesterday He helped me,
Today I'll praise His name,
Because I know tomorrow,
He'll help me just the same.

"Teach me, my Lord and King,
In all things Thee to see;
And what I do in anything
To do it as for Thee."

*This world we're livin' in
Is mighty hard to beat;
We get a thorn with every rose—
But ain't the roses sweet!*

THINK IT OVER

When your face is toward the sun, the shadows will always fall behind you.

———

The darkest hour has but 60 minutes!

———

It isn't the style of the Bible that makes it unpopular with moderns, but the fact that it cramps their style!

———

You cannot serve God and mammon; but you can serve God with mammon.

———

How can men expect to play the game of life unless they know what the goal posts are?

———

"I would rather fail in a cause that I know some day will triumph than to triumph in a cause I know some day will fail." —Woodrow Wilson

———

"The years have served to strengthen my faith in the Word of God, and I strongly endorse the practice of regular Bible reading for both inspiration and guidance in meeting the complex problems of daily life." —J. Edgar Hoover

———

The fellow who does things to count usually doesn't stop to count them.

———

We cannot know the future but we can know the One who holds the future.

———

A Christian should be like a good watch—open faced, busy hands, well regulated, and full of good works.

———

"If our Christian faith means anything to us, we should so expand and enlarge it that it will become a beacon light to the whole world."
—Congressman Paul Dague

———

There Are Those Who Are . . .

THE WISHBONES—Those who do all the wishing, but very little else.

THE JAWBONES—Those who do all the talking, but very little action.

THE KNUCKLEBONES—Those who knock everything that anyone else tries to do.

THE BACKBONES—Those who get under the load and do all the work.

MARTIN LUTHER: None can believe how powerful prayer is, and what it is able to effect, but those who have learned it by experience.

ROBERT C. McQUILKIN: It is suffering and then glory. Not to have the suffering means not to have the glory.

SIZZLING SENTENCES

"The strength of a country is the strength of its religious convictions."
—Calvin Coolidge

"My greatest thought is my accountability to God.
—Daniel Webster

"The best of all . . . God is with us." —John Wesley

Where there's a will there's a way, yes, but remember this: Where God's will is, that's the best way.

Remember that the milk of human kindness never curdles.

You can travel faster, and farther, and with more safety . . . on your knees.

Read your newspapers and you are up to date. Read your Bible and you are ahead of the times.

I have seen the past; I live in the present; I am not afraid of the future.
—Wm. Allen White

Things I Wish to Remember

That it pays to forget those things that are behind.

That what I would do for Christ must needs be done for others.

That a good name is rather to be chosen than great riches.

That the greatest thing in all the world is love.

That the way to find happiness is to forget self.

That there is no happiness in things.

That a word once spoken can never be recalled.

That no suffering is too great if it contributes to the building and nurture of Christian character.

That to correct one fault in myself is greater than to correct ten in my neighbor.

That yesterday is gone forever; tomorrow may never come; today, only, is mine.

That time is too precious to be used other than for God's glory.

The Ten Commandments

Above all else love God alone;
Bow down to neither wood nor stone.
God's name refuse to take in vain,
The Sabbath rest with care maintain.
Respect your parents all your days;
Hold sacred human life always.
Be loyal to your chosen mate;
Steal nothing, neither small nor great.
Report with truth your neighbor's deed;
And rid your mind of selfish greed.

—*Author unknown*

WORDS OF WISDOM

Be careful with half-truths; you might have told the wrong half.

If the world is getting smaller, why do they keep raising the postal rates?

If you must hammer, build something.

The darkest hour has but 60 minutes.

The middle letter of the word SIN is "I".

———

Great trials are often necessary to prepare us for great responsibilities.

———

The Lord wants our precious time, not our spare time.

———

It is far more important to put life into our years than to add years to our lives.

God's Will

It is God's will that I should cast
My care on Him each day (1 Peter 5).
He also asks me not to cast
My confidence away (Hebrews 10).
But, oh, how stupidly I act
When taken unaware;
I cast away my confidence,
And carry all my care.

—*T. Baird*

"Just one life,
'Twill soon be past:
Only what's done
For Christ will last."

This above all: To thine own self be true,
And it must follow as the night the day,
Thou canst not then be false to any man.

—*Shakespeare*

Sympathy is two hearts tugging at one load.

Courtesy is a great lubricant.

Brightening up the life of someone else will put a fresh shine on your own.

You can't change the past but you can ruin a perfectly good present by worrying over the future.

The world is moving so fast these days that the man who says it can't be done is generally doing it.

People seldom improve when they have no model but themselves to copy.

A place for everything and everything in its place.

If you don't stand for something, you fall for everything.

This and That

It is easier to preach ten sermons than to live one.

* * * * *

The most painful form of indigestion a man can have comes from swallowing his own words.

* * * * *

Winter is the season when you keep the house as hot as it was last summer when you complained about it being too hot.

* * * * *

Mankind owes most of its advancement to those who were not satisfied to leave well enough alone.

* * * * *

Some ministers are dying by DEGREES.

Things to Remember

You cannot kindle a fire in any other heart until it is burning within your own.

Let not your right hand know what your left hand doeth . . . But, be sure both your hands are occupied in doing the things that are worthwhile.

Hope, like a golden bell, rings out from the heart of the Bible, in the words of our Lord, who said, "Because I live, ye shall live also."

Nothing lies beyond the reach of prayer, except that which lies outside the will of God.

The sheep which keeps his eyes fixed on the Shepherd will never stray away from the fold.

The Bible has the answer to your questions.

The Gospel only—and only the Gospel—can save America, and the world.

Don't mistake religious indifference for tolerance.

Let's quit asking Congress for help—let's start getting on our knees and asking God for help.

Prayer
(Is Good for the Soul)

"O Lawd, give Thy servant this mornin' de eyes of de eagle and de wisdom of de owl, connect his soul with the Gospel telephone in de Central Skies, 'luminate his brow with de sun of heaven; pizen his mind with love for the people; turpentine his imagination; grease his lips with 'possum oil; loosen his tongue with de sledge hammer of Thy power; 'lectrify his brain with de lightnin' of de Word; put 'petual motion on his ahms; fill him plum full of the dynamite of Thy glory; 'noint him all over with de kerosene oil of Thy salvation and sot him on the fire.— Amen!"

—actual prayer delivered at Red Rock, Miss.

QUOTES

If you have no joy in your religion, there's a leak in your Christianity somewhere. —Billy Sunday

I shall allow no man to belittle my soul by making me hate him. —Booker T. Washington

A blow with a word strikes deeper than a blow with a sword. —Robert Burton

Reflect upon your present blessings, of which every man has many; not on your past misfortunes, of which all men have some. —Charles Dickens

Neither genius, fame, nor love show the greatness of the soul. Only kindness can do that. —Jean Baptiste Henri Lacor Daire

I never did anything worth doing by accident; nor did any of my inventions come by accident; they came by work. —Thomas A. Edison

That government is the strongest of which every man feels himself a part. —Thomas Jefferson

Personally, I am always ready to learn, although I do not always like being taught. —Winston S. Churchill

A man can succeed at almost anything for which he has unlimited enthusiasm. —Charles Schwab

Some people have just enough religion to make them uncomfortable. —John Wesley

The size of a man can be measured by the size of the things that makes him angry. —J. Kenfield Morley

The best medals are pinned on those who go "beyond the call of duty." —Robert E. Lee

True religion affords Government its surest support. —George Washington

"If you will become saturated with the knowledge of the Bible, you will have God's answer to every important question of men today."

President Woodrow Wilson said: "It is very difficult for an individual who knows the Scripture ever to get away from it. . . . It forms a part of the warp and woof of his life."

THE BOOK OF THE MONTH:
THE BOOK OF THE YEAR:
THE BOOK OF THE AGES—
IT'S THE BIBLE . . .

"I can see how it might be possible for a man to look down upon the earth and be an atheist, but I cannot conceive how a man could look up into the heavens and say there is no God."

—Abraham Lincoln

Think on These Things

It is better to be a cheerful one-legged octopus than a centipede with a grouch.

* * * * *

What we need is not more Christianity in books, but Christianity in boots.

He Is Able

He is able to *save* (Hebrews 7:25).

He is able to *keep you from falling* (Jude 24).

He is able to help them who are tempted (1 Corinthians 10:13).

He is able to *do for us more than we can ask or think* (Ephesians 3:20).

He is able to *make all grace abound* (2 Corinthians 9:8)

Today, I pray a sincere prayer;
That God may keep you in His care,
And give you peace, and smooth your
    way,
And guide you safely, day by day.

WELL SAID—

"Of all the things you wear, your expression is the most important."

———

To those you touch in life, you can be either a stepping stone or a stumbling block.

———

"You can't no more learn somethin' from anyone who don't know nothin' than you can come back from anywhere you ain't been."

———

Even though you are on the right track, you will be run over if you just sit there.

———

How can men expect to play the game of life if they do not know what the goal posts are?

———

"It's much better to make a wrong decision than none at all: for if you find that you have made a wrong decision, you can make another decision to correct it." —Harry Truman

———

"Christ's limitless resources meet our endless needs."

———

If you cross your bridges before you come to them, you'll still be on the same side of the river.

———

Hands build houses—hearts build homes.

———

If thou art willing to suffer no adversity, how wilt thou be the friend of Christ?

If prayer does not drive sin out of your life, sin will drive prayer out.

* * * * *

He stands best who kneels most.

* * * * *

God puts the Church in the world; Satan puts the world into the Church.

* * * * *

If God has called you, do not spend time looking over your shoulder to see who is following.

* * * * *

To realize the worth of the anchor we need to feel the storm.

* * * * *

Salvation may come quietly, but we cannot remain quiet about it.

* * * * *

Better never to have been born at all, than never to have been born again.

* * * * *

We ought so to live Christ as to compel others to think about Christ.

THINK IT OVER

It's not the size of the dog in the fight; it's the size of the FIGHT in the dog . . . that counts.

* * * * *

A mule cannot pull while he is kicking; and he cannot kick while he is pulling.

* * * * *

When it get dark enough, the stars always come out.

* * * * *

We are not to look at our faith but to God's faithfulness. We do not look on present circumstances but look at God's resources. We do not take thought for tomorrow—it is in God's hands.

The Eight Do-Mores

Do more than exist—live.
Do more than touch—feel.
Do more than look—observe.
Do more than hear—listen.
Do more than listen—understand.
Do more than think—ponder.
Do more than talk—say something.

—John Harsen Rhoades

Don't Forget That—

Every cloud will wear a rainbow if your heart keeps right.

Open the door of your heart to Christ and HE will open the windows of heaven for you.

"The light that shines the farthest shines brightest nearest home."

"There's a rainbow shining in the sky; You can always see it if you try."

The Bible is the sure anchor of the soul, the real bulwark of America, and the solid hope of the world!

REMEMBER: If it's in the Bible, it's *so!*

"You can learn a lot from studying the Bible—You can learn still more by practicing it."

If you want the *right* answer, it's in the Bible.

"The best binding for a Bible is shoe leather."

Think It Over

There are no hopeless situations—only there are men who have become hopeless.

No man ever choked to death swallowing his own pride.

QUOTABLE QUOTES

"All the good from the Savior of the world is communicated through this Book . . . all things desirable to man are contained in it." —Abraham Lincoln

"It is impossible to rightly govern the world without God and the Bible." —George Washington

"The Bible is the rock upon which our republic rests." —Andrew Jackson

"If we abide by the principles taught in the Bible, our country will go on prospering, and to prosper; but if we and our posterity neglect its instructions and counsel, there is no telling how great a catastrophe shall come upon us, and bury our glory in profound obscurity." —Daniel Webster

Satan can build a wall around us, and often does, but he can never put a lid on it. so, KEEP LOOKING UP!

If I Can

If I can plant some little seed of love
That later on will blossom in a smile;
It matters not however else I fail;
My life will be worthwhile.
If I can do some little kindly act
That later on may soothe some sad
    heart's pain,
It matters not what else I do. My life
Will not have been in vain.

—author unknown

The joy of life lies in the work of today and in the plans for the work tomorrow.

Words of Wisdom

Time was, is past;
Thou canst not it recall.
Time is, thou hast;
Employ the portion small.
Time future, is not;
And may never be.
Time present is the
Only time for thee.

—Lydia H. Sigourney

"Yesterday is gone;
tomorrow is uncertain;
today is here.
USE IT.

"God makes a promise. Faith believes it. Hope anticipates it. Patience quietly awaits it."

My All for Him

1. My Eyes . . . . Hebrews 12:2
   Fixed on Christ
2. My Ears . . . . Psalm 40:5-8
   Hearing and Heeding Him
3. My Hands . . . . Ephesians 4:28
   Busily Working for Others
4. My Feet . . . . Hebrews 12:1
   Running His Appointed Race
5. My Mind . . . . Isaiah 26:3
   Stayed on Him for Peace
6. My Heart . . . . 1 Peter 3:15
   Kept for His Occupancy
7. My Body . . . . Romans 12:1
   A Holy, Living Sacrifice

"Trust in the Lord with all thine heart; and lean not unto thine own understanding. In all thy ways acknowledge him, and he shall direct thy paths" (Proverbs 3:5, 6).

Things to Remember

You will never get ahead of anyone as long as you are trying to get even with him.

Before he can accumulate dollars, a man needs some sense.

Ben Franklin said that laziness travels so slowly that poverty soon overtakes it.

A good listener is not only popular everywhere, but after a while he knows something too.

To see a rival succeed without jealousy comes close to achieving greatness of character.

There's a lot to be said for the fellow who doesn't say it himself.

All men are born equal—but some outgrow it in time.

Success is getting what you want; happiness is wanting what you get.

The road to success is always under construction.

Killing time is not murder; it's suicide.

Very often the chip on a person's shoulder is only bark.

One of the hardest secrets for a man to keep is his opinion of himself.

Good judgment often comes from experience gained from poor judgment.

A totalitarian state is one where everything is compulsory that is not forbidden.

INSPIRED SENTENCE SERMONS

(From the Proverbs)

Trust in the Lord with all thine heart, and lean not unto thine own understanding. In all thy ways acknowledge Him, and He shall direct thy paths (3:5, 6).

Happy is the man that findeth wisdom, and he that getteth understanding (3:13).

The fear of the Lord is the beginning of wisdom (9:10).

A word fitly spoken is like apples of gold in pictures of silver (25:11).

A good name is rather to be chosen than great riches, and loving favor than silver and gold (22:1).

A merry heart doeth good like medicine (17:22).

A soft answer turneth away wrath: but grievous words stir up anger (15:1).

Righteousness exalteth a nation, but sin is a reproach to any people (14:34).

Boast not thy self of tomorrow; for thou knowest not what a day may bring forth (27:1).

The way of transgressors is hard (13:15).

Wine is a mocker; strong drink is raging; and whosoever is deceived thereby is not wise (20:1).

As a jewel of gold in a swine's snout, so is a fair woman which is without discretion (11:22).

Who can find a virtuous woman? For her price is far above rubies (31:10).

He that winneth souls is wise (11:30).

Keep thy heart with all diligence; for out of it are the issues of life (4:23).

A wise son maketh a glad father: but a foolish son is the heaviness of his mother (10:1).

Confidence in an unfaithful man in time of trouble is like a broken tooth, and foot out of joint (25:19).

He that covereth his sins shall not prosper: but whoso confesseth and forsaketh them shall have mercy (28:13).

GOLDEN THOUGHTS

Morale is when your hands and feet keep on working when your head says it can't be done. —Adm. Ben Moreell

The sweetest music isn't in oratorios, but in kind words. —Ralph Waldo Emerson

The reflections on a day well spent furnish us with joys more pleasing than ten thousand triumphs —Thomas a Kempis

Faith is to believe what we do not see, and the reward of this faith is to see what we believe. —St. Augustine

A kind heart is a fountain of gladness, making everything in its vicinity freshen into smiles. —Washington Irving

Lost, yesterday, somewhere between sunrise and sunset, two golden hours, each set with sixty diamond minutes. No reward is offered, for they are gone forever. —Thomas Mann

Goodness consists not in the outward things we do, but in the inward thing we are. —E. H. Chapin

Every noble life leaves the fiber of itself interwoven forever in the work of the world. —Ruskin

Bits of Humor . . .

Bible Riddles and Trick Questions

What creature was born without a soul, later possessed a soul, and then died without a soul? *(The whale that swallowed Jonah.)*

Of all the States in the Union, which is suggested in the Bible? *(Arkansas . . . "Noah looked out the ark and saw.")*

What is the first bank transaction? *(Pharaoh received a check on the bank of the Red Sea.)*

Which two Old Testament men took a flight through space? *(Enoch and Elijah.)*

Who took the first submarine ride? *(Jonah.)*

Who was the shortest man in the Bible? *(Bildad the "Shuhite".)*

Did Rebecca like baseball players? *(She went to the well with a pitcher.)*

Did Joshua have parents? *(He was the "sun of Nun".)*

What was Adam's longest day? *(When there was no Eve.)*

What animals carried the most baggage into the ark? *(The elephants carried their trunks.)*

What animals carried the most money into the ark? *(The skunk . . . each one entered with $1.01 . . . that is, four quarters and a scent.)*

What man qualified as the "straightest" man in the Bible? *(Joseph, because Pharaoh made a "ruler" out of him.)*

What was the first big league game? *(When the children of Israel defeated the giants.)*

Name three persons of the Bible who lived to be over 100 years old and who never wore eyeglasses. *(Any three centenarians.)*

Secrets to Success

"What is the secret of success?" asked the Sphinx.

"Push," said the Button.

"Never be lead," said the Pencil.

"Take pains," said the Window.

"Always keep cool," said the Ice.

"Be up to date," said the Calendar.

"Never lose your head," said the Match.

"Make light of your troubles," said the Fire.

"Do a driving business," said the Hammer.

"Don't be merely one of the hands," said the Clock.

"Don't try to be too sharp in your dealings," said the Knife.

"Find a good thing and stick to it," said the Stamp.

"Do the work that soots you," said the Chimney.

———

There is a line on the ocean where you lose a day when you cross it.

There's a line on most highways where you can do even better.

———

"A STICK of unexploded dynamite was found in the car." —From a news story.

Which brings up a question: Did anybody ever find an exploded stick of dynamite?

MONEY TALK

A silver Dollar to a Penny once said,
"What a poor little thing you are!
Just look at ME. See how big I am!
You won't go very far."

"O yes," said the Penny. "You're very,
   very big.
But I'm better than you, I know.
I go to church and Sunday school,
Where you very seldom go.

It's not how little or big you are;
What matters is what you do."
And what the Penny to the Dollar said,
Of folks is just as true.

—*Helen Howarth Lemn*

A Preacher's Prayer

Dear Lord, fill my mind
   With worthwhile stuff—
And nudge me hard
   When I've said enough.

Everyone has to commit a few blunders in order to understand his limitations.

* * * * *

It's a tough world. If you often tell lies, people won't trust you: if you always tell the truth, they won't like you.

Sam Jones, a noted preacher, once said, "If a man should come to haul logs with a team made up of a mule, a billy goat, a bumblebee, and a skunk, I would think him crazy; but the average preacher ofttimes has just such a team in his congregation to help (?) him—a stubborn kicker, a 'butter,' a stinger and a stinker." Just thank God if your church is different.

Bad Company

One evening in October
When I was far from sober,
And dragging home a load with
      manly pride;
My feet began to stutter,
So I lay down in the gutter,
And a pig came up and parked right
      by my side.
Then I warbled, "It's fair weather
When good fellows get together."
And a lady passing by was heard to
      say:
"You can tell a man who boozes
By the company he chooses."
Then the pig got up and slowly
      walked away.

What Kind Are You?

Some Christians are like wheelbarrows—not good unless pushed.

Some are like canoes—they need to be paddled.

Some are like kites—if you don't keep a string on them, they fly away.

Some are like footballs—you can't tell which way they are going to bounce next.

Some are like balloons—full of wind and likely to blow up unless handled carefully.

Some are like trailers—not good unless pulled.

The person who throws mud is losing ground.

Hard-Earned Wages

An artist who was employed to renovate and retouch the great oil paintings in an old church in Belgium, rendered a bill of $67.30 for his services. The church wardens, however, required an itemized bill, and the following was duly presented, audited and paid:

For correcting the Ten Commandments $5.12
For renewing heaven and adjusting stars 7.14
For touching up purgatory and restoring lost souls 3.06
For brightening up the flames of hell, putting new tail on
    the devil, and doing odd jobs for the damned 7.17
For putting new stone in David's sling, enlarging head of
    Goliath 6.13
For mending shirt of Prodigal Son and cleaning his ear 3.39
For embellishing Pontius Pilate and putting new ribbon on
    his bonnet 3.02
For putting new tail and comb on St. Peter's rooster 2.20
For re-pluming and re-gilding left wing of the
    Guardian Angel 5.18
For washing the servant of High Priest and putting carmine
    on his cheek 5.02
For taking the spots off the son of Tobias 10.30
For putting earrings in Sarah's ears 5.26
For decorating Noah's ark and new head on Shem 4.31
    TOTAL $67.30

Temperance . . .

Liquor, Tobacco, Etc.

The A B C
(All Blasting Curse)
of the Liquor Traffic

A —Arch foe of society

B —Baneful, blighting blast of the ages

C —Cruel, cancerous curse of civilization

D —Degrading, debauching, deadly and damning

E —Enslaving enemy of all its patrons

F —Ferocious fiend, and friend of no man

G —God-dishonoring, God-defying, and God-despising

H —Home-destroying, hell-enlarging, and heaven-hating

I —Incubator of iniquity, immorality, and insanity

J —Jilts joy, jibes justice, and jams jails

K —Kidnaps and kills boys and girls

L —Licentious, lawless, and loathsome

M —Merchant of mischief, misery and murder

N —Nefarious nuisance and nullifier of national honor

O —Oppressor of the poor and offense of the orphans

P —Pernicious promoter of prostitution, profligacy, and putrid politics

Q —Quagmire of corruption, quicksand of crime, and quick road to hell

R —Rotten, rancid, repulsive, ribald, ruthless, rapacious and revolutionary

S —Sin-soaked, soul-destroying, Satan-satisfying

T —Treacherous tyrant of trouble and tragedy

U —Uncivil, ungodly, ungovernable, and most unruly usurper in the universe

V —Vicious, venomous, villainous, violent, voracious, and vulturous

W —Wanton waster of wealth and wicked wrecker of womanhood

X —X-ray of death and doom

Y —Youth debauching, yoke-enthralling, yellow jaundice of society

Z —Zero of decency and the zorilla of damnation.

—Dale Crowley

I Do Not Drink Because—

I firmly believe that I will live a healthier, happier, and longer life because I abstain.

I can use the money to better advantage for myself and family than to spend it for alcoholic beverages.

I have an aversion for alcohol and detest its offensive odor on the breath of others.

I feel no compulsion to drink for I can face life and its problems better without alcohol than with it.

DRINK

Drink has drained more blood,
Hung more crepe,
Sold more houses,
Plunged more people into bankruptcy,
Armed more villains,
Slain more children,
Snapped more wedding rings,
Defiled more innocence,
Blinded more eyes,
Twisted more limbs,
Dethroned more reason,
Wrecked more manhood,
Dishonored more womanhood,
Broken more hearts,
Blasted more lives,
Driven more to suicide, and
Dug more graves than any other poi-
    soned scourge that ever swept its
    death-dealing waves across the
    world.

—Evangeline Booth

Death Laughs at Fools Who Drive and Drink

Death laughed at me in city streets;
    The red lights passed me by.
And warning signs were silly things
    For one about to die.

The empty bottle lay beneath
    My cold and numbing feet.
I failed to hear the warning cry
    And died there, in the street.

So now I lay upon a slab,
    My wisdom newly found.
But it's too late; they'll soon be here
    To put me underground.

* * * * * *

I wake to find 'twas just a dream
    Designed to make me think;
A dream that taught me how death laughs
    At fools who drive and drink.

—Pop Grey

WATER

Sweet, beautiful water—brewed in the running brook, the rippling fountain and the laughing rill—in the limpid cascade, as it joyfully leaps down the side of the mountain. Brewed in yonder mountain top, whose granite peak glitters like gold bathed in the morning sun—brewed in the fleecy foam and the whitened spray as it hangs like a speck over the distant cataract—brewed in the clouds of heaven, sweet, beautiful water! As it sings in the rain shower and dances in the hailstorm—as it comes sweeping down in feathery flakes, clothing the earth in a spotless mantle of white. Distilled in the golden tissues that paint the western sky at the setting of the sun, and the silvery tissues that veil the midnight moon— sweet, health-giving, beautiful water! Distilled in the rainbow of promise, whose warp is the raindrops of earth, and whose woof is the sunbeam of heaven—sweet, beautiful water.

(The above classic was written by one of the greatest orators in the cause of temperance in the 19th century, John B. Gough.)

Do-It-Yourself Tavern

"If you are a married man who absolutely must drink, start a saloon in your home. Be the only customer, and you won't have to buy a license. Give your wife twenty dollars to buy a gallon of booze. Remember, there are 69 glasses in a gallon. Buy your drinks from your wife. When your first gallon is gone, she will have $80.00 to deposit in the bank, and $20.00 to start business again. If you should live ten years, continue to buy booze from her, and then die with snakes in your shoes. She will have enough money to bury you respectably, bring up your children, buy a nice house and lot, marry a decent man, and FORGET ABOUT YOU!"

241

THE BAR

The Saloon is sometimes
  Called a Bar—that's true.

A Bar to Heaven, a Door to Hell,
  Whoever named it, named it well.

A Bar to Manliness and Wealth,
  A Door to Want and Broken Health.

A Bar to Honor, Pride and Fame,
  A Door to Sin and Grief and Shame.

A Bar to Home, a Bar to Prayer,
  A Door to Darkness and Despair.

A Bar to Honored useful Life,
  A Door to Brawling Senseless Strife.

A Bar to all that's true and brave,
  A Door to every Drunkard's Grave.

A Bar to Joys that home imparts,
  A Door to Tears and Aching Hearts.

A Bar to Heaven, a Door to Hell,
  Whoever named it, named it well.

—Written by a Life Convict in the
Joliet, Ill., prison

    The wages of sin is death, but the gift of God is eternal life, through Jesus Christ our Lord (Romans 6:23).

I Don't Drink

"Everybody's doing it." No, not yet!
  Because I'm "Somebody," don't
    forget!
Anyone with courage to stop and think,
  Is certainly "Somebody"!—I don't
    drink.
Many a "somebody" who didn't think,
  Became a "nobody" because of
    drink.
And you can follow what the crowds
  do;
  I'm trying to be a "Somebody"—
  How about you?

—Written by a high school student

A Boy Wanted

I want a boy at my saloon.
A man has died and now there's room
For a new boy to start right in
To live a life of shame and sin.

I want a boy from a fine home,
A boy who has a good income.
I want a boy with many friends,
For without boys my business ends.

I want a boy, some mother's boy,
Who is her comfort and her joy.
Such boys to me are worth the
    most—
For they are leaders of a host.

I want a boy who is not afraid
To start right on the downward grade;
A boy who's always brave,
For he must fill a drunkard's grave.

—N. L. Smith

The Drinkers 23rd Psalm

King Alcohol is my shepherd,
I shall always want.
He maketh me to lie down in the gutter.
He leadeth me beside trouble waters.
He destroyeth my soul.
He leadeth me in the paths of wicked-
    ness
For the effect's sake.
Yea, though I walk through the valley of
    poverty
And have delirium tremens,
I will cling to drink,
For thou art with me
To bite and sting and torment me.
Thou preparest an empty table
In the presence of my family.
Thou anointest my head with hellish-
    ness.
My cup of wrath runneth over.
Surely destruction and misery shall
    follow me
All the days of my life,
And I shall dwell in the house of the
    damned forever.

General Harrison's Toast

At a public dinner for General (afterward President) Harrison, one of the guests rather conspicuously "drank to his health." The general pledged his toast by drinking water.

Another man offered a toast, and said, "General, will you favor me by drinking a glass of wine?"

The general asked to be excused. Being again urged to join in a glass of wine, he rose and said, in a dignified manner, "Gentlemen, I have twice refused to partake of the wine cup. Not a drop shall pass my lips. I made a resolve when I started in life that I would avoid strong drink. That vow I have never broken. I am one of a class of seventeen young men who graduated at college together. The other sixteen members of my class now fill drunkards' graves—all from the pernicious habit of wine-drinking. I owe all my health, my happiness and prosperity to that resolution. Would you urge me to break it now?"

Beverage Alcohol
WHAT IT IS AND DOES

"Alcohol is an intoxicating, hypnotic, analgesic, anesthetic, narcotic, poisonous and potentially habit-forming, craving-producing or addiction-producing drug."

—Andrew C. Ivy, Ph.D., M.D., D.Sc., LL.D.
Head of the Department of Clinical Science,
University of Illinois

Alcohol has at least 600 good and necessary uses. Without it, present day science and industry would be tremendously handicapped, if not impossible. Its *beverage use*, however, is totally unnecessary and is the direct or related cause of many of the ills and tragedies of modern civilization.

Not So Easily "Fixed"

"Anywhere you wreck 'em,
We fix 'em," reads the sign.
When people smash their brand new cars
Mechanics are in line
To make the car look "good as new";

But who is advertising
A similar repair for FOLKS?
So isn't it surprising
That drinking people, driving cars
Won't stop to think a little;
For drivers' bodies, after all,
Are mighty soft—and brittle!
—Florence M. Stellwagen

Ingersoll on Alcohol

I believe that alcohol demoralizes those who make it, those who sell it, and those who drink it. I believe that from the time it issues from the coiled and poisonous worm of the distillery until it empties into the hell of crime, death and dishonor, it demoralizes everybody that touches it. I do not believe that anybody can contemplate the subject without becoming prejudiced against this liquid crime. All you have to do is to think of the wrecks upon either bank of this stream of death—of the suicides, of the insanity, of the poverty, of the ignorance, of the distress, of the little children tugging at the faded dresses of weeping and despairing wives, asking for bread; of the men of genius it has wrecked; of the millions who have struggled with imaginary serpents produced by this devilish thing. And when you think of the jails, of the almshouses, of the prisons, and of the scaffolds upon either bank—I do not wonder that every thoughtful man is prejudiced against the stuff called alcohol.

—Robert G. Ingersoll

LIQUOR DEFINED

Alcoholic liquor is:

1. A mocker saying, "Good Cheer," but leading men to prisons.

2. A cheat, receiving much value, but returning none.

3. A liar, promising to warm and strengthen, but sapping life instead.

4. A bandit, despoiling laborers of the profits of their toil.

5. A debaucher, whose haunt is hung with obscene pictures.

6. A thief, robbing the till of every honest merchant.

7. A corrupter, making mankind worse and never better.

8. A disturber, causing contention, strife, and disorder.

9. A murderer—alias a life giver—who deals out death.

10. A kidnapper, stealing boys from their homes and enslaving free men.

11. A ravager, whose wounded are in asylums, hospitals, and alms houses.

12. A poisoner, whose victims die in dire delirium.

13. A tyrant, ruling by a grasping habit that will not be thrown off.

14. A traitor, who daily betrays the flag of the land.

15. A despoiler, of health, happiness, home and country.

Why?

Liquor ads are adorned with pictures
    Of roses red and rare;
Of a beautiful girl in a bright red dress,
    With sunlight in her hair.

Why don't they picture the red of blood,
    Spilled on the highway wide,
Where the beautiful girl in the red, red dress
    Pays for the drunkard's ride?

—*Azalete Bolger Wells*

Startling Contrast Between Drinkers and Abstainers

Years ago a member of the British Parliament told his experience

The London "Daily Express" published the recollections of the Rt. Hon. David Kirkwood, M.P. It concerned boys who grew up together at Parkhead, Glasgow. All set out to "have a good time," some thought it was to be found in drinking and gambling, others refrained, joining a Temperance Youth Club. This is what happened to

The (so-called) "Jolly Twelve"
(all drinkers)

1. House agent, poisoned himself at 30.
2. Found dead at 30.
3. Committed suicide at 31.
4. Disappeared at 25.
5. Died in mental home at 30.
6. Drowned himself in Clyde at 26.
7. Poisoned himself at 32.
8. Did wrong and fled the country.
9. Jumped into the Clyde—drowned, 35.
10. Committed suicide, 36.
11. Committed suicide, 35.
12. ?

The Abstainers

1. Became manager, Beardmores Mills.
2. Manager, great engineering works.
3. Succeeded to father's business.
4. Controls successful business.
5. Engineer, retired well off.
6. Butcher's errand boy, now owns business.
7. Foreman, large building firm.
8. High position in leather factory.
9. Master builder, Glasgow.
10. Manager, important Glasgow business.
11. Myself.

Of the drinkers none lived beyond 36; of those who joined the Temperance Club, all lived to a good age, 63 being the earliest age of death. Every one of the latter class prospered.

244

A Fence or an Ambulance?

" 'Twas a dangerous cliff" as they freely
    confessed,
Though to walk near its crest was so
    pleasant.
But over its terrible edge there had
    slipped
A Duke and full many a peasant.
So the people said something would
    have to be done,
But their project did not at all tally.
Some said, "Put a fence 'round the edge
    of the cliff,"
Some, "An ambulance down in the val-
    ley."
But the cry for an ambulance carried the
    day,
For it spread to a neighboring city;
A fence may be useful or not it is true,
But each heart became full of pity
For those who slipped over the terrible
    cliff,
And the dwellers in highway and alley
Gave pounds and gave pence, not to put
    up a fence

But an ambulance down in the valley.
"For the cliff is all right if you're care-
    ful," they said,
"And if folks ever slip and are dropping
It isn't the slipping that hurts them so
    much
As the shock down below when they're
    stopping."
So, day after day, as the mishaps
    occurred,
Quick forth would the rescuers sally
To pick up the victims who fell from the
    cliff
With the ambulance down in the valley.
"Better guard well the young than
    reclaim them when old,"
For the voice of true wisdom is calling.
"To rescue the fallen is good, but 'tis
    best
To close up the source of temptation and
    crime
Than deliver from dungeon and galley.
Better to build a strong fence 'round the
    top of the cliff,
Than to put an ambulance down in the
    valley."

The Dangers of Smoking!

1. Smoking is a direct cause of cancer of the throat and cancer of the lungs!
2. A baby born of a smoking mother is weakened and sick, and is many times more susceptive to infection and disease!
3. The milk from the breasts of a smoking mother is laden with nicotine, and will poison her baby!
4. Poisons in tobacco actually destroy the brain cells of adolescents, and produce character changes which are rapidly increasing juvenile delinquency.
5. Smoking is a cause of coronary disease, the most deadly of the heart diseases.
6. Small quantities of tobacco smoke in the home injure the children and non-smokers of the family, as well as the one who smokes!
7. It is just as dangerous to expose an infant to tobacco smoke as it is to expose him to whooping cough, scarlet fever or polio!
8. Tobacco smoke aggravates and possibly aids in causing tuberculosis!
9. Many mothers have been DIRECTLY RESPONSIBLE for the death of their babies by smoking during pregnancy and by smoking while they nurse their infant!
10. Smoking is a direct cause of ulcers of the stomach.

A Tramp's Testimony

A tramp asked for a drink in a saloon. The request was granted, and when in the act of drinking the proffered beverage one of the young men present exclaimed: "Stop! Make us a speech! It is poor liquor that doesn't loosen a man's tongue."

The tramp swallowed down the drink, and as the liquor coursed through his blood, he straightened himself and stood before them with a grace and dignity which all his rags and dirt could not obscure.

"Gentlemen," he said, "I look tonight at you and myself, and it seems to me that I look upon the picture of my blighted boyhood. This bloated face was once as handsome as yours; this shambling figure once walked as proudly as yours, for I was a man of the world of men. I, too, once had a home and friends and position. I had a wife as beautiful as an artist's dream, but I dropped the priceless pearl of her honor and respect into a cup of wine, and, like Cleopatra, saw it dissolve, then quaffed it down in draught. I had children as sweet and pure as the flowers of spring and saw them fade and die under the blighting curse of a drunken father. I had a home where love lit its flame upon the altar and ministered before it, but I put out the holy fire, and darkness and desolation reigned in its stead. I had aspirations which soared high as the morning star, but I broke and bruised those beautiful forms and strangled them that I might hear the cries no more. Today I am a husband without a wife, a father without a child, a tramp without home, and a man in whom every impulse is dead. All have been swallowed up in maelstrom of drink."

The tramp ceased speaking. The glass fell from his nervous fingers, and shattered into a thousand fragments on the floor. The doors were pushed open and shut again, and when the group looked up, the tramp was gone.

(The above is recorded as the true experience of a prominent lawyer, but alas, THINK how many now that have homes as this man did but are traveling the same snare. "Be not deceived; God is not mocked: for whatsoever a man soweth, that shall he also reap" (Gal. 6:7).

Partners in Degradation

Said a beer to a cigarette,
"I'd like to make a good-sized bet
That I can get more scalps than you,
Although your victims aren't so few."
Said the cigarette to the beer flask,
"Well, that's easy as I could ask,
For I give kids their downward start,
Then you pitch in and do your part.
They come to you with burning thirst,
But I'm the fellow that sees 'em first;
So most of them should count for me.
I'll take the bet, it's a cinch, d'ye see?"
Then the beer can had this to say:
"I never looked at the thing that way,
But I confess you spoke the truth;
'Tis you who tackles the foolish youth.
You fill his system with dopey smoke,
I mould him into a first-class soak;
We work together far too well
To quarrel for even a little spell."
So the beer can and the cigarette
Shook hands together and offed the bet,
And away they sauntered side by side,
Hunting for victims far and wide.
In every corner of the nation,
Partners in crime and ruination.
So here's our warning, on the level:
"Shun them as you would the devil."

I bear no malice toward those engaged in the liquor business, but I hate the traffic.

I hate its every phase. I hate it for its intolerance. I hate it for its arrogance.

I hate it for its hypocrisy; for its cant and craft and false pretense.

I hate it for its commercialism; for its greed and avarice; for its sordid love of gain at any price.

I hate it for its domination of politics; for its corrupting influence in civic affairs; for its incessant effort to debauch the suffrage of the country; for the cowards it makes of public men.

I hate it for its utter disregard of law; for its ruthless trampling of the solemn compacts of state constitutions.

I hate it for the load it straps to labor's back; for the palsied hands it gives to toil; for its wounds to genius; for the tragedies of its might-have-beens.

I hate it for the human wrecks it has caused.

I hate it for the almshouses it peoples; for the prisons it fills; for the insanity it begets; for its countless graves in potters' fields.

I hate it for the mental ruin it imposes upon its victims; for its spiritual blight; for its moral degradation.

I hate it for the crimes it commits; for the homes it destroys; for the hearts it breaks.

I hate it for the malice it plants in the hearts of men; for its poison, for its bitterness, for the dead sea fruit with which it starves their souls.

I hate it for the brief it causes womanhood—the scalding tears, the hopes deferred, the strangled aspirations, its burden of want and care.

I hate it for its heartless cruelty to the aged, the infirm, and the helpless; for the shadow it throws upon the lives of children; for its monstrous injustice to blameless little ones.

I hate it as virtue hates vice, as truth hates error, as righteousness hates sin, as justice hates wrong, as liberty hates tyranny, as freedom hates oppression.

I hate it as Abraham Lincoln hated slavery. As he sometimes saw in prophetic vision the end of slavery and the coming of the time when the sun should shine and the rain should fall upon no slave in all the Republic, so I sometimes seem to see the end of this unholy traffic, the coming of the time when, if it does not wholly cease to be, it shall find no safe habitation anywhere beneath Old Glory's stainless stars.

—*J. Frank Hanley,*
Former Governor of Indiana

Is Drinking a Disease?

If alcoholism is a disease—

1. It is the only disease that is contracted by an act of the will;
2. It is the only disease that requires a license to propagate it;
3. It is the only disease that is bottled and sold;
4. It is the only disease that requires outlets to spread it;
5. It is the only disease that produces a revenue for the Government;
6. It is the only disease that provokes crime;
7. It is the only disease that is habit-forming.
8. It is the only disease that is spread by advertising; and
9. It is the only disease without a germ or virus cause, and for which there is no human corrective medicine.

—*American Businessmen's*
Research Foundation

Isn't It Strange?

I have walked in summer meadows
Where the sunbeams flashed and
broke,
But I never saw the cattle
Or any of the horses smoke.

I have watched the birds with wonder
When the world with dew is wet,
But I never saw a robin
Puffing at a cigarette.

I have fished in many a river
Where the sucker crop is ripe,
But never saw a catfish
Puffing at a briar pipe.

Man's the only living creature
That blows where'er he goes,
Like a booming tractor engine,
Smoke from mouth and nose.

If God had intended he would smoke
When He first invented man,
He would have built him on
A widely different plan.

He'd have fixed him with a stovepipe,
A damper and a grate,
And he'd had a smoke consumer
That was strictly up-to-date.

Smoking by Athletes: What Doctors Report

The American Medical Association has confirmed that coaches are right when they advise athletes not to smoke.

In a statement September 17 the association said, "There is no longer any room for doubt that athletes should not smoke. In a close finish between well-matched athletes, the nonsmoker has the edge." The reason: "The heavy smoker has trouble in breathing quickly and easily under heavy exertion."

The Confession of John Barleycorn

Alcohol is a self-confessed criminal. In fact, it is the world's greatest criminal. Listen to its confession:

"I am the greatest criminal in history. I have killed more men than have fallen in all the wars of the world. I have turned men into brutes. I have made millions of homes unhappy. I have transformed many ambitious youths into hopeless parasites. I make smooth the downward path for countless millions. I destroy the weak and weaken the strong. I make the wise man a fool, and trample the fool into his folly. I ensnare the innocent. The abandoned wife knows me; the hungry children know me; the parents whose child has bowed their gray heads in sorrow know me. I have ruined millions, and shall try to ruin millions more. My name is ALCOHOL."

General John J. Pershing Said:

"Banish the entire liquor industry from the United States; close every saloon and brewery; suppress drinking by severe punishment to the drinker; and, if necessary, death to the seller and maker, or both, as traitors, and the nation will suddenly find itself amazed at its efficiency and startled at the increase in its labor supply. I shall not go slow on prohibition, for I know what is the greatest foe of my men, greater than the bullets of the enemy."

"Woe unto him that giveth his neighbor drink, that puttest thy bottle to him and makest him drunk also . . . the cup of the Lord's right hand shall be turned unto thee, because of men's blood, and for the violence of the land, the city, and of all that dwell therein" (Habakkuk 2:15-17).

"Whoredom and wine and anew wine take away the heart" (Hosea 4:11).

Where Would He Go If He Lived Today?

During the frontier days, the driver of a covered wagon stopped his horses on the streets of a young town and called to a passing man, "Hey, any saloons in this place?"

"Sure, we've four," boastfully replied the man.

"Giddap!" the driver shouted, urging his horses on.

"Stop!" called the man.

"I can't stop here," replied the stranger. "I've got four boys in this wagon."

"Why?" again called the man. "What's your business?"

"My business is to raise these boys for God, and I can't do that in a town with four saloons." And he hurried his horses on, soon turning the bend in the road and passing out of sight.

TAKE YOUR PICK

There are Camels, and Luckies, and Viceroys
  Galore;
Fatimas, and Pall Malls, and brands by the score,
Their virtues extolled on waves of the air,
Enticing our boys, and our maidens fair.

To be happy and healthy, and prosperous we're told,
Just stop and relax and light up an Old Gold.
Now Winstons' the kind that make you feel good,
They satisfy, taste like a cigarette should.

Phillip Morris, L and M, Tarreyton, Kent,
All claim to be mild, yet have the same scent.
If smoke burns your throat, now don't be a fool,
The best thing to do is light up a Kool.

Smoke Marvel, Cavalier, Marlboro, Raleigh,
Till cancer rewards a fool for his folly.
A smoked-up liver, or nicotine heart,
The misery of bad health making its start.

Pleasure of smoking cannot compensate,
When T.B. lays you low, it then is too late.
Gran'pa and Gran'ma and little kid brother;
Uncle and Aunt, and now they've got mother.

Sound it out to the suckers, it's Satan's big lie,
But the biggest of all is "They Satisfy!"
"Thousands of filer traps"—that's a ringer;
Some kill you fast, these make you linger.

Millions to advertise, on with the show,
Television, magazine, billboard, radio!
So light up a fag, ill health is a joke,
Till you land in your casket—a victim of smoke.

—*David A. Beam*

Cigarettes—

- Waste your time
- Squander your money
- Reduce your efficiency
- Impair your success
- Jeopardize your safety
- Insult your friends
- Tarnish your skin
- Shatter your nerves
- Undermine your health
- Endanger your life
- Defile your body
- Stupefy your mind
- Corrupt your manners
- Deprave your senses
- Paralyze your conscience
- Demoralize your character
- Enslave your soul

LINCOLN SAID:

"The liquor traffic is a cancer in society, eating out the vitals and threatening destruction, and all attempts to regulate it will not only prove abortive, but will aggravate the evil; here must be no attempt to regulate the cancer; it must be eradicated; not one root must be left behind."

Ten Reasons Why I Smoke

1. It's such a clean, refined habit.
2. It makes my breath so pleasing to everybody.
3. It sets such a good example for children to follow.
4. It proves I have self control.
5. It makes my fingers and teeth so pretty and yellow.
6. It makes me look so manly.
7. I love to spit.
8. It starts fires, kills lives and destroys millions of dollars worth of forests and property. This is fun.
9. I want to see how much poison my body can take before I die.
10. It's my way of obeying God, Who says, "Keep thyself pure. Touch not the unclean thing."

"An ungodly man diggeth up evil, and in his lips there is a burning fire" *(Proverbs 16:27).*

The Judges Speak

Judge Torrence, former superintendent, Illinois State Reformatory: "I am sure cigarettes are ruining and making criminals of more boys and girls than liquor!"

Judge B. S. Shaw of Hart, Michigan: "In every instance of juvenile delinquency in this court I have found that the boys were cigarette users."

Judge Allen of Lisbon, North Dakota: "Every juvenile delinquent brought before me for the past 17 years has a been a cigarette smoker!"

Dr. Hutchinson of the Kansas State Reformatory: "Cigarettes are the cause of the downfall of more boys in this institution than all other vicious habits combined!"

Miss Winters, principal of one of the largest schools for delinquent girls in America: "Out of eleven hundred inmates, only 20 were non-smokers of cigarettes!"

King James I Warning

By the time of Rolfe's experiments, the use of tobacco had not become universal in all quarters. There was some stubborn opposition to its development in Virginia. No one had stronger feeling on the subject than King James I of England. In 1604 he had written:

And surely in my opinion, there cannot be a more base, and yet hurtfull corruption in a Countrey, then is the vile use (or other abuse) of taking *Tobacco* in this Kingdome, which hath mooved me, shortly to discover the abuses thereof in this following little Pamphlet.

The pamphlet to which he referred was his A COUNTERBLASTE TO TOBACCO, *which ended with a harsh warning:*

Have you not reason then to bee ashamed, and to forbeare this filthie noveltie, so basely grounded, so foolishly received and so grossely mistaken in the right use thereof? In your abuse thereof sinning against God, harming your selves both in persons and goods, and making also thereby the markes and notes of vanitie upon you: by the custome thereof making your selves to be wondered at by all forraine civil Nations, and by all strangers that come among you, to be scorned and contemned. A custome lothsome to the eye, hatefull to the Nose, harmefull to the braine, dangerous to the Lungs, and in the blacke stinking fume thereof, neerest resembling the horrible Stigian smoke of the pit that is bottomelesse.

—A Counterblaste to Tobacco by King James I

The Home . . .

Husband, Wife, Father, Mother, Children

A Christian Home

Where family prayer is daily said,
God's Word is regularly read,
And faith in Christ is never dead,
That is a Christian home.

Where father, mother, sister, brother,
All have true love for one another,
And no one ever hates the other,
That is a Christian home.

Where family quarrels are pushed aside
To let the love of God above
Ere darkness falls on eventide,
That is a Christian home.

Where Jesus Christ is host and guest,
Through whom we have eternal rest
And in Him are forever blest,
That is a Christian home.

Tell Her So

Amid the cares of married life,
In spite of toil and business strife,
If you value your sweet wife,
    Tell her so!

Prove to her you don't forget
The bond to which your seal is set;
She's of life's sweet the sweetest yet—
    Tell her so!

When days are dark and deeply blue,
She has her troubles, same as you;
Show her that your love is true—
    Tell her so!

Never let her heart grow cold—
Richer beauties will unfold;
She is worth her weight in gold!
    Tell her so!

Togetherness

Once two hearts are woven tightly
    In a heavenly embrace,
Life takes on a tender meaning,
    And things are not hard to face.

Gone are all the fears they harbored;
    In their place is faith anew.
Two hearts beating for one purpose
    Always have a brighter view.

When the rains of trouble wet life,
    Two hearts find a shelter warm
Wherein they can plan the future,
    And detour most any storm.

For togetherness is stronger
    Than the wildest winds of life;
Two hearts always will be equal
    To the highest waves of strife.

So it is and I am certain
    It will be till life is done.
Two hearts sing a song of gladness
    So much sweeter than just one.

THE FAMILY

The family is like a book:
    The children are the leaves,
The parents are the cover,
    Which protective beauty gives.

At first the pages of the book
    Are blank and smooth and fair;
But time soon writeth memories
    And painteth pictures there.

Love is the little golden clasp
    That bindeth up the trust.
Oh, break it not, lest all the leaves
    Should scatter and be lost.

What Makes a Home?

'Tis the gentle pitter-patter
Of wee feet upon the stair;
The sound of children's laughter
Gaily ringing through the air;
The shining eyes that smile at us,
Wee lips that hold a kiss,
Far sweeter than the nectar
That the bee from flower slips.
'Tis the fire's warm welcome
And the daylight's mellow glow,
Friendly books and easy chairs,
And the folks we like to know.
The love and light and laughter
That go singing through the gloam,
All telling us of peace within,
That makes a house a home.

—Elizabeth Brockway

To Husband and Wife

Preserve sacredly the privacies of your own house, your married state and your heart. Let no father or mother or sister or brother ever presume to come between you or share the joys or sorrows that belong to you two alone.

With mutual help build your quiet world, not allowing your dearest earthly friend to be the confidant of aught that concerns your domestic peace. Let moments of alienation, if they occur, be healed at once. Never, no never, speak of it outside; but to each other confess and all will come out right. Never let the morrow's sun still find you at variance. Renew and renew your vow. It will do you good, and thereby your minds will grow together contented in that love which is stronger than death, and you will be truly one.

Beatitudes for Married Couples

Blessed are husband and wife who continue to be considerate and loving, after the wedding bells have ceased to ring!

Blessed are the husband and wife who are as polite and courteous to each other as they are to their friends!

Blessed are the husband and wife who maintain a sense of humor!

Blessed are the married couples who ABSTAIN from alcoholic beverages!

Blessed are they who fulfill their marriage vows of a lifetime of fidelity and mutual helpfulness one to another!

Blessed are they who study God's Word and thank God for His multitude of blessings!

Blessed are the husband and wife who humbly dedicate their lives and their homes to Christ, and practice His teachings!

—Connecticut Counselor

Recipe for a Happy Marriage

1 cup consideration
2 cups milk of human kindness
1 gallon faith in God and each other
2 cups praise
1 reasonable budget with a generous
    dash of cooperation
1 cup of contentment
3 teaspoons of pure extract of "I am
    sorry"
1 cup each of confidence and encour-
    agement

"Flavor with frequent portions of recreation and a dash of happy memories. Stir well and remove any specks of jealousy, temper, or criticism. Sweeten well with generous portions of love and keep warm with a steady flame of devotion. Never serve with a cold shoulder or hot tongue."

—Grace Taylor

TO MY HUSBAND, DALE

As the wife of the author of Heart Blessings, *I wish to dedicate the following poem by Ben Murroughs to my husband.* —*Marguerite Crowley*

Together we will always be . . . whatever comes along! . . . tender hearts that beat as one . . . will sing a happy song . . . together through the storm and rain . . . and the darkest night . . . those who share a warm embrace . . . will find sweet delight . . . together in the morning sun . . . and when the stars break through . . . that's how it is when lovers . . . are forever true . . . together, what a wondrous word . . . for in it people find . . . the road that leads to happiness . . . and blessed peace of mind . . . "together," say it softly dear . . . the word gives hope to me . . . without it I am all alone . . . a lock without a key . . . but knowing you are by my side . . . deep in my heart I smile . . . together we will always be . . . and that's a long, long while.

TO MY PRECIOUS WIFE, MARGUERITE

(On our 36th Wedding Anniversary)

That was a gladsome hour for me
   Thirty and six years ago today—
When on that June the First
   You pledged "I do," "alway."

Darling, you have kept those vows,
   Through stormy days and calm,
And true to me you've been,
   And life has been a psalm.

There've been times of stress,
   And times of anxious strain,
But in courage you've been faithful—
   Did not murmur nor complain.

It's our true love for each other
   And God's unfailing grace
Which have brought us pleasant mem'ries
   That time cannot erase.

Could the clock of time roll back
   To that happy June the First,
The choice again to make dear,
   'Twould be you for me alway.

I am thankful for your patience,
   Your courage and your grace—
You're a constant inspiration
   With that love-light in your face.

—*Dale*

Heart of a Child

Whatever you write on the heart of a child,
   No water can wash away.
The sand may be shifted when billows are wild,
   And the efforts of time may decay.

   Some stories may perish,
   Some songs be forgot,
   But this graven record—
   Time changes it not.

Whatever you write on the heart of a child,
   A story of gladness or care
That Heaven has blessed or earth has defiled,
   Will linger unchangeably there.

The Answered Prayer

The way is dark and the road is long;
   Help me, dear Lord, for I cannot see!
Give me a light to guide me on;
   Teach me with patience to follow Thee!

* * * * * * *

My prayer Thou hast answered, O Lord, in
   Thy might,
   And my sadness is drearier still today,
For my little lad with the golden hair,
With eyes so blue and a face so fair,
   Has gone before me to light the way.
I can see him journeying up the height
   Over the narrow path and straight,
Which all must tread toward that mystic
   bourne;
Leaving his dear ones to sigh and mourn.
   He journeys alone toward the pearly
   gate.
I can see him, not as when strong and light
   Of foot he played with the children
   here,
But radiant with heavenly life and joy,
For the loving eyes of my angel boy
   Can never grow dim with pain or tear.
I shall meet him again on that heavenly
   height,
   For his light shall lead me along the
   way;
When the task that is given to me is done,
When the strife is ended, the battle won,
   I shall greet him there in the perfect day.

—Margaret Holland

Five Keys for a Happy Home

1. Give God the first hour of each day (Mark 1:35). Pray in the morning.
2. Give God the first day of the week (1 Cor. 16:2). Serve in your church to save your community.
3. Give God the first portion of your income (Prov. 3:9; 1 Cor. 6:2). Keep books on what you give to be sure you do not think you are giving more than you actually are.
4. Give God the first consideration in every decision (Matt. 6:33). This includes your choice of house, close friends, work, church, school, etc.
5. Give God's Son first place in your heart always (2 Cor. 8:5). Live in His presence as though He were the unseen guest in your house—He is, you know!

—Ord L. Morrow,
Good News Broadcaster

Gather the Children

Some would gather money
   Along the path of life,
Some would gather roses,
   And rest from worldly strife.
But I would gather children
   From among the thorns of sin,
I would seek a golden curl,
   And a freckled, toothless grin.
For money cannot enter
   In that land of endless day,
And roses that are gathered
   Soon will wilt along the way.
But, oh, the laughing children
   As I cross the sunset sea,
And the gates swing wide to heaven,
   I can take them in with me!

Heaven Every Day

We have a wonderful Guest
 At our house
Who makes our home a heaven
 Every day;
And this wonderful Guest
 At our house
Has promised us He'll
 Never go away.

He brought a lovely letter
 From His Father's house above,
And every day we read it,
 For it tells us of His love;
And when we go to sleep
 At night,
He sees that everything
 Goes right—
This wonderful Guest
 At our house,
Who makes our home a heaven
 Every day.

Chorus:
His name is JESUS, and because
 He loves us, one and all,
He'd love to visit your house
 If you'd like to have Him call.
So, if sometime you should decide,
 Just ask Him in, and He'll abide—
This wonderful Guest at our house,
 Who makes our home a heaven
 Every day.

All Ours, That's Marriage

My husband's home is my home
 As is his heart.
My husband's friends are my friends
 Nothing apart.
We own share and share alike.
My husband's cross is my cross
 As is his Hope.
Our hearts, our souls intertwine,
 Not yours, not mine.
All ours, that's marriage.

—Ivy Cunningham Sprowl

A Prayer for Your Home

God bless this house and all within it;
Let no harsh spirit enter in it.
Let none approach who would betray;
None with a bitter word to say.
Shield it from harm and sorrow's sting;
Here let the children's laughter ring.
Grant that these friends from year to year
Shall build their happiest memories here.

God bless this home and those who love it;
Fair be the skies which bend above it.
May never anger's thoughtless word
Within these sheltering walls be heard.
May all who rest beside this fire
And then depart, glad thoughts inspire;
And make them feel who close the door,
Friendship has graced their home once more.

God bless this house and those who keep it;
In the sweet oils of gladness steep it.
Endow these walls with lasting wealth,
The light of love, the glow of health,
The palm of peace, the charm of mirth,
Good friends to sit around the hearth;
And with each nightfall perfect rest—
Here let them live their happiest.

God Needed Another Angel

A little child was loaned to you
Just seven short years ago.
A baby boy—who brought you joy
That only Mothers know!

May you find solace and comfort
In "Lord, Thy will be done!"
As on thru life you cherish
The smile of the dear little one.

For the earthly life is ended
Of a child who was loved by all.
God needed another Angel,
That's why Jack answered the call.

My Wife's Hands

(As given over the Hour of Inspiration)

Her hands have so often ministered to my needs. So many times, and now for so many years, they have done the menial tasks of the homemaker, taking meticulous care of every detail about the house—cleaning, laundering, decorating, arranging the furnishings with all those extra touches, making the home so perennially attractive, making sure that her husband can live in an atmosphere of comfort and relaxation.

These hands, too, have provided so many delicious meals, arranging each detail at the table with professional finesse and yet with complete informality. So many meals, also, have her hands provided for our guests which in innumerable instances have been for the purpose of enhancing my happiness and promoting the interests of my work. And, oh, the tens of thousands of dishes, and pots and pans, and silverware these hands have washed!

And the million little every day things her hands have done, just for me. Even the exhilarating experience she grants me of simply holding her hands. What strength, reassurance and inspiration I get from this. For this pleasure is associated in memory with those earlier days of courtship; and, then, the night at the marriage altar when I placed the ring on her finger; and the countless times we have walked along together, hand in hand; and so many times we have at night closed our eyes for sleep with our hands interlocked. And when I have been ill those hands attended me, and when I have been discouraged, those hands on my brow have dispelled my heartache. Those hands have ministered to the needs of my children. Nothing in all of life has been so inspiring as to see those loving hands care for those precious little ones, providing for their every comfort and necessity.

In greeting friends, likewise, those hands have conveyed so much welcome and hospitality; and in clasping hands with them in a farewell so much sincere goodwill and friendship have been expressed.

And, oh, when her hands have so often been lifted up in prayer, it has brought blessing to my heart; and no doubt the dear Lord in heaven has been gladdened because of the expression of those hands.

Those soft, gentle hands, those hands of industry, those hands of hospitality; those hands of love—my wife's hands!

Published one year before she went to be with the Lord.
—D.C.

A BOY

Nobody knows what a boy is worth,
A boy at this work or play;
A boy who whistles around the place,
Or laughs in an artless way.

Nobody knows the worth of a boy,
And the world must wait to see;
For every man in an honored place,
Is a boy that used to be.

Nobody knows what a boy is worth,
A boy with his face aglow;
For hid in his heart there are secrets deep,
Not even the wisest know.

Nobody knows the worth of a boy,
A boy with his bare, white feet;
So have a smile and kindly word,
For every boy you meet.

—Exchange

How I Described "Her" Three Months Before the Marriage — to a Sister in Louisiana

(A keepsake found among my Marguerite's personal effects)

"God created everything and saw it was good, and for six thousand years He continued to create multiplied millions of human creatures, thousands upon thousands of whom were fair to look upon. Then, after this, God evidently decided to crown His creative work by bringing into being the finest, purest, truest, sweetest, loveliest specimen of womanhood that had yet honored the earth with her presence; and so heaven has blest us with one, Miss Marguerite McGee, who three months hence will be known ever afterward as Mrs. Dale S. Crowley. Amen and Selah! God has brought us together!

"She is the realization and consummation of all my fondest, fairest dreams. She is all and more than I have ever wished for, hoped for, and anticipated in the one whom I should cherish as a life companion—and you know how fastidious I have been in this respect. She has all the qualities and potentialities that fit and fully equip her for the place that she is taking, and more. In fact, it is difficult to understand just how it is possible for all the beautiful and noble and lofty qualities and traits and characteristics which she possesses to be converged into one person.

"She is as pure as the driven snow; she is as true as gold; she is as beautiful as an angel, and more lovely than a garden of fragrant roses. She is the quintessence of sweetness; and, as for her goodness, she is as near perfection as I ever hope to see in this world. She is Christlike in all points, being modest, humble, self-forgetful, faithful, patient, optimistic, zealous, courageous, having a heart full of love for God and for the world. Is it any wonder that I am so rejoicing to know also that her heart is full of love for *me?*

"A veritable flood of supernal glory has filled my soul these past few weeks, and particularly these past few days. Joy is vibrating in every fiber of my being. Who can describe it? No poet, no artist. It is sweeter as the days go by; and still sweeter as the moments fly."

Footnote to above: The descriptives above were all verified in forty-six years of happy married life. Not one word would I change, except that I came to appreciate her and love her more with every passing day. And I am sure that this love will be even deeper and richer throughout all eternity!

—Dale S. Crowley

The woman was made out of the side rib of man,
not made out of his head to rule over him,
but out of his side to be equal with him,
from under his arm to be protected,
and near his heart to be loved.

Please, Daddy, Let's Go

A little girl with shining eyes,
Her upturned face aglow,
Said, "Daddy, it's almost time
For Sunday School, you know;
Let's go and hear of Jesus' love
Of how He died for all,
To take them to His home above
Who on His name will call."

"Oh, no," said Daddy, "Not today;
I've worked hard all the week;
And I must have one day of rest,
I'm going to the creek,
For there I can relax and rest,
And fishing's fine they say;
So run along, don't bother me.
We'll go ANOTHER day."

Months and years have passed away,
But Daddy hears that plea no more—
"Let's go to Sunday School . . ."
Those childish days are o'er.
And now that Daddy's growing old,
And life is almost through,
He finds some time to go to church,
BUT, what does daughter do?:
She says, "Oh, Daddy, not today.

Was out almost all night;
I've got to get a little sleep;
Besides, I look a fright."
Then Daddy lifts a trembling hand
To brush away the tears;
Again he hears that pleading voice,
Distinctly through the years.
He sees a small girl's upturned face,
Upturned with eyes aglow,
Saying, "It's time for Sunday School,
Please, Daddy, won't you go?"

That Little Chap O' Mine

To feel his little hand in mine, so cling-
    ing and so warm,
To know he thinks me strong enough to
    keep him safe from harm;
To see his simple faith in all that I can
    say or do,
It sort o' shames a fellow, but it makes
    him better too.
And I am trying hard to be the man he
    fancies me to be,
Because I have this chap at home who
    thinks the world o' me.
I would not disappoint his trust for any-
    thing on earth,
Nor let him know how little I just natu-
    rally am worth.
But after all, it's easier, that brighter
    road to climb,
With the little hands behind me to push
    me all the time.
And I reckon I'm a better man that what
    I used to be
Because I have this chap at home who
    thinks the world o' me.

—Edith Gover Tarr Wheeler, 1901

A Little Fellow Follows Me

A careful man I want to be,
    A little fellow follows me.
I do not dare to go astray,
    For fear he'll go the self-same way.
I cannot once escape his eyes.
    Whate'er he sees me do, he tries.
Like me he says he's going to be,
    The little chap who follows me.
He thinks that I am good and fine,
    Believes in every word of mine.
The base in me he must not see,
    The little chap who follows me.
I must remember as I go,
    Through summer's sun and winter's
    snow;
I am building for the years to be
    That little chap who follows me.

—Taken from "In Your Hands" by
the Book House for Children

To Any Daddy

There are little eyes upon you,
And they're watching day by day.
There are little ears that surely
Take in every word you say.
There are little hands all eager
To do everything you do.
There's a little boy who's dreaming
Of the day he'll be like you!

You're that little fellow's idol,
You're the wisest of the wise.
In his little mind, about you
No suspicions e'er arise;
He believes in you devoutly,
Holds that all you say or do
He will say and do, in your way,
When he's all grown up like you.

There's a wide-eyed little fellow
Who believes you're always right;
His keen ears are always open
To catch your words, day or night.
You are setting an example,
Every day, in all you do,
For the little boy who's wanting
To grow up to be like you.

—*Isabelle Tucker*

MOTHER

The noblest thoughts my soul can claim,
The holiest words my tongue can frame,
Unworthy are to praise the name
    More sacred than all other.
An infant, when her love first came—
A man, I find it just the same;
Reverently I breathe her name,
    The blessed name of mother.

—*George Griffith Fetter*

Mothers

Mothers are the queerest things!
    'Member when John went away,
All but mother cried and cried
    When they said good-bye that day.
She just talked, and seemed to be
    Not the slightest bit upset—
Was the only one who smiled!
    Others' eyes were streaming wet.

But when John came back again
    On a furlough, safe and sound,
With a medal for his deeds,
    And without a single wound,
While the rest of us hurrahed,
    Laughed and joked and danced about,
Mother kissed him, then she cried—
    Cried and cried like all git out!

—*Edwin L. Sabin*

Dad's Greatest Job

I may never be as clever as my neighbors down the street,
I may never be as wealthy as some other men I meet;
I may never have the glory that some other men have had,
But I've got to be successful as a little fellow's dad.

There are certain dreams I cherish that I'd like to see come true.
There are things I would accomplish ere my working time is through;
But the task my heart is set on is to guide a little lad
And to make myself successful as that little fellow's dad.

I may never get earth's glory; I may never gather gold;
Men may count me as a failure when my business life is told;
But if he who follows after is a Christian, I'll be glad,
For I'll know I've been successful as a little fellow's dad.

TO ALL PARENTS

"I'll lend you for a little time, a child of mine," He said,
"For you to love the while he lives . . . and mourn for when he's dead;
It may be six or seven years, or twenty-two or three . . .
But will you . . . till I call him back, take care of him for me?
He'll bring his charms to gladden you; and shall his stay be brief,
You'll have his lovely memories as solace for your grief."

"I cannot promise he will stay, since all from earth return,
But there are lessons taught down there I want this child to learn;
I've looked the wide world over in my search for teachers true,
And from the throngs that crowd life's lanes . . . I have selected you.
Now will you give him all your love, nor think your labor vain?
Nor hate me when I come to call to take him back again?"

"I fancied that I heard them say, 'Dear Lord, Thy will be done!
For all the joy, thy child shall bring, the risk of grief we'll run . . .
We'll shelter him with tenderness, we'll love him while we may,
And for the happiness we've known, forever grateful stay;
But shall the angel call for him . . . much sooner than we've planned,
We'll brave the bitter grief that comes . . . and try to understand!!' "

—Edgar A. Guest

Parenthood

Someone to snuggle up close to me there;
    Somebody's head on the thick of my arm;
Someone to help with his cuddle-time prayer;
Someone believing I shield him from harm;
Somebody's dark-fearing hand I may hold
    Safe in my bigger one's sheltering keep;
Someone to guard till the morning light bold
    Rescue his eyes from the fetters of sleep.
Such are the yearnings that fill us all
    After those wonderful babies have grown;
These are the hungers that tug and call
    After the nestlings have feathered and flown;
Only this heart's-ease is comforting me,
    Missing my olden-time playfellow so;
He, in the years that shall presently be,
    Love like my love for himself shall know.

"Train up a child in the way he should go;
    And when he is old, he will not depart from it."

(Proverbs 22:6)

MacArthur's Prayer for His Son

According to the General's biographer and confidant, Maj. Gen. Courtney Whitney, the family repeated this MacArthur credo many times during early morning devotions.

"Build me a son, O Lord, who will be strong enough to know when he is weak, and brave enough to face himself when he is afraid; one who will be proud and unbending in honest defeat, and humble and gentle in victory.

"Build me a son whose wishes will not take the place of deeds; a son who will know Thee—and that to know himself is the foundation stone of knowledge.

"Lead him, I pray, not in the path of ease and comfort, but under the stress and spur of difficulties and challenge. Here let him learn to stand up in the storm; here let him learn compassion for those who fall.

"Build me a son whose heart will be clear, whose goal will be high, a son who will master himself before he seeks to master other men, who who will reach into the future, yet never forget the past.

"And after all these things are his, add, I pray, enough of a sense of humor, so that he may always be serious, yet never take himself too seriously. Give him humility, so that he may always remember the simplicity of true greatness, the open mind of true wisdom, and the meekness of true strength.

"Then I, his father, will dare to whisper, 'I have not lived in vain.' "

The Soul of a Child

"Each day we are carving, not upon stone or marble, but upon the lives of precious young boys and girls; therefore be careful with what tools you carve and how you use them."

The soul of a child is the loveliest flower
  That grows in the garden of God.
Its climb is from weakness to knowledge and
    power,
  To the sky from the clay and the clod.
To beauty and sweetness it grows under care,
  Neglected, 'tis ragged and wild.
'Tis a plant that is tender, but wondrously rare,
  The sweet, wistful soul of a child.
Be tender, O gardener, and give it its share
  Of moisture, of warmth, and of light,
And let it not lack for the painstaking care
  To protect it from frost and from blight.
A glad day will come when its bloom shall
    unfold.
  It will seem that an angel has smiled,
Reflecting a beauty and sweetness untold
  In the sensitive soul of a child.

A Girl's Prayer

Dear God, I would be beautiful!
  But if this may not be,
Oh, give me beauty of the soul,
  For deeper sight to see!

Dear God, I would be popular!
  But if this be not wise,
Let those who need me find me near
  To comfort or advise.

Dear God, I would go far in life,
  And do some noble thing!
But if I may not reach the heights,
  I'd cause some heart to sing.

Dear God, I would be dearly loved!
  But if this be denied,
Help me to love humanity
  Over all the world wide.

Dear God, I would be loveliness
  And grace personified!
Yet, help my life to shine for Thee,
  A splendid thing—all glorified!

—Bertha E. Wilson

Whose Delinquency?

We read in the papers
We hear on the air
Of killing and stealing,
And crime everywhere.
We sigh, and we say,
As we notice the trend,
"This young generation,
Where will it all end?"

But can we be sure
That it's their fault alone?
That maybe a part of it
Isn't our own?
Too much money to spend,
Too much idle time,
Too many movies
Of passion and crime;
Too many books
Not fit to be read;
Too much of evil
In what they hear said;
Too many children
Encouraged to roam
By too many parents
Who won't stay at home.

Kids don't make movies;
They don't write the books
That paint a gay picture
Of gangsters and crooks.
They don't make the
     liquor,
They don't run the bars,
They don't make the laws,
And they don't buy cars.
They don't make the drugs
That addle the brain;
It's all done by older folks
Greedy for gain.
And how many cases
We find that it's true
The label "Delinquent"
Fits older folks too.

—*Author unknown*

Send Them to Bed With a Kiss

O mothers, so weary, discouraged,
    Worn out with the cares of the day;
You often grow cross and impatient,
    Complain of the noise and the play.
For the day brings so many vexations,
    So many things going amiss;
But, mothers, whatever may vex you,
    Send the children to bed with a kiss!

The dear little feet wander often,
    Perhaps, from the pathway of right.
The dear little hands find new mischief
    To try you from morning till night;
But think of the desolate mothers
    Who'd give all the world for your bliss.
And, as thanks for your infinite blessings,
    Send the children to bed with a kiss!

For some day their noise will not vex you,
    The silence will hurt you far more;
You will long for their sweet childish voices,
    For a sweet childish face at the door;
And to press a child's face to your bosom,
    You'd give all the world for just this!
For the comfort 'twill bring you in sorrow,
    Send the children to bed with a kiss!

A Little Boy's Prayer

Last night my little boy confessed to me
Some childish wrong;
And kneeling at my knee,
He prayed with tears—
"Dear God, make me a man
Like Daddy—wise and strong;
I know You can."
Then while he slept
I knelt beside his bed,
Confessed my sins,
And prayed with low-bowed head:
"O God, make me a child
Like my child here—
Pure, guileless,
Trusting Thee with faith sincere!"

262

Make Childhood Sweet

Wait not till the little hands are at rest
　Ere you fill them full of flowers;
Wait not for the crowning tuberose
　To make sweet the last sad hours.
But while in the busy household band
Your darlings still need your guiding hand,
　Oh, fill their lives with sweetness!

Wait not till the little hearts are still
　For the loving look of praise;
But while you gently chide a fault,
　The good deed kindly praise.
The word you would speak beside the bier
Falls sweeter far on the living ear:
　Oh, fill young lives with sweetness!

Ah, what are kisses on clay-cold lips
　To the rosy mouth we press,
When our wee one flies to her mother's arms
　For love's tenderest caress!
Let never a worldly babble keep
Your heart from the joy each day should
　reap,
　Circling young lives with sweetness.

Give thanks each morn for the sturdy boys,
　Give thanks for the fairy girls;
With a dower of wealth like this at home,
　Would you rifle the earth for pearls?
Wait not for Death to gem Love's crown,
But daily shower life's blessings down,
　And fill young hearts with sweetness.

Remember the homes where the light has
　fled,
　Where the rose has faded away
And the love that glows in youthful hearts,
　Oh, cherish it while you may!
And make your home a garden of flowers,
Where joy shall bloom through childhood's
　hours,
　And fill young hearts with sweetness.

Too Little

Said a precious little laddie
　To his father one bright day,
"May I give myself to Jesus,
　Let Him wash my sins away?"

"Oh, my son, but you're too little;
　Wait until you older grow;
Bigger folk, 'tis true, do need Him,
　But little folk are safe, you know."

Said the father to his laddie,
　As a storm was coming on,
"Are the sheep all safely sheltered,
　Safe within the fold, my son?"

"All the big ones are, my father,
　But the lambs, I let them go,
For I didn't think it mattered;
　Little ones are safe, you know."

Oh, my brother! oh, my sister!
　Have you, too, made that mistake?
Little hearts that now are yielding
　May be hardened, then—too late.

Ere the evil days come nigh them,
　"Let the children come to Me
And forbid them not," said Jesus,
　"Of such shall My kingdom be."

WORTH OF A BOY

A DIAMOND in the rough
Is a diamond sure enough,
For before it ever sparkles
It is made of diamond stuff!
Of course, someone must find it,
Or it never will be found;
And then someone must grind it
Or it will never be ground.
And when it's found and when it's
　ground,
And when it's burnished bright,
That diamond's everlastingly
Just flashing out its light.
Oh, teacher, in the Sunday School,
Don't say, "I've done enough!"
That worst boy in your class may be
"A DIAMOND IN THE ROUGH!"

Ten Rules for a Successful Marriage

1. You must marry the right person, one you love and one who loves you, and both of you must be in love with Jesus Christ.
2. GIVE and TAKE is a necessity. Let love cover the disagreements which will come in any marriage.
3. Never carry into tomorrow the petty troubles of today. Forgive at the end of the day, and then forget.
4. Don't discuss your disagreements and personal problems with others. You will soon forget these quarrels, but others will remember them forever. Go to the LORD for the advice you need.
5. Try to live within your financial means. Don't try to keep up with some other couple; keep within your income. And be sure to set aside something for the Lord's work.
6. Keep your love as romantic as possible. Appreciate each other. Express that appreciation in actual love and affection in the home.
7. NEVER, NEVER, NEVER even think of divorce as a solution for your marriage problems. You took your vows "until death do us part." So often, divorce never settles anything.
8. Keep your eyes on the person you have married, and don't bother looking around for someone else. Wandering eyes benefit no marriage.
9. Read God's Word and pray together every day. To pray together is to stay together.
10. Let Christ shed the love of God abroad in your heart, and you will be sure to have love for each other.

Have Courage, My Boy, to Say No!

You're starting today on life's journey,
Alone on the highway of life.
You'll meet with a thousand temptations,
Each city with evil is rife.
The world in a state of excitement,
There's danger wherever you go;
But if you are tempted in weakness,
Have courage, my boy, to say—NO.

The siren's sweet smile may allure you,
Beware of her cunning and art;
Whenever you see her approaching,
Be guarded and haste to depart.
The inns and saloons are inviting,
Decked out in their tinsel and show.
Should you be invited to enter,
Have courage, my boy, to say NO.

Be careful in choosing companions,
Seek only the brave and the true;
And stand by your friends when in trial,
Ne'er changing the old for the new.
And when by false friends you are tempted
The taste of the wine cup to know,
With firmness, with patience, and kindness,
Have courage, my boy, to say—NO.

The bright, sparkling wine may be offered;
No matter how tempting it be,
From poison that stings like an adder,
My boy, have the courage to flee.
The gambling halls are before you,
Their lights, how they dance to and fro;
You may be invited to enter,
Do have courage, my boy, to say—NO.

In courage of faith lies your safety,
When you your long journey begin;
And trust in your heavenly Father
Will keep you unspotted from sin.
Temptations will go on increasing
As rivers from rivulets flow;
But if you are true to your Saviour,
You'll have courage, my boy, to say—NO.

—Anonymous

The New Year . . .

FLEETING YEARS

It seemed just yesterday when whistles blew,
  And sirens shrieked a mighty cheer,
When merry makers jammed the midnight streets
  To welcome in the glad New Year.

Only a little while since then it seems
  We faced the year with joyful heart.
And in the song and cheer of happy souls
  Our festive spirits were apart.

We looked with bright prospects upon the year
  To try what we had tried before;
To give to Christ and to lose humankind
  A yielded heart to serve Him more.

But now the year has swiftly fled away,
  And we are left with little done.
The many tasks that we had planned to do,
  It seems that we have just begun.

So swiftly flies the fleeting hours away;
  So soon the precious days are o'er;
Unless we hasten in the Master's work,
  We'll fail, just as we did before.

The old year's gone, but—in thy hand the new,
  Another chance has come to show.
As stewards of the year, we must not fail
  A faithful service to bestow.

We cannot stop the passing of the hours,
  Nor to our heart hold back the day.
Just as it came, so it must soon depart,
  And leave us on our weary way.

But one thing there is left for every man
  Within the harvest field to do.
And Grace is giv'n to carry out God's plan,
  Before the old year changes to the new.

—John W. Goodwin

Another Year for Thee

Another year is dawning!
  Dear Master, let it be,
In working or in waiting,
  Another year with Thee!

Another year of leaning
  Upon Thy loving breast,
Of even deeper trusting,
  Of quiet, happy rest.

Another year of mercies,
  Of faithfulness and grace;
Another year of gladness,
  In the shining of Thy face.

Another year of progress,
  Another year of praise;
Another year of proving
  Thy presence "all the days."

Another year of service,
  Of witness to Thy love;
Another year of training
  For holier work above.

Another year is dawning!
  Dear Master, let it be,
On earth, or else in heaven,
  Another year for Thee!

And I said to the man who stood
  at the gate of the year,
"Give me light that I may tread
  safely into the unknown."
And he replied: "Go out into the
  darkness and put thy hand
  into the hand of God.
That shall be to thee better than
  light and safer than a
  known way."

Message of the New Year

I asked the New Year for some motto sweet,
Some rule of life with which to guide my feet;
I asked and paused; he answered soft and low;
    "God's will to know."
"Will knowledge then suffice, New Year," I cried;
And, ere the question into silence died,
The answer came: "Nay, but remember, too,
    God's will to do."
Once more I asked, "Is there no more to tell?"
And once again the answer sweetly fell:
"Yes! this one thing, all other things above,
    God's will to love."

—Anonymous

Prayer for This Year

God give you FAITH this coming year!
   The faith that will not fail the keenest test;
That trusts and sings in midst of fire and storm;
   And dares rely upon His Word and rest.

God give you HOPE this coming year!
   The hopes that through the darkness sees afar—
The purifying hope that fondly waits
   The rising of the bright and Morning Star.

God give you LOVE this coming year!
   His own great love that burns out for the lost;
That intercedes, and waits, and suffers long—
   That never fails, nor stops to count the cost.

—Margaret D. Armstrong

GROWTH

I stood the children, straight and tall,
By last year's marks upon the wall.
Another year! How soon they go,
And see how fast the children grow!
And then I thought of how God's Word
Says, "Grow in grace and in the Lord."
And as I knelt with God alone,
He asked me gently, "Have you grown?"

New Year's Wishes

What shall I wish for?
   Treasures of earth?
Songs in the springtime,
   Pleasures and mirth?
Flowers on thy pathway,
   Skies ever clear?
Would this insure thee
   A Happy New Year?

What shall I wish for?
   What can be found
Bringing thee sunshine
   All the year 'round?
Where is the treasure,
   Lasting and dear,
That shall ensure thee
   A Happy New Year?

Faith that increaseth
   Walking in light;
Hope that aboundeth,
   Happy and bright;
Love that is perfect,
   Casting out fear;
These shall ensure thee
   A Happy New Year.

Peace in the Saviour,
   Rest at His feet,
Smile of His countenance,
   Radiant and sweet.
Joy in His presence!
   Christ ever near!
This will ensure thee
   A Happy New Year!

—Frances Ridley Havergal

I see not a step before me,
   As I tread on, another year;
But the past is still in God's keeping,
   The future His mercy shall clear,
And what looks dark in the distance
   May brighten as I draw near.

—Mary G. Brainerd

Facing a New Year

I know not what awaiteth me
  As dawns another year.
The path untrod I cannot see
  Yet knows my heart no fear.
Though dark the path may be, or light,
  A smooth or rugged way,
I ever shall be led aright
  While I for guidance pray.
I know not whether short or long
  My pilgrimage may be.
I'll daily praise my Lord in song
  For all His love to me.
And as the years shall onward roll
  And day by day be mine,
I'll seek to lead some precious soul
  To Christ, the way divine.
My God shall be my strength and stay
  While sojourning here below.
He will supply my need alway;
  His Word assures me so.
With joy I greet the opening year;
  It cannot bring me ill,
Since Christ, my Lord, is ever near,
  My soul with peace to fill.

The New Leaf

He came to my desk with a quivering lip;
The lesson was done.
"Dear Teacher, I want a new leaf," he said.
"I have spoiled this one."
I took the old leaf, torn and blotted,
And gave him a new one all unspotted,
And into his sad eyes smiled,
"Do better now, my child!"
I came to the Throne with a trembling
    heart;
The year's work was done.
"Dear Father, I want a new year," I said.
"I have spoiled this one."
He took the old year, torn and blotted,
And gave me a new one, all unspotted.
And into my sad heart smiled:
"Do better now, my child!"

—Helen F. Fisher

My Guide

The open door of another year
  I've entered by grace divine;
No ills I fear and no foes I dread,
  For a wonderful Guide is mine.
Through joy or chastening though He lead,
  In tears though my race be run,
Whate'er my lot, this my prayer shall be,
  "Not mine, but Thy will be done."

I walk by faith in my heav'nly Guide,
  With fearless, unfaltering tread.
Assured that He, who appoints my days,
  Will daily provide my bread.
He'll send more grace should afflictions
    come,
  And a staff for the pathways steep,
While o'er me ever by night and day
  My Father His watch will keep.

With perfect trust in His love and care,
  I'll walk to my journey's end;
And day by day He will strength renew,
  And peace to my heart will send.
O blessed Guide, walking all unseen,
  Yet close to my side alway,
Do Thou, who guidest my steps aright,
  Lead on to eternal day!

I Have Found Today

I've shut the door on Yesterday,
  Its sorrows and mistakes;
I've locked within its gloomy walls
  Past failures and heartaches;
And now I throw the key away
  To seek another room,
And furnish it with hope and smiles
  And every springtime bloom.
No thought shall enter this abode
  That has a hint of pain,
And every malice and distrust
  Shall never therein reign;
I've shut the door on Yesterday,
  And thrown the key away—
Tomorrow holds no doubt for me
  Since I have found Today.

"I Will Be With Thee"

As the old year now is waning,
    And the New Year comes in view,
Blessed Savior, we acknowledge
    Thou hast led us hitherto.

Hitherto Thy many mercies
    Have encompassed every day,
And we have Thy precious promise
    Thou wilt be with us all the way.

"Never leave thee nor forsake thee,"
    "Surely, I will be with thee,"
Promise of Thy blessed presence,
    Through each New Year still to be.

O, what peace and joy in knowing
    Thou art ever by our side,
And Thy loving hand of wisdom
    Will forever be our guide.

And what blessed reassurance
    That Thy mighty arm of power,
That same power that made the heavens,
    Guards and keeps us every hour.

What a merciful Redeemer!
    What a wondrous Savior, too!
What a gracious, loving Shepherd
    Who has led us hitherto.

Could we ever doubt Thy goodness?
    Could we doubt Thy loving care?
No! Thy matchless love and mercy
    Will be with us everywhere.

And Thy love and goodness to us
    Are beyond all human thought,
For Thou lovest without measure,
    Thine, with blood so dearly bought.

Entering another New Year,
    Pausing, we would contemplate
All Thy love's accomplished for us,
    All Thy mercies, O so great!

And we praise Thee for assurance
    Who has led us hitherto
That Thy presence will go with us,
    Every day the New Year through.

—Author unknown

My Year Book

The Master gave a "Book" to me
    With pages pure and white;
And then He said, "Most carefully
    Upon it you must write."

"No blot should mar a single page,
    Of such a volume fair,
Each word you write will always stay,
    Forever entered there."

For twelve brief months the "Book"
    was mine,
And then He came once more;
To give a new one all unsoiled,
    As He had done before.

He took the "Book" away from me,
    Although I begged of Him,
For just a moment more of time—
    I'd fill it to the brim.

With effort to correct a page,
    To cancel each bad spot;
But opportunity was gone,
    Old Years cannot be bought.

A New Year lies before me now,
    Its pages clean and white;
"Dear Lord," I cry, "Oh, take my hand
    And guide me as I write."

—G. Welker

MY LIFE

This coming year I'd like to be a
    friend of everyone;
I'd like to feel each day well spent at
    setting of the sun;
I'd like to be the kind of person
    everyone will love,
And make this world seem just a bit
    more like Heaven above.
I'd like in all my dealings to be true
    and just and fair;
That God will help me do these
    things shall be my daily prayer.

A New Year

I want a NEW year. New things are not patched.
So would I start my year all finely whole,
No gaps of dull omissions meanly closed
With poorly fitting fragments of dispatch;
No mendings of ignoble after-thought,
But all one piece of steady warp and woof,
A year entire, as all my years should be.

I want a NEW year. New things are not worn,
Not thin in places, ragged here and there,
And loose bits hanging down; no year all frayed
With fears and worries bare before its time;
But firm and confident, a brave new year.

I want a NEW year. Ah, but new things cost!
Well, I will pay the price of this new year:
The price of patience, and the price of time;
The price of prayers ascending to the God
Who was before all years began to be,
And will be through the new years as the old;
The price of partings from the lower aims,
Of stanch adhesion to the rugged best.

The price of life! I cannot pay the price.
Pay Thou for me, O Christ, my brother Christ!
Be Thou my patience; and be Thou my prayer;
Be Thou my strength of hard, laborious will.
From out Thine endless ages with my God
Bring newness to this little year of mine.
So shall it be Thy year and not my own,
Yet doubly mine, as I shall dwell with Thee;
Yes, doubly mine, as through it I shall pass
To Thine eternity forever new.

—*Amos R. Wells*

New Year's Wish

All that is beautiful, all that is best—
Joy of activity, calmness of rest,
Health for life's pilgrimage,
Strength for its strife,
Sunshine to brighten the pathway of life;
Courage to trust, tho' the skies be o'ercast,
Hope for the future born out of the past,
Love that is tender and friends who are true,
This is our New Year's wish for you.

Happy New Year

Throughout the New Year
   And each step of the way,
May Christ be your portion,
   Your joy and your stay.
With God's precious precepts
   Your daily delight,
To lead and encourage
   In paths that are right.

"The Lord is my Shepherd,"
   How precious the word!
He'll lead in green pastures,
   His promise we've heard.
"Beside the still waters,"
   What comfort and rest!
What peace there is found
   Leaning on Jesus' breast!

His goodness and mercy
   Each day may you prove,
His comforting presence,
   His infinite love!
With richest compassions
   Each morning anew,
May multiplied mercies
   Be showered over you.

"My cup runneth over,"
   His grace so abounds,
That fullest enjoyment
   In Jesus is found.
"The Lord is my portion,"
   This may your soul say,
And you will be happy
   Each step of the way.

God Is Faithful

I Corinthians 10:13

God will never fail us.
   He will not forsake:
His eternal covenant
   He will never break.
Resting on His promise,
   What have we to fear?
God is all-sufficient
   For the coming year.

—*F. R. Havergal*

NEW YEAR

O, year by year we well may be
  Deep exercised in soul to see
Just what is chaff and what is wheat,
  As valued at the judgment seat.

Look DOWN into the deep dark pit,
  Whence we were digged—O think
  of it!
Look BACK—we only render praise
For grace attending all our ways.

Look OUT upon the fields so white—
  The gladsome harvest just in sight!
Look UP—the objects of God's love
Are fed with manna from above.

Look ON—for Glory is in view,
  And Jesus waits to welcome you!
But do not ever look WITHIN,
  Upon the wretched source of sin.

How bright the coming days would be
  If only souls from self were free,
And had the mind and heart absorbed
  With CHRIST alone—their glorious
  Lord!

                        —E. J. C.

Farewell, Old Year,
  With goodness crowned,
A Hand divine hath set thy bound;
Welcome the New Year
  Which shall bring
Fresh blessings from
  My Lord and King.
The Old we leave without a tear,
The New we enter without fear.

                        —Anonymous

"The Lord thy God, He it is that doth
go with thee; He will not fail thee,
nor forsake thee" (Deut. 31:6). •

A New Year Prayer

O *New Year! New!* Spotless, undefiled!
Uncircumscribed as to holy aspirations
And lofty quest after God *in Christ!*
Fain would we understand thy full significance
And rightly interpret thy mighty content—
        For His Glory!
And all the while comforting others which
  are in any trouble,
By the comfort wherewith we ourselves
  are comforted of God!
O Jehovah God! We choose Thee, Thee
  only—
Thou art God, and beside Thee there is
  none else!
And so we would humbly bow and confess our sins.
Restore what is not our own; obey, serve,
  worship, adore Thee!
Hear Thou in heaven Thy dwelling place,
And show us, Thy blood-bought children,
  a token for good;
The cup that runneth over with Thy favor;
Thy tender mercies; Thy compassions that
  fail not;
Thy renewal of the inner man day by day,
Thy power, too, moment by moment, the
  whole year through.
Thy Will do we choose—day and night;
Thy Will would we know—step by step;
Thy Will would we love—with all our
  heart.
So do Thou teach us—guide us—help
  us—
From the first day unto the last!
Make us glad according to the days
  wherein
Thou hast afflicted us, and the years
  wherein
We have seen evil—Till He come!
        For Jesus' sake, Amen.

                        —EM - ME

Isaiah 9:6, 7

Special Days—

Easter, Resurrection . . .

In the end of the sabbath, as it began to dawn toward the first day of the week, came Mary Magdalene and the other Mary to see the sepulchre.

2 And, behold, there was a great earthquake: for the angel of the Lord descended from heaven, and came and rolled back the stone from the door, and sat upon it.

3 His countenance was like lightning, and his raiment white as snow;

4 And for fear of him the keepers did shake, and became as dead men.

5 And the angel answered and said unto the women, Fear not ye; for I know that ye seek Jesus, which was crucified.

6 He is not here: for he is risen, as he said. Come, see the place where the Lord lay.

7 And go quickly, and tell his disciples that he is risen from the dead; and, behold, he goeth before you into Galilee; there shall ye see him: lo, I have told you.

8 And they departed quickly from the sepulchre with fear and great joy; and did run to bring his disciples word.

9 And as they went to tell his disciples, behold, Jesus met them, saying, All hail. And they came and held him by the feet, and worshipped him.

10 Then said Jesus unto them, Be not afraid: go tell my brethren that they go into Galilee, and there shall they see me. —Matthew 28:1-10

"He Is Risen"

Christ the Lord is risen today,
Sons of men and angels say:
Raise your joys and triumphs high,
Sing, ye heavens, and earth reply.

Love's redeeming work is done,
Fought the fight, the battle won;
Lo! our Sun's eclipse is o'er;
Lo! He sets in blood no more.

Vain the stone, the watch, the seal;
Christ hath burst the gates of hell!
Death is vain forbids His rise;
Christ hath opened Paradise!

Lives again our glorious King;
Where, O Death, is now thy sting?
Once He died our souls to save:
Where thy victory, O Grave?

—Charles Wesley

Resurrection Morn

There was a morn, a glorious morn,
When Jesus Christ arose
Up from the sepulchre of rock,
A victor o'er His foes.

There was an hour, a blessed hour,
When Christ rose in my soul,
To break the bonds of Satan's might,
And all my life control.

Oh, love, oh, resurrection joy;
Oh, life of Christ within;
Our risen Lord, the victor
O'er death, and guilt, and sin.

Ah, look not back upon the tomb;
Rise with thy Lord today;
Receive Him in thy heart to dwell;
The Life, the Truth, the Way.

The Christ of Calvary
and the Empty Tomb

They led a Man to the judgment hall
Alone. His friends fled away.
He faced the taunts of the howling mob
As He suffered in silence that day.
Then bearing His cross He climbed a hill
To die there for you and for me.
But none of the hands of that rabble mob
Helped Him bear His Calvary.

Then down from the cross His body they took
And in sorrow they bore it away
To place it within a rich man's grave,
And their hearts were too anguished to pray.
In the hour of His need they failed the Lord.
How bitter their torment must be.
But now their hands reached up to lift
Him down from His Calvary.

But the grief of their sorrow changed to joy
With the word that an angel brought:
"Seek not in the grave for One who lives,
For salvation's work has been wrought."
The lives of His friends were changed that day
From fear they now were free.
And the rest of their lives they gladly gave
In sharing His Calvary.

I, too, to the cross of my Lord would come
And confess all my failings and fears,
And ask for grace to follow Him on
Where He leads me, down through the years.
I'll lift up the hands of my heart to Him
And share in His Calvary.
And some day in Heaven His hands of love
Will share all His glory with me.

—*Ramona Ray Woodson*

He Lives!

I know that my Redeemer lives!
What joy the best assurance gives!
He lives, He lives, who once was dead,
He lives, my everlasting Head!

He lives, to bless me with His love;
He lives, to plead for me above;
He lives, my hungry soul to feed;
He lives to help in time of need.

He lives and grants me daily breath;
He lives and I shall conquer death;
He lives my mansion to prepare.
He lives to bring me safety there.

He lives all glory to His Name;
He lives, my Saviour, still the same;
What joy the best assurance gives—
I know that my Redeemer lives.

"Because He Lives, We Too Shall Live"

In this restless world of struggle
    It is very hard to find
Answers to the questions
    That come daily to our mind—
We cannot see the future,
    What's beyond is still unknown,
For the secret of God's Kingdom
    Still belongs to Him alone—
But He granted us salvation
    When His Son was crucified
For life became immortal
    Because our Saviour died.
And to know life is unending
    And God's love is endless, too,
Makes each daily task we face
    Much easier to do.
For our Saviour's resurrection
    Was God's way of telling men
That in Christ we are eternal
    And in Him we live again.

—*Helen Steiner Rice*

Because I Live

If the Christ who died had
   stopped at the cross,
    His work had been incomplete.
If the Christ who was buried
   had stayed in the tomb,
    He had only known defeat.
But the way of the cross
   never stops at the cross,
    And the way of the tomb leads on
To victorious grace
   in the heavenly place
    Where our risen Lord has gone.

HE AROSE

Very early in the morning
   Before the break of day,
The morning star shone on the tomb
   Where our dear Saviour lay.

The earth was clothed with darkness;
   The shadows had not fled,
The city slumbered on that morn—
   They thought that He was dead.

It still was dark when He arose
   And stepped forth from the grave,
The victor over sin, and death
   With power your soul to save.

So shall it be when He returns
   And calls His own to rise;
While this old world is sleeping still,
   We'll meet Him in the skies.

—Anne Moore

CHRIST AROSE

Up from the grave He arose
   With a mighty triumph o'er His foes.
He arose a Victor from the dark domain,
   And He lives forever with His saints
    to reign:
Hallelujah, Christ arose!

—Robert Lowry

Resurrection Life

What whispers to the bulb, " 'Tis spring"?
Behold this shriveled, wrinkled thing—
It stirs and grows, bursts into bloom;
Its fragrance perfumes all the room.

Who tells the silent prisoner,
The little worm in tight cocoon,
"Wake up and work, and burst your
   bonds;
You will be winged and flying soon"?

Who tells the acorn in the ground
To keep on reaching toward the sky?
How could it dream that it would be
A spreading oak tree, wide and high?

Who speaks within my sickroom, where
I live, a prisoner of pain,
And tells me, though this body die,
This very flesh shall live again?

Because He rose, I too shall rise,
Shall rise and walk and dance and sing;
And there shall be no grief, no pain,
Nor any tears, remembering!

The Hope of Resurrection

Christ's resurrection changed Mary from a mourner into a messenger; it changed Thomas from a doubter into a believer; it changed Peter from a denier into a preacher, and it changed Paul from a persecutor into a missionary. For early Christians the Resurrection event became a Resurrection experience: a cleansing, life-changing, transforming experience!

Today, nearly 2,000 years later, that Resurrection event is still the greatest hope in a world of fear and confusion.

—Dr. Paul S. James

Mother's Day . . .

Mother's Day

Let us do today as she would have us do!
Let us be clean as she would have us be;
Let us be brave and fine and strong and true,
Fulfilling her dreams for you, her dreams for me.

Above the gift is the giver. Let us give
The precious substance of our life to make
The world a better place because we live:
Let us live worthily for her dear sake.

> —*Grace Noll Crowell*

To My Mother

Most of all the other beautiful things in life come by twos and threes, by dozens and hundreds; plenty of roses, stars, sunsets, rainbows, brothers and sisters, aunts and cousins, but only one mother in all the wide world.

> —*Kate Douglas Wiggin*

MOTHER'S DAY

Let every day be Mother's Day—
Make roses grow along her way
　And beauty everywhere.
Oh, never let her eyes be wet
With tears of sorrow or regret,
　And never cease to care.
Come grown up children, and rejoice
That you can hear your mother's voice.

A day for her? For you she gave
Long years of love and service brave.
　For you her youth was spent;
There was no weight of hurt or care
Too heavy for her strength to bear,
　She followed where you went;
Her courage and her love sublime
You could depend on all the time.

The Songs My Mother Sang

I hear them in the whispering winds,
　The forest's rhythmic strain,
The chime of bells, that sinks and swells,
　The patter of the rain.
I hear them in the vesper call
　Of birds from copse and tree;
Each note prolongs the dear old songs
　That mother sang to me.
I hear them in the ocean's voice,
　The prattle of the child,
The dashing rill, the fountain's trill,
　The tempests fierce and wild.
I hear them through the silent night,
　In dreams they echo free.
Since memory throngs with tender songs
　That mother sang to me.
I heard them when a babe I lay
　Upon her loving breast,
And when a child their charms beguiled
　My eager brain to rest.
I hear them now, and some last hour
　Across death's swelling sea
My soul shall wing, while angels sing
　The songs she sang to me.

> —*Lalia Mitchell*, in *Farm Journal*

274

There Still Are Mothers

Whatever else be lost along the way,
    There still are Christian mothers in all lands;
And now we pause to honor them today—
    These queens who have no scepters in their
      hands.
And yet who reign upon a firmer throne
Than any that the earth has ever known.

Rulers of life itself, with love as pure
    And true and selfless as the old earth knows,
Their trust in God unshakable and sure,
    Their faith implanted in their children grows
Into a living, lifting, shining thing
That through great stress can know no conquering.

There still are mothers who will ever hold
    The old sweet ways of truth and righteousness
Before their children's eyes; who long have told
    Christ's teachings to their young, to heal and
      bless.
Thank God for any mother, anywhere,
Who lives and serves, and finds her strength in
    prayer.

—Grace Noll Crowell

John Wesley's Tribute to His Mother

Take her for all and in all, I do not believe that any human being ever brought into the world, and carried through it a larger portion of original goodness than my dear mother. Everyone who knew her loved her, for she seemed to be made to be happy herself, and to make everyone happy within her little sphere. Her understanding was as good as her heart; it is from her that I have inherited that alertness of mind and quickness of apprehension without which it would have been impossible for me to have undertaken half of what I have performed. God never blessed a human creature with a more cheerful disposition, a more generous spirit, a sweeter temper, or a tenderer heart. I remember that when I first understood what death was, and began to think of it, the most fearful thought it induced was that of losing my mother; it seemed to me more than I could bear, and I used to hope that I might die first.

Mother Dear

Come and whisper soft and low,
    Mother dear,
As you used to long ago:
    "Mother's here!"
It will soothe my troubled breast,
It will lull me into rest,
For of all I love you best,
    Mother dear.

Oh, how long it seems tonight,
    Mother dear,
Since I saw your face, so bright,
    Hover near!
But I know I love you more
While the years are passing o'er
Than I ever have before,
    Mother dear.

How I fancy o'er and o'er,
    Mother dear,
All the happy days of yore
    With you near;
How you murmured soft and low,
As you kissed my cheek aglow:
"Precious child, I love you so!"
    Mother dear.

So my grateful heart shall beat,
    Mother dear,
With a love, though incomplete,
    Ever here;
And, though far away tonight,
Yet our spirits in their flight
Still may mingle with delight,
    Mother dear.

You have gone to be at rest,
    Mother dear,
In the mansions of the blest,
    Not a tear;
And upon that peaceful shore,
Where the storms of life are o'er,
We shall meet to part no more,'
    Mother dear.

—Oswald J. Smith

Mother—A Blessing

A wonderful blessing which everyone has,
  A gem much too precious to lose,
A flower so perfect we hardly can name it,
  E'en compared with a perfect white rose.
So here's to this one who inspires our good,
  This treasure, unlike any other:
God bless her and keep her, whatever betide,
  This Angel on Earth called—
    MOTHER.

My Mother's Prayers

Among the treasured pictures
  That I've hung on memory's wall,
There's one that's clearer than the rest
  And sweeter far than all:
'Tis a picture of my mother
  When I, a little chap,
Was folded in her loving arms,
  To slumber on her lap.

I felt her hands caress my head,
  I heard her softly say,
"Dear Jesus, take this little life
  And use it every day."
There must have been a mighty weight
  Behind that simple prayer,
For through the seasons, year on year,
  The picture lingers there.

And whether I'm on hill or plain
  Or on the deep blue sea,
The memory of that sacred scene
  Forever comforts me.
Among the treasured pictures
  That I've hung on memory's wall,
My mother's supplication
  Is the sweetest one of all.

Have You Written to Mother?

Pray, may I ask you, worthy lad,
  Whose smile no care can smother,
Though busy life throbs round about,
  Have you written home to mother?

Memories of Mother

My Mother's hand is on my brow,
Her gentle voice is pleading now;
Across the years so marred by ruin,
What memories of love steal in!

While others scorned me in their pride,
She gently drew me to her side;
When all the world had turned away,
My mother stood by me that day.

The memories of by-gone years,
My Mother's love, my Mother's tears,
The thought of all her constant care—
Doth bring the answer to her prayer.
                                    —Fred P. Morris

When Mother Prayed

I think that I shall never see,
This side of God's eternity,
A scene as lovely as the one
Which met my gaze when day was done.
In childhood years of long ago,
My mother sings, 'tis sweet and low.
Her face with love is all aglow.
She turns the pages of God's Word,
Her tender heart is deeply stirred.
She kneels, she prays, Oh, what a prayer!
I listen, lingering on the stair—
"God bless my boy"—I hear my name,
And there, within my heart, a flame
Begins to burn—'tis burning yet.
That hour I never shall forget!
My mother dear, at even kneels,
And prays for me. This morn there steals
A ray of warmth into my heart,
And now, like her, from cares apart,
I pray. Her prayers still follow me—
A torch, and by its gleam I see
My home across the crystal sea.
                                    —David F. Nygren

MOTHER'S PRAYERS

No formal prayers from mother's lips
Were ever heard to be.
No words that sounded elegant,
When mother prayed for me.

When mother prayed—I wonder still—
What happened up above.
Did heaven stop to listen in
As she poured forth her love?

My mother prayed for answers real.
Believed that God who hears
Would not deny her earnest cry,
Or turn aside from tears.

God answers yet my mother's prayers,
Though she is lost to view.
Sweet memories of precious days
They help to keep me true.

Thank God, He listened to her plea,
And saved my soul from sin.
In answer to a mother's prayers
That she her child might win.

—*G. Welker*

Mother o' Mine

If I were hanged on the highest hill,
I know whose love would follow me still;
If I were drowned in the deepest sea,
I know whose tears would come down to me;
If I were damned in body and soul,
I know whose prayer would make me
whole—
Mother o' mine! Mother o' mine!

—*Rudyard Kipling*

Mother, I Remember

Mother, when the night winds blow,
I remember long ago:
Lamplight falling on your hair,
And your children kneeling there.
Soft the dress-folds where we knelt,
I remember how they felt.

Mother, when the night winds cry,
I remember something high,
Something holy that we knew—
Kneeling there in front of you,
With your hands upon the Book
And your tender, trusting look.

Mother, though the world be cold,
I am warmed by all you told
When you taught us how to pray.
I am warmed day after day.
Faith you lit, no wind of doubt
Has been able to blow it out.

—*Helen Frazee-Bower*

WORDS

The greatest word is God.
The deepest word is Soul.
The longest word is Eternity.
The swiftest word is Time.
The nearest word is Now.
The darkest word is Sin.
The meanest word is Hypocrisy.
The broadest word is Truth.
The strongest word is Right.
The tenderest word is Love.
The sweetest word is Home.
The dearest word is MOTHER.

The Bravest Battle

The bravest battle that ever was fought!
  Shall I tell you where and when?
On the maps of the world you will find
    it not;
  'Twas fought by the mothers of men.

Nay, not with cannon or battle-shot,
  With a sword or noble pen;
Nay, not with eloquent words or thought
  From the mouths of wonderful men!

But deep in a walled-up woman's heart—
  Of a woman that would not yield,
But bravely, silently bore her part—
  Lo, there is that battlefield!

No marshaling troops, no bivouac song.
  No banner to gleam and wave;
But oh! these battles, they last so long—
  From babyhood to the grave.

Yet, faithful still as a bridge of stars,
  She fights in her walled-up town—
Fights on and on in the endless wars,
  Then, silent, unseen, goes down.

Oh, yet with banners and battle-shot,
  And soldiers to shout and praise!
I tell you the kingliest victories fought
  Were fought in those silent ways.

My Mother's Bible

This book is all that's left me now,
  Tears will unbidden start—
With faltering lip and throbbing brow
  I press it to my heart.
For many generations past,
  Here is our family tree:
My mother's hand this Bible clasped:
  She, dying, gave it to me.

Ah! well do I remember those
  Whose names these records bear,
Who round the hearthstone used to close
  After the evening prayer,
And speak of what these pages said.
  In tones my heart would thrill!
Though they are with the silent dead,
  Here are they living still!

Each guest upstarted at the word,
And laid a hand upon his sword,
  With fiery, flashing eye.
And Stanley said: "We crave the name,
Proud knight, of this most peerless dame,
  Whose love you count so high."

St. Leon paused, as if he would
Not breathe her name in careless mood,
  Thus lightly to another;
Then bent his noble head, as though
To give that name the reverence due,
  And gently said—"My mother"!

Too Late, Now!

"I am the most broken-hearted person on earth. I always found time to go every-where else but to see my dear old gray-haired parents. They sat home alone, loving me just the same. It is too late now to give them those few hours of happiness I was too selfish and too busy to give. And now when I go to visit their graves and look at the green grass above them, I wonder if God will ever forgive me for the heartaches I must have caused them. I pray that you will print this, Abby, to tell them and show their love and respect while there is still time. For it is later than you think." —TOO LATE

—From a "Dear Abby" column

Before It Is Too Late

If you have a gray-haired mother
  In the old home far away,
Sit you down and write the letter
  You put off from day to day.

Don't wait until her weary steps
  Reach heaven's pearly gate;
But show her that you think of her
  Before it is too late.

If you have a tender message
  Or a loving word to say,
Don't wait till you forget it
  But whisper it today.

We know what bitter memories
  May haunt you if you wait.
So make your loved one happy
  Before it is too late.

The tender word unspoken,
  The letters never sent,
The long forgotten messages,
  The wealth of love unspent.

For these some hearts are breaking,
  For these some loved ones wait.
Show them that you care for them
  Before it is too late.

        —Sent by Mrs. Gertrude Wright

My Mother

Who fed me from her gentle breast
And hushed me in her arms to rest,
And on my cheek sweet kisses prest?
  My mother.

When sleep forsook my open eye,
Who was it sung sweet lullaby
And rocked me that I should not cry?
  My mother.

Who sat and watched my infant head
When sleeping in my cradle bed,
And tears of sweet affection shed?
  My mother.

When pain and sickness made me cry,
Who gazed upon my heavy eye
And wept, for fear that I should die?
  My mother.

Who ran to help me when I fell,
And would some pretty story tell,
Or kiss the place to make it well?
  My mother.

Who taught my infant lips to pray,
To love God's holy word and day,
And walk in wisdom's pleasant way?
  My mother.

Mother's Translation of the Bible

There is a story about four clergymen who were discussing the merits of the various translations of the Bible. One liked the King James Version best because of its simple, beautiful English.

Another liked the American Revised Version best because it is more literal and comes nearer the original Hebrew and Greek.

Still another liked Moffatt's translation best because of its up-to-date vocabulary.

The fourth minister was silent. When asked to express his opinion, he replied, "I like my mother's translation best."

The other three expressed surprise. They did not know that his mother had translated the Bible.

"Yes, she did," he replied. "She translated it into life, and it was the most convincing translation I ever saw."

Mother Love

Long time ago, so I've been told,
    Two angels once met on the streets paved with gold.
"By the star in your crown," said the one to the other,
    "I see that on earth, you too, were a mother.

"And by the blue-tinted halo you wear,
    You, too, have known sorrow and deepest despair."
"Ah, yes," she replied, "I once had a son,
    A sweet little lad, full of laughter and fun."

"But tell of your child." "Oh, I knew I was blest
    From the moment I first held him close to my breast;
And my heart almost burst with the joy of that day. . . ."
"Ah, yes," said the other, "I felt the same way."

The former continued: "The first steps he took,
    So eager and breathless, the sweet, startled look
Which came over his face—he trusted me so. . . ."
    "Ah, yes," sighed the other, "How well do I know."

"But soon he had grown to a tall handsome boy,
    So stalwart and kind—and gave me such joy
To have him just walk down the street by my side."
    "Ah, yes," said the other, "I felt the same pride."

"How often I shielded and spared him from pain.
    And when he for others was so cruelly slain,
When they crucified him—and they spat in his face,
    How gladly would I have hung there in his place!"

A moment of silence—"Oh, then you are she—
    The Mother of Christ? and she fell on one knee.
But the Blessed one raised her up, drawing her near,
    And kissed from the cheek of the woman, a tear.

"Tell me the name of the son you loved so,
    That I may share with you your grief and your woe."
She lifted her eyes, looking straight at the other,
    "He was Judas Iscariot. I am his mother."

The Sphere of Woman

They talk about a woman's sphere as though it had a limit;
There's not a place in Earth or Heaven,
There's not a task to mankind given,
There's not a blessing or a woe,
There's not a whispered yes or no,
There's not a life, or death, or birth,
That has a feather's weight of worth—
　　Without a woman in it.

—C. E. Bowman

Are All the Children In?

I think ofttimes as the night draws nigh
Of an old house on the hill,
Of a yard all wide and blossom-starred
Where the children played at will.

And when the night at last came down,
Hushing the merry din,
Mother would look around and ask,
"Are all the children in?"

'Tis many and many a year since then,
And the old house on the hill
No longer echoes to childish feet,
And the yard is still, so still.

But I see it all, as the shadows creep,
And though many the years have been,
Even now, I can hear my mother ask,
"Are all the children in?"

I wonder if, when the shadows fall
On the last short, earthly day,
When we say goodbye to the world
　　outside,
All tired with our childish play,

When we step out into the Other Land
Where mother so long has been,
Will we hear her ask, as we did of old,
"Are all the children in?"

Mother Has Fallen Asleep

Mother was tired and weary.
Weary with toil and pain;
Put by her glasses and rocker,
She will not need them again.
Into heaven's mansions she's entered,
Never to sigh or to weep;
After long years with life's struggles,
Mother has fallen asleep.

Near other loved ones we laid her,
Low in the church yard to lie.
And though our hearts are near broken,
Yet we would not question "why?"
She does not rest 'neath the grasses
Tho' o'er her dear grave they creep;
She has gone into the Kingdom,
Mother has fallen asleep.

Rest the tired feet now forever,
Dear wrinkled hands are so still;
Blast of the earth shall no longer
Throw o'er our loved one a chill.
Angels through heaven will guide her,
Jesus will still bless and keep;
Not for the world would we wake her,
Mother has fallen asleep.

Beautiful rest for the weary.
Well deserved rest for the true;
When our life's journey is ended,
We shall again be with you.
This helps to quiet our weeping—
Hark! Angel music so sweet!
He giveth to His beloved,
Beautiful, beautiful sleep.

MOTHERS

I held her hands in mine last night . . . so very thin and worn . . . and they held mine just a tightly . . . as the day that I was born.

Those gentle and expressive hands . . . etched by work and care . . . have folded o'er my bedside . . . many times in humble prayer.

They've washed for me . . . they've fed me . . . they've helped me be a man . . . There's something of the Lord Himself . . . in *every* mother's hand.

Said a Little Boy:

"Mothers are wonderful people. They can get up in the morning before they smell bacon frying!"

—Author unknown

A Mother's Love

A Mother's love is something that no one can explain.
It is made of deep devotion of sacrifice and pain,
It is endless and unselfish and enduring, come what may.
For nothing can destroy it or take that love away.
It is patient and forgiving when all others are forsaking,
And it never fails or falters even though the heart is breaking. . . .
It believes beyond believing when the world condemns,
And it glows with all the beauty of the rarest, brightest gems.
It is far beyond defining, it defies all explanation. . . .
A many splendored miracle, man cannot understand
And another wondrous evidence of God's tender guiding hand.

—Helen Steiner Rice

MOTHER—DAUGHTER OF A KING

Dear little lady, this mother of mine,
The years may have left their sharp lines on her face
And bowed down her body, but she may be proud
That they have not marred her spirit's sweet grace.
Time, the great changer, puts his mark upon all;
There's never a person escapes this sad truth.
Fight hard as we will, the battle is lost,
For the ravage of years does away with our youth.
But "Favor is deceitful, and beauty is vain,"
She that loveth Jehovah shall know His dear praise,
The King's fairest daughter is glorious within,
And the King's image shines clear on her face.

—May Clutter

"Favour is deceitful, and beauty is vain; but a woman that feareth the Lord, she shall be praised."
—Proverbs 31:30

A Message From Mother

I have crossed the bourne of shadows,
   I have entered into rest.
I am happy with my loved ones
   In that land where all are blest.

I have anchored in the harbor,
   Where the storms of life are o'er,
Where the gleams of endless sunshine
   Break upon the heav'nly shore.

I have seen the golden city,
   With the jasper walls so bright;
Here we have eternal morning,
   And we never say, "Good Night."

I have heard the sweetest music
   From the angel choirs of love;
O how blest to be with Jesus
   In my Father's house above!

Yes, I left you; it was sudden,
   But it was the best for all.
It was God's will—I am happy—
   I but listened to His call.

Dearest husband, God will bless you
   As you journey down the way;
I shall wait and watch to meet you
   In this land of perfect day.

Loving children, you will miss me,
   But I love you more and more,
And we'll meet where there's no parting
   On this ever-golden shore.

Dry your tears and ease your heartache;
   Mother'll be your angel guide;
Be but faithful to your Savior
   And with Him you will abide.

Love God's church—there's nothing
   like it,
   Purchased with His precious life;
It will help you, it will bless you,
   It will keep you in the strife.

It was Mother's last great promise
   To attend the throne of grace;
Will you carry out my life work
   And be there in Mother's place?

Meet me, meet me in the morning,
   Here beside the crystal sea;
I shall linger near the border
   Till my loved ones are with me.

Thoughts About Mother

For unwearying patience and unchanging tenderness, the love of a true mother stands next to the love of our Father in Heaven.

* * * * *

"There is nothing sweeter than the heart of a pious mother."
   —Martin Luther

* * * * *

A mother is the only creature on earth who can cry when she is happy or laugh when she is heartbroken.

* * * * *

"Men make a camp; a swarm of bees a comb; birds make a nest; a woman makes a home."   —Arthur Guiterman

Come Home, It's Supper Time

When I was but a lad in days of childhood
    I used to play till evening shadows came;
Then winding down an old familiar pathway
    I heard my mother call at set of sun: "Come home,

Come home, it's supper time";
    The shadows lengthen fast;
"Come home, come home, it's supper time"—
    We're going home at last.

One day beside her bedside I was kneeling,
    And angel wings were winnowing the air:
She heard the call of Supper Time in Heaven,
    And now I know she's waiting for me there.

In visions now I see her standing yonder,
    And her familiar voice I hear once more,
"The banquet table's ready up in Heaven,
    It's Supper Time upon the golden strand."

My Mother's Prayers Have Followed Me

I grieved my Lord from day to day,
I scorned his love so full and free,
And though wandered far away
My mother's prayers have followed me.

I am coming home, I am coming home,
To live my wasted life anew.
For mother's prayers have followed me,
Have followed me the whole world
    through.

O'er desert wild, o'er mountain high
A wanderer I chose to be,
A wreck and condemned to die,
Still mother's prayers have followed
    me.

He turned my darkness into light,
This blessed Christ of Calvary.
I praise His name both day and night,
That my mother's prayers have fol-
    lowed me.

JUST ONE MOTHER

Beautiful things in this life
    Are manifold, 'tis true.
We count the stars by thousands,
    The birds and flowers, too.
The sunsets and the dawnings,
    Rare beauties far and near—
But all the wide world over
    There's just one MOTHER DEAR.

—*M. Carr*

GOD'S GIFT—MOTHER

God thought to give the sweetest gift
    In His Almighty Power to earth,
And deeply pondering what it should be,
    One hour, in fondest joy and love of heart,
    Outweighing every other,
He moved the gates of Heaven apart
    And gave to Earth a
    Mother.

My Mother

I used to think that I had nothing left
    To remind me of my mother, since her death.
I longed for some material earthly thing
    That to me ever memories of her would bring.
One day, while listening to my radio,
    I heard voices, singing songs I used to know—
"There's a land that is fairer than day,"
    And time stood still—and I was far away.
I was home again—the month was June,
    And all my world, it seemed in tune.
My mother was singing in the kitchen there—
    "Down at the Cross" and "Sweet Hour of Prayer":
Songs I used to know, and had forgotten, quite,
    Now came before me in a clearer light.
Memories came flooding of that happy past,
    Memories of mother that will forever last.

Somebody's Mother

The gayest laddie of the group,
He paused beside her and whispered low,
"I'll help you across, if you wish to go."
Her aged hand on his strong young arm,
She placed, and so without hurt or harm,
He guided her trembling feet along,
Proud that his own was firm and strong.

Then he went back to his friends again,
His young heart happy and well content.
"She's somebody's mother. Boys, you know,
For all she'd aged, poor and slow.
And I pray some fellow will lend a hand,
To help my mother,
If ever she's poor, and old, and gray."

Somebody's mother bowed her head in her home
That night, and the prayer she said was:
"God, be kind to the noble boy,
Who is somebody's son, and pride and joy."

Independence Day . . .

AMERICA

My country, 'tis of thee,
Sweet land of liberty,
  Of thee I sing:
Land where my fathers died,
Land of the pilgrims' pride;
From every mountainside
  Let freedom ring.

My native country thee,
Land of the noble free—
  Thy name I love:
I love thy rocks and rills,
Thy woods and templed hills;
My heart with rapture thrills
  Like that above.

Let music swell the breeze,
And ring from all the trees
  Sweet freedom's song:
Let mortal tongues awake,
Let all that breathe partake,
Let rocks their silence break—
  The sound prolong.

Our fathers' God! to Thee,
Author of liberty,
  To Thee we sing:
Long may our land be bright
With freedom's holy light;
Protect us by Thy might,
  Great God, our King!

—*S. F. Smith*

George Washington's Prayer

Almighty God, we make our earnest prayer that Thou wilt keep the United States in Thy holy protection; that Thou wilt incline the hearts of the citizens to cultivate a spirit of subordination and obedience to government; to entertain a brotherly affection and love for one another and for their fellow citizens of the United States at large. And finally that Thou wilt most graciously be pleased to dispose us all to do justice, to love mercy, and to demean ourselves with that charity, humility, and pacific temper of mind, which were the characteristics of the Divine Author of our blessed religion, and without an humble imitation of whose example in these things we can never hope to be a happy nation. Grant our supplication, we beseech Thee, through Jesus Christ, our Lord. Amen.

Daniel Webster Said:

"Finally, let us not forget the religious character of our origin. Our fathers were brought hither by their high veneration for the Christian religion. they journeyed by its light, and labored in its hope. They sought to incorporate its principles with the elements of their society and to diffuse its influence through all their institutions, civil, political, or literary. Let us cherish these sentiments, and extend this influence still more widely; in the full conviction, that that is the happiest society which partakes in the highest degree of the mild and peaceable spirit of Christianity.

"Remember that government of the people will be government for the people as long as there is government by the people."

Lincoln's 10 Guidelines

Tradition has it that it was Abraham Lincoln who gave us these ten guidelines, but we cannot be certain. Nevertheless these ten rules form the foundation for a successful constitutional republic and free enterprise economic system.

"You cannot bring about prosperity by discouraging thrift."

"You cannot help small men by tearing down big men."

"You cannot strengthen the weak by weakening the strong."

"You cannot lift the wage earner by pulling down the wage payer."

"You cannot help the poor man by destroying the rich."

"You cannot keep out of trouble by spending more than your income."

"You cannot further brotherhood of man by inciting class hatred."

"You cannot establish security on borrowed money."

"You cannot build character and courage by taking away man's initiative and independence."

"You cannot help men permanently by doing for them what they could and should do for themselves."

THIS IS MY SONG

This is my song, oh God of all the nations.
A song of peace for lands afar, and mine.
This is my home, the country where my heart is,
This is my hope, my dream, my shrine.
But other hearts in other lands are beating
With hopes and dreams the same as mine.
My country's skies are bluer than the ocean,
And sunlight beams on clover leaf and pine.
But other lands have sunlight, too, and clover,
And skies are sometimes blue as mine.
Oh, here my song, thou God of all the nations,
A song of peace for their land and mine.

What Kind of a "Nut" Is He?

He wants to run his own business.
He wants to select his own doctor.
He wants to make his own bargains.
He wants to buy his own insurance.
He wants to select his own reading matter.
He wants to provide for his own old age.
He wants to make his own contracts.
He wants to select his own charities.
He wants to educate his own children as he wishes.
He wants to make his own investments.
He wants to select his own friends.
He wants to provide his own recreation.
He wants to compete freely in the marketplace.
He wants to grow by his own efforts.
He wants to profit from his own errors.
He wants to compete with ideas.
He wants to be a man of good will.

What kind of a nut is he? He's an American who understands and believes in the Declaration of Independence, that's what kind.

Aren't you glad you are, too? And don't you wonder why so many of our fellow Americans are trying so hard to destroy the kind of life that has made us the aim and the envy of every other people on earth?

—Author unknown

Teach America to Pray

Lord, we would bow in need of Thee
Throughout this land from sea to sea;
From where Atlantic's breakers roar
To blue Pacific's golden shore.
Oh, may we all in longing say,
Lord, teach America to pray.

May we our sins to Thee confess,
Pleading in faith Thy righteousness.
May we again come to Thy throne,
Returning that which is Thine own.
Our broken hearts before Thee lay.
Lord, teach America to pray!

May our good land be true and just,
Her motto e'er "In God We Trust."
May she be guided by Thy Word,
Thy wisdom in her walls be heard.
May all who love her plead today,
Lord, teach America to pray!

And as her flag unfurls on high,
Its starry splendor to the sky,
May we, in grateful thanks to Thee
Who gave to us this land so free,
Preserve her freedom in Thy way.
Lord, teach America to pray!

To pray that cruel wars may cease,
That to the world may come Thy peace,
That ever, always, at Thy feet
We may attain communion sweet.
In loving trust to Thee we say,
Lord, teach America to pray!

—Edith A. Wilsey

Liberty

O liberty, a priceless gift
Of which so many are bereft.
'Twas bought with blood of men so
    brave,
And all they had they freely gave
The stars and stripes to raise aloft.
The path they trod—it was not soft;
But filled with pain and misery,
They died to give us LIBERTY.

—Lessie P. Perdue

THE FLAG

Here comes the flag
  Hail it!
Who dares to drag
  Or trail it?
Give it hurrahs—
Three for the stars
Three for the bars.
  Uncover your head to it!
  The soldiers who tread to it
  Shout at the sight of it,
  The justice and right of it,
  The unsullied white of it,
  The blue and the red of it,
  And tyranny's dread of it!

Here comes The Flag!
  Cheer it!
Valley and crag
  Shall hear it.
  Fathers shall bless it,
  Children caress it,
  All shall maintain it,
  No one shall stain it.
Cheers for the sailors that fought on
    the wave for it.
Cheers for the soldiers that always
    were brave for it.
Tears for the men that went down to
    the grave for it.
  Here comes The Flag!

—Arthur Macy

A Quotation to Remember

"Liberty lies in the hearts of men and women; when it dies there, no constitution, no law, no court can save it; no constitution, no law, no court can even do much to help it. While it lies there it needs no constitution, no law, no court to save it."

—Learned Hand, 1944

The Uncommon Man

I do not choose to be a common man. It is my right to be uncommon—if I can. I seek opportunity—not security. I do not wish to be a kept citizen, humbled and dulled by having the state look after me. I want to take the calculated risk; to dream and to build, to fail and succeed. I refuse to barter incentive for a dole. I prefer the challenges of life to the guaranteed existence; the thrill of fulfillment to the stale calm of utopia.

I will not trade freedom for beneficence nor my dignity for a handout. I will never cower before any master nor bend to any threat. It is my heritage to stand erect, proud and unafraid; to think and act for myself, enjoy the benefit of my creations and to face the world boldly and say, this I have done.

All this is what it means to be an American.

—Dean Alfange

Building of the Ship

Thou, too, sail on, O Ship of State!
Sail on, O UNION, strong and great!
Humanity with all its fears,
With all the hopes of future years,
Is hanging breathless on thy fate!
We know what Master laid thy keel,
What workman wrought thy ribs of steel,
Who made each mast, and sail, and rope,
What anvils rang, what hammers beat,
In what a forge, and what a heat
Were shaped the anchors of thy hope!
Fear not each sudden sound and shock;
'Tis of the wave, and not the rock,
'Tis but the flapping of the sail,
And not a rent made by the gale!
In spite of rock and tempest's roar,
In spite of false lights on the shore,
Sail on! nor fear to breast the sea!
Our hearts, our hopes, are all with thee.
Our hearts, our hopes, our prayers, our
    tears,
Our faith triumphant o'er the fears,
Are all with thee—are all with thee!

—Henry Wadsworth Longfellow
(born February 27, 1807)

Three Things

I know three things must ever be,
To keep a nation strong and free:
One is a hearthstone bright and dear
With busy, happy loved ones near.
One is a ready heart and hand
To love and serve and keep the land.
One is a worn and beaten way
To where the people go to pray.
So long as these are kept alive,
Nation and people will survive.
God, keep them, always, everywhere,
The hearth, the flag, the place of prayer.

The Land We Love the Most

Lord, while for all mankind we pray,
    Of every clime and coast,
O hear us for our native land—
    The land we love the most.

O guard our shores from ev'ry foe,
    With peace our borders bless,
Our cities with prosperity,
    Our fields with plenteousness.

Unite us in the sacred love
    Of knowledge, truth, and Thee;
And let our hills and valleys shout
    The songs of liberty.

—John R. Wreford

Pledge of Faith

America, my country, your very name
Sets my heart to singing and fans the flame
Of Freedom burning steadfast in my breast
To a fiery raging furnace that will not let me rest
Till all men shall respond to the flame within . . .

How to say, I love you? Where shall I begin?
I have loved you since the day, as a small child,
I watched the flag pass by and in my throat the wild,
Exultant beat of my heart throbbed to an old refrain,
Old as time the theme and for every man the same,
My flag—my country—my native land.

Have faith in these words. Speak them with pride.
Fling them in the face of those who have tried
To deprecate Freedom with words of negation.
Rejoice in the glory of being "One nation,
Under God, with Liberty and Justice for All."
United, we stand invincible; divided, we crumble and fall.

Ours, a great Republic, the best ever devised by man,
Where with divine unalienable rights each individual can,
If he so desires, aspire to the highest in self-expression,
Giving his best with no fear of oppression.
Man was not made to bear chains and crawl,
But before his God, to stand, proud and tall,
For, were we not in His image made?

My fellow Americans, be not afraid,
As from The Motherland you hear the loud cry:
"One world—our world—co-exist or die!"
This is the world's great battle, its hour of grave travail,
A gigantic, colossal struggle in which Freedom must prevail;
This is the crucial moment—the final testing place—
With the forces of good and evil locked in mortal embrace.
One must emerge triumphant. Who will the victor be?
Material, communist man or our Lady of Liberty?

America, my country, yours is a lovely name
That sets the world to singing and fans the flame
Of Freedom burning steadfast in men's breasts,
To a fiery raging furnace that will not let them rest
Till the bright, white light of freedom illuminates the world
And the flags of the captive nations are once again unfurled,
And ALL men have the right, as their flag is passing by,
To place their hands above their heart and oh! so proudly sigh,
My flag—my country—my native land!

—*Rita S. Brehm*

**This poem received the 1962 George Washington Honor Medal Award from
Freedoms Foundation, Valley Forge, Pa., as an "outstanding achievement
in bringing about a better understanding of the American Way of Life."**

The Battle Hymn of the Republic

Mine eyes have seen the glory of the coming of the Lord;
He is trampling out the vintage where the grapes of wrath are
  stored;
He hath loosed the fateful lightning of his terrible swift sword:
His Truth is marching on.

I have seen Him in the watch-fires of a hundred circling camps;
They have builded Him an altar in the evening dews and damps;
I have read His righteous sentence by the dim and flaring lamps;
His day is marching on.

He has sounded forth the trumpet that shall never call retreat;
He is sifting out the hearts of men before His judgment seat;
O be swift, my soul, to answer Him; be jubilant, my feet!
Our God is marching on.

In the beauty of the lilies Christ was born across the sea;
With a glory in His bosom that transfigures you and me;
As He died to make men holy, let us die to make men free,
While God is marching on.

He is coming like the glory of the morning on the wave;
He is wisdom to the mighty, he is succour to the brave;
So the world shall be His footstool, and the soul of time His slave:
Our God is marching on.

—Julia Ward Howe, 1862

Daniel Webster's Warning

". . . If disastrous war should sweep our commerce from the ocean, another generation may renew it; if it exhaust our treasury, future industry may replenish it; if it desolate and lay waste on our fields, still, under a new cultivation, they will grow green
again, and ripen to future harvest.

"It were but a trifle even if the walls of yonder Capitol were to crumble, if its lofty
pillars should fall, and its gorgeous decorations be all covered by the dust of the valley. All these may be rebuilt.

"But who shall reconstruct the fabric of demolished government? Who shall rear
again the well-proportioned columns of constitutional liberty?

"Who shall frame together the skillful architecture which unites national sover-
eignty with state rights, individual security, and public prosperity?

"No, if these columns fall, they will be raised not again. Like the Coliseum and the
Parthenon, they will be destined to a mournful and a melancholy immortality. Bitterer
tears, however, will flow over them than were ever shed over the monuments of Roman
or Grecian art; for they will be the monuments of a more glorious edifice than Greece
or Rome ever saw, the edifice of constitutional American liberty."

—Daniel Webster's Eulogy of Washington

OUR FLAG

Numbers 1:52

Our Flag is a glorious ensign,
Our Nation in epitome;
Its red . . . our blood,
Its stars . . . our world,
Its blue . . . our loyalty!

It is the Mayflower Compact;
It is Washington at Valley Forge;
Declaration of Independence
From the rule of tyrannical scourge;
It is Lawrence aboard the Chesapeake,
Calling, "Men, don't give up the ship!"
And MacArthur's grave, "I shall return!"
Stout heart, proud mien, and firm lip.
It is Eisenhower winning a beachhead;
And doughboys longing for home;
It is Flanders Fields with white crosses
    spread;
And Old Glory over Capitol Dome!

To the strains of the Star-Spangled
    Banner
Loyal hearts of all fifty states
Swell with pride as they sing of the
    splendor
And valor this epic relates.
But it is more than emblazoned emblem,

Or poem of our Land's history;
It is a prayer for continued freedom,
And prophetic of what we can be!

Our Flag is our great Constitution;
It is Lincoln's Gettysburg speech;
A brilliant banner of freedom
To sing, pray, worship and preach
Of God's Son, our blessed Redeemer,
Who died for us on the Cross
That we might know Him as Saviour
From sin and all of its dross.

Now, with this liberty threatened,
We must keep faith with our Flag;
Give our best to God and our country
And never let our interest lag.
We must pledge to it new allegiance,
The Republic too and then stand
One Nation under God, indivisible,
With justice for all in the land.

Our Flag is far more than a bunting,
This poem, and prayer, prophecy . . .
Is a Nation led of Almighty God,
American, Land of the Free!

—Jessie Whiteside Finks

Thanksgiving Day . . .

**"It is a good thing to give thanks unto the Lord,
and to sing praises unto thy name, O most high."**
Psalm 92:1

I Am Thankful!

I am thankful to be an American. It is a God-given privilege to dwell in a land where every citizen is free to worship God according to the dictates of his conscience; where everyone can vote his own political convictions at the polls; where there is freedom of speech, and freedom of the press; where there is the free enterprise system, under which every person can own property, and is not compelled to yield it to a despotic state. Yes, I am grateful to live in a country where there is the God-inspired doctrine that all men are created equal, and that every citizen is guaranteed "equal justice under the law."

I am thankful for our glorious flag. When I behold the stars and stripes, always a tingle of joy and pride courses through my spinal column, in the knowledge that "This is *my* flag," and I am overwhelmed with gratitude to Almighty God that as long as this flag ripples in the breezes, all the freedoms which we cherish shall be preserved. This flag represents the spilt blood of my fathers who died to obtain, under God, these freedoms. Forever, let us salute it with the spirit of thanksgiving, and with the holy resolve that its enemies shall never haul it down from its lofty ramparts.

I am thankful for the Bible, the Book upon which our nation was founded. It is evident to all who know history that America would never have known freedom except for the influence of the Word of God. Today, we would not have one vestige of freedom if the Bible had not been the guidebook and inspiration of our founding fathers. Today, if we were to turn away from the Bible, our country would be another godless Soviet state. Thank God for the Bible! The atheists have bombarded it, the agnostics have ridiculed it, the infidels have blasted it, the skeptics have sought to destroy it, the Roman hierarchy denied it to their people, the Modernist preachers have tried to scuttle it—in fact, all the agencies of Satan have hammered away at it. But it still stands as the imperishable, indestructible Word of the Eternal God. It still changes lives, transforms homes, elevates communities, blesses nations. Thank God for the Bible!

I am thankful for the church of the living God. I speak in the true Scriptural sense; that assembly of born again, called out ones who have been changed by the power of Christ, and who have been made members of the family of God. In spite of false pretenders, misguided religionists who misinterpret the truth, and willful apostates who seek to deceive the people by advocating the social gospel, and by denying the faith, the church goes on, conquering and to conquer; and as our Lord promises: "The gates of hell shall not prevail against it."

—Dale Crowley

Thanksgiving

Once again our glad thanksgivings
　　Rise before our Father's throne,
As we try to count the blessings
　　Of the year so swiftly flown;
As we trace the wondrous workings
　　Of His wisdom, power, and love
And unite our "Holy! Holy!"
　　With the seraphim above.

As we gather round our firesides
　　On this glad Thanksgiving Day,
Time would fail to count the blessings
　　That have followed all our way.
Grace sufficient, help and healing,
　　Prayer oft answered at our call;
And the best of all our blessings,
　　Christ Himself, our All in all.

He has blessed our favored country
　　With a free and bounteous hand;
Peace and plenty in our borders,
　　Liberty through all our land.
And although our sins and follies
　　Oft provoked Him to His face,
Mercy still restrains His judgments,
　　And prolongs our day of grace.

While we love to count the blessings,
　　Grateful for the year that's gone,
Faith would sweep a wider vision,
　　Hope would gaze yet farther on.
For the signals all around us
　　Seem with one accord to say,
"Christ is coming soon to bring us
　　Earth's last, best Thanksgiving Day!"

　　　　　　　　　　—A. B. Simpson

In Life's Garden

Count your garden by the flowers;
*　Never by the leaves that fall—*
Count your days by golden hours,
*　Don't remember clouds at all.*
Count your nights by stars—not shadows,
*　Count your life by smiles—not tears,*
And with joy through all your lifetime
*　Count your age by friends—not years.*

　　　　　　　　　　—Dixie Wilson

A Thanksgiving Prayer

We thank Thee, God, for blessings—
　The big ones and the small—
Thy tender love and mercy
　That guards and keeps us all—

The fresh awakening of joy
　That comes with morning light.
Sunlit hours to fill the day
　And restful sleep at night.

The hope, the beauty and the love
　That brighten each day's living—
We praise Thee—and our hearts are
　filled
　With joy—and with thanksgiving.

The pride that's found in work well
　done,
　The love of those who care,
The peace of mind, the sweet content
　That comes with quiet prayer.

Thanksgiving

I thank Thee, Lord, for eyes to see
The gracious gifts Thou sendest me.
All lovely things so fair and free.
I thank Thee, Lord, for eyes to see.

I thank Thee, Lord, for ears to hear
Thy faintest whisper, yet so clear,
That ever tells me Thou art near.
I thank Thee, Lord, for ears to hear.

I thank Thee, Lord, for lips to speak
Of One who died the lost to seek;
O lovely One so mild and meek.
I thank Thee, Lord, for lips to speak.

I thank Thee, Lord, that I can pray
For strength and counsel every day
To help me o'er life's rugged way.
I thank Thee, Lord, that I can pray.

I thank Thee, Lord, that now I bring
My heart to Thee—Redeemer, King,
That I may give Thee everything;
Accept and bless what now I bring.

　　　　　　　　　　—W. A. Ferguson

Thankful for Plenty

Plenty of Food. "Ye shall eat in plenty, and be satisfied" (Joel 2:26).

Plenty of Water. "Thou didst send plenteous rain" (Psalm 68:9).

Plenty of Goods. "He shall make thee plenteous in goods" (Deut. 28:11).

Plenty of Production. "The Lord thy God will make thee plenteous in every work of thine hand . . ." (Deut. 30:9).

Plenty in Store. "So shall thy barns be filled with plenty" (Prov. 3:10). "Bread enough, and to spare" (Luke 15:17).

Plentiful Mercy. "Slow to anger, and plenteous in mercy" (Psalm 103:8).

Plentiful Pardon. "Return unto the Lord, for He will abundantly pardon" (Isaiah 55:7).

Plentiful Peace. "And the peace of God, which passeth all understanding, shall keep your hearts and minds through Jesus Christ" (Phil. 4:7).

Plentiful Redemption. "With the Lord is plenteous redemption" (Psalm 130:7). "For God so loved the world that He gave His only begotten Son, that whosoever believeth in Him should not perish, but have everlasting life" (John 3:16).

Plentiful Grace. "And God is able to make all grace abound toward you, that ye always having all sufficiency for all things, may abound unto every good work" (2 Cor. 9:8).

Plentiful Resources. "Unto Him who is able to do exceeding abundantly, above all that we ask or think, according to the power that worketh in us" (Eph. 3:20).

Plenty for the Future. "Eye hath not seen, nor ear heard, neither have entered into the heart of man, the things which God hath prepared for them that love Him" (1 Cor. 2:9).

Thoughts for Thanksgiving

Ten lepers were healed,
But one only came
Back to the Master,
Praising His name.

Nine were forgetting
The mercy deed done.
No thought of their gain
Or joy they had won.

Ten lepers made clean
Their sick bodies healed . . .
But one giving thanks
At the Master's feet kneeled!

—*Mrs. Minerva Schultz*

For These I Am Thankful

There are so many things
To make life bright and gay.
That's why I sing a song
This glad Thanksgiving Day.

A baby's happy smile,
The handclasp of a friend,
A mother's love so true
Bring joys that never end.
The majesty of hills,
A tall and stately tree,
The wild and restless waves
Upon the mighty sea.

The fragrance of a rose,
The sun, the wind, the rain,
The silver stars, the moon,
A peaceful country lane.
The silence of the night,
The sparkling morning dew,
The music of the birds
That sing the whole day through.

For these and many more
I bring no price to pay.
Yet all these things are mine
This glad Thanksgiving Day.

—*Helen L. Hazel*

The Wonderful World

Great, wide, beautiful, wonderful World,
With the wonderful water round you curled,
And the wonderful grass upon your breast,
World, you are beautifully dressed.

The wonderful air is over me,
And the wonderful wind is shaking the tree—
It walks on the water, and whirls the mills,
And talks to itself on the tops of the hills.

You friendly Earth, how far do you go,
With the wheat fields that nod and the rivers
        that flow;
With cities and gardens, and cliffs and isles,
And people upon you for thousands of miles?

Ah! you are so great, and I am so small,
I tremble to think of you, World, at all;
And yet, when I said my prayers today,
A whisper inside me seemed to say,
"You are more than the Earth, tho' you are
        such a dot;
You can love and think, and the Earth cannot."

—William Brighty Rands (1823-1882)

Special Days—

Christmas . . .

A CHRISTMAS HYMN

Tell me what is this innumerable throng
Singing in the heavens a loud, angelic song?
These are they who come with swift and shining feet
From round about the throne of God, the Lord of Light to greet.

O, who are these that hasten beneath the starry sky,
As if with joyful tidings that through the world shall fly?
The faithful shepherds these, who greatly were afeared
When, as they watched their flocks by night, the heavenly host appeared.

Who are these that follow across the hills of night,
A star that westward hurries along the fields of light?
Three wise men from the east who myrrh and treasure bring
To lay them at the feet of Him, their Lord and Christ, and King.

What babe newborn is this that in a manger cries?
Near on her bed of pain His happy mother lies.
O, see! the air is shaken with white and heavenly wings—
This is the Lord of all the earth, this is the King of kings.

Tell me, how may I join in this holy feast
With all the kneeling world, and I of all the least?
Fear not, O faithful heart, but bring what most is meet;
Bring love alone, true love alone, and lay it at His feet.

—Richard Watson Gilder

Let Us Keep Christmas

Whatever else be lost
  Among the years,
Let us keep Christmas
  Still a shining thing.
Whatever doubts assail us,
  Or what fears,
Let us hold close one day,
  Remembering
Its poignant meaning
  For the hearts of men:
Let us get back
  Our childlike faith again.

—Grace Noll Crowell

Our King's Birthday

J esus, Son of God Eternal
E verlasting Lord is He,
S aviour of a world of sinners,
U niversal King to be,
S ought us, bro't us victory.

C hrist is due all adoration,
H umbly born to save our race,
R uler of the whole creation,
I ntercedes and gives us grace,
S aves us from sin's condemnation.
T ruly worthy of all praise!

297

Gift Wrapped in Swaddling Clothes

Gift wrapped in swaddling clothes
  Upon the cattle's hay,
Outside the inn where people feed,
  The Bread from Heaven lay.

The thorn-crowned Man in royal robes
  The populace refuse?
Acclaim instead a murderer,
  And Rome's rule o'er the Jews.

Enshrouded dead in Joseph's tomb,
  He lays the wraps aside,
Steps out to Kingship over all,
  And claims His church as bride.

Clothed now in majesty
  In heaven that Man I see,
Who came and loved and died and rose
  To give Himself for me.

—*Donald M. Taylor*

Christmas Prayer

Dear Christ, we thank Thee on this
  Christmas Day
For all the knowledge that we have of
  Thee.
Thank God for sending us His precious
  Son—
A Holy Gift to all humanity.
We thank Thee for our bodies, minds, and
  souls,
And for providing for their every need.
Oh, help us, Lord, to know and do Thy
  will
Throughout our lives, in every word and
  deed.
We thank Thee for our families, homes,
  and friends,
And all the joys that make life rich and
  free.
We kneel before Thee in adoring love
And gratitude, for all our gifts from Thee.

—*Jennie Wright*

Don't Leave Christ Out of Christmas!

GIFT OF LOVE

Christmas is a gift of love
  That can't be bought or sold.
It's ours just for the asking
  And it's worth far more than gold.

And this priceless gift of Christmas
  Is within the reach of all:
The rich, the poor, the young and old,
  The greatest and the small.

So take God's Christmas gift of love,
  Reach out and you receive;
And the only payment that God asks
  Is just that you believe.

—*Helen Steiner Rice*

The Gift That Keeps on Giving

There's a gift that keeps on giving.
Do you know the gift divine?
It's the Babe of Bethlehem's manger,
'Tis the Saviour, yours and mine.

For He brings so many blessings,
And they brighten all our way;
There's a gift that keeps on giving,
'Tis the Christ of Christmas Day.

There's a gift that keeps on giving;
One Who came from Heaven afar.
'Tis the Child the shepherds worshiped,
And the wise men saw His star.

He is Master and Redeemer,
And His voice our hearts obey.
There's a gift that keeps on giving,
'Tis the Christ of Christmas Day.

Christmas Tree of Everlasting Life

We
look
at this
tree, a sym-
bol of life
It reminds us of
the Savior's birth.
And it must always re-
mind us of His death on
Calvary's tree . . . for that is
why He came . . Thus within
this tree we must ever see the
shadow of the cross . . . and, lo . . . :
from the cross another tree we behold
which is called "the tree of life," in
heaven, there to forever remind us that
eternal life has been made possible by the
sacrificing of God's Son on the cross . . . Around
the world today the blessed Christmas carols
are sung, praising the day of His birth . . . and in
Heaven the "innumerable multitude" will sing redemption's song: "Unto Him who loved us and washed
our sins in His own blood" . . . "For God so loved the
world that He gave His only Begotten Son that whosoever believeth in Him should not perish but
Have everlasting life" . . . Today we rejoice
in the virgin-born Redeemer Who came from
Heaven's glory to the lowly manger at
Bethlehem, and from there to Calvary
to atone for our sins and thence
to the tomb of Joseph . . . where
HE
AROSE
THE
THIRD DAY
and ascended
into Heaven whence
HE IS COMING AGAIN TO
RECEIVE US UNTO HIMSELF!

—*Dale Crowley*

Let's Take the "X" Out of "Christmas"

Let's take the "X" out of "Christmas,"
And let's put Christ in again.
The day's the birthday of a King,
Not that of an unknown man.
The tinsel, the glitter, the glamour,
The noise of the parties gay
Have all but obscured the reason
That we celebrate the day.
We surely would not write "X-ian"
For the Christians here on earth.
Then why do many write "X-mas"
For the day of the Saviour's birth?
It's an honor that really is due Him
O'er that to a common man,
So let's take "X" out of "Christmas"
And let's put Christ in again.

—*Cyril W. Wommac*

Joy to the World! God's Gift

He did not use a silvery box
  Or paper green and red.
God laid His Christmas Gift to men
  Within a manger bed.
No silken cord was used to bind
  The Gift sent from above.
'Twas wrapped in swaddling clothes and
  bound
  In cords of tender love.
There was no evergreen to which
  His precious Gift was tied.
Upon a bare tree on a hill
  His Gift was hung . . . and died.
'Twas taken down from off the tree
  And laid beneath the sod.
But death itself could not destroy
  The precious Gift of God.
With mighty hand He lifted Him
  From out the stony grave.
Forevermore for every man
  A living Gift He gave.

For God so loved the world, that he gave his only begotten Son, that whosoever believeth in him should not perish, but have everlasting life (John 3:16)

The BEST Gifts Are Tied With "Heartstrings"!

What is the thought of Christmas?
  Giving.
What is the hope of Christmas?
  Living.
What is the joy of Christmas?
  Love.
No silver or gold is needed for giving,
If the heart is filled with Christmas love,
**For the hope of the world is kindly
  living,**
Learned from the joy of God above.

—*Laura Hooker*

I Have Seen the Star

I have seen the star up yonder,
  I have heard the angels sing;
I have seen the matchless wonder—
  Mary's Babe yet Heaven's King!

I have traced the lovely boyhood,
  And the noble, guileless youth
To the flower of perfect manhood,
  Full of wisdom, grace and truth.

I have wept amid the heartbreak
  Where He bled, my soul to save;
I have met Him in the dawn-break
  Of His rising from the grave.

I have felt His presence near me
  Mid the busy workday rush;
I have known it lift and cheer me
  In the twilight's solemn hush.

I have sensed Him all around me
  Here and there and everywhere;
I have felt His care surround me
  As I breathed a hurried prayer.

Yet although I knew His presence,
  He Himself remained unknown
Till I learned to wait in secret,
  He and I—each day—alone.

When Jesus Came

When Jesus came long years ago
To Bethlehem and a manger low,
The cattle kneeled near the Holy One
In homage there to God's dear Son.

As shepherds dwelt on distant hill,
A glory shone over rock and rill;
An angel stood in the midst of them—
The shepherds quaked for fear of him.

The angel said, "Why do ye fear?
From Heaven's throne tidings glad I
    bear!
For unto you there is born this night,
The Saviour-Lord, God's Child of Light!"

Their eyes beheld a wondrous glow
That filled the sky and the earth below,
While angel bands from the realms
    above
Hosannas sang of God's great love.

The echoes rang that holy morn:
O, earth, rejoice! Christ, the Lord, is
    born!
And peace, goodwill, toward sinful men,
For Christ is born in Bethlehem!

Three wise men found the manger
    place,
With rapture gazed on the Christ
    Child's face.
Then kneeling there on earthen floor
Gave gifts of gold, frankincense, myrrh.

Down through the years on Christmas
    morn
Men's hearts rejoice that the Christ was
    born,
And evermore praise His holy name
For grace and truth when Jesus came.

—Kathryn Bowsher

NO ROOM

No room for the Baby at Bethlehem's
    Inn—only a cattle shed.
No home on this earth for the dear
    Son of God—nowhere to lay
    His head.
Only a cross did they give to our
    Lord—only a borrowed tomb.
Today He is seeking a place in your
    heart,
Will you still say to Him, "No room"?

O Lord, in my heart there's a wel-
    come for Thee—gladly I now
    would say,
Come in, blessed Saviour, my heart
    and my life henceforth would
    own Thy sway.

Wishing You a Blessed Christmas

The blessedness of Christmas is all "wrapped up" in the person of Jesus. Our relationship to Him determines the measure of our blessing.

Blessing in His Name
Thou shalt call his name Jesus for he shall save His people from their sins (Matthew 1:21).

Blessing in His Purpose
I am come that they might have life, and that they might have it more abundantly (John 10:10).

Blessing in Receiving Him
But as many as received him, to them gave he power to become the sons of God, even to them that believe on his name (John 1:12).

Blessing in Belonging to Him
I am my beloved's, and his desire is toward me (Song of Solomon 7:10).
Is there greater joy than this?

Christ Makes Christmas Real

What makes Christmas? Is it a calendar date? Is it the giving and getting, the eating and drinking, the greeting cards, the Christmas tree, the holly, the colorful lights, the tinsel, the glamour?

What makes Christmas? Is it the story of Bethlehem, the manger, the Infant in swaddling clothes, the shepherds, the angels, the magi, the star, the nativity of the matchless Babe born of a virgin?

What makes Christmas? There can be but one answer: Fellowship with the Living CHRIST. For, alas, WHAT IS CHRISTMAS WITHOUT CHRIST?

It is the virgin mother without a supernatural Babe.

It is the swaddling clothes without the Infant Redeemer.

It is a manger-cradle without the Divine Occupant.

It is the angel choir without a song.

It is the lonely shepherds without a message from the skies.

It is the fruitless quest of the wise men on a hopeless mission.

It is the star of Bethlehem without promise or signification.

It is a perishing world without a Saviour!

It is a Bible without a message of hope!

It is a God of infinite power without love for dying sinners!

It is history and eternity without JESUS!

Therefore, it would mean that life is without purpose. We would struggle, toil, and suffer, and pass the days of our sojourn here, then die in our sins, only to face the fiery judgment of a righteous and holy God.

But thanks to our God forever, the message of the angels was TRUE: "Unto you is born this day in the city of David a Saviour, which is Christ the Lord" (Luke 2:11).

CHRIST makes Christmas REAL. For it is He who manifests the love of God, and makes real to us through faith His peace and joy. We have in Him a living Saviour who "saves to the uttermost all who come unto God by him" (Hebrews 7:25).

"For God so loved the world that he gave his only begotten Son that whosoever believeth in him should not perish, but have everlasting life" (John 3:16).

What makes Christmas real? THE LIVING CHRIST DWELLING IN OUR HEARTS!

—Dale Crowley

**"The Word was made flesh, and dwelt among us, and we beheld His glory, the glory as of the only begotten of the Father, full of grace and truth."
John 1:14**

First Christmas in Heaven

I've had my first Christmas in heaven,
A glorious, wonderful day!
I stood with saints of the ages
Who found Christ, the Truth, and the Way.

I sang with the heavenly choir:
Just think! I, who so long to sing!
And oh! what celestial music
We brought to our Saviour and King!

We sang the glad songs of redemption,
How Jesus to Bethlehem came,
And how they had called His name Jesus,
That all might be saved through His name.

We sang once again with the angels,
The song that they sang that blest morn,
When shepherds first heard the glad story
That Jesus, the Saviour, was born.

O, dear one, I wish you had been here:
No Christmas on earth could compare
With all the rapture and glory
We witnessed in Heaven so fair.

You know how I always loved Christmas;
It seemed such a wonderful day,
With all of my loved ones around me,
The children so happy and gay.

Yes, now I can see why I loved it,
And, oh, what a joy it will be,
When all of my loved ones are with me,
To share in the glories I see.

So, dear ones on earth, here's my greeting:
Look up till the day dawn appears,
And oh, what a Christmas awaits us,
Beyond all our partings and tears.

—*Dr. Albert S. Reitz*

When Christmas Comes Again

Some of us may not be here
    When Christmas comes again—
Spread around your words of cheer
    To ev'ry one you can.
Look with joy to Christmas time
    And sing in sheer delight;
Listen to the bells that chime
    Their gladsome—"Silent Night."
In such happy Christmas days
    Be you a friend indeed—
Know the joy your giving pays,
    To help some friend in need.
All may join the Yuletide cheer
    And give as best they can—
Some of us may not be here
    When Christmas comes again.
Why defer until too late
    The good we could have done?
Why forget, or pause, or wait,
    And thus be friend to none?
Tho' some never understand
    The good we tried to do—
Blessings, love for others planned
    Come back to me and you.
Then remember friend or foe
    And, tho' your gift be small,
Let your love to others flow,
    Ere comes the last low call.
Some kind deed or word of cheer
    May ease the sting of pain—
Some of us may not be here
    When Christmas comes again.

**"Boast not thyself of tomorrow, for thou
knowest not what a day may bring forth."**
Proverbs 27:1

Miscellaneous . . .

The Monkey's Viewpoint

Three monkeys sat in a coconut tree
   Discussing things as they're said to be.
Said one to the others, "Now, listen, you two,
   There's a certain rumor that can't be true—
That man descended from our noble race.
   The very idea! It's a dire disgrace.
No monkey ever deserted his wife,
   Starved her baby, and ruined her life.
To leave the babies with others to bunk,
Or pass them on from one to another
   Till they scarcely know who is their mother
And another thing—you'll never see
   A monk build a fence 'round a coconut tree,
And let the coconuts go to waste.
   Why, if I put a fence around this tree,
Starvation would force you to steal from me.
   Here's another thing a monk won't do:
Go out at night and get in a stew!
   Or use a gun, or club, or knife
To take some other monkey's life.
   Yes, man descended—the ornery cuss,
But could he really descend from us?"

DARWINISM

Don't be discouraged, poor little fly.
You'll be a chipmunk by and by.
And years after, I can see,
You'll be a full grown chimpanzee.
Next I see, with prophet's ken,
You'll take your place in the ranks of
   men.
Then in the great, sweet by-and-by,
We'll be angels, you and I.
Why should I swat you, poor little fly?
Prophetic chum of my home on high.
That's what Darwin says, not I.

           —*Nelson*

God's Weather

Sunshine is healthful,
   Wind is invigorating,
Rain is refreshing,
   Snow benefits crops,
Heat makes cold attractive,
   Cold makes heat appreciated;
ALL weather is God's weather.
THANK GOD FOR TODAY!

HEADS UP!

   Now here—let us wake up, sing up, preach up, pray up, PAY up and stay up—but never give up, or let up or back up, or shut up until Christ who was caught up shall come and call up the BRIDE—made up of redeemed sinners to whom the Lord was lifted up! So "heads up" (Luke 21:28) while the glorious cause of Christ is BUILT up."

About Cussing

It grieves me, friend, to hear my Maker's
   name
Thus spoken without reverence or shame.
Be thou a man, thy noble rank maintain;
Appeal to God, but not in words profane;
Scorn to be rougher or thus impolite,
'Tis neither brave nor wise, 'Tis far from
   right;
You would not knowingly speak thus in
   death,
Reflect—your Maker now could stop
   your breath;
For self respect, for friends you should
   forbear;
God in heaven commands, "Thou shalt
   not swear."

"Blessed Are They"—

1. Who seek the Lord (Psalm 119:2).
2. Whom God chooses (Psalm 65:4).
3. Who believe (Galatians 3:9).
4. Whose sins are forgiven (Romans 4:7).
5. Who hunger and thirst after righteousness (Matthew 5:6).
6. Who avoid the wicked (Psalm 1:1).
7. Who endure temptation (James 1:12).
8. Who suffer for Christ's sake (Luke 6:22).
9. Who delight in His Word (Psalm 121:1).
10. Who frequent God's house (Psalm 84:4).
11. Who are poor in spirit (Matthew 5:3).
12. Who are merciful (Matthew 5:7).
13. Who are faithful (Revelation 16:15).
14. Who wait for the Lord (Isaiah 30:8).
15. Who watch for the Lord (Luke 12:27).
16. Who die in the Lord (Revelation 14:18).
17. Who have part in the first resurrection (Revelation 20:6).
18. Who have not seen, and yet have believed (John 20:29).

—*J. T. Bougher*

What Did You Say?

I have always wondered just why it is,
But find no one who will truly explain,
Why people, when talking, for some reason
Persist in using God's name in vain.

The trend seems to be on the increase
For you hear it wherever you go.
Some people who are dull and uncultured
Will blaspheme just to make a big show.

Now if someone took the name of your
     mother
Or your wife, in a slanderous way,
I'm sure you'd be startled and angry
And would have some choice words to say.

So when tempted to use profane language,
Think what the good Lord would have said.
Then if you feel that you must say some-
     thing,
Just say "hallelujah" instead.

—*Ralph Blakeney*

THE PASTOR'S WIFE

In the shadow of the parsonage
     Stands a figure oft obscure,
Just behind the faithful pastor
     Is his wife, devout and pure.
She is with him every moment
     Helping make his work progress,
And you can't discount her portion
     In his measure of success.
Oft behind the scene of action,
     Often never seen or heard,
Yet she stands forever ready
     Just to give a helping word.
It is not in active service
     That her worth is really shown,
But in bearing heavy burdens
     That to others are unknown.
With encouragement and vision
     She must urge God's servant on,
When the shadows are the darkest
     And his courage's almost gone.
With her home forever open
     And her work quite never done,
She is ever his lieutenant
     In the battles fought and won.

—*T. R. Buzzard*

305

A Preacher on the Fence

2 Timothy 4:2

From out the millions of the earth,
  God often calls a man
To preach His Word, and for the truth
  To take a loyal stand.
'Tis sad to see him shun his cross,
  Nor stand in its defense,
Between the sides of right and wrong:
  A preacher on the fence.

Before him are the souls of men,
  Destined for heaven or hell;
An open Bible in his hand,
  And yet he dare not tell
Them all the truth as written there,
  He fears the consequence;
The shame of heaven, the joy of hell,
  A preacher on the fence.

Some Church Statistics

5% of church folks never existed
10% cannot be found
20% never pray
25% never attend church services
30% never read the Bible
40% never give
50% never go to church on Sunday night
60% never give to missions
75% never accept any responsibility
85% never go to prayer meeting
90% never have any prayer in the home
95% never witness for Christ to the lost

Let us be like the bird, for a moment perched
On a frail branch while he sings.
He feels it bend, but he sings his song,
For he knows that he has wings.

—Victor Hugo

From a Tadpole to a Ph.D.

Once I was a tadpole, grubbing in the mire;
Till I became ambitious and started to aspire.
I rubbed my tail so hard against a sunken log,
It disappeared completely and I became a frog.

I struggled from my puddle and jumped upon land.
And the feeling within me was glorious and grand;
It made me kind of frisky, so I hopped around a tree
Till I landed in the branches as happy as could be.

And there I spent some aeons, evoluting without fail,
Till I became a monkey and grew another tail.
But still I had ambitions, as the aeons quickly sped.
I climbed down from the tree and walked the earth instead.

My tail got tired with trailing on the hard earth every day,
And twice within my "process" that appendage passed away.
Once again I evoluted, and believe it, if you can,
I awoke one summer morning and found myself a man!

Now, you tadpoles, in the mire, just think what you may be.
If you'll only in your puddles start to climb the family tree.
I'm the genus homo, "finished" for all the world to see,
For when I told my story I was given a Ph.D.

What the Churches Need

More tithes and fewer drives.
More workers and fewer shirkers.
More action and less faction.
More backers and fewer slackers.
More praying and less straying.
More of God's plans and less of man's.
More divine power and less human "pow-wows."
More burden bearers and fewer tale bearers.
More fighting squads and fewer tightwads.
More tongues of fire and fewer fiery tongues.
More zealous effort and less jealous thought.
More love for the Word and less love for the world.
More seeking for Grace and less seeking for place.
More holiness of life and less bickering and strife.
More fasting and praying and less feasting and playing.
More religion in politics and less politics in religion.

—Pastor James Thorne

In the Modern Direction

"You're quite out of date,"
Said young Pastor Bate
To one of our faithful old preachers
Who had carried for years,
In travail and tears,
The Gospel to poor sinful creatures.

"You still preach on Hades,
And shock cultured ladies,
With your barbarous doctrine of blood;
You're so far behind
That you'll never catch up;
You're a flat tire stuck in the mud."

For some little while
A sweet bit of a smile
Enlightened the old pastor's face.
Being made the butt
Of ridicule's cut
Didn't ruffle his sweetness or grace.

Then he turned to young Bate,
So suave and sedate:
"Catch up! did my hears hear you say?
Why, I couldn't succeed
If I doubled my speed;
For, my friend, I'm not going your way."

—Elim Evangel

The Christian's Daily Dozen

First, turn your heart to God for grace
Before you look on any face.
Next, breathe a word of thankful greeting
To Him who watched while you were
   sleeping.
Next say a verse or hum an air
To make an atmosphere of prayer.
At length, when mind is keenly turning,
Repeat some new verse you are learning.
Then it will surely clear your vision
To voice in words, the day's decision;
To talk with Christ about your work,
For Heaven can never bless a shirk.
And now, prepared the day to meet,
Arise and stand upon your feet.
Then, from the table while you're dress-
   ing,
Glean something from the Book of
   Blessing!
And, for the climax of all motion,
Fail not to kneel in sweet devotion.
So go forth with smile to greet
The first and every heart you meet.
And all day long your soul will thrive,
And men will thank God you're alive.

—Bishop R. S. Cushman

The Faithful Pastor

He held the lantern, stooping low,
So low that none could miss the way,
   And yet so high, to bring in sight
That picture fair—the world's great
    Light,
That gazing up—the lamp between—
   The hand that held it scarce was seen.

He held the pitcher—stooping low
To lips of little ones below,
   Then raised it to the weary saint
And bade him drink when sick and faint!
They drank—the pitcher thus between,
   The hand that held it scarce was seen.

He blew the trumpet soft and low
To call the waiting soldiers near,
   And then with louder notes and bold
To raze the walls of Satan's hold!
The trumpet coming thus between,
   The hand that held it scarce was seen.

And then the Captain says, "Well done,
Thou good and faithful servant, come
   Lay down the pitcher and the lamp.
Lay down the trumpet—leave the
    camp,"
The weary hands will then be seen,
   Clasped in those pierced Ones
    Naught between.

God's Best Things

God has His best things for the few
   Who dare to stand the test;
God has His second best for those
   Who will not have His best.

I want, among the victor's throng
   To have my name confessed;
And hear the Master say, "Well done,
   My child, you did your best."

        —*Found among personal effects*
              of Marguerite Crowley

Three Kinds of Christians

There are three kinds of Christians: the rowboat type, the sailboat type, and the steamboat type.

The rowboat sort are humanistic, self-dependent, trying to get on with their own resources. But as those resources are limited, the progress is limited.

The sailboat type depend on the winds. If the winds are with them, if people are constantly complimenting and encouraging them, they get on. But if the patting on the back stops, they stop.

Then there is the steamboat type—those who have power on the inside, and they go on whether winds are favorable or unfavorable.

"TEEN" COMMANDMENTS

1. Don't let your parents down; they brought you up.
2. Choose your companions with care; you become what they are.
3. Be master of your habits or they will master you.
4. Treasure your time; don't spend it, invest it.
5. Stand for something or you'll fall for anything.
6. Select only a date who would make a good mate.
7. See what you can do for others; not what they can do for you.
8. Guard your thoughts; what you think, you are.
9. Don't fill up on this world's crumbs; feed your soul on Living Bread.
10. Give your all to Christ; He gave His all for you.

           —*Western Messenger*

BE A "SQUARE"

A "Square"! One of the good old words, that's gone the way of love and modesty and patriotism. Something to be snickered at, or outright laughed at. Why? — it used to be that there was no higher compliment you could pay a man than to call him a "square shooter."

The "ad man's" promise of a "square deal" was once as binding as an oath on the Bible. But today, a "square" is a guy who volunteers when he doesn't have to—he's the guy who gets his "kicks" from trying to do a job better than anyone else. A "boob" who gets so lost in his work he has to be reminded to go home.

A "Square" is a guy who doesn't want to stop at a bar and get "juiced up," because he prefers to go to his own home, his own dinner table, his own bed. He hasn't learned to cut corners or "goof off." This "nut" even gets all "choked up" when he hears children singing "My Country, 'Tis of Thee." He believes in God and says so in public.

Some of the "Old Squares" were Nathan Hale, Patrick Henry, George Washington, and Ben Franklin.

Some of the "New Squares" are Glenn, Grissom, Shepard, Cooper, Schirra. John Glenn says he gets a funny feeling down inside when he sees the flag go by. Says he's proud to say he belonged to the Boy Scouts and the YMCA. How "Square" can you get?!!

A "Square" is a guy who lives within his means, whether the Joneses do or not; and thinks his Uncle Sam should too. He doesn't want to "fly now and pay later."

A "Square" is likely to save some of his own money for a "rainy day" rather than count on using yours.

A "Square" gets books out of the library instead of from the corner news stand.

He tells his sons it is more important to play fair than it is to win—imagine!

A "Square" is a guy who reads Scripture and prays, even when there's no one around to be impressed.

He thinks Christmas trees should be green and that Christmas gifts should be lovingly hand picked.

He wants to see America first in everything.

He believes in honoring his mother and father and "do unto others" and that kind of stuff.

He thinks he knows more than his "teenagers" about "car freedom and curfew." So will all you "Gooney Birds," who fit that description, please stand up—you "Missfits," in this "Brave New Age." You dismally disorganized, improperly apologetic, ghosts of the past—stand up and be counted.

You "Squares" who turn the wheels and pick the fields, and move mountains, and put rivets in our dreams.

You "Squares" who dignify the human race. You "Squares" who hold a thankless world in place.

STAND UP!

—Paul Harvey

DIVINE DETERGENT NEEDED

"Though you wash yourself with lye and use much soap, the stain of your guilt is still before me, saith the Lord God" (Jer. 2:22).

HOWEVER: "If we confess our sins, He is faithful and just to forgive us our sins, and to cleanse us from all iniquity" (1 John 1:9).

Are you soft-soaping God? "Duz" you just "Dreft" along the "Tide"? "Vel" now is the time for "All" to "Cheer" up. If you want real "Joy" the "Trend" is to "Breeze" to church regularly on Sunday mornings. But too many people "Woodbury" their heads in the pillows or work in their yards like "Handy Andy" forgetting that the Lord's Day as made for "Lestoil."

Where our Lord reigns, the "Dove" of peace will never need to send out an "S.O.S." Don't trust "Lux," good or bad. Shall we "Dial" you and remind you of those "Ivory" palaces up yonder?

This is not just idle "Bab-O"! Worship will "Ad" to your "Life-buoy"! So why not be faithful and "Whisk" yourselves out of bed Sunday mornings, dress up "Spic & Span" and "Dash" like a "Comet" to God's house of prayer! Singing "Praise" to God will bring a "Cleanser" to your soul. "Pledge" yourself and "Pride" of a clear conscience will be yours. Your life will then become full of real "Zest."

(We do not know who wrote the foregoing article. It is submitted by Phyllis M. Harlan who copied it from a local church bulletin.)

For a Peaceful World

If we would keep our freedom and survive,
We must hold high the torch of truth.
Integrity must govern all the acts
Of every man. Right can, and must prevail!
Hold fast your faith in God's great power!
His power will never fail!
No atom bomb, or human tool
Can blot out that which God creates.
And only as men obey God's laws,
Can peace be found. Only so,
Can all mankind survive.

—Mary H. Oliver

Some persons are tortured to death by pin pricks. A small worm may bring destruction to a giant oak tree. A small leak will sink a mighty ship. Small trifles, if not brought under control, may cripple our thinking and retard our realization of the full possibilities of our lives. Every person must find spiritual elevation if he would rise above the irritations of daily living. What is the motivation for your life?

CHANNING'S SYMPHONY

To live content with small means; to seek elegance rather than luxury; and refinement rather than fashion; to be worthy, not respectable, and wealthy, not rich; to study hard, think quietly, talk gently, act frankly; to listen to stars and birds, to babes and sages, with open heart; to bear all cheerfully, do all bravely, await occasion, hurry never; in a word, to let the spiritual, unbidden and unconscious grow up through the common. This is to be my symphony.

—William Henry Channing

The Blessed B's for the Believer As Found in Romans 12:9-16

1. Be consistent. "Let love be without hypocrisy" (v. 9).
2. Be loving. "Be kindly affectioned one to another" (v. 10).
3. Be zealous. "Not slothful in business; fervent in spirit; serving the Lord" (v. 11).
4. Be hopeful. "Rejoicing in hope" (v. 12).
5. Be patient. "Patient in tribulation" (v. 12).
6. Be prayerful. "Continuing instant in prayer" (v. 12).
7. Be generous. "Distributing to the necessity of saints; given to hospitality" (v. 13).
8. Be magnanimous. "Bless them which persecute you; bless and curse not" (v. 14.
9. Be brotherly. "Rejoice with them that do rejoice and weep with them that weep" (v. 15).
10. Be humble. "Keep in harmony with one another; instead of being ambitious, associate with humble folk; never be self-conceited" (v. 16, Moffat).

—*Cliff Robinson*

A Striking Contrast

Man calls sin an accident;
God calls it an abomination.
Man calls sin a blunder;
God calls it blindness.
Man calls sin a defect;
God calls it a disease.
Man calls sin a chance;
God calls it a choice.
Man calls sin an error;
God calls it enmity.
Man calls sin a fascination;
God calls it a fatality.
Man calls sin a luxury;
God calls it leprosy.
Man calls sin a liberty;
God calls it lawlessness.
Man calls sin a trifle;
God calls it a tragedy.
Man calls sin a mistake;
God calls it madness.
Man calls sin a weakness;
God calls it willfulness.

Thank God for Youth

Thank God for Youth with the strength to lift,
And the will to serve, and the heart to pray;
Thank God for the marvelous wonder-gift of Youth today.

There are paths to be straightened within our land.
There are darkened ways that have need of light,
Thank God for the Youth of earth who stand
    Foursquare for right.

There is need for a vision of undimmed eyes;
There is need for hands that are clean and strong;
For backs that are straight, and hearts that are wise;
For lips with a song.

Thank God for Youth with its latent powers;
Thank God for Youth that yet may bring
Out of these failures that have been ours
    Some better thing.

—*Grace Noll Crowell*

FORGIVENESS

My heart was heavy, for its trust had been
    Abused, its kindness answered with foul wrong;
So, turning gloomily from my fellowmen,
    One summer Sabbath Day I strolled among
The green mounds of the village burial-place;
    Where, pondering how all human love and hate
    Find one sad level; and how, soon or late,
Wronged and wrongdoer, each with meekened face,
    And cold hands folded over a still heart,
Pass the green threshold of our common grave,
    Whither all footsteps tend, whence none depart,
Awed for myself, and pitying my face,
    Our common sorrow, like a mighty wave,
    Swept all my pride away, and, trembling, I forgave!

—John Greenleaf Whittier

Prayer to Be a True Christian

Of myself I am an empty vessel.
Fill me so that I may live the life of the
    Spirit,
The life of Truth and Gladness,
The life of Beauty and Love,
The life of Wisdom and Strength.
And guide me today in all things:
Guide me to the people I should meet or
    help,
To the circumstances in which I can best
    serve Thee;
Whether by my actions or my sufferings.
But, above all, make Christ to be formed
    in me.
That I may dethrone self in my heart
And make Him King:
So that He is in me, and I in Him,
Today and forever. Amen.

—Adapted from a prayer by
the Bishop of Bloemfontein

It is very late in the afternoon
of the day of decision

Five Points for the GROWING Christian

Read your Bible daily
As newborn babes, desire the sincere milk of the word, that ye may grow thereby (1 Peter 2:2).

Keep looking to Jesus
And whatsoever ye do in word or deed, do all in the name of the Lord Jesus, giving thanks to God and the Father by him (Colossians 3:17).

Pray without ceasing
And I say unto you: Ask, and it shall be given you; seek, and ye shall find; knock, and it shall be opened unto you (Luke 11:9).

Confess Him to others
Whosoever therefore shall confess me before men, him will I confess also before my father which is in heaven (Matthew 10:32).

Do something for Jesus
And the King shall answer and say unto them, Verily I say unto you, Inasmuch as ye have done it unto one of the least of these my brethren, ye have done it unto me (Matthew 25:40).

—Faith, Prayer & Tract League

The Unknown Soldier's Prayer

Look, God, I have never spoken to You,
But now I want to say, "How do You do?"
You see, God, they told me You didn't exist,
And, like a fool, I believed all this.

Last night from a shell hole I saw Your sky—
I figured right then they had told me a lie.
Had I taken time to see things You made,
I'd have known they weren't calling a spade a
      spade.

I wonder, God, if You'd shake my hand;
Somehow, I feel that You will understand.
Funny I had to come to this hellish place
Before I had time to see Your face.

Well, guess there isn't much more to say,
But I'm sure glad, God, I met You today.
I guess the "zero hour" will soon be here,
But I'm not afraid since I know You're near.

The signal! Well, God, I'll have to go;
I like You lots, this I want You to know.
Look, now, this will be a horrible fight—
Who knows, I may come to Your house
      tonight.

Though I wasn't friendly to You before,
I wonder, God, if You'd wait at Your door.
Look, I'm crying! Me! Shedding ears—
I wish I had known You these many years.

Well, I have to go now, God. Good-bye!
Strange, since I met You, I'm not afraid to
      die.

—*Frances Angermayer*

God Loveth Thee

God loveth thee—then be content;
Whate'er thou hast, His love hath sent;
Come pain or pleasure, good or ill,
His love is round about thee still.
Then murmur not, nor anxious be,
Rest thou in peace, God loveth thee!

A Parable of Trees

Once upon a time a man built his house on a spot which commanded a view to the distant mountains and a vast expanse of heaven's blue skies. Then he said to himself, "I must have trees to shelter and adorn my house; trees make any place more lovely." So he planted a number of fine trees, and these grew up and were admired. But the trees were too many, and were planted too closely, and by their lofty tops and interlacing branches shut out the distant view. The mountains were no longer visible from the house, and scarcely a glimpse of the sky could be had.

It is often that way with men's lives. They gather about them earthly interests in order to make their lives more beautiful, more comfortable, more influential until after a while the glorious mountains of heaven are shut out and heaven itself grows dim and unreal.

A Godly Man

One righteous man.
What is he worth?
Far above all the
Diamonds on earth.
Blessed is the man
Whose God is the Lord,
Who lives by His power
And feeds on His Word.
For this man shall prosper,
His soul cannot die.
His treasures, the riches
Of earth cannot buy.

—*Betty Dulin*

IT IS NOT EASY

To apologize,
To begin over,
To be unselfish,
To take advice,
To admit error,
To face a sneer,
To be charitable,
To keep on trying,
To be considerate,
To avoid mistakes,
To endure success,
To profit by mistakes,
To forgive and forget,
To think and then act,
To keep out of the rut,
To make the best of little,
To subdue an unruly temper,
To maintain a high standard,
To shoulder a deserved blame,
To recognize the silver lining—
But it always pays.

—Ohio Educational Monthly

PULLING TOGETHER

Two old mules, now get this dope,
    were tied together with a piece of rope.
Said one to the other, "You come my way
    while I take a nibble of this new-mown hay."

"I won't" said the other, "You come with me,
    for I, too, have some hay, you see."
So they got nowhere, just pawed up dirt,
    and how, how that old rope did hurt!
Then they faced about, those stubborn mules,
    and said, "We're just too much like human
    fools.
Let's pull together, I'll go your way,
    then come with me and we'll both eat hay."

Well, they ate their hay, and liked it too,
    and swore to be comrades good and true.
As the sun went down, they were heard to say,
    "Ah, this is the end of a perfect day—
We must pull together—'tis the only way."

TWO RECIPES

Here are two tried and tested recipes for the family chef. They were originally published by Marshall Field and Co. to accompany a film on social relations and were sent to us by Dr. Albert C. Baker, rector of the Trinity Episcopal Church, Bessemer, Alabama.

Recipe for a Happy Day

1 cup friendly words
2 heaping cups understanding
4 heaping teaspoons time and patience
Pinch of warm personality
Dash of humor

Instructions for mixing: Measure words carefully. Add heaping cups of understanding; use generous amounts of time and patience. Cook with gas on front burner. Keep temperature low—do not boil! Add dash of humor and a pinch of warm personality. Season to taste with spice of life. Serve in individual molds.

Recipe for a Terrible Day

Take a pint of ill humor;
Add one or more unfortunate incidents.
Set over a good fire.
When boiling point is reached, add a
    tablespoon of temper.
Baste from time to time with sarcasm.
Cook until edges curl.
Add handful of haughty words;
As mixture curdles, stir furiously.
Warning: Do not cover—may blow top!
    Serve while sizzling.

The Gospel Alphabet

A All have sinned and come short of the glory of God (Rom. 3:23).

B Behold, the Lamb of God, that taketh away the sin of the world (John 1:29).

C Come unto me, all ye that labor and are heavy laden, and I will give you rest (Matt. 11:28).

D Draw nigh to God, and he will draw nigh to you (James 4:8).

E Even so, it is not the will of your Father which is in heaven that one of these little ones should perish (Matt. 18:14).

F For by grace are ye saved through faith, and that not of yourselves: it is the gift of God (Eph. 2:8).

G God so loved the world that he gave his only begotten Son, that whosoever believeth on him should not perish, but have everlasting life (John 3:16).

H Him that cometh to me I will in no wise cast out (John 6:37).

I I am the way, the truth and the life; no man cometh unto the Father, but by me (John 14:6).

J Jesus answered and said unto them, This is the work of God, that ye believe on him whom he hath sent (John 6:29).

K Knock, and it shall be opened unto you (Matt. 7:7).

L Look unto me, and be ye saved, all the ends of the earth (Isa. 45:22).

M My grace is sufficient for thee (2 Cor. 12:9).

N Now is the accepted time; behold, now is the day of salvation (2 Cor. 6:2).

O Open thou mine eyes, that I may behold wondrous things out of thy law (Psalm 119:18).

P Peace I leave with you: My peace I give unto you: not as the world giveth, give I unto you. Let not your heart be troubled, neither let it be afraid (John 14:27).

Q Quicken me according to thy word (Psalm 119:154).

R Rest in the Lord, and wait patiently for him (Psalm 37:7).

S Seek, and ye shall find (Matt. 7:7).

T The blood of Jesus Christ his Son cleanseth us from all sin (1 John 1:7).

U Unto you is born this day in the city of David a Saviour which is Christ the Lord (Luke 2:11).

V Verily, verily I say unto you, He that believeth on me hath everlasting life (John 6:47).

W What shall it profit a man, if he shall gain the whole world and lose his own soul? (Mark 8:36.

X Except a man be born again, he cannot see the kingdom of God (John 3:3).

Y Ye are not your own; ye are bought with a price (1 Cor. 6:19, 20).

Z Zealous of good works (Titus 2:14).

Encouragement From a Rooster

The Lord will use any Christian following rules adhered to by the rooster:

1. The rooster rises early, and immediately begins his God-given task—crowing.

2. The rooster does not refuse to crow because he cannot sing like a canary; but he does crow as if to him, at least, his work was the most important in the world.

3. He does efficiently that which is never praised. Whoever heard anyone asking, "Did you listen to that rooster crow? Hasn't he a charming voice?"

4. He awakens sleepers. Unpopular, but often necessary.

5. He is the proclaimer of good news: A new day with glorious opportunities and responsibilities has dawned.

6. He is dependable. He is persistent. He is an excellent advertiser.

7. He never complains about having to do the same common task, and he does not worry about compensation or the recognition that he should have.

—Wheeler City Rescue Mission Tract

God's Bill of Exceptions

1. Except (unless) a man be born again, he cannot see the kingdom of God (John 3:3).
2. Except (unless) ye repent, ye shall all likewise perish (Luke 13:3).
3. Except (unless) your righteousness shall exceed the righteousness of the scribes and Pharisees, ye shall in no case enter into the kingdom of heaven (Matt. 5:20).
4. Except (unless) ye be converted, and become as little children, ye shall not enter the kingdom of heaven (Matt. 18:3).

The Little Black Dog

I wonder if Christ had a little black dog
   All curly and wooly like mine;
With two long silky ears, and a nose
   round and wet,
   And two eyes brown and tender that
   shine.

I'm afraid that He hadn't,
   because I have read
How He prayed in the garden alone,
For all His friends and disciples had fled—
   Even Peter—the one called a stone.

And I am sure that the little black dog
   With heart so tender and warm,
Would never have left Him to suffer
   alone,
   But creeping right under His arm

Would have licked the dear fingers in
   agony clasped,
   And counting all favors but loss,
When they took Him away would have
   trotted behind
   And followed Him right to the Cross.

God's Wave Length

There's ever a call that is coming
Over a broadcasting station above;
Tune in your heart and listen
To God tell of His wonderful love.
The receiver must be in good order,
The wires not rusted with sin;
You won't need much amplification,
When His message comes rolling in.
But if Satan has got into your heart,
And ruined the works out of spite,
Ask God to renew your receiver;
He'll give you one that works right.
Then keep your receiver in order,
Tuned to God's own wave length;
Close the circuit if Satan is calling,
And God will add much to your
   strength.

—Alfred Disbrow

My Body

Thank You, God, for this body.
For the things it can feel,
The things it can sense.
Thank You for the wondrous things it
can do.
For the bright vigor of my body at the
day's beginning,
For its weariness at the day's end.
Thank you for its pain—
If only to sting me into awareness of my
own existence upon earth.
I look upon Your creation in amazement,
For we are indeed fearfully and wonder-
fully made.
All its secret, silent machinery—the
meshing and churning—
What a miracle of design!
Don't let me hurt it, God,
Or scar it or spoil it,
Or overindulge or overdrive it.
But don't let me coddle it, either, God.
Let me love my body enough to keep it
agile
And able and well and strong.

Psalm of the Welfare State

The government is my shepherd
Therefore, I need not work.
It alloweth me to lay down on a good
job.
It leadeth me beside still factories.
And it destroys all my initiative.
It leadeth into the path of a parasite
for politic's sake.
Yea, though I walk through the valley
of laziness and deficit-spending,
I will fear no evil, for the govern-
ment is with me.
It prepareth an economic Utopia for me,
by appropriating the earnings
Of my own grandchildren.
It filleth my head with false security;
my insufficiency runs over.
Surely the Government should care
for me all the days of life here on
earth!!!
And I shall dwell in a fool's paradise
forever.

—Los Angeles Medical Society Bulletin

YOUTH

Youth is not a time of life. It's a state of mind. It's a test of the will, a quality of imagination, a vigor of emotions, a predominance of courage over timidity, of the appetite for adventure over love of ease.

Nobody grows old by merely living a number of years. People grow old only by deserting their ideals. Years wrinkle this skin, but to give up enthusiasm wrinkles the soul. Worry, doubt, self-distrust, fear and despair. . . . these are the quick equivalents of the long, long years that bow the head and turn the growing spirit back to dust.

Whether 70 or 16, there is, in every being's heart, the love of wonder, the sweet amazement of the star and the starlike things and thoughts, the undaunted challenge of events, the unfailing childlike appetite for "What next?"

You are as young as your faith, as old as your doubt . . . as young as your self-con-fidence, as old as your fear . . . as young as your hope, as old as your despair.

So long as your heart receives messages of beauty, cheer, courage, grandeur and power from the earth, from man and from the infinite, so long are you young.

When all the wires are down, and all the central places of your heart are covered with the snows of pessimism and the ice of cynicism, then, and only then, are you grown old indeed . . . and may God have mercy on your soul.

—Gen. Douglas MacArthur

Your House of Happiness

Take what God gives, O friend of mine,
And build your house of happiness.
Perchance some have been given more,
But many have been given less.
The treasure lying at your feet,
Whose value you but faintly guess,
Another builder looking on
Would barter heaven to possess.
Have you found work that you can do?
Is there a heart that loves you best?
Is there a spot somewhere called home,
Where spent and worn your soul can
    rest?

A friend, a tree, a book, a song,
A dog which loves your hand's caress,
A story of health to meet life's needs;
Oh, build your house of happiness.
Trust not tomorrow's dawn to bring
The dreamed-of joy which we await.
We have enough of pleasant things
To house our souls in goodly state.
Tomorrow, time's relentless stream
May bear what now we have away.
Take what God gives, O friend,
And build your house of happiness
    today.

To Those Having Birthdays

*Count not your age by the years
    you live,
But by the happiness you give.
The friends you make, the good you
    do,
The confidence that's placed in you,
The little things that, day by day,
Bring cheer to others on life's
    way—
And count this birthday one more
    mile
Upon the road of things worthwhile.*

Who Are You?

The following definitions were taken from a recent church publication.

1. A PILLAR—One who worships regularly, gives freely of both time and money.

2. A SUPPORTER—One who gives time and money if he likes the pastor.

3. A LEANER—One who uses the church for funerals, baptisms and marriages, but gives no time or money to support the church.

4. A SPECIAL—One who helps and gives occasionally for something that appeals to him.

5. An ANNUAL—One who dresses up, looks serious, and goes to church on Easter.

6. A SPONGE—One who takes all the blessings and benefits, but gives nothing to support the church.

7. A TRAMP—One who goes from one church to another but supports none.

8. A GOSSIP—One who talks freely about everyone and everything in the church except Jesus Christ.

9. A SCRAPPER—One who takes offense at everything, and is always criticizing everybody, and is always ready for a church fight.

RELIGION is the INBORN LONGING of the human soul for GOD and for COMPANIONSHIP with Him. It is as fundamental as life itself, as enduring as the human race.

—*John D. Rockefeller, Jr.*

TEN LITTLE OPERATORS

Ten little operators
Feeling fit and fine,
One tripped over a telephone wire,
Then there were nine.

Nine little operators
Thought they'd be late.
One ran with high heels on,
Then there were eight.

Eight little operators
Looking up to Heaven.
One fell down an elevator shaft,
Then there were seven.

Seven little operators
Putting in hard licks.
One threw her cords around,
Then there were six.

Six little operators,
Glad to be alive.
One slipped on the floor,
Then there were five.

Five little operators
Going through a door.
One slammed it on another,
Then there were four.

Four little operators,
One scratched her knee.
Didn't go for first aid,
Then there were three.

Three little operators
Crossed the avenue.
One didn't see the car,
Then there were two.

Two little operators
Took stairways on the run.
One missed her footing,
Then there was one.

One little operator
Thought of the other nine,
Began to practice SAFETY,
Now she's doing fine.

("Operators," in this sense of the
word, is now obsolete.)

Things That Endure

Honor and truth and manhood—
    These are the things that stand,
Though the sneer and jibe of the cynic tribe
    Are loud through the width of the land.
The scoffer may lord it an hour on earth,
    And a lie may live for a day.
But truth and honor and manly worth
    Are things that endure alway.

Courage and toil and service,
    Old, yet forever new—
These are the rock that abides the shock
    And holds through the storm, flint-true.
Fad and folly, the whims of an hour,
    May bicker and rant and shrill;
But the living granite of truth will tower
    Long after their rage is still.

Labor and love and virtue—
    Time does not dim their glow;
Though the smart may say, in their languid
    way,
    "Oh, we've outgrown all that, you know!"
But a lie, whatever the guise it wears,
    Is a lie as it was of yore.
And a truth that has lasted a million years
    Is good for a million more!

—Ted Olson

Revival Formula

If all the sleeping folk will wake up,
And all the lukewarm folk will fire up,
And all the dishonest folk will confess up,
And all the disgruntled folk will sweeten up,
And all the discouraged folk will cheer up,
And all the depressed folk will look up,
And all the estranged folk will make up,
And all the gossipers will shut up,
And all the dry bones will shake up,
And all the soldiers stand up,
And all the church members pray up,
Then and only then we can have REVIVAL.

I'd Rather Walk By Faith

Sometimes a lonely road I tread,
  Sometimes the path is rough;
But I'd rather walk along by faith,
  To me this is enough.

I'd rather walk along by faith
  Though others walk by sight;
My father knows where I must go,
  He'll guide my steps aright.

I'd rather walk along by faith,
  No dangers lurk ahead,
And those who travel in His steps
  Have naught of harm to dread.

Though others go their way by sight,
  And trust in lands and gold,
I'd rather walk along by faith
  And have His wealth untold.

I'd rather walk along by faith
  And never halt or quail,
For He who guides me on the way
  I know will never fail.

—Dale Crowley

"For we walk by faith, and not by sight" (II Cor. 5:7).

You Can't Fool God!

You can fool the general public,
You can be a subtle fraud,
You can hide your little meanness,
But you can't fool God!

You can advertise your virtues,
You can self-achievement laud,
You can load yourself with riches,
But you can't fool God!

You can criticize the Bible,
You can be a selfish clod,
You can lie, swear, drink and gamble,
But you can't fool God!

You can magnify your talent,
You can hear the world applaud;
You can boast yourself somebody,
But you can't fool God!

Keep On Keeping On

If the day looks rather gloomy,
And your chances rather slim,
If the situation's puzzling
And the prospect's very grim,
If perplexities keep pressing
Till hope is nearly gone,
Just bristle up and grit your teeth
And keep on keeping on.

Forgetting never wins a fight
And fuming never pays;
There is no use in brooding
In these pessimistic ways;
Just smile bravely and cheerfully
Though hope is nearly gone.
And bristle up and grit your teeth
And keep on keeping on.

There is no use in growling
And grumbling all the time,
When music's ringing everywhere
And everything's a rhyme;
Just keep on smiling cheerfully
If hope is nearly gone,
And bristle up and grit your teeth
And keep on keeping on.

The Road Home

There's a big road in the city,
  They call the Great White Way
Where the bright lights,
  The glaring white lights,
Turn the night into day.

But you're lonely when you walk it,
  For you want once more to find
In the shadows, in the darkness,
  The old road you left behind.

It's the old road back to homeland,
  It's the outcast's only goal
Where the ever cruel white lights
  Cast no shadow o'er your soul.

It's the old road back to homeland,
  It's the road you want to roam,
With the hand of God to guide you . . .
  It's the road to home sweet home.

EXCUSES

In summertime it is too hot,
In winter it's too cold;
In spring and fall when the weather's nice
There's some place to go—
Either to the mountains or to the beach,
Or visit some old friend;
Or stay at home and hope that some of
   the relatives will drop in.

A headache every Sunday morn,
And a backache Sunday night;
But by the time on Monday
You're feeling quite all right.
But maybe some of the children had a
   cold—
Pneumonia, you suppose—
So all the family had to stay at home,
And blow the poor child's nose!

On Sunday morn the battery's weak,
And the old car just won't run,
But pleasure riding Sunday afternoon is
   oh, so much fun.
Then you get back home Sunday
   evening
Too tired to come to church.
But you push the old car off early
   Monday morning
In time to get to work.

The preacher is too young,
Or some say he's too old.
His sermons are not plain enough,
Or either they're too bold.

His voice is too quiet like,
Or else he's too loud;
He needs to have more dignity,
Or else he's too proud.

His sermons are too long;
Or some say they're too short.
He ought to gently wave his hand,
Instead of stomp and snort.
And you'd think that the preacher
Must be a very stuck up man,
For you heard some woman say,
"He didn't even shake my hand."

The church seats are uncomfortable,
And the choir sings too loud—
Besides, you get so nervous
When you get in a big crowd.
The doctor's told you, you must take
   care,
For big crowds set you back.
But, of course, you go to the ball game,
You claim it helps you to relax.

CHORUS:
Excuses, excuses; you'll hear them
   every day.
The devil will supply you, if from
   church you'll stay away.
When people come to know the Lord,
   the devil always loses,
And so to keep them from the church he
   offers them EXCUSES.

—from Evangelist Harold Leake's album

---

*Blessed is the man that walketh not in the counsel of the ungodly,
nor standeth in the way of sinners, nor sitteth in the seat of the
scornful. But his delight is in the law of the Lord; and in his law doth
he meditate day and night. And he shall be like a tree planted by the
rivers of water, that bringeth forth his fruit in his season; his leaf
also shall not wither; and whatsoever he doeth shall prosper.*

Psalm 1:1-3

The Christian's Riches

In CHRIST we have—
A LOVE that can never be fathomed;
A LIFE that can never die;
A RIGHTEOUSNESS that can never be
    tarnished;
A PEACE that can never be understood;
A REST that can never be disturbed;
A JOY that can never be diminished;
A HOPE that can never be disappointed;
A GLORY that can never be clouded;
A HAPPINESS that can never be interrupted;
A LIGHT that can never be darkened;
A STRENGTH that can never be enfeebled;
A BEAUTY that can never be marred;
A PURITY that can never be defiled;
A WISDOM that can never be baffled;
RESOURCES that can never be
    exhausted.

The Pilgrim Way

But once I pass this way,
And then—no more.
But once, and then the Silent Door
Swings on its hinges—
Opens, closes,
And no more
I pass this way.
So while I may,
With all my might,
I will assay,
Sweet comfort and delight
To all I meet upon the Pilgrim Way.
For no man travels twice
The Great Highway
That climbs through darkness up to
    Light—
Through Night
To Day.

—*John Oxenham*

Lord, Show Me How!

If I can right a human wrong,
If I can help to make one strong,
If I can cheer with smile or song—
    Lord, show me how.

If I can sow a fruitful seed,
If I can help someone in need,
If I can do a kindly deed—
    Lord, show me how.

If I can feed a hungry heart,
If I can make a better start,
If I can fill a nobler part—
    Lord, show me how!

Four things a man must learn to do if he
would keep his record true:
    To think without confusion clearly;
    To love his fellowman sincerely;
    To act from honest motives purely;
    To trust in God and heaven securely.

—*Henry Van Dyke*

The Fear of God

GREAT GOD ABOVE, FATHER OF
    MEN,
Naught but THEE need we fear.
For all on THEE we must depend
Throughout each passing year.

THOU governest and THOU alone.
All men must bow to THEE,
For THOU controllest from THY
    THRONE
Time and Eternity.

GOD grant us by THY LIGHT DIVINE
Life's lessons so to see
That we may feel toward all mankind
A deeper sympathy.

And may our pathway to Life's end
In the rays of the setting sun
In their beautiful reflection blend
The good deeds we have done.

—*Frank Stollenwerck*

Milton on His Blindness

They charge me with poverty, because I never desired to become rich dishonestly; they accuse me of blindness, because I have lost my eyes in the service of liberty; they tax me with cowardice, and while I had the use of my eyes and my sword I never feared the boldest among them; finally, I am upbraided with deformity, while no one was more handsome in the age of beauty. I do not even complain of my want of sight; in the night with which I am surrounded the light of the Divine presence shines with a more brilliant luster. God looks down upon me with tenderness and compassion, because I can now see none but Himself. Misfortune should protect me from insult, and render me sacred; not because I am deprived of the light of heaven, but because I am under the shadow of the Divine wings which have enveloped me with this darkness.

—John Milton's Letter to a Foreign Friend

Tax Free

A tax assessor came one day to a poor pastor to determine the amount of taxes the pastor would have to pay.

The following conversation took place:

"What property do you possess?" asked the assessor.

"I am a very wealthy man," replied the minister.

"List your possessions, please," the assessor instructed.

"First, I have everlasting life, John 3:16.

"Second, I have a mansion in heaven, John 14:2.

"Third, I have peace that passeth understanding, Philippians 4:7.

"Fourth, I have joy unspeakable, 1 Peter 1:8.

"Fifth, I have divine love which never faileth, 1 Corinthians 13:8.

"Sixth, I have a faithful, pious wife, Proverbs 31:10.

"Seventh, I have healthy, happy, obedient children, Exodus 20:12.

"Eighth, I have true, loyal friends, Proverbs 18:24.

"Ninth, I have songs in the night, Psalm 42:8.

"Tenth, I have a crown of life, James 1:12."

The tax assessor closed his book, and said, "Truly you are a very rich man, but your property is not subject to taxation."

"GOOD-BYE"

(Said to have been written by Ah Foo Lin, a Chinese student, in a friend's album.)

There is a word of grief the sounding token;
   There is a word bejeweled with bright tears,
The saddest word fond lips have ever spoken;
   A little word that breaks the chain of years;
Its utterance must ever bring emotion,
   The memories it crystals cannot die,
'Tis known, in every land, on every ocean—
   'Tis called "Good-bye."

A Little Prayer

If any little word of mine
   May make a life the brighter;
If any little song of mine
   May make a heart the lighter,
God help me speak the little word,
   And take my bit of singing,
And drop it in some lonely vale
   To set the echoes ringing.

God Is Able

1. God is able to perform that which He promised (Rom. 4:21).
2. God is able to deliver us (Dan. 3:17).
3. God is able to give us grace to bear temptation (1 Cor. 10:13).
4. God is able to make all grace abound toward us (2 Cor. 9:8).
5. God is able to do abundantly above all that we ask or think (Eph. 3:20).
6. God is able to subdue all things (Phil. 3:21).
7. God is able to keep that which I have committed unto Him (2 Tim. 1:12).
8. God is able to succour them that are tempted (Heb. 2:18).
9. God is able to save to the uttermost (Heb. 7:25).
10. God is able to keep us from falling (Jude 24).
11. God is able to make the weakest one stand (Rom. 14:4).

—Pastor L. R. Shelton

God's Sunshine

Never since the world began
Has the sun ever stopped shining.
His face very often we cannot see,
And we grumble at his inconsistency.
But the clouds were to blame, not the sun,
For behind the clouds he was still shining.
And so behind life's darkest cloud
God's love is always shining.
We veil it, at times, with our faithless fears,
And darken our sight with our foolish tears,
But in time the atmosphere always clears,
For His love is always shining.

—Author unknown

God, grant me the serenity to accept the things I cannot change,
Courage to change the things I can,
and wisdom to know the difference.

God's Job for You

The Lord had a job for me, but I had so much to do,
I said, "You get somebody else—or wait till I get through."
I don't know how the Lord came out, but He seemed to get along—
But I felt kind of sneaking like—knowed I'd done God wrong.
One day I needed the Lord, needed Him myself—needed Him right away;
And He never answered me at all, but I could hear Him say,
Down in my accusing heart—"I'se got too much to do;
You get somebody else, or wait until I get through."
Now, when the Lord, He have a job for me, I never tries to shirk,
I drops what I have on hand and does the good Lord's work;
And my affairs can run along, or wait till I get through,
Nobody else can do the job that God's marked out for you.

—Paul Lawrence Dunbar

TROUBLE IN THE AMEN CORNER

(As read on the Hour of Inspiration)

It was a stylish congregation, you could see they'd been around.
And they had the biggest pipe organ of any church in town.
But over in the amen corner of that church sat Brother Eyre,
And he insisted every Sunday, on singing in the choir.
He was poor but gentle lookin', and his hair like snow, was white.
And his old face beamed with sweetness, when he sang with all his might.
His voice was cracked and broken, age had touched his vocal chords,
And nearly every Sunday he'd get behind and miss the words.
Well, the choir stormed and blustered, Brother Eyre sang too slow,
And he used the tunes in style a hundred years ago.
At last the storm cloud burst, and the church was told in time
That Brother Eyre must stop his singing or the choir was gonna resign.
So the pastor appointed a committee, I think it was three or four,
And they got in their big, fine car and drove up to Eyre's door.
They found the choir's great trouble sitting there in an old armchair,
And the summer's golden sunbeams lay upon his snow white hair.
He was singing Rock of Ages in a cracked voice, soft and low,
But the angels understood him, and that's all he cared to know.
Said York, "We're here, Dear Brother, with the vestry's approbation,
To discuss a little matter that affects the congregation.
Now we don't want the singing except what we've bought,
The newest tunes are all the rage, the old ones stand for naught.
And so we have decided, are you listening, Brother Eyre?
You'll have to stop your singing, it's messing up our choir."
The old man raised his head, a sign that he did hear,
And on his cheek the three men caught the glitter of a tear.
His feeble hands pushed back the locks as white as silky snow,
And he answered the committee, in a voice both soft and low.
"I've sung the Psalms of David nearly 80 years," said he.
"They've been my staff and comfort, all along life's dreary way.
I'm sorry I disturbed the choir, I guess I'm doing wrong,
But when my heart is filled with praise, I can't keep back a song.
I wonder of beyond the time that's breaking at my feet,
In that far off heavenly temple, where my Master I shall meet.
Yes, I wonder, if when I try to sing the songs of God up higher,
I wonder if they'll kick me out, up there, for singing in heaven's choir."
A silence filled the little room, the old man bowed his head.
The committee went on back to town, but Brother Eyre was dead.
The choir missed him for a while, but he was soon forgot.
A few churchgoers watched the door, but the old man entered not.
Now our brother's voice is silent, and his critics don't complain;
For he's gone to the land of glory for that heavenly refrain:
Far away his voice is sweet as he sings his heart's desire,
Where there are no stern committees, and no fashionable choirs.

—*Archie Campbell*

THE CONTRAST

Unbelief and Its Answer

Out of the night that covers me
Black as the pit from pole to pole,
I thank whatever gods may be
For my unconquerable soul.

In the fell clutch of circumstance
I have not winced nor cried aloud;
Under the bludgeonings of chance
My head is bloody, but unbowed.

Beyond this place of wrath and tears
Looms but the horror of the shade;
And yet the menace of the years
Finds, and shall find me unafraid.

It matters not how strait the gate,
How charged with punishment the
    scroll;
I am the master of my fate;
I am the captain of my soul.

        —Wm. Henley's "Invictus"

Out of the light that dazzles me,
Bright as the sun from pole to pole,
I thank the God I know to be
For Christ the conqueror of my soul.

Since His the sway of circumstance
I would not wince nor cry aloud.
Under that rule which men call chance
My head with joy is humbly bowed.

Beyond this place of sin and tears—
That life with Him! and His the aid,
Despite the menace of the years,
Keeps, and shall keep me unafraid.

I have no fear though strait the gate,
He cleared from punishments the
    scroll;
Christ is the Master of my fate,
Christ is the Captain of my soul.

        —"My Captain" by Dorothea Day

If God Forgot the World for Just One Day

Then little children would not laugh and play;
Birds would not in the leafy woodlands sing,
And roses would not beautify the spring.
No gentle showers throughout the summer long,
No autumn fields to cheer the heart with song,
No rising sun, no moon to give its light,
No placid lake reflect the stars of night.
No friend to help us on the toilsome road,
No one to help us bear the heavy load.
No light to shine upon the pilgrim way,
No one to care, or wipe the tear away.
No listening ear to hear the lost one call,
No eye to see the righteous battler fall.
No balm of Gilead to dull the throbbing pain,
No one to comfort and the heart sustain.
Millions would die in unforgiven sin,
With none to bring the lost and straying in;
Yes, this great universe would melt away,
If God forgot the world for just one day.

        —W. H. B. Kirshner

I am sorry for the men who do not read the Bible every day; I wonder why they deprive themselves of the strength and of the pleasure. It is one of the most singular books in the world for every time you open it, some old text that you have read a score of times suddenly beams with a new meaning. There is no other book that I know of, of which this is true; there is no other book that yields its meaning so personally, that seems to fit itself so intimately to the very spirit that is seeking its guidance.

        —Author unknown

"The Heavens Declare the Glory of God"

(Psalm 19:1)

You ask me how I know it's true
  That there is a living God—
A God who rules the universe,
  The sky . . . the sea . . . the sod;
A God who holds all creatures
  In the hollow of His hand;
A God who put *Infinity*
  In one tiny grain of sand;
A God who made the seasons—
  Winter, Summer, Fall and Spring,
And put His flawless rhythm
  Into each created thing;
A God who hangs the sun out
  Slowly with the break of day,
And gently takes the stars in
  And puts the night away;
A God whose mighty handiwork
  Defies the skill of man,
For no architect can alter
  God's *Perfect Master Plan*—
What better answers are there
  To prove His Holy Being
Than the wonders all round us
  That are ours just for the seeing.

—*Author unknown*

OUR OWN

If I had known in the morning
How wearily all the day
  The words unkind
  Would trouble my mind
I said when you went away,
I had been more careful, darling,
  Nor given you needless pain;
But we vex "our own"
With look and tone
  We might never take back again.
For though in the quiet evening
You may give me the kiss of peace,
  Yet it might be
  That never for me
The pain of the heart should cease.

How many go forth in the morning
  That never come home at night,
And hearts have broken
For harsh words spoken
  That sorrow can ne'er set right.
We have careful thoughts for the stranger,
And smiles for the sometime guest,
  But oft for "our own"
  The bitter tone,
Though we love "our own" the best.
Ah! lips with curve impatient,
  Ah! brow with that look of scorn,
'Twere a cruel fate
Were the night too late.
  To undo the work of morn.

—*Margaret E. Sangster*

We Can't Ask God

—For help if we are not making any effort.
—For strength if we have strength we are not using.
—For guidance if we are ignoring the guidance we now have.
—For prosperity if we cannot be trusted with it.
—For faith when we are afraid to act on what we already know.
—For forgiveness if we continue hating someone.
—For mercy if we intend to commit the same sin again.

—*Roy L. Smith*

Face to Face

I had walked life's path with an easy tread,
  I followed where comforts and pleasures
    led—
Until one day in a quiet place
  I met my Master face to face.

With station and rank and wealth as my goal
  Much tho't for the body, but none for the
    soul,
I had entered to win in life's mad race
  When I met my Master face to face.

I built my castles, reared them high,
  Until their towers pierced the sky
I had sworn to rule with an iron mace
  When I met my Master face to face.

I met Him and knew Him and blushed to see
  That His eyes of sorrow were fixed on me;
I faltered and fell at His feet that day
  And all my castles vanished away.

They melted and vanished, and in their place
  I saw naught else but Jesus' face;
I cried aloud, "O make me meet
  To follow the footsteps of Thy wounded
    feet.

My thought is now for the souls of men,
  I lost my life to find it again,
Ere since alone in that quiet place
  I met my Master face to face.

What Is Your Body Worth?

THE CHEMICAL ANALYSIS
OF THE HUMAN BODY
Sulphur—enough to rid a dog of fleas.
Lime—enough to whitewash a chicken coop.
Fat—enough for six bars of soap.
Iron—enough for a six-penny nail.
Phosphorus—enough for 20 boxes of
  matches.
Sugar—enough for 10 cups of coffee.
Potassium—enough to explode a toy cannon.
Total Value—87 cents
That's all you are worth!

I Shall Not Want

I shall not want rest.
  He maketh me to die down in
  green pastures.
I shall not want refreshment.
  He leadeth me beside the still
  waters.
I shall not want forgiveness.
  He restoreth my soul.
I shall not want guidance.
  He leadeth me in the paths of
  righteousness for His name's
  sake.
I shall not want companionship.
  Yea, though I walk through the
  valley of the shadow of death, I
  will fear no evil: for Thou art
  with me.
I shall not want comfort.
  Thy rod and Thy staff they com-
  fort me.
I shall not want food.
  Thou preparest a table before me
  in the presence of mine enemies.
I shall not want joy.
  Thou anointest my head with oil.
I shall not want anything.
  My cup runneth over.
I shall not want anything in this life.
  Surely goodness and mercy shall
  follow me all the days of my life.
I shall not want anything in eternity.
  And I will dwell in the house of
  the LORD for ever.

—Mrs. J. R. Mott

A Prayer

All through the day, O Lord, let
me touch as many lives as possible
for Thee; and every life I touch do
Thou by Thy Spirit quicken,
whether through the word I speak,
the prayer I breathe, or the life I
live.

The Land of Beginning Again

I wish for the Land of Beginning Again
    Where I could start life all anew;
Where confusion and strife
That filled this poor life
    Could not dampen my way like the dew.

If I could forget how I've stumbled along,
    How I've fumbled and faltered and failed,
How I've veered each day
From the service way,
    And from duties have halted and quailed.

My ear has been dull to the call of the world
    With its sorrows, and heartaches, and needs;
So taken up with self
I've had time for naught else,
    No time to cheer others with helpful deeds.

If I could erase all the dark things of life,
    If I could make right all the wrongs—
Every unkind word spoken,
Every good intention broken,
    It would turn all my sighs into songs.

Oh, God, to that Land of Beginning Again
    Let me come thru these penitent tears;
Let me start life anew,
Let Thy rich grace endue
    Me for service thru life's golden years.

—Dale Crowley

Every task, however simple,
    Sets the soul that does it free;
Every deed of love and mercy,
    Done to man, is done to Me.
—Van Dyke

God Bless You

I know no word more fitting to address you,
    No song, no poem I've ever heard
Is sweeter than just "God bless you."
    In these three little words may you find
All the joy the whole wide earth possesses,
    For there can truly be no joy
Unless indeed, God blesses.

I might wish you wealth or wish you health,
    Or that good fortune might caress you.
But wealth might bring sorrow,
    Or even health fail tomorrow:
So I simply say, "God bless you."

THE DIVINE WARNING

There is a time, we know not when, a point, we know not where,
That marks the destiny of men, for glory or despair.
There is a line, by us unseen, that crosses every path,
That marks the boundary between God's patience and His wrath.
To pass that limit is to die, to die as if by stealth;
It does not dim the beaming eye, or pale the glow of health.
The conscience may be still at ease, the spirit light and gay;
That which is pleasing still may please, and care be thrust away.
But on the forehead God has set indelibly a mark
Unseen by man, for man as yet is blind and in the dark.
And yet the doomed man's path below, like Eden, may have bloomed;
He did not, does not, will not know or feel that he is doomed.
He thinks and feels that all is well, and every fear is calmed;
He lives, he dies, he wakes in hell, not only doomed but damned!
O where is this mysterious bourne by which our path is crossed,
Beyond which God Himself hath sworn that he who goes is lost?

The Zigzag Path

We climbed the height by the zigzag path
　　And wondered why, until
We understood it was made zigzag
　　To break the force of the hill.

A road straight up would be too steep
　　For the travellers' feet to tread;
The thought was kind in its wise design
　　Of a zigzag path instead.

It is often so in our daily life—
　　We fail to understand
That the twisting way our feet must tread
　　By love alone was planned.

Then murmur not at the winding way,
　　It is our Father's will
To lead us home by the zigzag path
　　To break the force of the hill.

—Author unknown

WAIT

If but one message I may leave behind,
One single word of courage for my kind,
It would be this, oh brother, sister, friend,
Whatever life may bring, what God may send,
No matter whether clouds lift soon or late,
Take heed and wait.
Despair may tangle darkly at your feet,
Your faith be dimmed, and hope, once
　　cool and sweet,
Be lost, but suddenly above a hill,
A heavenly lamp, set on a heavenly sill,
Will shine for you and point the way to go,
How well I know.
For I have waited through the dark, and I
Have seen a star rise in the darkest sky
Repeatedly—it has not failed me yet!
And I have learned God never will forget
To light His lamp. If we but wait for it,
It will be lit.

—Grace Noll Crowell

330

INDEX TO TOPICS

335

Another
Unusal...
Inspirational...
Enlightening...
Important Book

FROM THE CROWLEYS

Books to GROW by!

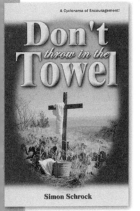

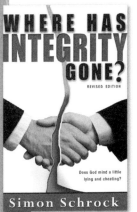

Notes

Notes

Notes